Oracle 9i Cram Sheet

This Cram Sheet contains last-minute reminders you can review briefly before the exam starts. You cannot take this cram sheet with you into the exam!

THE ITERATIVE SYSTEM DEVELOPMENT CYCLE

1. *Strategy and Analysis*—Analyze user requirements and produce system specification.
2. *Design*—Technical design documentation, a product of *Strategy and Analysis*.
3. *Build and Document*—Convert *Design* into executable software code and data structures.
4. *Transition*—User acceptance testing and bug removal.
5. *Production*—Applications release and support passed to production support.

BASIC TERMINOLOGY

- SQL—Structured Query Language.
- DML—Data Manipulation Language (ROLLBACK allowed).
- DDL—Data Definition Language (ROLLBACK not allowed).

THE SELECT STATEMENT

The SELECT statement is used to retrieve data from a database. A SELECT statement is also known as a query because it *queries* a database.

- Simple SELECT:

```
SELECT *¦<column> [AS
<name>¦"name"][,...] FROM
[<schema>.]<table>;
```

- Add an alias:

```
SELECT [<alias>.]*¦[<alias>.]<column>
[,...]
FROM [<schema>.]<table> [<alias>];
```

- Retrieve unique (DISTINCT) items:

```
SELECT DISTINCT¦UNIQUE [(]<col-
umn>[,...][)] FROM
[<schema>.]<table>;
```

The WHERE Clause

The optional WHERE clause is used to filter rows in a query, an UPDATE command, or a DELETE command.

- Simple comparison:

```
SELECT * FROM [<schema>.]<table>
[WHERE
[<schema>.][[<table>.]¦[<alias>.]]<co
lumn>
    <comparison>[...]<column>];
```

- Conjunctive comparison using logical conditions:

```
SELECT * FROM [<schema>.]<table>
[WHERE
[<schema>.][[<table>.]¦[<alias>.]]<co
lumn>
    <comparison>[...]<column>
AND [NOT]¦ OR [NOT] [...]<column>
<comparison>[...]<column>
AND [NOT]¦ OR [NOT] ... ];
```

- The UPDATE and DELETE commands:

```
UPDATE [<schema>.]<table> SET ...
[WHERE
[<schema>.][[<table>.]¦[<alias>.]]<co
lumn>
    <comparison>[...]<column> ...];

DELETE FROM [<schema>.]<table>
[WHERE
[<schema>.][[<table>.]¦[<alias>.]]<co
lumn>
    <comparison>[...]<column> ...];
```

The ORDER BY Clause

The optional ORDER BY clause is used to sort rows returned by a query, and it can also be a part of the OVER clause for analysis.

- Simple sorting:

```
SELECT * FROM [<schema>.]<table>
[WHERE]
[ORDER BY {[<alias>.]<column>¦<posi-
tion>}[,...]];
```

- Ascending (the default) and descending sorts:

```
SELECT * FROM [<schema>.]<table>
[WHERE]
[ORDER BY {[<alias>.]<column>
[ASC¦DESC]
    ¦<position>
[ASC¦DESC]}[,...[ASC¦DESC]]];
```

- Sorting NULL values (by default returned last):

```
SELECT * FROM [<schema>.]<table>
[WHERE]
[ORDER BY {[<alias>.]<column>
[ASC¦DESC][NULLS {FIRST¦LAST}]
    ¦<position> [ASC¦DESC][NULLS
{FIRST¦LAST}]}[,...[ASC¦DESC]]];
```

- The OVER clause:

```
SELECT {<column> [AS OVER() [ORDER
BY]...]}[,...]
```

```
FROM <table> [WHERE][ORDER BY];
```

The GROUP BY Clause

The optional GROUP BY clause is used to summarize, aggregate, and analyze groupings returned from queries. Any SELECT list elements not included in aggregation functions must be included in the GROUP BY list of elements. This includes both columns and expressions. At least one element of the SELECT list of elements must be subjected to an aggregation function.

- Simple GROUP BY:

```
SELECT * FROM [<schema>.]<table>
[WHERE]
[GROUP BY
[<alias>.]<column>[,...]][ORDER BY];
```

- Filtering groups with the optional HAVING clause (similar syntax to that of the WHERE clause):

```
SELECT * FROM [<schema>.]<table>
[WHERE]
[GROUP BY ... [HAVING <column> <com-
parison> <column> [,...]]]
[ORDER BY];
```

- Extending the GROUP BY clause with OLAP functionality using the ROLLBUP, CUBE, and GROUPING SETS clauses:

```
SELECT * FROM [<schema>.]<table>
[WHERE]
[GROUP BY ... [HAVING ...]
[ROLLUP(<column>,[...])¦CUBE(<column>
[,...])
     ¦GROUPING
SETS((<group>)[,...])][ORDER BY];
```

JOINING TABLES

Tables can be joined such that results from one or more tables appear in the same query result. Joins can be an outer join, a Cartesian Product (a cross join), a table joined to itself (a self join), or a semi join.

- Oracle join syntax is placed into the WHERE clause using the (+) operator (outer join operator), determining the side of an outer join deficient in information:

```
SELECT * FROM <table>
[WHERE <column> <comparison> <column>
[(+)]]
     ¦[WHERE <column>[(+)] <compari-
son> <column>]
AND [NOT]¦ OR [NOT] ... ][GROUP
BY][ORDER BY];
```

- ANSI join syntax is placed into the FROM clause using the JOIN keyword:

```
SELECT * FROM <table> [JOIN <table>
[JOIN <table> ...]]
[WHERE][GROUP BY][ORDER BY];
```

- ANSI join syntax allows the CROSS JOIN clause to create a Cartesian Product between two tables:

```
SELECT *
FROM <table> [[CROSS] JOIN <table>
[[CROSS] JOIN <table> ...]]
[WHERE][GROUP BY][ORDER BY];
```

- ANSI join syntax can use the NATURAL keyword to create both inner and outer joins, joining tables on columns with the same name in the different tables:

```
SELECT *
FROM <table> [[NATURAL] JOIN <table>
[[NATURAL] JOIN <table> ...]]
[WHERE][GROUP BY][ORDER BY];
```

- ANSI join syntax can utilize the USING clause to specify exact column names to join on, avoiding joins on same-named columns with different meanings:

```
SELECT *
FROM <table> [JOIN <table>
USING(<column>[,...])
     [JOIN <table> ...] USING(<col-
umn>[,...])]
[WHERE][GROUP BY][ORDER BY];
```

- ANSI join syntax can utilize the ON clause to specify exact column names to join on, specifically when different-named columns are required in the join, usually requiring a table or alias reference:

```
SELECT *
FROM <table> a [JOIN <table> b
     ON (a.<column>=b.<column> [AND
[NOT]¦ OR [NOT] ... ] [,...])
          [JOIN <table> c] ON(...)]
[WHERE][GROUP BY][ORDER BY];
```

SPECIALIZED QUERIES

- Subqueries can return single values (scalar), multiple columns or multiple rows, or both. Subqueries can be used in a SELECT clause elements list, the FROM clause, the WHERE clause, the ORDER BY clause, an INSERT statement VALUES clause, an UPDATE statement set clause, or a CASE statement expression. Also tables and views can be created using subqueries.
- The WITH clause allows prepared execution of subquery results. Results can then be utilized by the primary calling query:

```
WITH query1 AS (subquery), query2 AS
(subquery)
SELECT * FROM query1 JOIN query2
JOIN query3;
```

- Hierarchical queries allow hierarchical representations of hierarchical data. The hierarchy can be accessed from the root node or a starting point within the hierarchy (the START WITH clause). The CONNECT BY clause allows linking between a column in the current row and another value in a parent (the PRIOR operator) row:

```
SELECT <column>, LEVEL FROM <table>
START WITH <condition>
CONNECT BY <current_row> <parent_col-
umn>
     = PRIOR <parent_row>
```

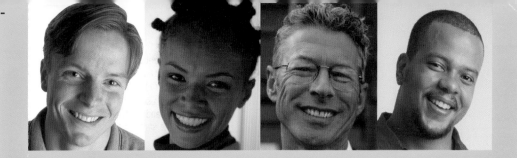

Oracle 9i SQL

Gavin Powell

800 East 96th Street • Indianapolis, Indiana 46240

Oracle 9i SQL Exam Cram 2

International Standard Book Number: 0-7897-3248-3

Library of Congress Catalog Card Number: 2004108919

Printed in the United States of America

First Printing: September 2004

07 06 05 04 4 3 2 1

Trademarks

Warning and Disclaimer

Bulk Sales

Que Publishing offers excellent discounts on this book when ordered in quantity for bulk purchases or special sales. For more information, please contact

U.S. Corporate and Government Sales

1-800-382-3419

corpsales@pearsontechgroup.com

For sales outside the U.S., please contact

International Sales

international@pearsoned.com

Publisher
Paul Boger

Executive Editor
Jeff Riley

Acquisitions Editor
Carol Ackerman

Development Editor
Steve Rowe

Managing Editor
Charlotte Clapp

Project Editor
Andy Beaster

Copy Editor
Cheri Clark

Indexer
Larry Sweazy

Proofreader
Juli Cook

Technical Editors
Arup Nanda
Jenne Shimko

Publishing Coordinator
Pamalee Nelson

Multimedia Developer
Dan Scherf

Interior Designer
Gary Adair

Cover Designer
Anne Jones

Page Layout
Interactive Composition Corporation

Graphics
Tammy Graham
Laura Robbins

Que Certification • 800 East 96th Street • Indianapolis, Indiana 46240

A Note from Series Editor Ed Tittel

You know better than to trust your certification preparation to just anybody. That's why you, and more than 2 million others, have purchased an Exam Cram book. As Series Editor for the new and improved Exam Cram 2 Series, I have worked with the staff at Que Certification to ensure you won't be disappointed. That's why we've taken the world's best-selling certification product—a two-time finalist for "Best Study Guide" in CertCities' reader polls—and made it even better.

As a two-time finalist for the "Favorite Study Guide Author" award as selected by CertCities readers, I know the value of good books. You'll be impressed with Que Certification's stringent review process, which ensures the books are high quality, relevant, and technically accurate. Rest assured that several industry experts have reviewed this material, helping us deliver an excellent solution to your exam preparation needs.

Exam Cram 2 books also feature a preview edition of MeasureUp's powerful, full-featured test engine, which is trusted by certification students throughout the world.

As a 20-year-plus veteran of the computing industry and the original creator and editor of the Exam Cram Series, I've brought my IT experience to bear on these books. During my tenure at Novell from 1989 to 1994, I worked with and around its excellent education and certification department. At Novell, I witnessed the growth and development of the first really big, successful IT certification program—one that was to shape the industry forever afterward. This experience helped push my writing and teaching activities heavily in the certification direction. Since then, I've worked on nearly 100 certification related books, and I write about certification topics for numerous Web sites and for *Certification* magazine.

In 1996, while studying for various MCP exams, I became frustrated with the huge, unwieldy study guides that were the only preparation tools available. As an experienced IT professional and former instructor, I wanted "nothing but the facts" necessary to prepare for the exams. From this impetus, Exam Cram emerged: short, focused books that explain exam topics, detail exam skills and activities, and get IT professionals ready to take and pass their exams.

In 1997 when Exam Cram debuted, it quickly became the best-selling computer book series since "*...For Dummies*," and the best-selling certification book series ever. By maintaining an intense focus on subject matter, tracking errata and updates quickly, and following the certification market closely, Exam Cram established the dominant position in cert prep books.

You will not be disappointed in your decision to purchase this book. If you are, please contact me at etittel@jump.net. All suggestions, ideas, input, or constructive criticism are welcome!

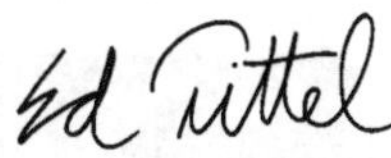

About the Author

Gavin Powell BSc. Comp. Sci., OCP DBA (Oracle Certified Professional) has 15 years of diverse experience in database administration and database development, both relational and object databases. His applications development experience is procedural and object-oriented. Consulting experience includes software vendors, Internet dotcoms, accounting, banking and financial services, the travel industry, construction, retail, mining, shipping, education, and in a general advisory capacity. Gavin is the author of five other Oracle titles, including three Oracle certification titles.

Software Used During the Writing of This Book

- A Win2K Oracle 9.2 (release 9.2.0.1.0) installation was used to test all examples in this book.
- ERWin was used to create schema entity relationship diagrams (ERDs).
- Powerpoint, Visio, and Paintshop were used to draw graphics.
- The original manuscript was written in Microsoft Word.

Other Sources of Information

- http://www.oracle.com
- http://www.oracle.com/education/certification
- http://otn.oracle.com *or* http://technet.oracle.com
- http://www.oracledbaexpert.com
- http://www.oracledbaexpert.com/oracle/ocp/index.html
- http://www.amazon.com for other Oracle titles

Other Titles by the Same Author

- *Oracle SQL Jumpstart with Examples* (ISBN: 1555583237). Written by Gavin Powell, with Carol McCullough-Dieter. A complete Oracle SQL Reference for 10*g*.
- *Oracle Performance Tuning for 9i and 10g* (ISBN: 1555583059). More than 700 pages of performance tuning for Oracle Database, covering data modeling, Oracle SQL, and physical/configuration tuning.
- *Introduction to Oracle SQL Tutorials* (ISBN: 1932072241). Oracle Certification videos for exam 1Z0-001 on CD-ROM.
- *Oracle Database Administration Fundamentals I* (ISBN: 1932072535). Oracle Certification videos for exam 1Z0-031 on CD-ROM.
- *Oracle Database Administration Fundamentals II* (ISBN:1932072845). Oracle Certification videos for exam 1Z0-032 on CD-ROM.

About the Technical Reviewers

Carol McCullough-Dieter. Carol has 20 years of Oracle database administration, programming, systems design, and consulting experience. Carol is also the author of 12 books on Oracle, including *Oracle9i for Dummies*.

Arup Nanda. Arup is an OCP DBA, co-author *of HIPAA Auditing for Oracle Database Security*, director of CT Oracle User Group, editor of *Select Journal*, contributor to other Oracle-related magazines, and a speaker at conferences. Arup also was selected as the 2003 DBA of the Year by *Oracle Magazine*.

Mathew Newfield. Mathew is Director of Security Services and IT Infrastructure for TruSecure Corporation, running Oracle8i and Oracle9i installations.

Jenné Shimko. An experienced Oracle DBA, Jenné Shimko has 14 years' experience as an Oracle DBA, data and applications integration specialist, multimedia developer, computer instructor, and researcher. She is also a contributing Oracle author, presenter, and technical editor. Currently, Jenné works at a supercomputing center.

We Want to Hear from You!

As the reader of this book, *you* are our most important critic and commentator. We value your opinion and want to know what we're doing right, what we could do better, what areas you'd like to see us publish in, and any other words of wisdom you're willing to pass our way.

As an executive editor for Que Publishing, I welcome your comments. You can email or write me directly to let me know what you did or didn't like about this book—as well as what we can do to make our books better.

Please note that I cannot help you with technical problems related to the topic of this book. We do have a User Services group, however, where I will forward specific technical questions related to the book.

When you write, please be sure to include this book's title and author as well as your name, email address, and phone number. I will carefully review your comments and share them with the author and editors who worked on the book.

Email: feedback@quepublishing.com

Mail: Jeff Riley
Executive Editor
Que Publishing
800 East 96th Street
Indianapolis, IN 46240 USA

For more information about this book or another Que Certification title, visit our website at www.examcram2.com. Type the ISBN (excluding hyphens) or the title of a book in the Search field to find the page you're looking for.

Contents at a Glance

Table of Contents

Chapter 6
Joining Tables 103

Chapter 7
Groups and Summaries (GROUP BY) 125

Chapter 8
Subqueries and Other Specialized Queries 145

Introduction

Welcome to *Oracle9i SQL Exam Cram 2!* This book covers the Oracle certification exam Introduction to Oracle9i SQL (1Z0-007). This exam is the first in a series of Oracle certification tracks, and subsets thereof, covering both database administration and application development. The most current of the different Oracle certification tracks for Oracle9i as of the writing of this book are shown in Figure 1. Exam 1Z0-007 is highlighted in the diagram.

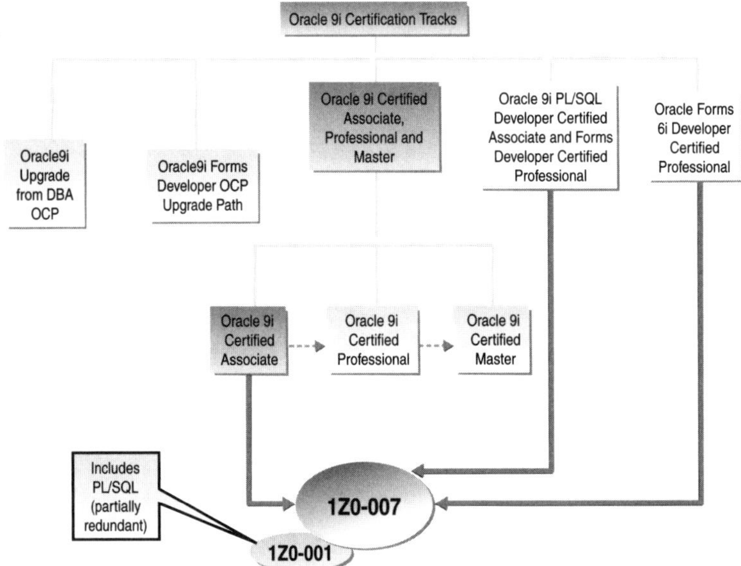

Figure 1 Certification tracks for Oracle9i.

This book covers only the 1Z0-007 exam. 1Z0-007 is included in a number of Oracle certification tracks. Oracle certification tracks consist of multiple exams. As shown in Figure 1, the 1Z0-007 exam can be the starting exam for three different Oracle certification tracks:

- ➤ Oracle9i Certified Professional
- ➤ Oracle9i PL/SQL Developer
- ➤ Oracle Forms 6i Developer

There are several points to emphasize about the Oracle9i certification tracks shown in Figure 1:

- ➤ 1Z0-007 applies to three Oracle9i certification tracks, namely Oracle Certified Professional (database administration), Oracle Certified Developer, and Oracle Forms Developer.
- ➤ Oracle9i Certified Associate (OCA) includes only the first two tests in the Oracle9i Certified Professional track for database administration.
- ➤ Oracle9i Certified Professional (OCP) includes all four OCP tests required for database administration certification.
- ➤ Oracle9i Certified Master (OCM) extends the OCP qualification, including numerous very advanced and detailed topics.
- ➤ 1Z0-001 is a redundant form of 1Z0-007 but is still available. 1Z0-001 includes PL/SQL as well as SQL.

OCA is a subset track of the OCP track.

This book is one of the *Exam Cram 2* series of books, and it will help start you on your way to becoming an Oracle Certified Professional (OCP).

This introductory chapter discusses the basics of OCP exams. Included are sections covering preparation, taking an exam, a description of this book's contents, how this book is organized, and finally author contact information.

Practice exams in this book should provide a fairly accurate assessment of the level of expertise you need to obtain to pass the test. *Answers and explanations are included for all test questions.* Other sample tests can be found elsewhere. It is best to obtain a level of understanding equivalent to a consistent pass rate of 85% or more before taking the test. The pass rate is usually around 70% and that is a *scrape!* Pass rates vary for each certification test and for different versions of Oracle. The 85% is a good figure to aim at because practice tests are often easier than the real exams.

Let's begin by looking at preparation for an exam.

How to Prepare for an Exam

Previous hands-on experience is not a prerequisite for taking the 1Z0-007 Oracle certification exam, but it would give a basic grounding of knowledge. Prepare for this exam by reading this book. Additionally, invest in some practice tests to assess your skills level.

Some people have passed the 1Z0-007 exam simply by reading an exam cram type of book. I would encourage you to read other Oracle SQL books and even the SQL reference manual in the Oracle documentation. Oracle documentation is immense but provides an excellent reference source. Oracle documentation is bundled with Oracle software and is available online from the Oracle Technology Network at this uniform resource locator (URL):

http://otn.oracle.com

I have a group of web pages on my website at the following URL:

http://www.oracledbaexpert.com/oracle/ocp/index.html

This group of web pages covers material for the 1Z0-007 exam. I have had one report of someone passing the 1Z0-007 exam simply by reading these web pages of mine.

I would not recommend using only a single book or source of information when attempting to pass the 1Z0-007 exam.

Practice Tests

The all-important practice test is enormously useful with respect to Oracle certification tests. Practice tests are an excellent resource, allowing you to decide when you are ready to take an exam. Oracle Corporation has partnered with a company called Self Test Software. There are a multitude of other companies providing Oracle certification practice tests. Self Test Software and some of these other companies are listed here:

- **Self Test Software.** Find this at http://www.selftestsoftware.com or from the Oracle Corp. website.
- **Boson.** This company's website is http://www.boson.com.

- **Transcender.** This company's website is http://www.transcender.com.
- **MeasureUp.** Find this company at http://www.measureup.com.

There is not much you need to know about practice tests other than that they are a worthwhile expense for two reasons. First, they help you diagnose areas of weakness. Second, they are very useful for getting used to the format of questions. Oracle certification exams cover all areas of their respective curriculums. Self Test Software Oracle practice tests are $99 for each Oracle certification practice test and consist of more than 200 questions. Check individual company documentation for recommended pass rate requirements before taking an exam.

Now let's discuss taking a certification exam.

Taking a Certification Exam

The culmination of exam preparation should be registration for an exam. At present, the first Oracle Certification exam costs $90 and the others are $125.

The first exam, 1Z0-007, can be taken online or at a recognized testing center, whereas all others can be taken only at a recognized testing center.

Registering for an exam can be done online or by telephone. Check websites for telephone numbers. In North America all Oracle certification tests are administered by a company called Thompson Prometric. You can find information on registration from the following sources:

- **Thompson Prometric.** The Thompson Prometric website is at http://www.prometric.com. Register for an exam online or by telephone.
- **Oracle Corporation.** Oracle's website contains links and certification information at http://www.oracle.com/education/certification. Follow the Education link from Oracle's main site at http://www.oracle.com. A plethora of information on Oracle certification is available, including how to register with Prometric. There is also information on how to take the 1Z0-007 exam online.

The other prominent provider of certification exams is Pearson VUE. This company's website is at http://www.vue.com. Currently this company does not have any Oracle testing, but this situation will probably change in the near future.

Scheduling a Certification Exam

To schedule a certification exam, you need to locate a convenient test site and then actually schedule a test. Location is important because you might want a site close to either your workplace or your home. Many locations allow testing after hours such as during the evenings and over weekends.

Not all testing locations provide after-hours testing time slots. Check with the location before making an examination appointment. If details about available testing times are not available on the Prometric website, you might want to call that particular testing location first.

The duration of the 1Z0-007 examination is 2 hours and 15 minutes. You must schedule the examination 24 hours in advance and not more than 8 weeks ahead. Contact the testing center directly for possible same-day testing availability. To reschedule or cancel an examination, 24 hours notice is usually required. When scheduling an exam, you need to have the following details available:

- Your name and mailing address.
- Your previous testing ID (when registering on the website). If you have not taken a test before, you will have to create a testing ID. Booking over the telephone will require a unique identifier such as a Social Security number.
- The name and the testing code for the exam, in this case, Introduction to Oracle9i: SQL, 1Z0-007.
- Some form of advance payment method (such as a credit card).

Arriving at the Exam Location

As with any examination, you should arrive at the testing center early. Be prepared! You will need identification such as a driver's license, green card, or passport. Any photo ID will suffice. Two forms of ID are usually required. The testing center staff will need proof that you are who you say you are and that someone else is not taking the test for you. Yes, apparently that sort of thing has happened in the past.

In the Exam Room

Do not take anything into the examination room with you that could cause you to be accused of cheating. During one test I took, I was not allowed to keep my cell phone on me, for obvious reasons. I had to leave it at the front desk and remember to collect it afterwards. Things such as computers, piles of papers, Oracle SQL reference manuals, and personal electronic gadgets are not allowed.

After the Exam

Examination results are usually available in printed form from the front desk after you have finished the test. You should be able to trigger extra printouts of certificates from the computer you take the test on. The front desk should have those extra copies. Ask for them!

Additionally, all examination results are sent to Oracle, but keep your test results just in case.

Retaking a Test

For most types of certifications, retaking a test usually requires a short period to prepare for the test again. This is obviously the sensible approach to take. Oracle certification examinations are no exception. You must wait at least 30 days to take a failed examination once again. If you fail an exam and need to retake it, use previous test results indicating areas of weakness to guide you as to what to brush up on. Additionally, invest in some practice tests if you have not already done so. There is much to be said for "getting used to" a testing format.

Now let's talk briefly about this book.

About This Book

The ideal reader for an *Exam Cram 2* book is someone seeking certification. However, it should be noted that an *Exam Cram 2* book is a very easily readable, rapid presentation of facts. Therefore, an *Exam Cram 2* book is also extremely useful as a quick reference manual.

Most people seeking certification use multiple sources of information. Oracle Corporation documentation is extremely detailed and very useful. Practice tests can help indicate when you are ready. There are also various types of Oracle books available from retailers.

Numerous elements are used in this book apart from the actual logical step-by-step learning progression of the chapters themselves. *Exam Cram 2* books use elements such as exam alerts, tips, notes, and practice questions to make the information easier to read and absorb.

Reading this book from start to finish is the best approach because each chapter builds gradually on previous chapters, becoming more complex as the book progresses.

Use the cram sheet to remember last-minute facts immediately before the exam. Use the practice questions to test your knowledge. You can always brush up on specific topics in detail by referring to the table of contents and the index. Even after certification this book can be used as a rapid-access reference manual.

Chapter Elements

Each *Exam Cram 2* book has chapters following a predefined structure. This structure makes *Exam Cram 2* books easy to read and provides a familiar format for all *Exam Cram 2* books. These are the elements typically used:

- Opening hotlists
- Chapter topics
- Exam alerts
- Notes
- Tips
- Sidebars
- Cautions
- Exam prep questions and answers
- "Need to Know More?" sections

Bulleted lists, numbered lists, tables, and graphics are also used if and where appropriate. Sometimes a picture really can paint a thousand words. Tables can help associate different elements with each other visually.

Now let's take a look at each of the elements in detail.

- **Opening Hotlists.** The start of every chapter contains a list of terms you should understand. A second hotlist identifies all the techniques or skills that will be covered in the chapter.

- **Chapter Topics.** Each chapter contains details of all subject matter listed in the table of contents for that chapter. The objective of an *Exam Cram 2* book is to cover all the important facts without too much detail. It is an exam cram. When examples are required, they will be included.
- **Exam Alerts.** Exam alerts address exam-specific, exam-related information. An exam alert will address content that is particularly important, tricky, or likely to appear on the exam. Exam Alerts look like this:

Make sure you remember that the **ROLLBACK** command will undo any uncommitted DML activity for the current session.

- **Notes.** Notes typically contain useful information that is not directly related to the current topic under consideration. In order not to break up the flow of the text, they are set off from the regular text.

This is a note. You have already seen several notes.

- **Tips**. Tips often provide shortcuts or better ways to do things.

NVL2 is a little-known function in SQL that acts a little like a combination of **NVL** and **DECODE**. **NVL2** can be used to determine whether a column value is **NULL** by returning one value if **NULL** and another if not.

- **Sidebars.** Sidebars are longer asides, often describing real-world examples or situations.

This Is a Piece of Code

Sidebars can include descriptions of complex situations, case-studies, or real-world examples. They also can include code, such as this:

```
SELECT M.NAME "Movie", A.NAME "Actor"
FROM MOVIE M JOIN ACTOR A USING(M.MOVIE_ID)
WHERE M.NAME LIKE 'The %';
```

- **Cautions.** Cautions apply directly to the use of the technology being discussed in the Exam Cram. For example, pointing out the dangers involved in the use of a particular command and how to avoid damaging a database server you may be working on would constitute a caution.

Deleting all rows in an extremely large table can affect system performance and upset your clients. You could also destroy production data!

- **Exam Prep Questions and Answers.** The end of every chapter contains a list of about 10 exam practice questions, similar to those in the actual exam. Each chapter contains a list of questions relevant to that chapter, including answers and explanations. Test your skills as you read.
- **"Need to Know More?" Sections.** This section appears in Appendix B, describing any other possible relevant sources of information. The best place to look for Oracle certification information is the Oracle Corp. website at http://www.oracle.com/education/certification.

Other Book Elements

Most of this *Exam Cram 2* book on Oracle SQL follows the consistent chapter structure already described. However, there are also various important elements not part of the standard chapter format. These elements apply to the entire book as a whole:

- **Practice Exams.** In addition to exam preparation questions at the end of each chapter, two full practice exams are included at the end of the book.
- **Answers and Explanations for Practice Exams.** These chapters follow each practice exam in a separate chapter and provide answers and explanations to the questions in the exams.
- **Glossary.** The glossary contains a listing of important terms used in this book, with explanations. All hotlist items are included in the glossary.
- **Cram Sheet.** The cram sheet is a quick-reference, tear-out cardboard sheet of important facts, useful for last-minute preparation. Cram sheets often include a simple summary of those facts most difficult to remember.
- **CD.** The book's CD contains an innovative test engine powered by MeasureUp, giving you yet another effective tool to assess your readiness for the exam. MeasureUp practice tests are available in Study, Certification, Custom, Missed Question, and Non-Duplicate

Question modes, plus they provide feedback on all correct and incorrect answers. For more MeasureUp practice exams, visit the website at www.measureup.com.

Chapter Contents

The following list provides an overview of the chapters:

- *Chapter 1: Getting Started with Oracle Database*. This chapter introduces basic relational data modeling, various Oracle SQL tools, and new features for Oracle9i. Any changes for Oracle9i are indicated as such by the appearance of the 9i icon in the margins next to the text for the entire book.
- *Chapter 2: Retrieving Data (SELECT)*. This chapter makes things interesting by jumping straight into the basic syntax of data retrieval, additionally briefly introducing some specifics.
- *Chapter 3: Filtering (WHERE) and Sorting Data (ORDER BY)*. This chapter covers filtering of rows using the WHERE clause and sorting of retrieved data using the ORDER BY clause. The WHERE clause applies to both queries and most DML commands; the ORDER BY clause applies to queries only.
- *Chapter 4: Operators, Conditions, Pseudocolumns, and Expressions*. This chapter builds on basic selecting, filtering, and sorting by introducing all operators, conditions, pseudocolumns, and expressions. Operators and conditions are used in expressions. Pseudocolumns contain information in Oracle database not available from tables.
- *Chapter 5: Single Row Functions*. This chapter describes single row functions. Single row functions can operate within or as expressions on each row of a SQL statement.
- *Chapter 6: Joining Tables*. This chapter shows all the numerous methods of joining tables and row sets into merged output results.
- *Chapter 7: Groups and Summaries (GROUP BY)*. This chapter covers grouping of output row sets. Grouping of data includes simple aggregation summary and more complex analysis. Advanced topics are introduced but not analyzed because they are out of scope.
- *Chapter 8: Subqueries and Other Specialized Queries*. This chapter covers all the aspects of subquery processing, including how subqueries are constructed and where they can be used. Additionally, other specialized, more obscure query types are only briefly introduced because they are out of scope.

- *Chapter 9: SQL*Plus Formatting*. This chapter covers advanced formatting using SQL*Plus tools for database administrators, developers, and report writers.
- *Chapter 10: Changing Data (DML)*. This chapter describes how to change data in an Oracle database, concluding with details on transactional control. Transactional control is most important to user concurrency and maintaining consistency of data in a database.
- *Chapter 11: Tables, Datatypes, and Constraints (DDL)*. This chapter examines the details of table creation and maintenance. Tables contain multiple columns where columns have specific datatypes. Constraints are used to control access to, within, and between both tables and occasionally views.
- *Chapter 12: Views, Indexes, Sequences, and Synonyms (DDL)*. This chapter looks at views, indexes, sequences, and synonyms. Views are an overlay or logical window onto data in underlying tables. Indexes contain small columnar sections of tables. Sequences are Oracle internal auto-counter objects. Synonyms provide transparent access to objects across schemas and multiple databases. Other database objects such as materialized views and index-organized tables are out of scope.
- *Chapter 13: Security (DDL)*. This chapter deals with Oracle database security issues. Details included cover schemas (users), privileges, roles for grouping privileges, and finally granting and revoking of privileges.
- *Chapter 14: Practice Test #1*. This is a full-length practice exam.
- *Chapter 15: Answer Key to Practice Test #1*. This chapter contains the answers and explanations for the first practice exam.
- *Chapter 16: Practice Test #2*. This is a second full-length practice exam.
- *Chapter 17: Answer Key to Practice Test #2*. This chapter contains the answers and explanations for the second practice exam.

Contacting the Author

Hopefully this book will provide you with the tools you need to pass the first Oracle certification exam. Feedback is appreciated. The author can be contacted at the following email addresses:

- gjtpowell@earthlink.net
- questions@oracledbaexpert.com

Thank you for selecting my book and I hope you like it. Good luck!

Self-Assessment

This Self Assessment section allows you, the reader, to decide whether you are ready to take the 1Z0-007 Oracle certification exam. Let's dispense with any waffle and get straight to the point. Are you ready?

Oracle9i SQL in the Real World

Oracle database is the most popular commercial database. Its install base probably occupies at least 50% of the relational database market, at least in terms of capitalization, on a global scale.

Capitalization implies the amount of money spent on Oracle database software, a possibly misleading measure.

In short, there is no denying the popularity of Oracle database and Oracle software in general. Current economic conditions dictate that there is possibly still a large Oracle8i install base in existence. However, as Oracle Corp. continues to upgrade and introduce new features, most installations will eventually upgrade to Oracle9i and beyond.

The number of people seeking Oracle certification is fairly substantial. Many developers want to be DBAs, and many existing DBAs want to become certified. It's all about three things: excitement, stress, and money, in that order. Yes, some people do actively seek out stressful working situations. Many people thrive on the excitement. The 1Z0-007 is the first exam in multiple certification tracks. It is likely that both developers and DBAs are continually seeking to pass this test.

The Ideal Oracle9i SQL Candidate

The ideal candidate has a college education and is very likely to need at least some experience with Oracle. That Oracle experience can be database administration or Oracle SQL development. However, these skills are not essential to take or pass the test.

Obviously, the best qualification is a Computer Science degree or perhaps a degree in a related field such as mathematics. A degree is not a prerequisite to take the test. Neither is practical work experience. There are plenty of successful certification candidates without a Computer Science degree or much commercial experience. I have never come across a certified DBA without a degree and with no experience, but I am sure they do exist. The first Oracle certification test, 1Z0-007, is not that difficult to pass. Then again, some words of caution might be in order:

- For all Oracle certification tests, the amount of material to absorb is truly immense. The exams are usually about 2 hours in duration and consist of 60 questions.
- The pass mark is generally high at over 70%. To get at least 70% you have to know everything, and I mean everything! Getting a result of well over 70% requires the ability to think rapidly, in addition to having a very deep understanding of the topic. As of the writing of this book, pass rates for Oracle certification exams can be found on the Internet at the URL http://www.oracle.com/education/certification/index.html?dba9i_exam.html.

So who is the ideal candidate to pass the 1Z0-007 Oracle certification exam? Try to answer this question by putting yourself to the test.

Put Yourself to the Test

In this section you will answer some simple questions. To begin with, you should try to determine how much time and work you have to invest to pass the 1Z0-007 Oracle certification exam. The truth is that the less experience and education you have, the more difficult it will be for you to pass, and thus the harder you will have to work. However, as I said earlier in this chapter, the 1Z0-007 exam is not that difficult. Someone with an extremely high IQ and photographic memory could quite possibly scrape by this test simply by reading this book. Unfortunately, most people do not have that level of intelligence. It will require at least some work, no matter what your inherent or learned skill set is.

Let's examine your educational background and your hands-on experience, and test your exam readiness.

Your Educational Background

This section examines educational backgrounds from little schooling through to university and Oracle-specific courses.

- Do you have a photographic memory?

  If yes, you might have a vague chance of passing simply by reading this book. Then again, a certain amount of understanding is required to beat a pass rate of 70% in any type of exam. The problem with learning by heart is that you probably will not have the faintest idea what to do when faced with an employer expecting results.

- Did you finish schooling?

  You might have the required skills, assuming that your schooling included some fairly sophisticated computer skills. Subject areas such as mathematics and logic would be a great help. The same applies as in the preceding point about employers expecting instant results.

- Did you attend some type of technical school or computer cram course?

  This question applies to low-level or short-term computer courses. Many of these courses are extremely basic or very focused in one particular area. If the focus of these courses was SQL, relational databases, and particularly Oracle, you might survive the exam.

- Do you have a college or university degree?

  In terms of education, a college or university degree is the best background to have. Often the intention of a university-level education is to teach you how to think. Not only how to think but to think in a certain way, as a professional in a specific field of thought. A university education is not necessarily specific, like a 3 month computer cram course is, but it is the best form of education. A computer science degree is the better option, but mathematics or even subject areas such as physics can be useful.

- Have you completed any Oracle courses? Have you read Oracle texts?

  Oracle Corp. and many independent schools exist that teach Oracle coursework. This would help perhaps better than anything, assuming you have the basic educational background, work experience, or high intelligence level to absorb large amounts of complex course material.

That's education, and the requirements are again by no means absolute. An education can give you a very good grounding in any endeavor—the higher the level of education, the better.

Your Hands-on Experience

So what about experience? What about hands-on commercial work experience? What is your work history? We can assess this by examining various layers of your work experience:

- Do you work in the computer industry?

  Are you a programmer; developer; data model designer; systems analyst; or database, systems, or network administrator? General use of end-user products such as MS Access or Excel should probably be excluded. Work experience really needs involve the nitty-gritty details of coding on and maintenance of computer systems. Skills such as data model design and systems analysis are somewhat removed from expert use of Oracle SQL, but not always.

- How long have you worked as a developer or computer administrator?

  Six months probably won't cut it. A few years would be useful. Have you done development or database and systems administration work? What level is this work experience at? Have you used power tools such as Crystal Reports, or have you written Oracle SQL code? Do you know how to start up an Oracle database? If some Oracle database files went missing, would you know how to recover the database? Do you know how to retrieve 10 rows from an Oracle database table containing 100 million rows without completely killing database performance?

- Do you have experience working with relational databases? If so, how much?

  Any relational database applies such as Sybase, Ingres, DB2, or even SQL Server. There are many relational databases in commercial use. Experienced DBAs and developers with extensive relational database work experience generally do not have too much trouble crossing over to Oracle. However, Oracle database is structurally much more complex than other relational databases. Oracle Corp. is the most successful relational database vendor by a long shot. The result is much more money for investment in development of Oracle database and a plethora of available tools. The result is that Oracle SQL is much more complex and versatile than SQL is in all other relational databases. Even DBAs with years of experience in other relational databases need to do quite a lot of work to pass Oracle certification exams. I would know because I used Ingres database for years before crossing over to Oracle database.

Testing Your Exam Readiness

Undoubtedly, practice exams are one of the best options for testing your readiness. Practice exams help in various ways:

- Practice exams highlight weak spots for further study.
- Practice exams give you a general perspective on question format. Practicing exams in the format in which they will be presented in the examination room can help enormously on the day of the test. Otherwise, the particular format of Oracle certification multiple-choice questions could easily deteriorate into a multiple-guess test.
- Practice exams allow a general assessment of readiness by giving you a percentage. Practice test questions are much easier than the real thing. Make sure you get well above the pass mark of 70% on practice test questions before diving into the actual exam. Also, don't simply run through the practice questions until you know them all by heart, because that will not help. In general, I have found that practice exams assess knowledge of topics. Questions in the real exam force you to think, thus requiring a fairly high level of understanding. In other words, you are unlikely to pass simply by memorizing all the practice questions, even if you do have a photographic memory and an Einsteinian IQ!

Assessing Your Readiness for the 1Z0-007 Exam

So now let's tie all these things together. At this point you may be completely confused. For the purposes of clarity, I will use a process of comparison. I will talk about my personal experience with Oracle certification tests.

As far as I know, my IQ is well above average but perhaps a slice of cheese short of a sandwich when it comes to reaching genius level. So, no, I do not have a photographic memory. I did complete my schooling. I spent six years at good universities obtaining parts of two completely disparate degrees, one of those being a Computer Science degree. I did not achieve fantastic results at the university due to too many distractions. College students know all about the distractions of college or university life.

I have a few short computer courses under my belt, but these I considered as getting my foot into various doors along the way. In general, I have a lot of education, but as I said I am no genius. I worked with the Ingres relational database and other relational databases for about 10 years before crossing over to Oracle. It took me about 4 months to absorb all the material required to pass the 1Z0-007 Oracle certification exam. Perhaps this information will help you judge your readiness before you jump in without looking and spend $90 only to fail the exam.

The best method might be to do a single practice test every few days or weeks, depending on your study schedule. When you get a high enough percentage on average, you are ready for the exam.

Let's get started with Oracle database and Oracle SQL.

Getting Started with Oracle Database

Terms You Need to Understand

- ✓ RDBMS (relational database management system)
- ✓ Table or entity
- ✓ Row or tuple
- ✓ Column
- ✓ Primary key
- ✓ Foreign key
- ✓ Iterative
- ✓ Strategy and analysis phase
- ✓ Design phase
- ✓ Building and documentation stage
- ✓ Transition phase
- ✓ Production phase
- ✓ SQL (Structured Query Language)
- ✓ DML (Data Manipulation Language)
- ✓ DDL (Data Definition Language)
- ✓ SQL*Plus
- ✓ SQL*Plus Worksheet
- ✓ iSQL*Plus
- ✓ Oracle Enterprise Manager

Concepts You Need to Master

- ✓ Normalization
- ✓ Denormalization
- ✓ Referential Integrity
- ✓ System Development Cycle

This chapter introduces basic relational data modeling, Oracle SQL (SELECT, DML, and DDL), various Oracle SQL tools, and new features for Oracle9i SQL. Also included is the MOVIES schema used for all examples throughout this book, plus a brief description of syntax conventions used.

What Is an RDBMS?

RDBMS is an abbreviation for *relational database management system*. A relational database contains tables with data. The management system part is the part allowing you access to that database and the power to manipulate both the database and the data contained within it. A relational database is called a relational database due to setlike relationships established between tables. These relationships are based on the rules of Normalization.

This leads us to relational data modeling.

Basic Relational Data Modeling

Relational data modeling is a simple, or perhaps sometimes not so simple, method of establishing or building relationships between tables. A table contains rows of data. Rows are divided into columns. The objective of the relational data model is twofold. First, application of the rules of Normalization applies structure to data. The most important aspect of Normalization is removal of duplication from the database. Second, enforcement of Referential Integrity ensures, among other things, that data never becomes orphaned and potentially inaccessible.

Normalization is the process of simplifying the structure of data. Denormalization is the opposite of Normalization, usually executed for the sake of performance of data warehouses or reporting. Normalization increases granularity and Denormalization decreases granularity. Granularity is the scope of a definition for any particular thing. The more granular a data model is, the easier it becomes to manage. However, over-granular structures tend to create complexity and hurt performance.

A subsidiary process sometimes required but often neglected is a step called Denormalization. Denormalization is used in data warehouse databases or when the application of the rules of Normalization has been over-zealously applied. So three topics have been mentioned in this section: Normalization, Referential Integrity, and Denormalization. Let's look at each topic in turn.

An entity is synonymous with *a table*. In general, *an entity* refers to a data model and *a table* refers to a database.

Normalization

Normalization consists of various Normal Forms. In practice only 1st, 2nd, and 3rd Normal Forms are useful, and even 3rd Normal Form is often used over-zealously, producing too much granularity. 4th Normal Form and beyond are rare and are often impractical commercially.

Normal Forms are the steps contained within the process of Normalization. Normal Forms are cumulative such that a data model in 3rd Normal Form is in both 2nd and 1st Normal Forms, but not 4th or 5th Normal Form.

1st Normal Form eliminates repeating groups (rows containing repeated column values) by dividing a single entity into two separate entities, connecting the two new entities with a one-to-many relationship. Both entities get primary keys. A primary key uniquely identifies each row in a table. The entity on the "many" side of the relationship has a foreign key. The foreign key column contains primary key values of the entity on the "one" side of the relationship. A 1st Normal Form transformation is shown in Figure 1.1.

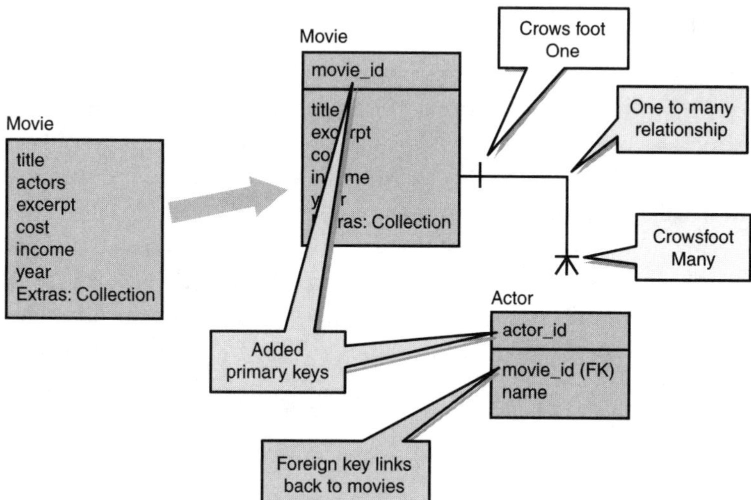

Figure 1.1 A 1st Normal Form transformation.

In Figure 1.1 movie titles duplicated by multiple actors are removed by separating movies and actors into two entities. In Figure 1.2 it should be clear that movie title repetitions are removed by creation of a one-to-many relationship between movies and their respective actors.

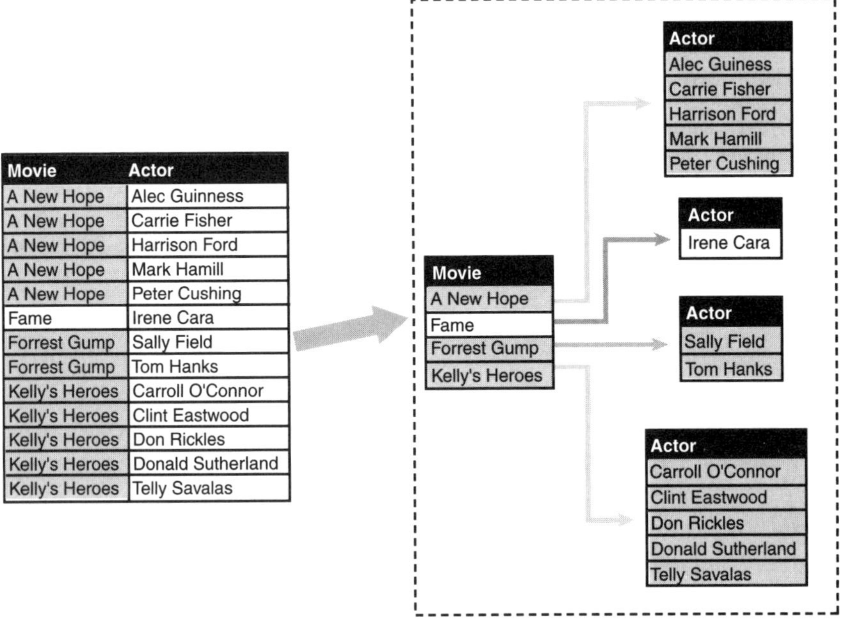

Figure 1.2 A 1st Normal Form one-to-many relationship.

2nd Normal Form eliminates redundant data by separating an entity into two entities in which the 1st Normal Form entity contains columns not dependent on the primary key, or only a part of a composite primary key. Unlike 1st Normal Form, in which repetitive rows are spread to a new entity, for 2nd Normal Form repeated rows are consolidated to a new entity. In simpler terms, 2nd Normal Form creates many-to-one relationships between dynamic and static data, separating static data into the new entity. A many-to-one relationship is identical to a one-to-many relationship. The term is reversed for descriptive purposes only. A 2nd Normal Form transformation is shown in Figure 1.3.

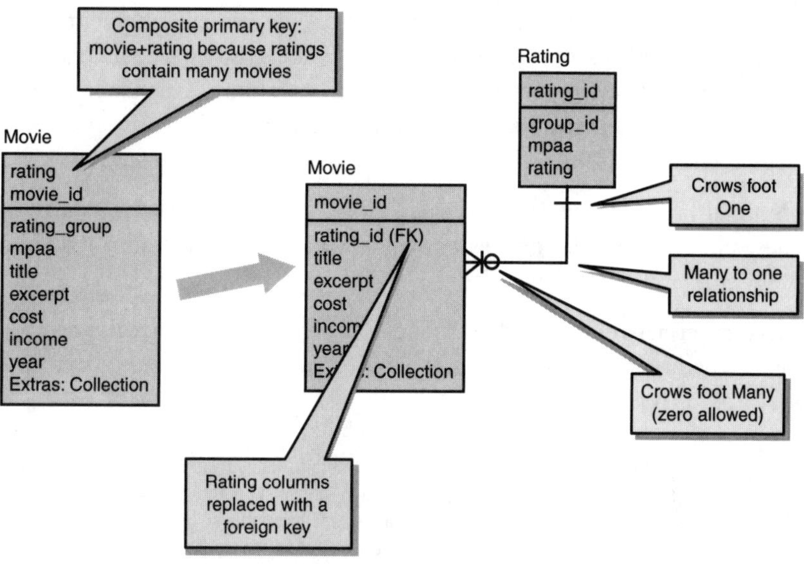

Figure 1.3 A 2nd Normal Form transformation.

One important point to note about the specific transformation in Figure 1.3 is the possibility of zero on the many side of the relationship. What this means is that there does not have to be a movie in the movie table for every rating. For instance, movies in my database are rated as PG, PG-13, and R, but I have no movies rated as NC-17 (no children under 17). Figure 1.4 shows that there are some ratings not assigned to any movies and that rating information other than the MPAA code is removed from the movie table.

Movie	Rating
Young Frankenstein	PG
The Phantom Menace	PG
A New Hope	PG
The Empire Strikes Back	PG
Return of the Jedi	PG
Patton	PG
The Perfect Storm	PG-13
Waterworld	PG-13
Forrest Gump	PG-13
Blazing Saddles	R
Midnight Express	R
Fame	R
Scent of a Woman	R
Serpico	R
Kelly's Heroes	U
Richard III	U
Scarface	U

MPAA	RATING
G	General
NC-17	No Children Under 17
NR	Not Rated
PG	Parent Guidance
PG-13	Parent Guidance Under 13
R	Restricted
U	Unrated
	Family Viewing

Figure 1.4 A 2nd Normal Form many-to-one relationship.

3rd Normal Form expects all nonkey fields to be dependent on the primary key with no transitive dependencies. What is a transitive dependency? A transitive dependency implies that when a given column X depends on the key and column Y depends on column X, then column Y depends on the key through column X. Column Y is transitively dependent on the key.

4th Normal Form disperses multivalued facts in a single entity into separate entities, and 5th Normal Form essentially covers anything already missed by 1st, 2nd, 3rd, and 4th Normal Forms.

Most commercial relational data models rarely use 3rd Normal Form or beyond. Dividing data into too many parts (granularity) can cause performance issues for relational databases.

As a personal simplification, I like to call many-to-many relations and their link entity resolutions 3rd Normal Form. This is quite obviously complete hogwash! However, looking at the inscrutability of the accepted descriptions for the different Normal Forms, perhaps my simplification of Normalization makes data model design a little easier. After all, I have been designing relational data models for years. Most of what I do is instinctive, and I never really think in terms of applying the rules of Normalization, based on precise Normal Form terminology.

The most important thing about data modeling is in understanding what data is about. You must know what the data is describing, and you should understand the business application. One of my biggest problems with Normal Forms is that it tends to partially ignore the nature of data from a business perspective, the meaning of data. Application of Normal Forms tries to abstract data by concentrating on syntax (rules) and disregarding semantics (meaning). In reality it is very difficult to totally abstract a commercial business application by a set of mathematical rules. Mathematics is perfection. The real world is far from perfect and is certainly not predictable enough to be completely abstracted into mathematics, other than complete chaos!

Specific questions about Normalization and Normal Forms are extremely unlikely in OCP exams, but an understanding is essential to being able to describe the use of primary and foreign keys.

Referential Integrity

Referential Integrity validates one-to-many relationships. This validation is a process of making sure that related primary and foreign key column values actually exist. For instance, a foreign key value cannot be added to a table unless the related primary key value exists in the parent table. Similarly, deleting a primary key value necessitates removing all rows in subsidiary tables containing that primary key value in foreign key columns.

Additionally, it follows that preventing the deletion of a primary key row is not allowed if a foreign key exists elsewhere.

Cascading deletions from primary to foreign keys is possible, but you must explicitly request cascading deletions when deleting a primary key row in a table.

Beware of deleting rows from tables using cascading primary and foreign key constraints. Also beware of using certain DDL commands, including cascading options such as **DROP TABLE <table> CASCADE CONSTRAINTS**, **DROP USER <user> CASCADE**, or **DROP TABLESPACE <tablespace> INCLUDING CONTENTS**. Results can be extremely upsetting!

Referential Integrity is enforced in one of three ways. Referential Integrity can be implemented in an Oracle database using constraints or triggers, and even outside the database in application coding. The most effective method for implementing Referential Integrity in an Oracle database is by using constraints (see Chapter 11, "Tables, Datatypes, and Constraints (DDL)"). Constraints are centralized, standardized, the best option for performance, and easy to change.

Denormalization

Denormalization is a very interesting topic. Denormalization is the opposite of Normalization and with numerous other possible additions. Denormalization can sometimes involve the undoing of Normal Forms, particularly 3rd Normal Form and beyond. Denormalization is primarily used in an Oracle database for data warehousing and reporting. Denormalization also includes special database objects for presorting and prejoining data, avoiding construction of sorts and joins when data is accessed. The following list briefly details specialized Oracle Database objects such as clusters, index organized tables (IOTs), and materialized views:

- Oracle Database clusters combine commonly used columns, usually from multiple tables, into a single, presorted, and even prejoined physical chunk of data. Clusters are normally used to create joins and sort data in advance, avoiding repeated processing of joins and sorts already contained within clusters.
- An IOT is a table built as an index. Normally, an index contains a small subset of table columns. For an IOT, all rows and all columns are contained within an index.
- A materialized view physically contains data, generally as a summary or straight copy of underlying table data. Do not confuse materialized

views with views. Where a materialized view creates a snapshot copy of data, a view overlays existing data in real-time. A snapshot copy of data is a picture of data at a specific point in time. Materialized views are commonly used in data warehouses or sometimes even to maintain partial remote database copies.

Denormalization Does Include Use of Views

Views Denormalize only as a logical overlay and are thus logical and not physical Denormalization. Therefore, views do not serve to increase performance by way of consolidating over-granular data. Denormalization is nearly always a case for performance improvement. Using views for Denormalization purposes is meaningless.

Other Denormalizing, or granularity reduction, techniques involve making copies or summaries of parts of tables in other tables, among other options, including the following techniques:

- Duplicating columns across tables to avoid joins.
- Summarizing totals into parent tables.
- Separating huge amounts of historical data from small amounts of active data. This is often the primary function of a data warehouse. A data warehouse is often a collection of historical data, transferred from and destroyed in a transactional (OLTP) database.
- Physical separation of columns into separate tables based on highly disparate access rates.
- Caching of data performed on middle tier or client browser tier machines.

Questions on Denormalization will not be found in OCP exams, but a conceptual understanding is essential.

The Object-Relational Data Model

The object-relational data model is the combination of relational and object data models, two completely contradictory methodologies. The object-relational data model takes various forms:

- The object-relational data model sometimes attempts to emulate an object model in a relational database by using surrogate keys. Surrogate keys allow the removal of foreign keys from composite primary keys by adding a table-wide unique primary key.

- Objects can be stored into relational database rows (tuples) as binary objects. Binary objects either are physically stored inline with rows or are stored as both direct and indirect pointers external to tables.
- Recent enhancements to Oracle database allow inclusion of collections into tables. Effectively, an object collection allows multiple iterations within a single table row to be stored in each row (or pointed to—see the preceding bullet). This practice, of course, completely contradicts relational data modeling and Normalization by removing a one-to-many relationship between a primary and subset foreign key table.

That is more than enough about data modeling to give you a general understanding.

Database Design and Modeling the Oracle Way

Oracle documentation often includes topics such as the System Development Cycle, distinct steps, and an iterative process.

The distinct steps of the iterative System Development Cycle may be included in this OCP exam.

Oracle Corp. classifies the System Development Cycle as consisting of five distinct steps. The term *iterative* is used to imply that the distinct steps can be revisited more than once, either in part or as a whole, and not necessarily in sequence. The System Development Cycle steps are shown here:

1. *Strategy and Analysis*—This step analyzes user requirements and produces a system specification.
2. *Design*—The design stage covers technical design documentation. Technical design documentation is a direct successor to and produced from the user requirements and system specifications.
3. *Build and Document*—Building implies the conversion of the technical design document into executable software code and data structures.

Thus the building process is construction of Oracle databases and software applications.

4. *Transition*—A transition implies user acceptance testing and any final modifications as a result of discrepancies (bugs) found during testing.

5. *Production*—The production stage is the final stage in which applications actually come into use in the real world. Application support is passed over to production support, and applications are released to the general user population.

Aside from the System Development Cycle, Oracle Corp. also likes to vary the appearance of tables and relationships as represented in entity relationship diagrams (ERD). These graphics are shown in Figure 1.5.

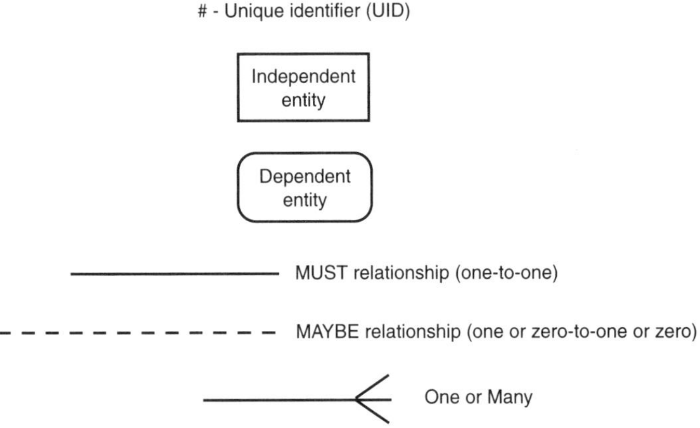

Figure 1.5 Relational data modeling the Oracle way.

What Is Oracle SQL?

Let's briefly examine Oracle SQL. SQL, pronounced either "ess-queue-ell" or "sequel", is an abbreviation for the term *Structured Query Language*.

SQL is used to access the data in a relational database by way of retrieving columns from both a single data source and combinations of data sources. Ultimately, a data source is a table, but both logical and physical layers can be used as data sources, mapping between SQL commands and underlying tables. Those physical and logical layers can be database objects such as physically presorted index organized tables or logical overlays such as views.

The roots of SQL lie in a relational database access language devised for a relational database from IBM called System R. System R was used to access data in tuples (table rows) from the original IBM relational database, the precursor of DB2. The ideas for System R SQL originated with the inventor of the relational data model.

One interesting difference with Oracle SQL and SQL used by other relational databases is the separation in Oracle Database of what are called Data Manipulation Language (DML) and Data Definition Language (DDL) commands. DML commands can be undone (rolled back); DDL commands cannot be rolled back. DDL commands commit automatically. DML manipulates data and thus DML commands are used to change data in the database.

DDL commands cannot be undone using a **ROLLBACK** command or otherwise.

DDL implies changing database objects such as the structure of tables themselves. More generally, DDL commands are used to change database metadata. Metadata is the data about the data, the tables, the indexes, the views, and any other database object. For example, changing columns in a table is a change to metadata.

Let's get back to SQL. The most primitive form of SQL was a theory of a reporting language devised by the inventor of the relational data model. The roots of SQL lie with retrieval of sets of data. This means that SQL was intended as a language to retrieve many rows from one or many tables at once, producing a result set. SQL was not originally intended to retrieve individual rows from relational databases as exact row matches in transactional or OLTP databases. On the contrary, SQL can now be used to do precisely this, and very efficiently.

In essence, SQL was developed as a shorthand method of retrieving information from relational databases, and it has become the industry standard over the past 20 years. Here is an example of a query (a question posed to the database that asks for certain information) written in SQL:

```
SELECT TITLE "Movie", NAME "Actor"
FROM MOVIE JOIN PART USING (MOVIE_ID)
    JOIN ACTOR USING (ACTOR_ID)
ORDER BY 1, 2;
```

The SELECT command is actually neither a DML command nor a DDL command. Why? The SELECT statement is used exclusively to retrieve data from an Oracle database. DML commands change data and DDL commands change metadata. Because a SELECT command only retrieves without changing anything, it is by definition neither a DML nor a DDL command.

Tools

Oracle provides user-friendly interactive tools for executing SQL commands and maintaining an Oracle database. These tools have several variations:

- *SQL*Plus*—SQL*Plus can be executed either from a shell using SQLPLUS.EXE or in a window using SQLPLUSW.EXE.
- *SQL*Plus Worksheet*—SQL*Plus Worksheet comes packaged with Oracle Enterprise Manager and provides a much more user-friendly form of SQL*Plus.
- *iSQL*Plus*—iSQL*Plus implies "Internet SQL*Plus" and is a browser-enabled form of SQL*Plus. iSQL*Plus can be used just like SQL*Plus, running SQL commands and generating reporting in HTML format.
- *Oracle Enterprise Manager*—This tool provides a complete suite of tools and programs for accessing, maintaining, tuning, and administering an Oracle database.

SQL*Plus

SQL*Plus can be executed either from a shell as SQLPLUS.EXE or from a Windows interface as SQLPLUSW.EXE. In both cases a username, password and database or network name are required to connect to an Oracle database.

The simplest network naming method is something Oracle calls the Transparent Network Substrate (TNS). TNS is defined by a configuration file on a client machine called `$ORACLE_HOME/network/admin/tnsnames.ora`.

On a Win2K box the variable **$ORACLE_HOME** is defaulted to **c:\oracle\ora*nn***, ***nn*** representing the version release of Oracle software (*92* or *10*).

The configuration shown below is a sample configuration file from my client machine. This particular configuration contains two databases, one called TEST and the other called OLTP. These two databases are on two separate machines called 2000server and 1300server, respectively. The database names happen to be the same as the network names for the sake of simplicity.

```
TEST =
  (DESCRIPTION =
    (ADDRESS_LIST =
      (ADDRESS = (PROTOCOL = TCP)(HOST = 2000server)(PORT = 1521))
    )
    (CONNECT_DATA =
      (SERVER = DEDICATED)
      (SERVICE_NAME = TEST)
    )
  )

OLTP =
  (DESCRIPTION =
    (ADDRESS_LIST =
      (ADDRESS = (PROTOCOL = TCP)(HOST = 1300server)(PORT = 1521))
    )
    (CONNECT_DATA =
      (SERVER = DEDICATED)
      (SERVICE_NAME = OLTP)
    )
  )
```

On the database server side there is a listener process "listening" for incoming connection requests from client machines, or the database server. The configuration file for the listener and TNS resides on the server as `$ORACLE_HOME/network/admin/listener.ora`. A sample listener configuration file (`LISTENER.ORA`) is shown here:

```
LISTENER =
  (DESCRIPTION_LIST =
    (DESCRIPTION =
      (ADDRESS_LIST =
        (ADDRESS = (PROTOCOL = TCP)(HOST = 2000server)(PORT = 1521))
      )
    )
  )

SID_LIST_LISTENER =
  (SID_LIST =
    (SID_DESC =
      (GLOBAL_DBNAME = TEST)
      (ORACLE_HOME = C:\oracle\ora92)
      (SID_NAME = TEST)
    )
  )
```

To connect to SQL*Plus from a shell, type the following command in a shell:

```
SQLPLUS SYSTEM/password@TEST;
```

From within SQL*Plus type this:

```
CONNECT SYSTEM/password@TEST;
```

To disconnect type the following:

```
DISCONNECT;
EXIT;
```

Connecting to a different user while already connected will execute a disconnection from the currently connected user.

Connecting to the database using the Windows form of SQL*Plus requires execution of the program SQLPLUSW.EXE from either a command line or a menu interface. Connecting using SQLPLUSW.EXE is simple, as shown in Figure 1.6.

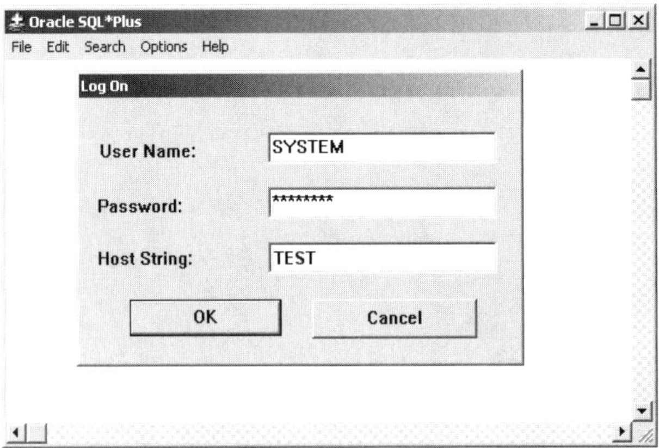

Figure 1.6 Connecting to an Oracle database in **SQL*PLUSW.EXE**.

Figure 1.6 shows that a connection requires a username, password, and host string. The host string is the same as a network name, in our case TEST.

If you have problems connecting to a database, talk to your database administrator. Communicating with an Oracle database can be much more complex and potentially problematic than described in this chapter.

SQL*Plus Worksheet

Connecting to an Oracle database using SQL*Plus Worksheet requires the same username, password, and network name combination as for SQL*Plus. The only difference in launching is that the Worksheet must be launched from a menu, from within Oracle Enterprise Manager, or within a shell using the following command:

```
oemapp worksheet
```

Finding and describing menus is not in the scope of an *Exam Cram 2* book.

Figure 1.7 shows our previously used connection parameters, this time using SQL*Plus Worksheet.

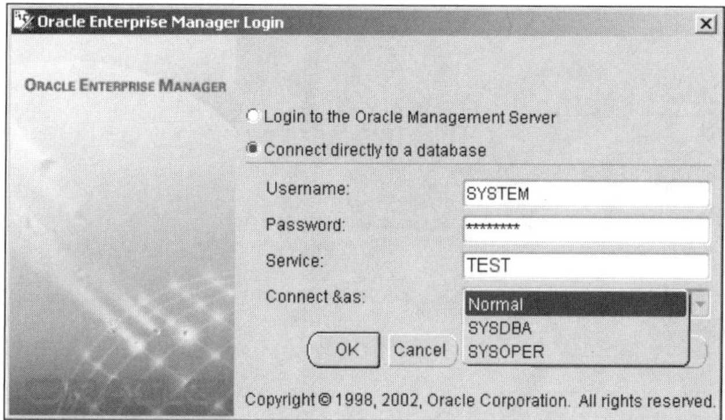

Figure 1.7 Connecting to an Oracle database in SQL*Plus Worksheet.

Once again, Figure 1.7 shows username, password, and network name values. There are two differences:

- Optionally log in to an Oracle Management Server process or connect directly to a database. The Oracle Management Server is intended for multiple Oracle database installation, enterprise level use.
- A database administration user with SYSDBA and/or SYSOPER privileges can connect with these high-level privileges. Otherwise, simply connect as *Normal*. The SYSDBA privilege is usually granted only to the SYS user and is used for serious tasks such as restarting an Oracle database.

A connection will not be allowed with the **SYS** user unless the **SYSDBA** or **SYSOPER** privileges are used.

iSQL*Plus

Oracle9i comes with a mini web server process called Oracle HTTP Server. The HTTP server process allows communication between a browser and an Oracle database. Connecting to an Oracle database using iSQL*Plus is very similar to using SQL*Plus and SQL*Plus Worksheet.

To connect to an Oracle database using iSQL*Plus, open a browser such as Internet Explorer and type in a uniform resource locator (URL) in the following form:

http://<mymachine>.<mydomain>:7778/isqlplus

For my database the URL looks like this:

http://2000server:7778/isqlplus

The connection to the database is shown in Figure 1.8.

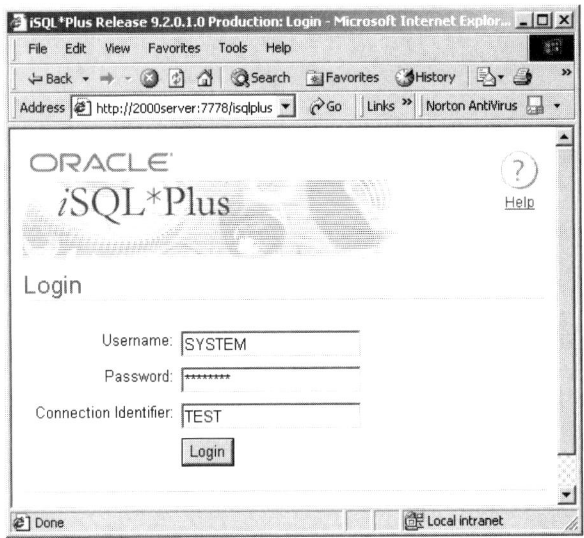

Figure 1.8 Connecting to an Oracle database in iSQL*Plus.

In the case of Figure 1.8, I am connecting to iSQL*Plus using the same username, password, and database server machine.

If you have problems connecting with iSQL*Plus, contact your database administrator.

Oracle Enterprise Manager

A detailed dissertation of Oracle Enterprise Manager software is not required in this book. What I will do is describe its capabilities in general. Those capabilities are formidable and are contained within an excellent graphical user interface (GUI). The easiest way to access Oracle Enterprise Manager is by launching the Console, either from a menu or by executing the following shell command:

```
oemapp console
```

The Console will allow access to the multifarious array of applications available from within Oracle Enterprise Manager. Oracle Enterprise Manager truly is an enterprise-wide Oracle software management tool, as its name describes, even though it can be a little flaky at times.

Oracle Enterprise Manager allows for many enterprise-wide benefits. Descriptive terms commonly used are terms such as single point management, scalability and distribution, extensible, fully automated, intelligent, and easy to use. “Easy to use” is a contradiction in terms. An enormous array of capabilities naturally introduces immense complexity.

The capabilities of Oracle Enterprise Manager conjure up terms such as automated job control, fire and forget event detection, automated discovery, paging and email to the database administrator in the middle of the night, extensive security, and far-reaching reporting capabilities of both preemptive and reactive kinds.

Yes, lots of long words! What can be done with the Console? Here is a list:

- Navigation across all applications and databases within an enterprise
- Job scheduling
- Automated event management and detection
- Instance management
- Schema management
- Security management
- Storage management
- Distribution management
- Data warehouse management
- Workspaces management
- XML management

The Console offers numerous wizards to make tasks easier. Additionally, there are several add-on packages allowing for comprehensive and sometimes intuitive diagnostics, tuning, and change management.

Be careful using wizards or any of the add-on packages. Learn how to use these features on a noncritical database first, preferably a database nobody else is using. Some of the wizards and add-on packages and most of the other Console features mentioned in the preceding bulleted list can make quite drastic changes to a database. If you do something nasty, your DBA might not let you within 100 miles of any database again, *ever!* Or worse! Be careful. Most DBAs are very careful and methodical people. Be careful and methodical, starting now!

Oracle SQL New Features for Oracle9i

In this section we will briefly list new features in Oracle9i for Oracle SQL. Any items without a chapter reference in this book are out of scope but are included to encourage further reading. The term "out of scope" means that a topic is not included in the exam and does not necessarily precisely fit in with the subject matter of Oracle SQL. However, some out-of-scope items are included due to a requirement for essential background knowledge or because they are just interesting. This section lists and briefly describes features for Oracle SQL new to Oracle Database 9i.

Any features new to Oracle9i are referenced by the 9i icon in all other chapters of this book.

General

This first section includes some Oracle9i changes not included in the 1Z0-007 OCP exam and is for informational purposes only. Details of the out-of-scope items will not be detailed in subsequent chapters. It is, however, important to know that these capabilities exist.

- There are a multitude of XML capabilities, which are not relevant to the 1Z0-007 OCP exam and are thus not covered in this book (see my other book *Oracle SQL Jumpstart with Examples*, ISBN: 1555583237).
- Numerous new privileges are introduced, and all are beyond the scope of this book.
- Almost all SQL*Plus features are now supported in iSQL*Plus, allowing for web-based reporting (see Chapter 9, "SQL*Plus Formatting").

SQL Statements

This section is divided into two sections: DML commands and DDL commands.

DML Commands

- The SELECT Command.
  - *ANSI SQL Standards*—ANSI standard join format and other ANSI SQL standards are now supported in Oracle SQL (see Chapter 6, "Joining Tables").
  - *The* ROLLUP *and* CUBE *Clauses*—The GROUP BY clause can be extended to include ROLLUP and CUBE OLAP type functionality (see Chapter 7, "Groups and Summaries [GROUP BY]").
  - *The* WITH *Clause*—A name can be assigned to a subquery block using the WITH clause. This name can be used elsewhere in a query to access the resulting row set (see Chapter 8, "Subqueries and Other Specialized Queries").
  - *Flashback Queries*—Flashback queries can now be executed using special SQL commands (see Chapter 8).
- DEFAULT *Values*—The INSERT and UPDATE commands now allow access to default values (see Chapter 10, "Changing Data [DML]").
- *The* SET TRANSACTION *Command*—Transactions can now be named explicitly (see Chapter 10).
- *The* MERGE *Command*—A new DML command called MERGE can be used to merge rows from a source into a target table. Non-existent rows are inserted into the target table and existing rows are updated (see Chapter 10).

DDL Commands

There are numerous DDL command enhancements, many of which involve database administration. Database administration activities do not apply to this course. Only relevant topics are covered in appropriate chapters.

- The CREATE TABLE and ALTER TABLE commands.
  - *Renaming Columns and Constraints*—Columns and constraints can be renamed using the ALTER TABLE command (see Chapter 11).
  - Constraint maintenance now caters for indexing.
  - External tables manage data stored outside an Oracle database (see my other book *Oracle SQL Jumpstart with Examples*, ISBN: 1555583237).
  - List partitions and range-list composite partitions are now allowed (see my other book *Oracle SQL Jumpstart with Examples*, ISBN: 1555583237).

- XMLType-based tables can be created for containing XML structured documents (see my other book *Oracle SQL Jumpstart with Examples*, ISBN: 1555583237).

- *View Constraints*—Views can now include constraints (see Chapter 12) and subviews when using objects. Both the CREATE VIEW and the ALTER VIEW commands apply.
- Synonyms—The CREATE SYNONYM command now includes objects.

Datatypes

- *The* TIMESTAMP *Datatype*—The TIMESTAMP datatype (see Chapters 4, 5, and 11) supports time-zone–sensitive dates and times. INTERVAL YEAR TO MONTH and INTERVAL DAY TO SECOND express values in years and months plus days and seconds respectively (see Chapter 5 and Chapter 11).
- Oracle-supplied datatypes include datatypes that are often application-specific, such as the Any datatype, XML, and Spatial and Media datatypes. These datatypes are too specific for this book.

Expressions

New expression capabilities include expression-embedded CASE statements, cursor expressions using CURSOR (subquery) syntax and scalar subqueries returning an expression, and datetime and interval expressions (see Chapter 4, "Operators, Conditions, Pseudocolumns, and Expressions").

Conditions

The IS OF type condition checks the type of the instance of an object. In object parlance, an instance of an object is created from a class.

Built-In Functions

There are many new functions for Oracle9i, and a few existing functions have been enhanced. See Chapter 5 for single row functions and Chapter 7 for aggregation and analytic functions.

The MOVIES Schema

In this section we will introduce a schema called the MOVIES schema. It is important to acquaint yourself with this schema because the MOVIES schema tables are used for all examples throughout this book, and as part of the first chapter let's take a look at what makes up this schema. Figure 1.9 shows you the schema ERD visually.

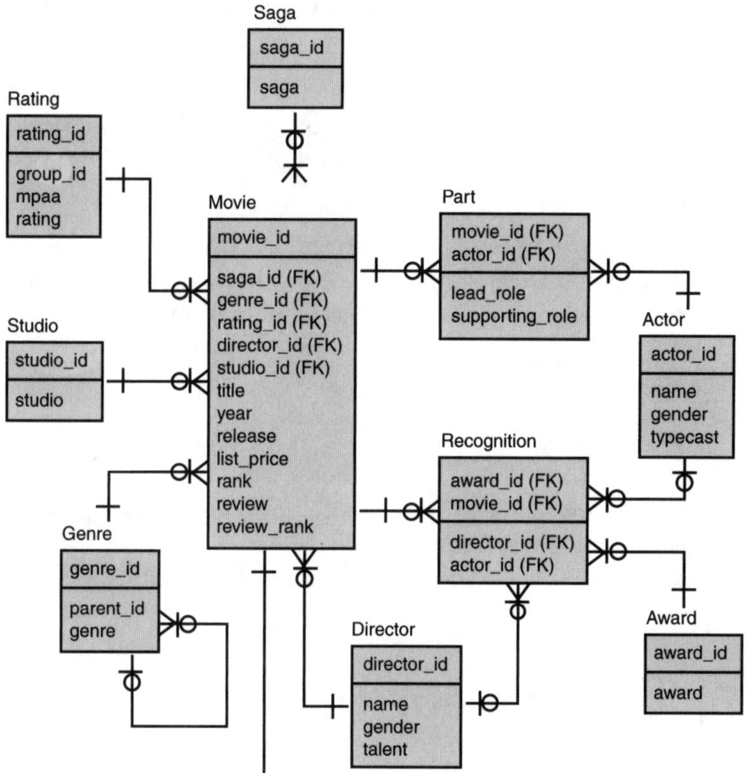

Figure 1.9 The **MOVIES** schema ERD.

The **MOVIES** schema may be expanded and altered throughout this book to accommodate different types of examples. A data warehouse section is introduced in Chapter 7, in the section "Expanding the **MOVIES** Schema."

The basic Online Transaction Processing (OLTP) type tables for the MOVIES schema are given in the following list:

- MOVIE—Lists different movies with foreign keys to many other tables.
- ACTOR—Lists different actors who act in movies.

- DIRECTOR—Lists different directors.
- AWARD—Lists different types of awards given to movies.
- STUDIO—Lists different studios making movies.
- RATING—Contains ratings for movies, such as PG-13.
- GENRE—Contains a hierarchical structure of movie genres. For instance, an Espionage movie, which is categorized as Suspense, is in turn categorized as an Action movie. In reality, movie genres require multiple inheritance, but the current data structure is adequate for the purposes of this book.
- SAGA—Contains groups for movies falling into sagas of multiple movies. For instance, all the Star Wars movies are part of the Star Wars saga of movies.
- PART—Contains the cast of actors in a movie. This table is a many-to-many join resolution between movies and actors, because there are many actors in a movie and actors can also appear in multiple movies.
- RECOGNITION—Is a many-to-many join resolution entity between movies and awards, because a movie can have many awards and a single award can be allocated to many movies.

Scripts to create the **MOVIES** schema and add data to tables can be found on my website at the following URL:

www.oracledbaexpert.com/oracle/OracleSQLExamCram2/index.html

Syntax Conventions Used in This Book

This section examines syntax conventions used throughout this book in both syntax diagrams and coding examples. Syntax diagrams in this book will use the Backus-Naur Form syntax notation convention. Backus-Naur Form is a de facto standard for most computer texts. The following list details syntax standards used in this book, very close to Backus-Naur syntax formatting conventions:

- Optional [...]—For example, a WHERE clause is syntactically optional in a SELECT statement:

```
SELECT * FROM <table> [ WHERE <column> = ... ];
```

- At least one of { ... | ... | ... }—For example, the SELECT statement retrieval list has to include an asterisk (*), retrieval of all columns in a table, or a list of one or more columns:

  ```
  SELECT { * | { <column>, ... } } FROM <table>;
  ```

Where we use curly braces to represent at least one iteration, pure Backus-Naur notation represents zero or more iterations.

- Angle brackets < ... >—Angle brackets are substitution variables. For example, in the line

  ```
  SELECT * FROM <table>;
  ```

  <table> would be replaced with a table name:

  ```
  SELECT * FROM MOVIE;
  ```

- OR |—The pipe character (|) represents an OR conjunction. In other words, either option on either side of the pipe character can be selected:

  ```
  SELECT { * | { <column>, ... } } FROM <table>;
  ```

The next chapter looks at retrieving data from a database using the SELECT statement.

Exam Prep Questions

1. What does the abbreviation RDBMS represent?

   ❑ A. Relative Database Mining System

   ❑ B. Real Database Management System

   ❑ C. Relational Database Mining System

   ❑ D. Relational Database Management System

   ❑ E. None of the above

   Answer D is correct. RDBMS stands for relational database management system. All answers other than E are nonsensical.

2. What does the abbreviation SQL represent?

   ❑ A. Simple Query Language

   ❑ B. Simple Questioning Language

   ❑ C. Structured Questioning Language

   ❑ D. Structured Query Language

   ❑ E. None of the above

   Answer D is correct. SQL stands for Structured Query Language. All answers other than E are nonsensical.

3. Place the following steps of the System Development Cycle in the correct order:

   ❑ 1. Design

   ❑ 2. Transition

   ❑ 3. Strategy and Analysis

   ❑ 4. Build and Document

   ❑ 5. Production

   The correct order is 3, 1, 4, 2, and 5. Those steps are Strategy and Analysis, Design, Build and Document, Transition, Production.

4. Which is the most effective method of enforcing Referential Integrity?

   ❑ A. Using triggers

   ❑ B. Cached on client tier machine memory

   ❑ C. Using constraints

   ❑ D. In application code

   ❑ E. None of the above

   C is the correct answer. Constraints are the better method because they are centrally controlled and easiest to maintain. A is not correct because using triggers will hurt performance and triggers require coding maintenance. Constant coding maintenance introduces new bugs. B is not correct because caching on client memory machines is irrelevant to Referential Integrity. In past versions of Oracle Database, D would have been the correct answer. However, enforcing data integrity using application coding can make applications complex, top-heavy, convoluted, and difficult (expensive) to maintain. Constraints are centralized, are easy to maintain, and can be changed once for many applications. E is incorrect because C is correct.

5. What does the abbreviation DML represent?
   - ❑ A. Data Munching Language
   - ❑ B. Data Manipulative Language
   - ❑ C. Database Manipulation Language
   - ❑ D. Data Manipulation Language
   - ❑ E. None of the above

   Answer D is correct. DML stands for Data Manipulation Language. All answers other than E are nonsensical.

6. What does the abbreviation DDL represent?
   - ❑ A. Data Dumping Language
   - ❑ B. Database Definitional Language
   - ❑ C. Database Definition Language
   - ❑ D. Data Definition Language
   - ❑ E. None of the above

   Answer D is correct. DDL stands for Data Definition Language. All answers other than E are nonsensical.

7. Select all correct answers:
   - ❑ A. DML allows metadata changes using only the **ROLLBACK** command.
   - ❑ B. DML allows metadata changes using only the **COMMIT** command.
   - ❑ C. DDL allows metadata changes.
   - ❑ D. DML does not allow metadata changes.
   - ❑ E. DML allows table data changes.

   DML changes table data and DDL changes metadata. Therefore, A, B, and D are incorrect. On the same basis, C and E are correct.

8. Select all correct answers:
   - ❑ A. All DDL commands can be rolled back.
   - ❑ B. All DML commands can be rolled back.
   - ❑ C. Both A and B.
   - ❑ D. Neither A nor B.
   - ❑ E. Both DML and DDL commands can be rolled back.

   DML commands can be rolled back and DDL commands cannot be rolled back. Thus, A is false and B is true. It follows that C, D, and E are all false. B is the only correct answer.

9. What are the three most essential parameters for connecting to a database using tools such as SQL*Plus, iSQL*Plus, SQL*Plus Worksheet, and the Oracle Enterprise Manager Console?

   - ❑ A. Some fast typing
   - ❑ B. A network name
   - ❑ C. The **SYSDBA** privilege
   - ❑ D. The correct password
   - ❑ E. The required username

   Answers B, D, and E are correct because a username, its password, and a network name are required to connect to an Oracle database. The **SYSDBA** privilege is usually required only for the **SYS** user. Answer A is ridiculous. C is incorrect because the **SYSDBA** privilege is correct only when one is connecting as **SYS** or another user assigned this privilege.

10. Which of these commands could succeed in connecting to an Oracle database?

    - ❑ A. `CONNECT SYS/password@TEST;`
    - ❑ B. `CONNECT SYS/password@TEST AS SYSDBA;`
    - ❑ C. `CONNECT SYS/password@TEST AS SYSOPER;`
    - ❑ D. All of the above
    - ❑ E. None of the above

    The commands in B and C are correct because the **CONNECT** command requires the **SYSBDA** or **SYSOPER** privilege to succeed. Thus, A will fail and D and E are incorrect.

Retrieving Data (SELECT)

Terms You Need to Understand

- ✓ The **SELECT** statement
- ✓ The **FROM** clause
- ✓ Query
- ✓ Column and column list
- ✓ Schema
- ✓ Expression
- ✓ Alias
- ✓ **DISTINCT** versus **ALL**
- ✓ **NULL**

Concepts You Need to Master

- ✓ What a query is
- ✓ What an expression is
- ✓ The difference between a column and an expression
- ✓ Simple queries
- ✓ The **DUAL** table
- ✓ The effect of **NULL** values on the result of expressions
- ✓ The **DISTINCT** clause
- ✓ Repeating groups

This chapter jumps straight into the basic syntax of data retrieval using the Oracle SQL SELECT statement, additionally briefly introducing some specifics.

What Is a Query?

A *query* is a statement interrogating the database and returning information. Most often tables are interrogated and rows from those tables are returned. Queries can be both simple and complex. Some complex Oracle SQL queries can do some very interesting things indeed.

SELECT Statement Syntax and Query Capabilities

Let's begin by introducing the basics of the SELECT statement, including syntax, how columns are selected, using aliases, and what can be selected from an Oracle database. The syntax for the basic SELECT statement is simple, as shown in Figure 2.1.

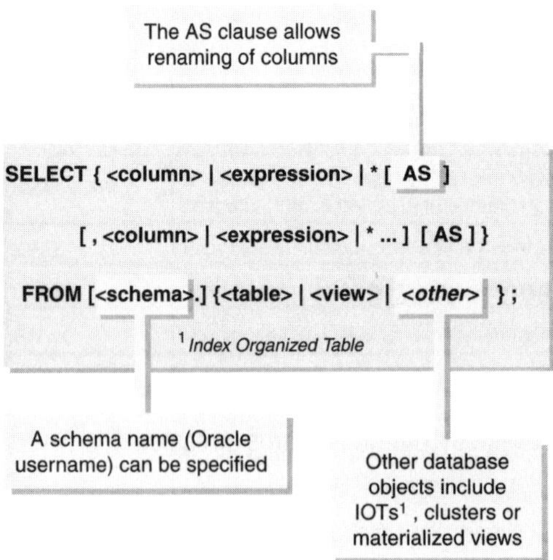

Figure 2.1 Basic **SELECT** statement syntax.

Following is a synopsis of the syntax diagram as shown in Figure 2.1:

➤ The SELECT list is the list of items retrieved.

- The SELECT list can consist of an asterisk (*), one or more columns or expressions. An asterisk is used as a substitution character representing all available columns in the object or objects retrieved from.
- The AS clause allows renaming of columns within the scope of a query. Renamed columns can be referenced later in the query in a limited fashion, they change header names and allow COLUMN command (see Chapter 9, "SQL *Plus Formatting") access.
- When referencing a column or a table they can be referenced using a schema name. This allows users to access tables belonging to other users (a user and a schema are the same thing).
- Various database objects can be select from as shown by <other>: table, view, IOT, cluster, materialized view.

Memorize and understand the content of all syntax diagrams in this book. OCP exams have very specific syntax questions and expect an understanding of all syntax!

Selecting Columns from Tables

As shown in Figure 2.1 one, many, or all columns, or even an expression, can be retrieved using a SELECT statement.

This example selects a single column:

```
SELECT TITLE FROM MOVIE;
```

This example selects three columns:

```
SELECT TITLE, YEAR, RANK FROM MOVIE;
```

This example selects all columns in the MOVIE table using the asterisk (* or star character):

```
SELECT * FROM MOVIE;
```

The following example also selects all columns but lists all the columns by name instead of using the * (asterisk). In this case the preceding example is better, although the next example may be slightly more efficient.

The asterisk or * character is used in Oracle SQL syntax in two places: in the select list of a **SELECT** statement when all columns are to be retrieved, and as a multiplication operator in arithmetic expressions.

```
SELECT MOVIE_ID, SAGA_ID, GENRE_ID, RATING_ID, DIRECTOR_ID, STUDIO_ID,
TITLE, YEAR, RELEASE, LIST_PRICE, RANK, REVIEWS, REVIEW_RANK
FROM MOVIE;
```

The next example retrieves the product of two columns, the product being an expression:

```
COL PROJSALES FORMAT $9,999,990.99 HEADING "Projected Sales"
SELECT TITLE, LIST_PRICE * RANK AS PROJSALES FROM MOVIE;
```

The first line in the preceding query is something new. The COL command is allowing me to format my output for readability. Figure 2.2 shows the result of this query.

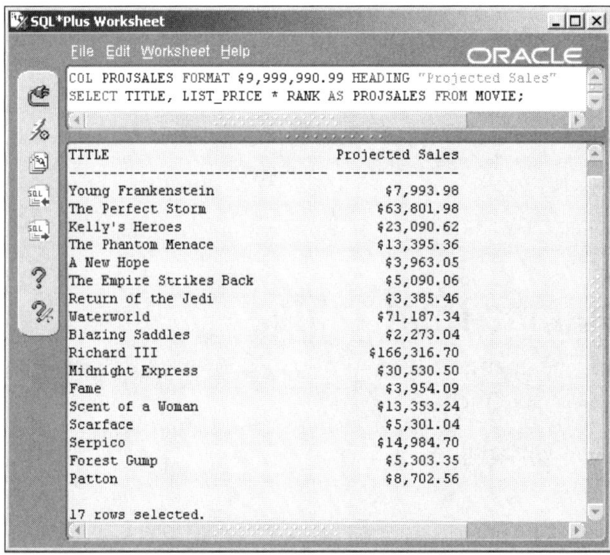

```
COL PROJSALES FORMAT $9,999,990.99 HEADING "Projected Sales"
SELECT TITLE, LIST_PRICE * RANK AS PROJSALES FROM MOVIE;

TITLE                            Projected Sales
-------------------------------- ---------------
Young Frankenstein                     $7,993.98
The Perfect Storm                     $63,801.98
Kelly's Heroes                        $23,090.62
The Phantom Menace                    $13,395.36
A New Hope                             $3,963.05
The Empire Strikes Back                $5,090.06
Return of the Jedi                     $3,385.46
Waterworld                            $71,187.34
Blazing Saddles                        $2,273.04
Richard III                          $166,316.70
Midnight Express                      $30,530.50
Fame                                   $3,954.09
Scent of a Woman                      $13,353.24
Scarface                               $5,301.04
Serpico                               $14,984.70
Forest Gump                            $5,303.35
Patton                                 $8,702.56

17 rows selected.
```

Figure 2.2 Some simple column formatting.

Notice in Figure 2.2 how the product expression result is renamed using the AS clause to PROJSALES. The PROJSALES column has specific formatting applied to it using the SQL*Plus COL formatting command executed immediately before the query:

```
COL PROJSALES FORMAT $9,999,990.99 HEADING "Projected Sales"
```

The COL command or COLUMN command imposes a money format with a floating $ sign, plus the heading Projected Sales, on to the PROJSALES expression result column.

SQL*Plus formatting is covered in detail in Chapter 9, "SQL*Plus Formatting."

The next example shows retrieval from a table accessed through the `MOVIES` schema name:

```
SELECT TITLE FROM MOVIES.MOVIE;
```

Specifying a schema name is usually optional and is an absolute requirement only when retrieving from an accessible table in a different schema. There is no harm in specifying the schema name for the currently connected user. In this case the `MOVIES` schema is the currently connected user.

Using Aliases

The next thing is to use what is called an alias. As shown in the syntax diagram in Figure 2.3, an alias is a shorthand or secondary name, which can be applied to a table if defined in the `FROM` clause. An alias can be used to access columns retrieved in the query.

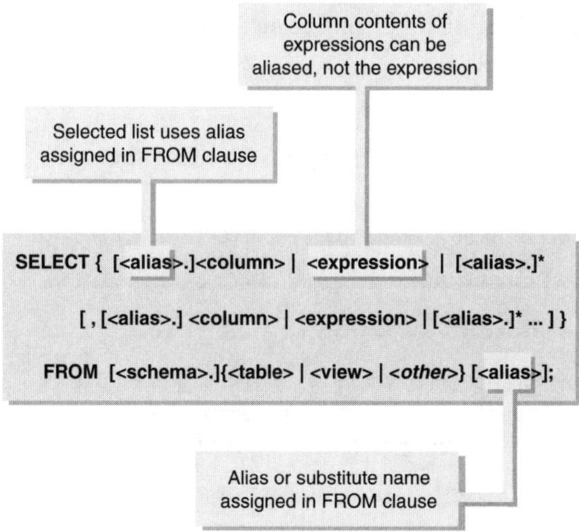

Figure 2.3 Basic **SELECT** statement syntax using aliases.

Following is a synopsis of the syntax diagram shown in Figure 2.3:

- An alias can be defined for a table or object in the FROM clause.
- Columns can be accessed within the SELECT list, ORDER BY clause, WHERE clause, and other clauses using columns prefixed by an alias, in the form `<alias>.<column>`. Depending on the contents of the query, aliases declared for tables do not always have to prefix a column.
- If multiple tables are retrieved, then multiple aliases can be used.
- Only columns can be aliased because they refer to an aliased table. Expressions containing multiple columns cannot be aliased as a whole, only the columns within those expressions. So for the expression `(<column1> * <column2>)`, `<alias>.(<column1> * <column2>)` is syntactically invalid, whereas `(<alias>.<column1> * <alias>.<column2>)` is valid.

The next example shows the use of an alias on a table, forcing a column in that table to be accessed using the alias:

```
SELECT M.TITLE, M.RANK FROM MOVIE M;
```

It is not always essential to include the alias for a column:

```
SELECT TITLE, RANK FROM MOVIE M;
```

However, this next example will cause an error because a specified alias has not been declared in the FROM clause:

```
SELECT M.TITLE, M.RANK FROM MOVIE;
```

The alias does not apply to the expression, the expression being the result of the product of the two aliased columns:

```
SELECT M.TITLE, M.LIST_PRICE * M.RANK AS PROJSALES FROM MOVIE M;
```

Clearing **COLUMN** Command Settings in SQL*Plus

The previously declared **COL** command formatting will still apply, assuming that it was not cleared either by clearing the column (see Chapter 9) or by exiting and restarting the tool.

This next query would cause an error because you cannot access the expression with the alias, but only the columns within the expression as shown in the preceding example:

```
SELECT M.TITLE, LIST_PRICE * RANK AS M.PROJSALES FROM MOVIE M;
```

You can also access a column from a table using the table name as the alias, as opposed to using a shorthand alias, declaring or not declaring the alias:

```
SELECT MOVIE.TITLE FROM MOVIE;
SELECT MOVIE.TITLE FROM MOVIE MOVIE;
```

Understand how to use aliases.

Okay. So that's aliases. One of the real powers in using aliases lies with join queries. Join queries are covered in Chapter 6, "Joining Tables."

Selecting from Other Database Objects

You can query various database objects, such as tables, views, IOTs, clusters, or materialized views. For example, the following `CREATE VIEW` command creates a very simple view specifying all movie `TITLE` column values only. The subsequent line of code queries the view.

```
CREATE OR REPLACE VIEW TITLES AS SELECT TITLE FROM MOVIE;
SELECT * FROM TITLES;
```

Views are covered in Chapter 12, "Views, Indexes, Sequences, and Synonyms (DDL)."

Types of Queries

Before we get into some of the nitty-gritty of using the `SELECT` statement, I want to quickly describe different types of queries. Different types of queries all use variations on the `SELECT` statement, both simple and complex. The objective of this section is to briefly present all the available query types and provide references to which chapters each query type is discussed in. Different types of available Oracle SQL queries can be classified loosely as shown here:

- *Simple Query*—This is a query simply retrieving one or more columns and/or expressions from a single table or other selectable database object. The following query selects all rows from the `MOVIE` table.

  ```
  SELECT TITLE, RANK FROM MOVIE;
  ```

- *Filtered Query*—Filtering implies selecting a subset of rows or removing a subset of rows from the source. Filtering is done in Oracle using the `WHERE` clause (see Chapter 3). This query returns only movies with a popularity ranking of less than a thousand.

  ```
  SELECT TITLE, RANK FROM MOVIE WHERE RANK < 1000;
  ```

- *Sorted Query*—Sorting a query involves reordering the sequence in which rows are returned using the ORDER BY clause (see Chapter 3). The following query re-sorts the rows in descending order of rank, returning the most popular movies (lowest ranking) last and most visibly:

```
SELECT TITLE, RANK FROM MOVIE ORDER BY RANK DESC;
```

- *Grouping, Summary, and Analysis*—These types of queries can get extremely complex and utilize the GROUP BY clause (see Chapter 7). The GROUP BY clause has numerous extensions such as the HAVING clause; OLAP functionality in the ROLLUP, CUBE, and GROUPING SETS extensions; and an enormous capability to utilize functions for various intricate forms of analysis. In short, the GROUP BY clause is comprehensive and powerful but can be very complex. The following example is a simple summary query finding the average rank for all movies, summarized by YEAR made:

```
SELECT YEAR, AVG(RANK) FROM MOVIE GROUP BY YEAR;
```

- *Joins*—A joined query implies that the rows from more than a single row source (table) are merged together. Joins can be built in various ways (see Chapter 6). Joins can become extremely complex. This query is a simple join query producing what is known as an intersection (natural join) between the MOVIE, PART, and ACTOR tables:

```
SELECT TITLE "Movie", NAME "Actor"
FROM MOVIE JOIN PART USING (MOVIE_ID)
    JOIN ACTOR USING (ACTOR_ID)
ORDER BY 1, 2;
```

- *Subquery*—Subqueries can be built in numerous shapes and forms. A subquery is, as the term implies, one query called from another (see Chapter 8). In the following two sample subqueries, the first example finds all unused ratings and the second example returns all movies without recognition (no awards achieved):

```
SELECT RATING FROM RATING WHERE RATING_ID NOT IN
    (SELECT RATING_ID FROM MOVIE);

SELECT TITLE FROM MOVIE WHERE MOVIE_ID NOT IN
    (SELECT MOVIE_ID FROM RECOGNITION);
```

- *Table and View Creation*—Tables and views can be created using what could be called a subquery or an inline view (see Chapter 8 and Chapter 12). In the first of the following examples, a new table is created from the join used previously. The second example uses the same query to create a view.

```
CREATE TABLE CAST AS
    SELECT TITLE "Movie", NAME "Actor"
    FROM MOVIE JOIN PART USING (MOVIE_ID)
        JOIN ACTOR USING (ACTOR_ID)
    ORDER BY 1, 2;

CREATE VIEW CAST_VIEW AS
    SELECT TITLE "Movie", NAME "Actor"
    FROM MOVIE JOIN PART USING (MOVIE_ID)
        JOIN ACTOR USING (ACTOR_ID)
    ORDER BY 1, 2;
```

- *Hierarchical Query*—These queries are used to return a representation of hierarchical data, generally in a single table (see Chapter 8, "Subqueries and Other Specialized Queries"). The MOVIES schema contains two tables with hierarchical data, the GENRE and RATING tables. The RATING table is not a true hierarchy because it contains only two levels. The GENRE table, on the other hand, contains multiple hierarchical levels. The following query will return the Classic genre subtree (including all Classic genre child genres) within the hierarchical structure of the GENRE table:

```
SELECT GENRE, PARENT_ID, LEVEL
FROM GENRE
START WITH GENRE = 'Classic'
CONNECT BY PRIOR GENRE_ID = PARENT_ID;
```

- *Composite Query*—These queries use the set operators UNION, UNION ALL, INTERSECT, and MINUS to concatenate row sets from two queries into a single query (see Chapter 8). The resulting column list, including any selected expressions, must match by both number of selected items and datatypes. This example simply retrieves all rows from both the DIRECTOR and the ACTOR tables as a UNION:

```
SELECT ACTOR_ID, NAME FROM ACTOR
UNION
SELECT DIRECTOR_ID, NAME FROM DIRECTOR;
```

- *Top-N Query*—A Top-N query retrieves the top-*n* rows from a query (see Chapter 3). It uses what is called an inline view (see Chapter 8) to retrieve rows initially. An inline view is a subquery embedded in the FROM clause of a calling query. For example, this query retrieves only the first three movies selected from the MOVIE table:

```
SELECT * FROM
(SELECT TITLE FROM MOVIE ORDER BY TITLE)
WHERE ROWNUM < 4;
```

Some Things We Can Do with SELECT

Now let's go and make use of the SELECT statement in various ways, demonstrating a few things you need to know and understand. This section describes some specific aspects of using the SELECT statement in Oracle SQL. These aspects include the use of the DUAL table, the behavior of NULL values, and the use of the DISTINCT clause.

The DUAL Table

The DUAL table is a dummy (temporary table) used for executing any SQL command not requiring a database object such as a table or a view as a row source. SQL commands create an internal cursor. This internal cursor is a chunk of memory reserved for the result of a query. As a result, the structure of a SELECT statement requires the format SELECT * FROM <table>, and thus anything not selected from a table is required to be selected from the DUAL dummy table. The following example selects from the DUAL table:

```
SELECT * FROM DUAL;
```

The **DUAL** table contains a single row containing a single column with the value **X**.

The DUAL table is often used to retrieve values such as the currently connected user and the current date. The next two examples retrieve just that:

```
SELECT USER FROM DUAL;

SELECT SYSDATE FROM DUAL;
```

Both USER and SYSDATE are single row functions (see Chapter 5, "Single Row Functions"). The next example simply returns the listed string:

```
SELECT 'Welcome to Exam Cram 2 for Oracle SQL!' FROM DUAL;
```

NULL Values

What is NULL? NULL is both a value and a PL/SQL command. NULL is nothing and does nothing. PL/SQL is not in this exam, so we will ignore NULL with respect to PL/SQL. NULL represents nothing. NULL is not the same as a space character or a zero value. A NULL valued column is a column that has never been initialized with any value. Functions and expressions deal with NULL in the following ways:

- Most functions will return `NULL` when passed `NULL`:

```
SELECT SUM(NULL) FROM DUAL;
```

- An expression containing `NULL` will return `NULL`:

```
SELECT 5 * NULL FROM DUAL;
```

Here are some important points to remember about `NULL`:

- `NULL` is tested for using the condition operator `IS [NOT] NULL` (see Chapter 3 and Chapter 4).
- The function `NVL(<expression>, <replace>)` is used to replace `NULL` expressions with the replacement value (see Chapter 3 and Chapter 5). The SQL*Plus environmental setting `SET NULL` has the same effect in SQL*Plus (see Chapter 9).
- `NULL`s behave unexpectedly when sorting such that `NULL` values always sort last in an ascending sort order (see Chapter 3).
- `NULL` values are not included in a BTree index (see Chapter 12).

The DISTINCT Clause

The `DISTINCT` clause functions by returning the first element of each repeating group from multiple repeating groups. The syntax for the `DISTINCT` clause is shown in Figure 2.4.

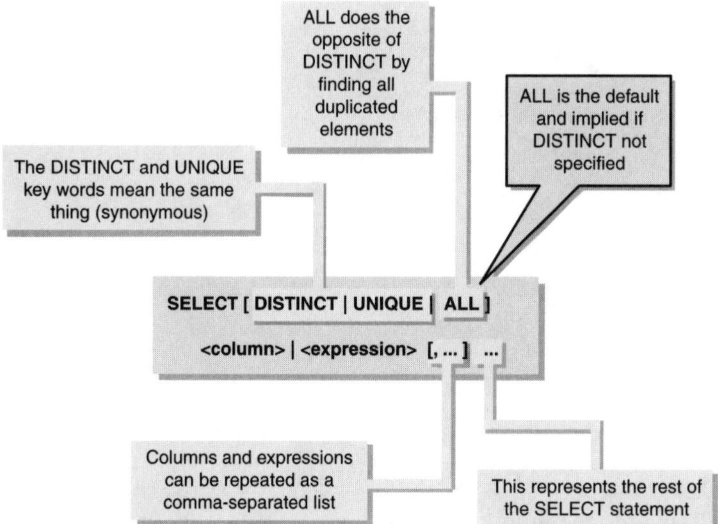

Figure 2.4 Syntax of the **SELECT** statement **DISTINCT** clause.

Following is a synopsis of the syntax diagram as shown in Figure 2.4:

- The `ALL` key word is the default and will retrieve all rows including all repetitions.
- The `DISTINCT` and `UNIQUE` clauses are synonymous. In other words they perform exactly the same function.
- The `DISTINCT` clause retrieves all of the unique rows from a query, depending on what is referenced by the `DISTINCT` clause. `DISTINCT` does this by first sorting all rows in the order of the `DISTINCT` clause, and then retrieving the first row from each set of repetitions.
- The `DISTINCT` clause can retrieve unique values based on a single column or expression and multiple columns or expressions.

The `DISTINCT` or `UNIQUE` clause is a `SELECT` clause modifier allowing retrieval of unique elements only, from a query row set. The best way to explain the use and behavior of the `DISTINCT` clause is by example.

First, let's make it blatantly obvious what `DISTINCT` does. Two examples are demonstrated in Figure 2.5.

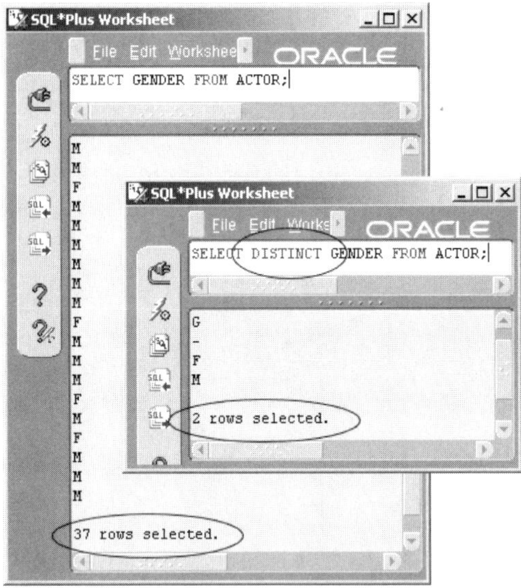

Figure 2.5 Using **DISTINCT** versus not using **DISTINCT**.

In Figure 2.5 one example selects all duplicated gender values of actors, and the other selects only the unique (`DISTINCT`) gender values (`M` for Male and `F` for Female).

The next example would return only rows with unique combinations of GENDER and TYPECAST:

```
SELECT DISTINCT GENDER, TYPECAST FROM ACTOR;
```

One more point to make about the DISTINCT clause has to do with the way that the DISTINCT clause operates on a SELECT statement. The DISTINCT clause has to operate on a resulting row set. In other words, all duplicated rows are retrieved before the execution of the DISTINCT clause. Why? The DISTINCT clause must have duplicated rows sorted in order to extract the first of each repeating group. This tells us two things about the DISTINCT clause. First, using the DISTINCT clause is inefficient, and second, the DISTINCT clause executes an inherent or automatic sort. Sorting is by nature inefficient, because sorting operates on a resulting row set and is not applied as rows are retrieved. The examples in Figure 2.6 demonstrate that DISTINCT clause results are returned as sorted results (see Chapter 4, "Operators, Conditions, Pseudocolumns, and Expressions").

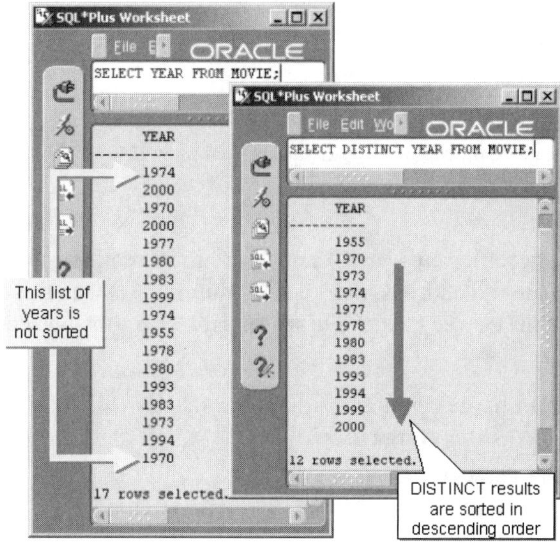

Figure 2.6 **DISTINCT** executes sorting automatically.

This completes coverage of the SELECT statement and the very basics of how we retrieve data from an Oracle database using Oracle SQL. The next chapter will expand the SELECT statement and examine filtering and sorting of SELECT statement results.

Exam Prep Questions

1. What types of database objects can rows be retrieved from, using the **SELECT** statement?

   - ❑ A. Table
   - ❑ B. Materialized view
   - ❑ C. Primary and foreign keys
   - ❑ D. Row column
   - ❑ E. View
   - ❑ F. IOT (index organized table)
   - ❑ G. A **DISTINCT** clause

   Tables, views, IOTs, clusters, and materialized views can have rows retrieved from them using a **SELECT** clause. Thus, answers A, B, E, and F are correct. Answers C and D are nonsensical, and the **DISTINCT** clause is a modifier clause for the **SELECT** statement.

2. Which one of these five answers is the best answer when executing this command in SQL*Plus?

   ```
   SELECT * FROM schema.MOVIE;
   ```

   - ❑ A. There is nothing wrong.
   - ❑ B. The **FROM** clause is incorrect.
   - ❑ C. The word **schema** must be replaced with the username **MOVIES**.
   - ❑ D. The * (asterisk) is syntactically incorrect.
   - ❑ E. This command is correct.

   Answer C is correct. Therefore, answers A and E are incorrect. Answer D is not erroneous because * (asterisk) selects all columns. Answer B is also a correct answer, but answer C is the more specific and thus better answer.

3. Disregarding any column names, which of these commands will cause an error when connected as the **SYSTEM** user?

   - ❑ A. **SELECT * FROM MOVIES.MOVIE;**
   - ❑ B. **SELECT * FROM MOVIES.ACTOR;**
   - ❑ C. **SELECT TITLE FROM MOVIES.MOVIE;**
   - ❑ D. **SELECT NAME FROM MOVIES.ACTOR;**
   - ❑ E. None of the above

   The correct answer is E. All commands are valid because the **SYSTEM** user will have complete access to all **MOVIES** schema tables. The **SYSTEM** user has access to all user tables, even the **SYS** user.

4. Which single line in this **SELECT** statement should be altered to remove the error, line A, B, or C?

❑ A. **SELECT M.TITLE**

❑ B. **, M.RANK**

❑ C. **FROM MOVIE;**

Line C is incorrect because the alias is used in the columns and the alias is not specified with the table. Lines A and B could have the alias removed from columns, but this would be altering more than a single line.

5. Which lines can be changed to make this **SELECT** statement function? Select one answer from the list.

```
1.SELECT M.TITLE
2. , LIST_PRICE * RANK
3.    AS M.PROJSALES
4. FROM MOVIE M;
```

❑ A. 4

❑ B. 2

❑ C. 1, 3, and 4

❑ D. 1, 2, 3, and 4

❑ E. 1, 2, and 4

C is correct. Answer A is incorrect because the alias from the **FROM** clause has been removed, and because the alias is present in line 1 and line 3. Answer B is incorrect because adding aliases to the two columns in line 2 would help, but line 3 would need to be changed as well to remove the alias from the name of the expression. Answer C is correct because the alias can be completely removed. Answer D is incorrect because line 2 requires no changes if the alias is removed elsewhere. Answer E is incorrect because line 3 must be changed. In summary, line 3 should not have an alias at all because it renames a column and is not an expression. In addition you can either remove the alias from line 1 and line 4 or add it to the two columns in line 2.

6. If you were connected as the **MOVIES** user, which of these queries would cause errors?

❑ A. **SELECT TITLE FROM MOVIE MOVIE;**

❑ B. **SELECT MOVIE.TITLE FROM MOVIE;**

❑ C. **SELECT MOVIE.TITLE FROM MOVIE MOVIE;**

❑ D. **SELECT TITLE FROM MOVIES.MOVIE;**

❑ E. None of the above

None of the queries causes an error so the last answer, E, is correct, making A, B, C, and D incorrect.

7. What does this query return?

```
SELECT * FROM DUAL;
```

- ❑ A. **NULL**
- ❑ B. **27**
- ❑ C. **Oracle 9.2.0.2.3**
- ❑ D. **X**
- ❑ E. None of the above

The query returns the value **X** in a column called **DUMMY**. Answer D is correct; thus, A, B, C, and E are incorrect.

8. What will the following query return?

```
SELECT 5*RANK*NULL FROM MOVIE;
```

- ❑ A. Nothing
- ❑ B. **NULL**
- ❑ C. All rows in the **MOVIE** table
- ❑ D. All rows in the **MOVIE** table, all with **NULL** values for each row
- ❑ E. All of the above
- ❑ F. None of the above

Answer D is correct because any arithmetic expression containing a **NULL** will return a **NULL**. Also, the expression is applied to every row in the **MOVIE** table, so all **MOVIE** table rows are returned with **NULL** values replacing each returned row. Therefore, answers A, B, C, E, and F are incorrect.

9. If there are two unique values in a table column (**COLUMN1** in **TABLE1**) and there are three rows, which keyword should be removed in the following query to return all three rows?

```
SELECT DISTINCT COLUMN1 FROM TABLE1;
```

The answer is the keyword **DISTINCT**. The **DISTINCT** keyword removes duplicate values from a resulting row set.

10. If we have two possible genders, male and female, with the **GENDER** column defined as **NOT NULL**, which of these queries potentially returns more than two rows?

- ❑ A. **SELECT DISTINCT GENDER FROM ACTOR;**
- ❑ B. **SELECT UNIQUE GENDER FROM ACTOR;**
- ❑ C. **SELECT GENDER FROM ACTOR;**
- ❑ D. **SELECT ALL GENDER FROM ACTOR;**

Both C and D will return more than two rows only if there are more than two rows in the **ACTOR** table. Note that the only possible values are **male** or **female**, and thus no **NULL** values are present. Therefore, A and B queries are correct because they will both return two rows because **DISTINCT** and **UNIQUE** are synonymous.

Filtering (WHERE) and Sorting Data (ORDER BY)

Terms You Need to Understand

- ✓ The **WHERE** clause
- ✓ The **ORDER BY** clause
- ✓ Filtering
- ✓ Sorting
- ✓ Comparison condition
- ✓ Logical condition
- ✓ Top-N query
- ✓ Ascending sort
- ✓ Descending sort

Concepts You Need to Master

- ✓ Filtered queries
- ✓ Sorted queries
- ✓ Precedence of logical conditions
- ✓ What the available comparison conditions are
- ✓ What the available logical conditions are
- ✓ Comparison conditions compare expressions
- ✓ Logical conditions allow for multiple comparisons
- ✓ What equi, anti, and range comparison conditions are
- ✓ The use of **LIKE**, **IN**, **EXISTS**, **BETWEEN**, **ANY**, **SOME**, and **ALL** comparison conditions
- ✓ Logical condition precedence: **()**, **NOT**, **AND**, **OR**
- ✓ **NULL** values and sorting
- ✓ Sorting methods

This chapter covers filtering of rows using the WHERE clause and sorting of retrieved data using the ORDER BY clause. The WHERE clause applies to both queries and most DML commands; the ORDER BY clause applies to queries only.

Filtering with the WHERE Clause

The WHERE clause extends the syntax of the SELECT statement, allowing filtering of rows returned from a query.

A **WHERE** clause is applied to a query during the initial reading process, regardless of whether reading of rows involves I/O, reading from database buffer cash, or both. Other clauses, such as the **ORDER BY** clause, are applied after all rows are retrieved. Thus, applying **WHERE** clause filtering first limits the number of rows sorted by an **ORDER BY** clause, for instance. Proper use of **WHERE** clause filtering is good coding practice, leading to better-performing queries in general.

WHERE Clause Syntax

The preceding chapter examined the basics of the SELECT statement with respect to retrieving data from the database. The basic SELECT statement is made up of a SELECT clause, with a list of items to be retrieved, plus a FROM clause. In its simplest form the SELECT clause specifies columns in a table, and the FROM clause specifies the table from which column values are to be selected.

The WHERE clause allows inclusion of wanted rows and filtering out of unwanted rows. The syntax for the WHERE clause is shown in Figure 3.1.

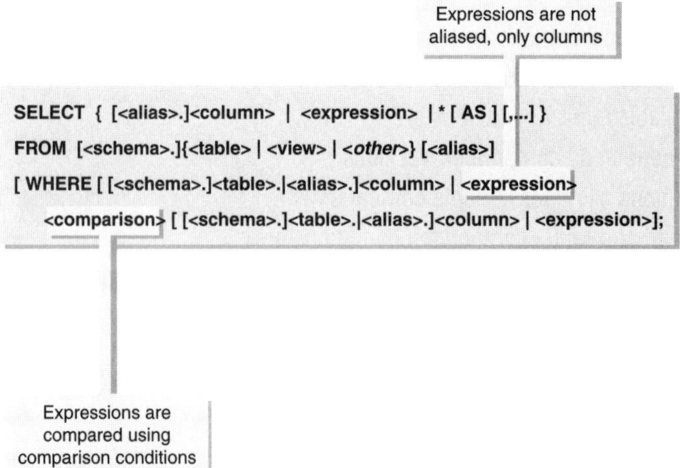

Figure 3.1 **WHERE** clause syntax.

Following is a synopsis of the syntax diagram shown in Figure 3.1:

- The WHERE clause is an optional addition to a SELECT command. The WHERE clause can also be used in both UPDATE and DELETE DML commands.
- The WHERE clause is used to filter out unwanted rows from the resulting row set or retain required rows.
- The WHERE clause in its simplest form is a simple comparison between two expressions. An expression can be a simple column, or include schema and table or view names, aliases, and even another expression.

Figure 3.1 shows a number of important points.

A WHERE clause is structured as follows:

```
WHERE <expression> <comparison> <expression>
```

The following example finds all movies ranking at less than 1000:

```
SELECT TITLE, RANK FROM MOVIE WHERE RANK < 1000;
```

The WHERE clause is shown in the preceding example and in the following example such that the two expressions RANK and 1000 are compared using the comparison condition <. RANK is a column in the MOVIE table and 1000 is an expression:

```
WHERE RANK < 1000
```

It follows that both sides of the comparison condition can be table columns:

```
SELECT TITLE, RANK, REVIEW_RANK FROM MOVIE WHERE RANK > REVIEW_RANK;
```

Additionally, both sides of the comparison condition can be expressions:

```
SELECT TITLE, RANK, REVIEW_RANK FROM MOVIE WHERE RANK/100 > 0.5;
```

There are a multitude of conditions, and it is necessary to examine all possible comparison conditions available for use in the WHERE clause.

Comparison Conditions

Comparison conditions allow for two expressions to be compared with each other in various ways. These different methods of comparison depend on the comparison condition used, as listed here:

- **Equi (=), Anti (!=, <>), and Range (<, >, <=, >=).** Equi implies equality (=) between two expressions that are being compared. Anti implies that two expressions being compared are not equal to each other (!= or <>). Range implies that one expression is greater than (>), less than (<), less than or equal to (=>), or greater than or equal to (>=).

Syntax:

```
<column> | <expression> { = | != | > | < | >= | <= }
    <column>  | <expression>
```

For example:

```
SELECT TITLE, RANK FROM MOVIE WHERE RANK = 1000;
SELECT TITLE, RANK FROM MOVIE WHERE RANK <= 1000;
SELECT TITLE, RANK FROM MOVIE WHERE RANK >= 1000;
SELECT TITLE, RANK FROM MOVIE WHERE RANK < 1000;
SELECT TITLE, RANK FROM MOVIE WHERE RANK > 1000;
SELECT TITLE, RANK FROM MOVIE WHERE RANK != 1000;
```

- **[NOT] LIKE.** `LIKE` uses special wild card characters performing pattern matching between expressions. The `%` (percentage) character attempts to match zero or more characters in a string, and the _ (underscore) character matches exactly one character in a string.

The underscore character _ is also known as the *underbar character*.

Syntax:

```
<column> | <expression> LIKE <column> | <expression>
```

For example, this query finds all movies with the vowel *e* anywhere in the movie title:

```
SELECT TITLE FROM MOVIE WHERE TITLE LIKE '%e%';
```

The next query finds all movies beginning with a capital letter *A*:

```
SELECT TITLE FROM MOVIE WHERE TITLE LIKE 'A%';
```

This query finds only movies with the vowel *e* in the second character position of their title:

```
SELECT TITLE FROM MOVIE WHERE TITLE LIKE '_e%';
```

In contrast, the following query finds all movies without the vowel *e* in the second character position of their title:

```
SELECT TITLE FROM MOVIE WHERE TITLE NOT LIKE '_e%';
```

Queries using strings in expressions are case-sensitive, and thus uppercase *A* is different from lowercase *a* just as uppercase *E* is different from lowercase *e*.

- **[NOT] IN.** `IN` is used to test for membership of an expression within a set or list of expressions.

Oracle calls **IN** a membership condition.

Syntax:

```
<column> | <expression> IN
    ( <column> | <expression> [,<column> | <expression> [, ... ] ] )
```

For example:

```
SELECT TITLE, YEAR FROM MOVIE WHERE YEAR IN (1998, 1999, 2000);
```

Using strings:

```
SELECT NAME, TYPECAST FROM ACTOR WHERE TYPECAST IN
    ('Drama', 'Horror', 'Musical');
```

Using the negative form of `IN`:

```
SELECT NAME, TYPECAST FROM ACTOR WHERE TYPECAST NOT IN
    ('Drama', 'Horror', 'Musical');
```

IN is best used for short lists of literal values.

- **[NOT] EXISTS.** Like `IN`, the `EXISTS` comparison condition is used to test for membership of an expression within a set or list of expressions.

Syntax:

```
EXISTS ( <column> | <expression> [,<column> | <expression> [, ... ] ] )
```

Don't forget that **EXISTS** has no expression on the left, only on the right.

For example, this query will find all rows because the subquery always exists:

```
SELECT TITLE, YEAR FROM MOVIE WHERE EXISTS
    (SELECT 'all years' FROM DUAL);
```

A better use for EXISTS is typically to validate the calling query against the results of a subquery. The following query finds all movies with no recognition:

```
SELECT M.TITLE FROM MOVIE M WHERE NOT EXISTS
 (SELECT MOVIE_ID FROM RECOGNITION WHERE MOVIE_ID = M.MOVIE_ID);
```

An equivalent query using IN would be as follows:

```
SELECT TITLE FROM MOVIE WHERE MOVIE_ID NOT IN
 (SELECT MOVIE_ID FROM RECOGNITION);
```

Subqueries are covered in detail in Chapter 8, “Subqueries and Other Specialized Queries.”

- **[NOT] BETWEEN.** BETWEEN verifies expressions between a range of two values.

  Syntax:

  ```
  <column> | <expression> [ NOT ] BETWEEN <column> | <expression>
      AND <column> | <expression>
  ```

  The first of the following examples finds all values between and including a range of 900 to 1000 and is the equivalent of the second example using simple range conditions and a conjunction:

  ```
  SELECT TITLE, RANK FROM MOVIE WHERE RANK BETWEEN 900 AND 1000;

  SELECT TITLE, RANK FROM MOVIE WHERE RANK >= 900 AND RANK <= 1000;
  ```

  The second of the preceding two queries uses the AND logical condition. Logical conditions (conjunctions) are discussed in the next section.

  This next example will produce no rows at all because there is no such range beginning at 1000, counting upwards to 900:

  ```
  SELECT TITLE, RANK FROM MOVIE WHERE RANK BETWEEN 1000 AND 900;
  ```

This is a potential trick question: **BETWEEN 1000 AND 900** is invalid but does not cause an error in SQL*Plus.

This example finds rows between a range of string values:

```
SELECT NAME, TYPECAST FROM ACTOR WHERE TYPECAST BETWEEN 'Odd' AND
'Shakespearian';
```

Oracle calls **BETWEEN** a range condition.

- **ANY, SOME, and ALL.** These comparisons all check an expression for membership in a set or list of elements. ANY and SOME are the same and allow a response when any element in the set matches. ALL produces a response only when all elements in a set match an expression.

  Syntax:

```
<column> | <expression> [ = | != | < | > | <= | >= ]
    { ANY | SOME | ALL } <column> | <expression> [, <column>
        | <expression> [, ... ] ]
```

  Both of the following two examples will produce the same result, returning all movies made in the years 1998, 1999, and 2000:

```
SELECT TITLE, YEAR FROM MOVIE WHERE YEAR = ANY(1998, 1999, 2000);

SELECT TITLE, YEAR FROM MOVIE WHERE YEAR = SOME(1998, 1999, 2000);
```

  This example would produce no result because there are no movies made in all three of the years 1998, 1999, and 2000:

```
SELECT TITLE, YEAR FROM MOVIE WHERE YEAR = ALL(1998, 1999, 2000);
```

- **IS [NOT] NULL.** NULL values are tested for using the IS NULL comparison. In testing for NULL, IS NULL implies equal to NULL and IS NOT NULL implies not equal to NULL. In other words, = NULL and != NULL are both syntactically invalid and will cause errors.

  Syntax:

```
<column> | <expression> IS [ NOT ] NULL
```

  The following two queries will include only NULL values and exclude only NULL valued TYPECAST actors, respectively:

```
SELECT GENDER, TYPECAST, NAME FROM ACTOR
    WHERE TYPECAST IS NULL ORDER BY GENDER, TYPECAST;

SELECT GENDER, TYPECAST, NAME FROM ACTOR WHERE TYPECAST IS NOT NULL
    ORDER BY GENDER, TYPECAST;
```

The function **NVL(<expression>, <replace>)** is used to replace **NULL** expressions with the replacement value (see Chapter 5, "Single Row Functions"). The SQL*Plus environmental setting **SET NULL** has the same effect in SQL*Plus (see Chapter 9, "SQL*Plus Formatting").

Make sure you understand all comparison conditions.

The preceding list covers WHERE clause comparison conditions. You can also join multiple comparisons together using conjunctions, otherwise known as logical conditions.

Logical Conditions

Logical conditions expand SELECT statement WHERE clause syntax, as shown in Figure 3.2.

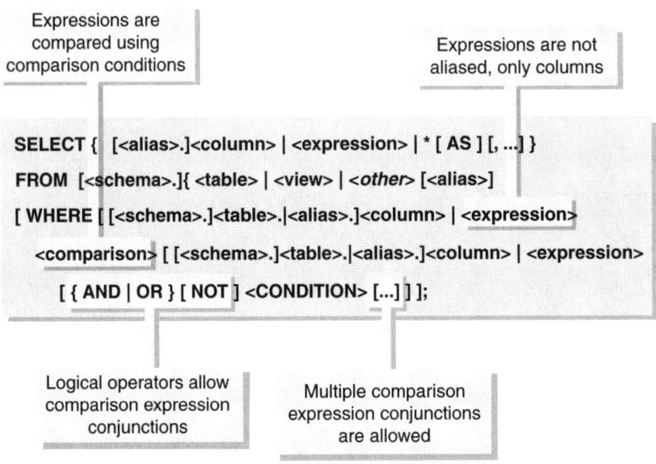

Figure 3.2 **WHERE** clause syntax with logical condition conjunctions.

Following is a synopsis of the syntax diagram as shown in Figure 3.2:

- ➤ Different pairs of one or more expressions can be linked together in the same WHERE clause using the logical operators NOT, AND and OR.
- ➤ NOT has highest precedence (is processed first), followed by AND and then OR.

Logical conditions can be used to form conjunctions or concatenations between multiple comparisons in a WHERE clause. There can be any number of comparison conjunctions. As shown in Figure 3.2 there are two logical conditions: AND and OR. Both AND and OR can also have the optional NOT clause applied, resulting in the opposite.

NOT by itself, as well and **AND** and **OR**, is sometimes classified as a logical condition, even though it only reverses **AND** and **OR**.

AND requires that both of two comparison expressions must be true for a true result. OR requires that only one of two comparison expressions must be true for a true result.

The following lines are syntax examples of AND and OR:

AND requires that both `<expression1>` and `<expression2>` are true:

```
<expression1> AND <expression2>
```

OR requires that either `<expression1>` or `<expression2>` is true:

```
<expression1> OR <expression2>
```

Make sure you understand the use of **AND**, **OR**, and **NOT** logical conditions.

The precedence of logical conditions by default is first left to right, followed by NOT, AND, and finally OR.

Remember the precedence sequence of logical conditions: **()**, **NOT**, **AND**, **OR**.

Precedence is explained from a mathematical perspective in Chapter 4, "Operators, Conditions, Pseudocolumns, and Expressions." Additionally, the rules of precedence apply where parentheses (round brackets) can be used to change the order of resolution of an expression, or increase the precedence of a bracketed part of an expression. Thus, the use of parentheses can change the order of evaluation of NOT, AND, and OR. The term *precedence* means that one part of an expression is forced to be executed before other parts.

The following syntax demonstrates precedence further. `<expression1>` is evaluated first, followed by `<expression2>` and finally `<expression3>`:

```
<expression1> OR <expression2> AND <expression3>
```

In the next example, `<expression1>` is still evaluated first, but it is compared using `OR` with the result of `<expression2>` and `<expression3>`, not simply `<expression2>`, followed by a spurious `AND` conjunction with `<expression3>`:

```
<expression1> OR (<expression2> AND <expression3>)
```

Questions on the precedence of logical conditions using parentheses are very likely.

This simple example returns movies with regular rankings of greater than 1000 that have a review ranking of greater than 4, two different types of rankings:

```
SELECT TITLE, RANK, REVIEW_RANK, YEAR FROM MOVIE WHERE RANK > 1000
OR REVIEW_RANK > 4;
```

Figure 3.3 shows the result of the following two examples:

```
SELECT TITLE, RANK, REVIEW_RANK, YEAR FROM MOVIE
WHERE YEAR = 2000 AND RANK > 1000 OR REVIEW_RANK > 4;

SELECT TITLE, RANK, REVIEW_RANK, YEAR FROM MOVIE
    WHERE YEAR = 2000 AND (RANK > 1000 OR REVIEW_RANK > 4);
```

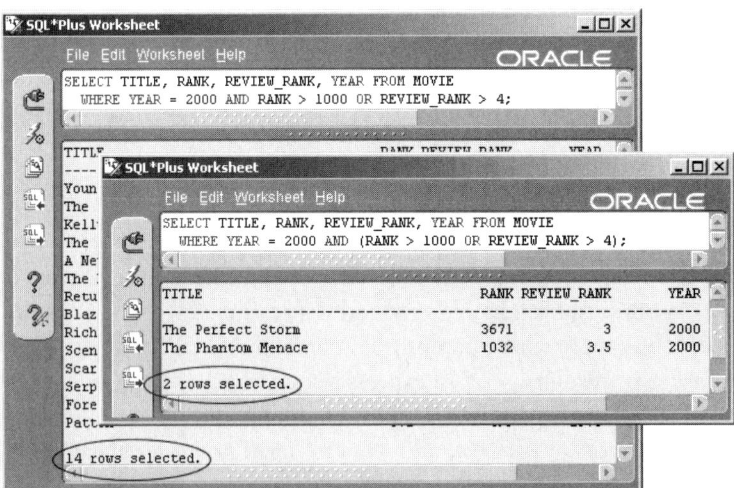

Figure 3.3 Precedence and logical conditions.

Note in Figure 3.3 how the two different queries retrieve different numbers of rows. This is a direct result of the use of parentheses, changing the precedence (sequence of evaluation) of the logical conditions `AND` and `OR`.

Don't get confused! Comparison and logical conditions are sometimes known as comparison and logical operators. Oracle documentation uses the terms *comparison* and *logical conditions.*

The Importance of Precedence

The syntax

```
<expression1> OR <expression2> AND <expression3>
```

evaluates differently from this:

```
<expression1> OR (<expression2> AND <expression3>)
```

The importance of precedence generally determines that a clause without proper precedence such as **p OR q AND r** will produce a spurious result. On the other hand, **p OR (q AND r)** forces **q AND r** to be evaluated before comparison with **p**. This implies that **p OR** the result of **q AND r** produces a true response. For example, if **p=round**, **q=large**, and **r=four-sided**, then testing for a large rectangle will succeed, and correctly so. On the other hand, **p OR q AND r** will fail because a large four-sided rectangle cannot possibly be both round and four-sided. Mathematically, **p OR (q AND r)** implies that either **p** is true or the combination of **q AND r** is true; **p** does not have to be true. On the contrary, **p OR q AND r** effectively implies **(p OR q) AND r**, a completely different expression, stating that **q** can be false if **r** is true and the expression will still yield a true result, which is false. Fascinating, huh?

Top-N Queries

When database tables become extremely large, making estimates is sometimes best done using a simple sampling method. Top-N queries can provide a measure of sampling to avoid regularly reading millions of rows to answer simple questions. This can be achieved using what is called an inline view and a pseudocolumn called ROWNUM (see Chapter 4).

A ROWNUM simply returns the sequence number for each row returned in a query, in the order in which rows are returned by that query. Thus, the 1st row has a ROWNUM value of 1 and the 10th row has a ROWNUM value of 10.

An inline view is a type of subquery in which the subquery is embedded in the FROM clause of a calling query (see Chapter 8).

The following query is a Top-N query. All movie titles are selected in the subquery. The query result is trimmed to only four rows before passing over the network. The result is a small sample subset of the potentially much larger inline query.

```
SELECT * FROM
   (SELECT TITLE FROM MOVIE ORDER BY TITLE)
WHERE ROWNUM < 4;
```

There are two important points to remember about Top-N queries:

➤ WHERE ROWNUM > n produces a NULL result. The following example will return a result of "no rows selected" (NULL).

```
SELECT * FROM (SELECT TITLE, RANK, REVIEW_RANK, YEAR FROM MOVIE
    ORDER BY RANK DESC)
WHERE ROWNUM > 4;
```

WHERE ROWNUM > n will produce no rows. This is a likely trick question!

➤ Top-N queries can be confused by application of an ORDER BY clause. The ROWNUM pseudocolumn filters out all rows but those specified as being less than a specified value. If a sort order is applied to the calling query containing the ROWNUM filter as opposed to the subquery, a spurious result could occur. This is aptly demonstrated in Figure 3.4.

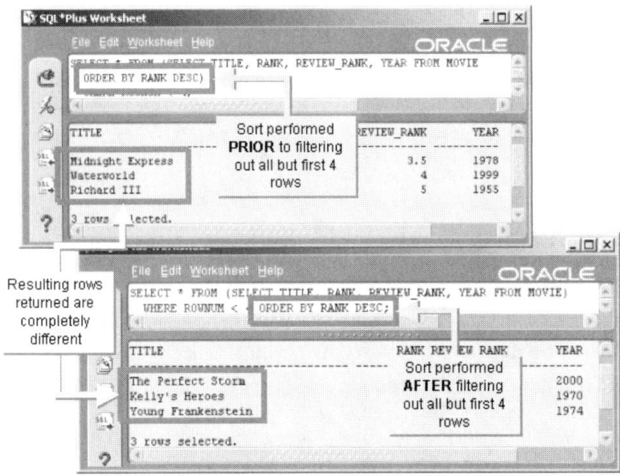

Figure 3.4 Top-N queries and placing an **ORDER BY** clause within an inline view subquery.

Remember to place an **ORDER BY** clause in the inline view subquery section of a Top-N query. You need to sort results before the **ROWNUM** comparison.

Figure 3.4 shows a notable difference between placing an ORDER BY clause in an inline view and placing it outside of an inline view. The reason is that the ORDER BY clause in a query will always be executed on the filtered result.

In other words, the WHERE clause is always executed before the ORDER BY clause. Obviously, placing an ORDER BY clause inside the inline view resolves this issue.

Sorting with the **ORDER BY** Clause

So far in this chapter, we have expanded the SELECT statement (including the FROM clause) with the WHERE clause for filtering. Now we will expand the SELECT statement further with the ORDER BY clause. The ORDER BY clause is used to sort rows returned by a query.

The **ORDER BY** clause is always executed on filtered query results, namely after the **WHERE** clause. Obviously, if there is no **WHERE** clause, this does not apply.

ORDER BY Clause Syntax

The syntax for the SELECT statement, including details of the optional ORDER BY clause, is shown in Figure 3.5.

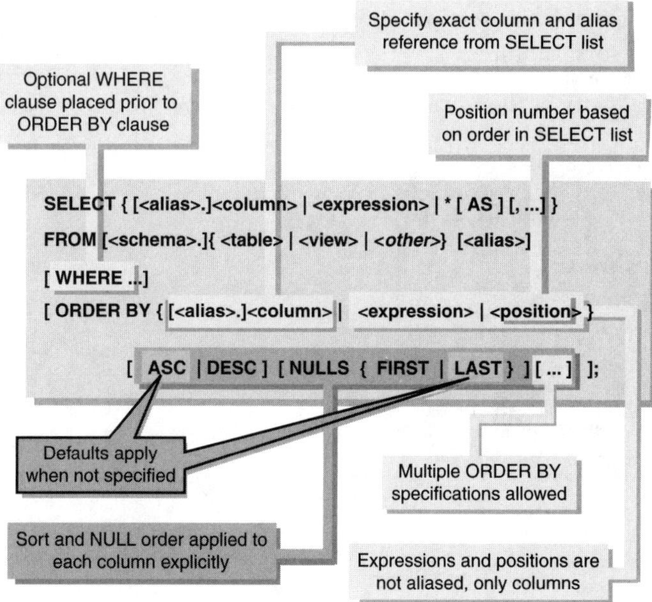

Figure 3.5 **ORDER BY** clause syntax.

Following is a synopsis of the syntax diagram as shown in Figure 3.5:

- The ORDER BY clause is optional and is used for sorting filtered row sets. Thus, a WHERE clause will always appear before an ORDER BY clause.
- Elements in the ORDER BY clause can refer to columns, aliased columns, expressions (those expressions can be in the SELECT list or not), or positions of elements in the SELECT list.
- Each element in an ORDER BY clause is sorted in ascending order by default. Each element can be forcibly sorted individually in ascending order (ASC) or descending order (DESC).
- By default, in ascending order, NULL values will always be sorted last and thus appear last. In descending order NULL values will appear first. Sorted order of NULL values can be overridden using the NULLS FIRST clause and the NULLS LAST clause (the default). NULLS FIRST returns NULL values at the start of a query, and NULLS LAST returns NULL values at the end of a query.

Sorting Using the ORDER BY Clause

Rows in a query are sorted according to the sequence of elements listed in the ORDER BY clause, from left to right. Therefore, the leftmost ORDER BY clause element is the most significant sort parameter, and the rightmost element is the least important sort parameter.

Figure 3.6 shows a query of the ACTOR table sorting by TYPECAST within GENDER.

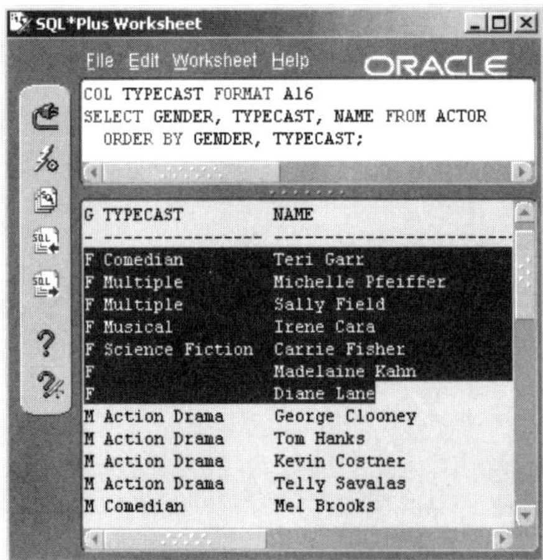

Figure 3.6 The sequence of **ORDER BY** clause sorting.

In Figure 3.6 we can see that all females (F) are sorted before all males (M). The TYPECAST column is sorted within GENDER. As a result, Teri Garr as a Comedian appears before George Clooney as an Action Drama actor.

Sorting Methods

The following example sorts on a single column:

```
SELECT TITLE, RANK, REVIEW_RANK, YEAR FROM MOVIE ORDER BY TITLE;
```

The next example sorts on multiple columns, not in the order in which the columns are selected:

```
SELECT TITLE, RANK, REVIEW_RANK, YEAR FROM MOVIE
    ORDER BY YEAR,TITLE, RANK;
```

This example sorts columns both in the selected columns list and not in that list but in the accessed MOVIE table:

```
SELECT TITLE, RANK, REVIEW_RANK, YEAR FROM MOVIE
ORDER BY REVIEWS, LIST_PRICE, YEAR, TITLE, RANK;
```

The next query will produce exactly the same result as the preceding query using positions of select list elements. YEAR is in fourth position, TITLE is in first position, and RANK is in second position:

```
SELECT TITLE, RANK, REVIEW_RANK, YEAR FROM MOVIE
ORDER BY REVIEWS, LIST_PRICE, 4, 1, 2;
```

If you change the sequence of select list elements, you have to change position numbers as well. This query produces the same rows as before but with the columns in a different order:

```
SELECT YEAR, TITLE, RANK, REVIEW_RANK FROM MOVIE
ORDER BY REVIEWS, LIST_PRICE, 1, 2, 3;
```

You can sort using aliased columns, even including those not in the select list:

```
SELECT M.TITLE, M.LIST_PRICE * M.RANK AS PROJSALES FROM MOVIE M
ORDER BY M.YEAR, M.TITLE;
```

And following from the previous query, we can sort using expressions in the select list:

```
SELECT M.TITLE, M.LIST_PRICE * M.RANK AS PROJSALES FROM MOVIE M
ORDER BY PROJSALES;
```

You can even sort using an expression not in the query select list:

```
SELECT M.TITLE, M.LIST_PRICE * M.RANK AS PROJSALES FROM MOVIE M
ORDER BY M.YEAR / 1000;
```

Sorting using expressions implies that PL/SQL user-defined procedures can be used to sort with as well. PL/SQL is out of the scope of this book.

It follows that we can combine different sorting methods in the same ORDER BY clause. The following example is sorted by a column select list position, a column name in the select list, a column name in the tables but not in the select list, and finally an expression:

```
SELECT TITLE, RANK, REVIEW_RANK, YEAR, LIST_PRICE * RANK AS PROJSALES
FROM MOVIE
ORDER BY 4, TITLE, RELEASE, PROJSALES;
```

Sorting Modifiers

We can modify the way in which each column within an ORDER BY clause is sorted as shown in Figure 3.5, the ORDER BY clause syntax diagram, by using the ASC | DESC and NULLS { FIRST | LAST } optional modifiers.

If you look closely at Figure 3.6 again, you will see that the last two females, Madelaine Kahn and Diane Lane, have no TYPECAST setting. Their TYPECAST column values are NULL because they have not been set to anything, not even a space character. The default setting is NULLS LAST, meaning that NULL values are sorted last, as in Figure 3.6. If we wanted to specify NULLS LAST explicitly, we could use the following query modification:

```
SELECT GENDER, TYPECAST, NAME FROM ACTOR
ORDER BY GENDER, TYPECAST NULLS LAST;
```

You could return the NULL TYPECAST rows at the beginning of the females by using the following modification:

```
SELECT GENDER, TYPECAST, NAME FROM ACTOR
ORDER BY GENDER, TYPECAST NULLS FIRST;
```

Now we can reorder the same query. Specify both of the individual columns as being ordered in descending order, placing males before females. Also, specify all TYPECAST values in reverse alphabetical order and NULLS FIRST:

```
SELECT GENDER, TYPECAST, NAME FROM ACTOR
ORDER BY GENDER DESC , TYPECAST DESC NULLS FIRST;
```

A **NULL** value is logically undefined and thus cannot be sorted, and can be placed only at the start of a sort (**NULLS FIRST**) or at the end of a sort (**NULLS LAST**).

This chapter has expanded the SELECT statement with the WHERE clause and the ORDER BY clause to cater for filtering and sorting of returned rows, respectively. The next chapter is the first of two chapters examining some Oracle SQL reference material, essential at this stage, covering operators, conditions, pseudocolumns, and expressions.

Exam Prep Questions

1. What is the symbol < called in this query?

```
SELECT TITLE, RANK FROM MOVIE WHERE RANK < 1000;
```

- ❑ A. Logical operator
- ❑ B. Comparison condition
- ❑ C. Comparison operator
- ❑ D. Logical condition
- ❑ E. None of the above

Answer B, comparison condition, is the correct answer. A, logical operator, should be called a logical condition, and those are **NOT**, **AND**, and **OR**. C contradicts B and is thus incorrect. Because B is correct, E is incorrect.

2. This query will cause an error. Why?

```
SELECT TITLE, RANK, REVIEW_RANK FROM MOVIE WHERE RANK/100 > 0.5;
```

- ❑ A. **RANK/100** cannot be compared with 0.5 using the > operator.
- ❑ B. The **FROM** clause is incorrect.
- ❑ C. The **WHERE** clause should appear before the **FROM** clause.
- ❑ D. Too many columns are selected.
- ❑ E. The query will not cause an error.

There is nothing wrong with this query, and thus answer E is correct. The **WHERE** clause, its expression, and the **FROM** clause are fine; thus A, B, and C are not correct answers. D is incorrect because there is no limitation on the number of columns selected; the only limitation is that they must exist.

3. What will this query find? Select the best answer.

```
SELECT TITLE FROM MOVIE WHERE TITLE LIKE 'B%e%';
```

- ❑ A. All rows with **TITLE** beginning with the letter *B*.
- ❑ B. It will cause an error.
- ❑ C. All movies containing an *e* in their title.
- ❑ D. The intersecting rows from answers A and C.
- ❑ E. None of the above.

Answer D is correct because it is the "best" answer. The query will return only movie titles beginning with *B* and containing an *e*. Both answer A and answer C are partially correct because only some rows could be returned for each due to the possibility of rows without both characters. Both answer B and answer E are therefore incorrect as well.

4. Which of these answers are correct? Select three answers.

- ❑ A. Both **IN** and **EXISTS** can compare two expressions.
- ❑ B. **IN** compares two expressions.
- ❑ C. **IN** compares a single expression against a list of values.

- ❑ D. **EXISTS** compares a single expression with a Boolean (true or false) result.
- ❑ E. All of the above.

IN compares two expressions; **EXISTS** produces a Boolean result for a single expression. Therefore, A is wrong, and E is thus incorrect as well. B, C, and D are all correct.

5. Assume that the **MOVIE** table contains titles with **YEAR** column values in all three of the years 1998, 1999, and 2000. Which of these queries produces the least number of rows?

   - ❑ A. **SELECT TITLE FROM MOVIE WHERE YEAR = ANY(1998,1999,2000);**
   - ❑ B. **SELECT TITLE FROM MOVIE WHERE YEAR = SOME(1998,1999,2000);**
   - ❑ C. **SELECT TITLE FROM MOVIE WHERE YEAR = ALL(1998,1999,2000);**

   C is correct because it will produce zero rows. A and B will produce at least three rows each (at least one for each year). Why? **ANY** and **SOME** require that the **YEAR** must match at least one of the three years 1998, 1999, and 2000. **ALL**, on the other hand, requires that every movie must have three values in the **YEAR** column: **1998**, **1999**, and **2000**. This is of course impossible, and thus C produces no rows at all, the least number of rows.

6. What type of a query is this?

   ```
   SELECT * FROM
       (SELECT TITLE FROM MOVIE ORDER BY RANK DESC) WHERE ROWNUM < 4;
   ```

   Valid answers are Top-N, TopN, Top-N query, TOPN query, in uppercase, lowercase, or mixed case.

7. How many rows will this query find?

   ```
   SELECT * FROM
       (SELECT TITLE FROM MOVIE ORDER BY RANK DESC)
   WHERE ROWNUM > 4;
   ```

   Valid answers are 0, zero, none, no rows, in any case. **ROWNUM > 4** is invalid. Only **ROWNUM < 4** is valid. This is because **ROWNUM** is a pseudocolumn generated as the query is produced. It is impossible to tell what is greater than when values greater than **4** have not yet been reached.

8. How many rows will this query produce?

   ```
   SELECT TITLE, RANK FROM MOVIE
       WHERE RANK BETWEEN 1000 AND 900;
   ```

   Valid answers are 0, zero, none, no rows. Why? **RANK BETWEEN 1000 AND 900** equates to the expression: **RANK >=1000 AND RANK <= 900**. We cannot find **>=1000** and **<=900** using **BETWEEN**.

9. What is wrong with this query?

```
SELECT TITLE FROM MOVIE
    WHERE YEAR = 2000 AND RANK > 1000 OR REVIEW_RANK > 4;
```

- ❑ A. Not enough columns are selected.
- ❑ B. The second and third comparisons should be replaced with **BETWEEN**.
- ❑ C. Precedence!
- ❑ D. There is nothing wrong with this query.
- ❑ E. None of the above.

The correct answer is C; the problem is precedence and lack of parentheses, `(... AND ...)`. A coder examining this query should spot the lack of parentheses before anything else.

10. For this query, if some rows have **NULL** valued **GENDER** columns, where will those **NULL** valued rows appear in the sorted order?

```
SELECT GENDER, TYPECAST, NAME FROM ACTOR
    ORDER BY TYPECAST DESC NULLS FIRST;
```

- ❑ A. First
- ❑ B. Last
- ❑ C. Never
- ❑ D. In the middle

The correct answer is A. By default, **NULL** values are not sorted and Oracle Database returns them at the end of a query, appearing as the final rows returned. Both the **DESC** and the **NULLS FIRST** clauses force **NULL** rows to be returned as the beginning rows of the query. Therefore, answers B, C, and D are all incorrect.

Operators, Conditions, Pseudocolumns, and Expressions

Terms You Need to Understand

- ✓ Operator
- ✓ Condition
- ✓ Pseudocolumn
- ✓ Expression
- ✓ **ROWID**
- ✓ **ROWNUM**

Concepts You Need to Master

- ✓ Expressions are combinations of other expressions, operators, conditions, and pseudocolumns
- ✓ The rules of precedence
- ✓ The concatenation operator (||)
- ✓ Different expression types
- ✓ Composition of a **ROWID**

This chapter introduces details for all Oracle SQL operators, conditions, pseudocolumns, and expressions. Operators allow the composition of multiple expressions. Conditions allow comparison between expressions. Pseudocolumns contain information in Oracle databases not available from tables and can be embedded in expressions. Expressions are combinations of other expressions, operators, conditions, and pseudocolumns.

Precedence

In Chapter 3, "Filtering (WHERE) and Sorting Data (ORDER BY)," we covered some details on precedence as related to logical conditions: AND, OR, and NOT. At the start of this chapter, it is necessary to explain precedence in more general terms.

The rules of mathematical precedence imply that various types of things, such as arithmetical operators, contain different levels of precedence.

The word *precedence* implies that one expression has priority over another, and that expression is executed first.

For example, with respect to arithmetic operators there are six simple rules:

- * and / (multiplication and division) have higher precedence than + and - (addition and subtraction).

  `4 + 5 * 3 = 19` and not `27` because even though + occurs to the left of *, * has higher precedence.

- Arithmetic expressions are generally resolved from left to right, assuming that rules 1 and 3 are not contradicted; for example

  `4 + 5 * 3 * 2 = 34` because the two * operators are executed left to right, before the + operator.

- Enclosing parts of expressions in parentheses or `( <expression> )` causes the expression between parentheses to be executed first. Nested layers of parentheses cause the lowest nested layers to be executed first, still executing the arithmetic expression from left to right.

  `( 4 + 5 ) * 3 = 27` because the parentheses cause + to occur first.

  `3 * ( 4 + 5 ) = 27` as well because once again the parentheses force + to be resolved first, even though * is on the left.

`( ( 4 + ( 5 * 3 ) ) * 2 ) = 38` because + is executed before the second * due to the nested parentheses. Note also that the entire expression is enclosed in parentheses, meaningless mathematically but not erroneous.

- * and / have the same precedence.
- + and - have the same precedence.
- Functions have higher precedence than all the rest (see Chapter 5).

Functions Have Higher Precedence Than * and /

Oracle SQL only has four arithmetic operators: *****, **/**, **+**, and **-**. Oracle SQL does not, for instance, have an arithmetic operator for an exponent, such as raising 2 to the power of **3:** $2^3 = 8$. An exponent actually has higher precedence than * and /, for obvious reasons. Oracle uses a built-in function to calculate an exponent. Therefore, functions have higher precedence than * and /. Thus, $5 * 2^3 = 40$ and not **1000**.

This example in Oracle SQL could be coded this way:

5 * POWER(2,3).

Operators

This section lists the types of operators. Operators are used to perform operations on arguments passed to them. Operators can be divided into arithmetic operators, the concatenation operator, set operators, and hierarchical query operators. Table 4.1 shows the types of operators, including descriptions and examples.

Table 4.1 SQL Operators in Oracle

Operator	Operator Information
Arithmetic Operators	Arithmetic operators are used to perform simple arithmetic calculations on numeric values: ➤ * *and* /. Multiplication and division have equal precedence but higher than addition and subtraction. ➤ + *and* -. Addition and subtraction also have equal precedence but lower than multiplication and division.

(continued)

Table 4.1 SQL Operators in Oracle *(continued)*

Operator	Operator Information
Concatenation Operator	Oracle SQL has a special string concatenation operator denoted by two pipe characters, ll. The following example concatenates two columns from different tables with an extra string added in between: **SELECT NAME‖' directed '‖TITLE** **FROM MOVIE NATURAL JOIN DIRECTOR;**
Set Operators	Set operators merge multiple compatible queries into a single resulting row set (see Chapter 8). The following are examples of Set Operators: ➤ **UNION**—Returns unique rows from two queries. ➤ **UNION ALL**—Returns all rows from two queries, including duplications. ➤ **INTERSECT**—Returns only rows common to both queries. ➤ **MINUS**—Returns all distinct rows in the first query not in the second query.
Hierarchical Query Operator	The hierarchical query operator **PRIOR** works in tandem with the **CONNECT BY** clause, causing a column in a currently processed row to be connected with a row in a column from a parent row (see Chapter 8).

Conditions

This section lists the types of conditions. In its simplest form, a condition is used to test the existence of a condition, between two expressions. Conditions can be divided into comparison conditions, logical conditions, XML conditions, and object collection conditions. Table 4.2 shows the types of conditions, including descriptions and examples.

Table 4.2 SQL Conditions in Oracle

Condition	Condition Information
Comparison Conditions	Comparison conditions are primarily used in a **WHERE** clause (see Chapter 3). Comparison conditions are used to compare the values of two expressions: ➤ Equi (=), Anti (**!=**, **<>**), and Range (**<**, **>**, **<=**, **>=**)—Simple equality (Equi), inequality (Anti), and range conditions. ➤ **[NOT] LIKE**—Pattern matching. ➤ **[NOT] IN**—Set membership between expressions. ➤ **[NOT] EXISTS**—Set membership producing a Boolean result. ➤ **[NOT] BETWEEN**—Range search between two values, inclusive of end points. ➤ **ANY**, **SOME** and **ALL**—Set membership conditions. ➤ **IS [NOT] NULL**—**NULL** value test condition.
Logical Conditions	Logical conditions are primarily used in a **WHERE** clause (see Chapter 3) and allow combining or merging of multiple expressions to find a Boolean result based on whether either expression or both expressions yield a true result: ➤ **NOT**—An expression being false yields **true**. ➤ **AND**—Two expressions being true yields **true**. ➤ **OR**—One of two expressions being true yields **true**.

(continued)

Table 4.2 SQL Conditions in Oracle *(continued)*

Condition	Condition Information
XML Conditions	An XML document contains a hierarchical or upside-down treelike structure. ➤ **EQUALS_PATH**—Searches the entire path of an XML document from the root node. **<n>** forms a correlation for **EQUALS_PATH** using the **PATH** and **DEPTH** ancillary functions. Syntax: **<expression> = EQUALS_PATH (<column>, <path> [, <n>])** ➤ **UNDER_PATH**—Searches a relative path of an XML document. **<n>** means the same as for **EQUALS_PATH**. Syntax: **<expression> = UNDER_PATH (<column>, <path> [, <n>])**
Object Collection Conditions	Tests the type of an object (see Chapter 11). Syntax: **<expression> IS [NOT] OF [TYPE]**

Pseudocolumns

This section examines *pseudocolumns*. A pseudocolumn is selected from by use of a SELECT command, much like a table is accessed via a standard syntax SELECT statement, typically selected from the DUAL table or embedded within a query or DML statement. There are five pseudocolumns:

- ROWID—A relative row pointer most commonly used internally by Oracle Database. For instance, indexes contain values of indexed columns plus a ROWID pointer value back to the row in the table indexed.

A **ROWID** is a relative pointer to a row in an Oracle database. A **ROWID** is a concatenated set of values comprising relative address pointers to a data object (a segment or table), a datafile within a tablespace, a block, and a row within a block. A **ROWID** might contain a different format if the row is located outside the database.

- ROWNUM—A sequence number for rows returned by a query as the rows are returned.
- <sequence>.CURRVAL and <sequence>.NEXTVAL—The current and next values for a sequence (see Chapter 12).

Executing **<sequence>.CURRVAL** without executing **<sequence>.NEXTVAL** first will cause an error.

- LEVEL—Returns the level of a row in a hierarchical query (see Chapter 8, "Subqueries and Other Specialized Queries").
- XMLDATA—Allows access to the underlying storage structure of binary stored XML documents.

Pseudocolumns *cannot* be altered with DML statements.

9i Expressions

This section examines the types of expressions for Oracle SQL. Simply put, an expression is a combination of other expressions or values, evaluating to a single value. Expressions can be categorized into simple expressions, compound expressions, expression lists, CURSOR expressions, and finally CASE expressions. Here is a list of the types of expressions:

- *Simple Expression*—A single value such as a number, a string, or a pseudocolumn. Pseudocolumns were discussed previously in this chapter. In the following example all the expressions, each on a separate line, in the select list of the SELECT statement are simple expressions. The LENGTH(TITLE) expression is a simple expression but is sometimes called a function expression.

```
SELECT  ROWNUM
     , ROWID
     , TITLE
     , 1000
     , NULL
     , MOVIE_SEQ.NEXTVAL
     , LENGTH(TITLE)
FROM MOVIE;
```

- *Compound Expression*—A combination or concatenation of multiple simple expressions. For example, both of the elements selected here are compounds of multiple simple expressions:

```
SELECT  5 * 10 * (3 + 2)
     , 'Rank is '||TO_CHAR(RANK) "Rank"
FROM MOVIE;
```

- *List of Expressions*—A list of comma-delimited expressions, those expressions being any other expression type. Both of the preceding examples for simple and compound expressions contain expression lists in their SELECT statement select lists.
- 9i CURSOR *Expression*—A cursor can be nested inside a calling SQL statement and can be passed to a function as a REF CURSOR. The following example demonstrates a nested cursor expression:

```
SELECT  M.TITLE
    ,CURSOR(SELECT NAME FROM DIRECTOR WHERE DIRECTOR_ID=M.DIRECTOR_ID)
FROM MOVIE M;
```

- 9i CASE *Expression*—A CASE statement can be embedded in a SQL statement and is thus an inline CASE statement expression. A CASE statement is a similar programming construct to that of an IF-THEN-ELSE statement. Figure 4.1 shows the syntax for the CASE expression embedded in a SELECT statement.

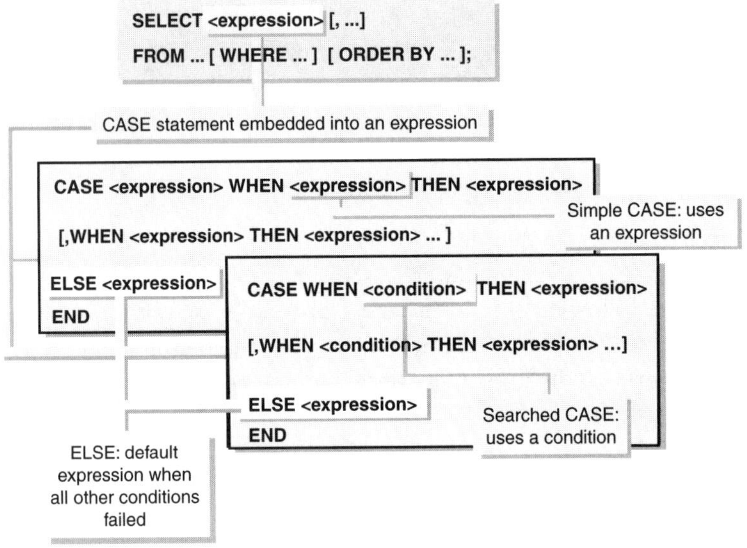

Figure 4.1 Embedded SQL expression **CASE** statement syntax.

Following is a synopsis of the syntax diagram shown in Figure 4.1:

- A CASE statement can be embedded into an expression.
- There are two types of CASE statement. The first is called a simple CASE statement and the second a searched CASE statement.

- A simple CASE statement contains a single condition with multiple possible expressional options:

  ```
  CASE x WHEN 1 THEN ... WHEN 2 THEN ... ELSE ...
  ```

- A searched CASE statement contains a condition for each WHEN clause:

  ```
  CASE WHEN x = 1 THEN ... WHEN x = 2 THEN ... ELSE ...
  ```

- The ELSE condition is executed when all preceding CASE options have failed, and only then.
- In general, a CASE statement will execute one option, and then abandon testing all other options.

For example, the following query contains a simple CASE statement expression:

```
SELECT      NAME
    , CASE GENDER
      WHEN 'F' THEN 'Female'
      WHEN 'M' THEN 'Male'
      ELSE 'Unknown'
      END
FROM ACTOR;
```

This next example contains a searched CASE statement expression:

```
SELECT      NAME
    , CASE
        WHEN GENDER = 'F' THEN 'Female'
        WHEN GENDER = 'M' THEN 'Male'
        ELSE 'Unknown'
      END
FROM ACTOR;
```

A **CASE** statement expression can be a substitute for **DECODE**, **COALESCE**, and **NULLIF** functions (see Chapter 5, "Single Row Functions").

- *Datetime Expression*—Places a date into varying datetime datatypes such as LOCAL, DBTIMEZONE, or SESSIONTIMEZONE, among others. The first example finds my local time timestamp:

  ```
  SELECT CAST(SYSDATE AS TIMESTAMP) AT LOCAL FROM DUAL;
  ```

9i The **TIMESTAMP** datatype is new to Oracle9i.

The next two examples find timestamps for my session (SESSIONTIMEZONE) and database time zone (DBTIMEZONE) settings, respectively:

```
SELECT CAST(SYSDATE AS TIMESTAMP) AT TIME ZONE SESSIONTIMEZONE
FROM DUAL;

SELECT CAST(SYSDATE AS TIMESTAMP) AT TIME ZONE DBTIMEZONE FROM DUAL;
```

You can verify session and database time zone settings with the following queries:

```
SELECT SESSIONTIMEZONE FROM DUAL;

SELECT DBTIMEZONE FROM DUAL;
```

The next query finds 24-hour clock times in PST (Pacific Standard Time), GMT (Greenwich Mean Time: 0° longitude), and my local time zone. I live in the EST time zone (Eastern Standard Time).

```
SELECT  TO_CHAR(CAST(SYSDATE AS TIMESTAMP) AT LOCAL, 'HH24:MI') "EST"
 ,TO_CHAR(CAST(SYSDATE AS TIMESTAMP) AT TIME ZONE 'PST','HH24:MI') "PST"
 ,TO_CHAR(CAST(SYSDATE AS TIMESTAMP) AT TIME ZONE 'GMT','HH24:MI') "GMT"
FROM DUAL;
```

The next query is useful for resolving the previous query in that it shows me names of all possible time zones:

```
SELECT * FROM V$TIMEZONE_NAMES;
```

V$TIMEZONE_NAMES is a database performance view. You can gain access to metadata and performance views by asking your administrator to assign you the **SELECT_CATALOG_ROLE** role. An example of a metadata view is **DBA_TABLES** and an example of a performance view is **V$TABLESPACE**.

- *Interval Expression*—These expressions can be used to express intervals between dates. This example returns Year-Month and Day-Second intervals between the movie release date and SYSDATE (current date on my machine) for all movie titles in the MOVIE table:

```
COL TITLE FORMAT A24
COL MONTHS FORMAT A24 HEADING "Years/Months"
COL SECONDS FORMAT A24 HEADING "Days/Seconds"
SELECT TITLE, RELEASE, SYSDATE
    , (SYSDATE - RELEASE) YEAR TO MONTH AS MONTHS
    , (SYSDATE - RELEASE) DAY TO SECOND AS SECONDS
FROM MOVIE WHERE RELEASE IS NOT NULL;
```

- *Scalar Subquery Expression*—A scalar subquery is an expression, returning a single column value from one row where no rows returned results in a

`NULL value`. In the following `INSERT` command, the subquery `(SELECT MAX(SAGA_ID)+1 FROM SAGA)` always returns a single value:

```
INSERT INTO SAGA(SAGA_ID,SAGA) VALUES((SELECT MAX(SAGA_ID)+1 FROM
SAGA),'A Saga');
```

If there are zero rows in the `SAGA` table, the subquery will return a `NULL` value.

- *Object Expressions*—Various object methodology expressions such as type constructors, variables, and object access expressions. Object expressions are out of the scope of this book.

The next chapter looks at single row functions in Oracle SQL.

Exam Prep Questions

1. What type of expression is the number 802?

   - ❑ A. Compound expression
   - ❑ B. Datetime expression
   - ❑ C. Function expression
   - ❑ D. Regular expression
   - ❑ E. None of the above

   A, B, C, and D are all incorrect. Thus, E is the correct answer. The number 802 is a simple expression. A compound expression contains multiple simple expressions, a datetime expression produces a date, a function expression contains a function, and a regular expression uses the pattern matching processing to parse and replace contents of strings.

2. Where can **CURSOR** and **CASE** statement expressions be nested?

   - ❑ A. In any DDL command
   - ❑ B. In any DML command
   - ❑ C. In a subquery
   - ❑ D. In a **REF** cursor function parameter
   - ❑ E. In a calling SQL **SELECT** statement, as long as it is not a subquery

   Answer E is correct. **CURSOR** and **CASE** statement expressions can be nested only in **SELECT** statement select lists, as long as they are not subqueries. A, B, and C are incorrect because DDL and any DML commands are not included in answer E's result. D is incorrect because it applies to only **CURSOR** and not **CASE** expressions.

3. Which line has an error?

   - ❑ A. `SELECT CASE`
   - ❑ B. `WHEN 'F' THEN 'Female'`
   - ❑ C. `WHEN 'M' THEN 'Male'`
   - ❑ D. `ELSE 'Unknown' END FROM ACTOR;`

   Line 1 has an error because the **GENDER** condition is absent. Line 1 should be constructed as `SELECT CASE GENDER`.

4. Which of the following is an interval expression?

   - ❑ A. `TO_CHAR(TO_DATE('31/12/2003'))`
   - ❑ B. `TO_DATE(TO_CHAR('31-DEC-2003'))`
   - ❑ C. `TO_CHAR(CAST(SYSDATE AS TIMESTAMP) AT TIME ZONE 'PST', 'HH24:MI')`
   - ❑ D. `None of the above`

   D is the correct answer. A, B, and C are not interval expressions; they are all datetime expressions.

5. What is the result of this query?

```
SELECT (SYSDATE - (SYSDATE-365)) YEAR TO MONTH FROM DUAL;
```

- ❑ A. `+000000001-01`
- ❑ B. `+000000002-00`
- ❑ C. `+000000365-00`
- ❑ D. `+000000001-00`
- ❑ E. None of the above

Answer D is correct returning a value representing 1 year and zero days. This value is obtained by subtracting 1 year (365 days) from the **SYSDATE**. A represents 1 year and 1 day. B represents 2 years. C represents 365 years. E is incorrect because D is correct.

6. What is the correct sequence of values in a **ROWID**?

- ❑ A. Datafile, tablespace, block, row
- ❑ B. Datafile, block, tablespace, row
- ❑ C. Segment, datafile, block, row
- ❑ D. None of the above

The answer is C. A **ROWID** is a concatenated set of values comprising relative address pointers to a data object (a segment or table), a datafile within a tablespace, a block, and a row within a block.

Single Row Functions

Terms You Need to Understand

- ✓ Single row function
- ✓ String function
- ✓ Datetime function
- ✓ Conversion function

Concepts You Need to Master

- ✓ Single row functions
- ✓ Differences between string, number, datetime, and conversion functions
- ✓ Where functions can be used
- ✓ Nesting functions in other functions
- ✓ Number conversion function formatting
- ✓ Date conversion function formatting

This chapter describes single row functions. Single row functions operate within or as expressions on each row of a SQL statement. By definition, a function is a piece of compiled or interpreted code used to do some processing and return a value. Because a function returns a value, it can be embedded into an expression.

What Is a Function?

A function is a programming unit returning a single value, allowing values to be passed in as parameters. The parameters can change the outcome or return the result of a function. The beauty of a function is that it is self-contained and can thus be embedded in an expression. By definition, in Oracle SQL an expression is a SQL code command or even another function.

Types of Functions

In general, functions in Oracle SQL are divided into five groups, the first group being the topic of this chapter, namely, single row functions. Other function types are aggregate functions, which create groups of rows; analytic functions, which also group but allow in-depth data analysis; object reference functions, allowing access to special object pointers; and finally user-defined functions, such as those you create using a programming language such as PL/SQL.

- *Single Row Functions*—Single row functions can be used to execute an operation on each row of a query. In other words, a single row function can be used to execute the same operation for every row a query retrieves.
- *Aggregate Functions*—These functions summarize repeating groups in a row set into distinct groups, aggregating repetitive values into items such as sums or averages. See Chapter 7.
- *Analytic Functions*—Unlike aggregates, which summarize repetitions into unique items, analytics create subset summaries within aggregates. See Chapter 7.
- *Object Reference Functions*—These functions use pointers to reference values. Commonly, object reference functions either reference objects or dereference values from objects. See Chapter 11, "Tables, Datatypes, and Constraints (DDL)."
- *User-Defined Functions*—Custom functions can be built using PL/SQL, allowing extension of the large library of Oracle SQL built-in functionality. PL/SQL is beyond the scope of this book.

Where Can Functions Be Used?

If you recall, a function is an expression in itself and thus belongs anywhere an expression does, as shown by the LENGTH function in this example:

```
SELECT LENGTH('This is a string') FROM DUAL;
```

Or it can be within an expression, as shown by the LENGTH function embedded in the SUBSTR function in this example:

```
SELECT SUBSTR('This is a string', 6, LENGTH('is a')) FROM DUAL;
```

The following list describes some places where functions might appear:

- SELECT statement item selection list
- WHERE and ORDER BY clauses
- GROUP BY and HAVING clauses (see Chapter 7)
- CONNECT BY and START WITH clauses in hierarchical queries (see Chapter 8)
- INSERT command VALUES clause and UPDATE command SET clause (see Chapter 10)

A function is an expression. Expressions can be embedded in other expressions. Therefore, a function can call another function, be embedded in another function, or be nested in another function.

Single Row Functions

Now let's focus on the subject matter of this chapter. Recall that a single row function was defined as a function that can be used to execute an operation on each row of a query. Let's start this journey by discovering the different classifications for single row functions:

- *String Functions*—These functions take a string as a parameter and return a number or a string.
- *Number Functions*—A number is passed in, usually returning a number.
- *Datetime Functions*—These functions accept date value parameters.
- *Conversion Functions*—These functions convert between different datatypes.
- *Miscellaneous Functions*—Odd functions fall into this category.

String Functions

A string function takes a string as a parameter and returns either a number or a string result. Thus, string functions can be broken down into string functions that return numbers and string functions that return strings.

String Functions Returning Numbers

This type of function will have a string passed into it, but the resulting output is a number. The following bulleted list details all string functions that return numbers:

- ASCII(<character>)—ASCII(' ') returns the ASCII numeric value for a space character: 32.

- INSTR(<string>, <substring> [, <position> [, <occurrence>]])—INSTR returns the numeric position of a substring within a string. INSTR('This world is round', 'is') returns 3 because the first occurrence of is begins in position 3 as part of the word This.

  Position allows searching from a position within a string. For example, this query finds the first occurrence of the word is in the string, from the word This. The result of 3 is returned:

  ```
  SELECT INSTR('This world is round, it is not flat.','is') FROM DUAL;
  ```

  In this next example, the INSTR function begins searching for is from position 15, missing two occurrences of the string is, including the one in the first word, This. The query returns 25:

  ```
  SELECT INSTR('This world is round, it is not flat.','is',15) FROM DUAL;
  ```

  Occurrence applies to which duplicate substring to select, if any. For example, search from position 5, including both occurrences of is but ignoring the first:

  ```
  SELECT INSTR('This world is round, it is not flat.', 'is',5,2)
      FROM DUAL;
  ```

  We can also search backward from the end of the string using a negative value for the position. This query searches from position -1. Position -1 is the last character in the string:

  ```
  SELECT INSTR('This world is round, it is not flat.', 'is',-1) FROM DUAL;
  ```

  In this example, position -30 is used to search backward through the string to find the position of the string is in the first word of the string, This, once again back at position 3:

  ```
  SELECT INSTR('This world is round, it is not flat.', 'is',-30)
      FROM DUAL;
  ```

The **INSTR** function is not new to Oracle9i but has been enhanced.

- `LENGTH(<string>)`—`LENGTH('This is a string')` returns the length of the string, 16 characters.

  `LENGTH(INSTR('This world is round, it is not flat.', 'is', 15))` returns a string length of 2 characters because the value returned by `INSTR` is `25`. The `LENGTH` function expects a string, but an implicit type conversion changes the input from a numeric to a string.

The **LENGTH** function is not new to Oracle9i but has been enhanced.

For the **ASCII** function, the **<character>** parameter can be an expression but must evaluate to a single character in the ASCII character set. The only prerequisite is that the expression must evaluate to the required datatype or equivalent of the parameter. Similarly, these points apply to all functions in that all parameters can be expressions and resulting datatypes must be appropriate matches.

String Functions Returning Strings

Previously, you discovered functions in which a string was passed into a function and a number was returned as a result. In this section, you will discover some strings that pass a string into the function and also get a string returned. The following bulleted list highlights these functions:

- `CHR(<n>)`—The `CHR` function returns the ASCII string equivalent of an ASCII numeric value. In other words, when you press the spacebar on your keyboard, the computer interprets the spacebar as the number 32. Computers understand numbers rather than characters. If you recall from the definition of the ASCII function earlier in this chapter, the ASCII function returns the ASCII numeric value for a space character: `32`. The `CHR` function is the opposite of the ASCII function. Thus, whereas `ASCII(32)` returns a space character, `CHR(' ')` returns the number `32`.
- `CONCAT(<string>, <string>)`—This function concatenates two strings. For example, `CONCAT('This is ','a string')` returns `This is a string`.
- `INITCAP(<string>)`—This function capitalizes the first letter in each word. `INITCAP('This is a string')` returns `This Is A String`.

- LOWER(<string>) and UPPER(<string>)—These two functions convert strings to lowercase and uppercase, respectively. LOWER('This is a string') returns this is a string. Similarly, UPPER('This is a string') returns THIS IS A STRING.

NLS_LOWER, **NLS_UPPER**, and **NLS_INITCAP** apply to different national language character sets. Similarly, **NLSSORT** applies alphanumeric sorting sequences for different languages.

- LPAD(<string>, <n> [, <replace>]) and RPAD(<string>, <n> [, <replace>])—These functions pad or fill a string to length <n> from the left or right side of a string, optionally replacing with a replacement string. The replacement string defaults to a space character. In this example the LPAD function will fill or pad the string out to 20 characters:

  ```
  SELECT LPAD('This is a string', 20, '01') FROM DUAL;
  ```

  Because the string is less than 20 characters in length, it is padded from the left with the replacement characters 01 twice, returning 0101This is a string.

  It follows that this example returns the same string, increased in length to 20 characters, padded on the right of the string with space characters:

  ```
  SELECT RPAD('This is a string', 20, ' ') FROM DUAL;
  ```

  Therefore, the result is This is a string   .

- LTRIM(<string>, <string>), RTRIM(<string>, <string>), and TRIM([[LEADING¦TRAILING¦BOTH] <character> FROM] <string>)—These functions trim or remove characters from strings from the left, from the right, or from both sides of a string. For example, LTRIM('   This is a string') removes spaces from the beginning of the string, resulting in the output This is a string. No more spaces!

  RTRIM('   This is a string ', ' g') removes spaces from the end of the string only, plus removes the last g character (the second trim string is specified as ' g', a space character followed by the character g). The output would be '   This is a strin', removing the g character and leaving three spaces at the start of the string. The RTRIM function trims from the right side of the string, unlike the already seen LTRIM function, which trims from the left side of the string.

  TRIM(BOTH ' ' FROM '   This is a string   ') removes spaces from both the beginning and the end of the string, not the spaces between the words. Thus the result would be This is a string.

- SUBSTR(<string> [, [-]<position> [, <n>]])—This function extracts substrings from other strings. <position> implies the start position from the start of the string, a negative <position> counts from the end of the string, and <n> denotes a number of characters to extract. SUBSTR('This is a string', 6, 4) returns is a (six characters from the start, for four characters in length).

  SUBSTR('This is a string', -11, 4) does the same except from the end of the string, also returning the string is a.

The **SUBSTR** function is not new to Oracle9i but has been enhanced.

- REPLACE(<string>, <search> [, <replace>]) and TRANSLATE(<string>, <search> [, <replace>])—The REPLACE function replaces character groupings, and the TRANSLATE function translates characters to other characters.

  For example, REPLACE('This is a string', ' ', '') returns Thisisastring because all space characters (' ') have been replaced with NULL (''). Also, TRANSLATE('This is a string', 'ia', 'IA') returns ThIs Is A StrIng because any occurrence of lowercase letters i or a are translated into uppercase letters I or A, respectively.

- SOUNDEX(<character>)—This function returns phonetic representations of characters. SOUNDEX('See') is equivalent to the string Sea.

You might wonder why some functions listed in Oracle docs are not included here, and ultimately in the exam. The reason is that there are a multitude of XML functions, which could be viewed as single row string functions. XML functions are out of the scope of this book and this exam.

Number Functions

A number function performs calculations with numbers, including calculations even as simple as those you learned in mathematics classes when you were a child. With number functions, a number is passed in, usually returning a number. For example, an absolute value calculation is a number function because it converts any whole number into a positive value. Number functions can be broken down into those performing simple calculations, trigonometry, and logarithms. So number functions could be used as simple calculators or even perform trigonometric and logarithmic calculations.

Simple Calculators

A simple calculator executes a simple calculation on an input number value. The following list gives you some simple calculator functions:

- ABS(<n>)—An absolute value function always returns a positive value. For example, ABS(-5) and ABS(5) both return 5. ABS(0) returns 0.
- POWER(<n>, <exponent>) and SQRT(<n>)—The POWER function raises <n> to the power of <exponent>. For example, POWER(2, 3) returns 8, or 2 * 2 * 2 = 8. In mathematical notation, POWER(2, 3) is represented as 2^3 = 8. SQRT(<n>) returns the square root of a number. For example, SQRT(4) returns 2 because 2 * 2 = 4, or 2^2 = 4.
- CEIL(<n>) and FLOOR(<n>)—The CEIL function returns a whole number rounded up, and FLOOR returns a whole number rounded down, regardless of the value of decimals. Thus, CEIL(5.11) returns 6 and FLOOR(5.99) returns 5. With normal mathematical rounding, 5.99 rounded to zero decimal places would be 6, and 5.11 would round down to 5. Thus, the CEIL and FLOOR function perform the opposite. In mathematical lingo, any decimal .5 and above is rounded up and others are rounded down.
- ROUND(<n>, [<decimal places>]) and TRUNC(<n>, [<decimal places>])—The ROUND function rounds up or down when a decimal place is >= 5 or < 5, respectively. The TRUNC function simply chops off decimal places with no rounding. <decimal places> defaults to 0 if not specified. ROUND(10.234) returns 10, ROUND(10.5) returns 11, ROUND(10.2) returns 10, and ROUND(10.125, 2) returns 10.13, rounding the digits 25 in the second and third decimal places up to a single digit of 3. TRUNC(10.234) returns 10, TRUNC(10.5) returns 10, TRUNC(10.2) returns 10, and TRUNC(10.125, 2) returns 10.12. The TRUNC function does not round as the ROUND function does; it truncates or chops off.
- MOD(<numerator>, <denominator>)—This function finds a modulus or remainder by dividing the numerator by the denominator. In mathematical lingo the numerator is a number to be divided by, and the denominator is a number to be divided with. In other words, when you're calculating 100/2 (division), 100 is the numerator and 2 is the denominator. MOD(4,2) returns 0 because 2 divides into 4 exactly with nothing left over. MOD(5,2) returns 1 because 2 divides into 5 twice, making 4, and 5 – 4 = 1, returning the remainder or modulus of 1. MOD(9,5) returns 4, similarly because 9/5 = 1, with 4 remaining.
- SIGN(<n>)—The SIGN function returns the sign of a number, -1 for negative, 1 for positive, and 0 for 0. SIGN(-5) returns -1, SIGN(5) returns 1, and SIGN(0) returns 0. For example, the following query would classify all

movies made before the year 2000 as Old, those in the year 2000 as Y2K, and those after the year 2000 as New:

```
SELECT TITLE, YEAR, DECODE(SIGN(YEAR-2000),-1,'Old',0,'Y2K',1,'New')
FROM MOVIE ORDER BY YEAR;
```

- BITAND(<n>, <n>—This function performs a bitwise logical AND operation on two integers.

Understanding what a bitwise **AND** operation is or what it does is not a requirement for the exam. The fact that the **BITAND** function exists is a requirement. Therefore, no example is provided.

- 9i WIDTH_BUCKET(<expression>, <min>, <max>, <buckets>)—This function allows construction of equal-width histogram data.

You won't be required to understand what a histogram is for the exam. You will, however, be required to know that the **WIDTH_BUCKET** function exists. Therefore, no example is provided.

Trigonometry

What is trigonometry? Trigonometry is the mathematics of computational geometry. Or, as the *Oxford English Dictionary* says, it's "*the branch of mathematics concerned with the relations of the sides and angles of triangles and with the relevant functions of any angles. Origin: the Greek word* trigonos *meaning three-cornered.*" The following functions provided in Oracle SQL allow for trigonometric calculations:

- SIN(<n>), COS(<n>) and TAN(<n>)—These functions perform Sine, Cosine, and Tangent functions.
- ASIN(<n>), ACOS(<n>), ATAN(<n>), and ATAN2(<n>)—The opposite of SIN, COS, and TAN: ArcSine, ArcCosine, and ArcTangent.
- SINH(<n>), COSH(<n>), and TANH(<n>)—These are hyperbolic Sine, Cosine, and Tangent functions.

The understanding of what trigonometric functions produce is trigonometry, which is mathematics and not Oracle SQL. Therefore, no examples are provided. Knowing that these functions exist and knowing that they mean Sine, Cosine, or Tangent are required for this exam. But you do not have to know specifically what a Sine function means or what it does precisely, or even its application. The test will not have trick questions such as asking you the Sine of 2 Pi radians. However, you will be expected to know that typing in **SINE(90)** rather than **SIN(90)** will produce a syntax error in SQL*Plus. In other words, memorize the syntactically correct forms of functions.

Logarithms

What is a logarithm? In simple terms, if

$10^2 = 100$

then

$\log 100 = 2$

In actuality, log 100 is really $\log_{10}100 = 2$, because if the default base of 10 is used, then it is omitted in the mathematical notation. Therefore, if

$2^3 = 8$

then

$\log_2 8 = 3$

So what is a logarithm? A logarithm is a logarithmic function or an inverse exponent. An inverse is an opposite. The POWER function, seen earlier in this chapter, is an exponent. An exponent is a number to which another numbered is raised. Thus, the inverse exponent or logarithm is the number to which a number was raised to the power of, namely, the exponent. Or, as the *Oxford English Dictionary* puts it, "*a logarithm is a quantity representing the power to which a fixed number (the base) must be raised to produce a given number. Origin: the Greek words* logos *meaning reckoning or ratio, plus* arithmos *meaning number.*"

- `LOG(<base>, <n>)`—A logarithm is the number to which the `<base>` must be raised to get `<n>`. Thus, `LOG(10,100)`, mathematically written as LOG 100, returns `2` because $10^2 = 100$. The default `<base>` is always 10. `LOG(2,8)`, mathematically written as $\text{LOG}_2 8$ (log 8 to base 2), returns `3`, because $2^3 = 8$.
- `LN(<n>)`—`LN` is the natural logarithm of a number with the base being the constant *e* ($e = 2.71828183$).
- `EXP(<n>)`—`EXP` is the opposite of `LN`, calculating *e* to the power of `<n>` or $e^{<n>}$.

Knowing the meanings of logarithmic functions is mathematics and not Oracle SQL. Memorize only the syntactical forms of functions. Additionally, examples of **LN** and **EXP** functions are not included because they are once again mathematics and not Oracle SQL.

Date Functions

Date functions accept date value parameters and produce dates and times. Various date functions allow you to retrieve dates from a database and format date values, such as changing from American format (MM/DD/YYYY) to British format (DD/MM/YYYY). You can also change date values and extract parts of dates.

Date functions can be divided into sections dealing with date retrieval, parts of dates, and time zones.

Simple Date Retrieval Functions

These functions simply get dates and times from the Oracle SQL engine such as the date in the database, or the operating system, even adding timezone details and modifications. These functions are shown in the following bulleted list:

- `SYSDATE` and 9i `CURRENT_DATE`—Both functions return current date and time, except that `CURRENT_DATE` returns the date and time for the time zone of the connected session (see the `SESSIONTIMEZONE` function in the "Time Zones" section).
- 9i `CURRENT_TIMESTAMP(<precision>)` and 9i `LOCALTIMESTAMP(<precision>)`—Both produce a timestamp except that the `CURRENT_TIMESTAMP` function returns it with a time zone as well. Figure 5.1 shows what a timestamp looks like.

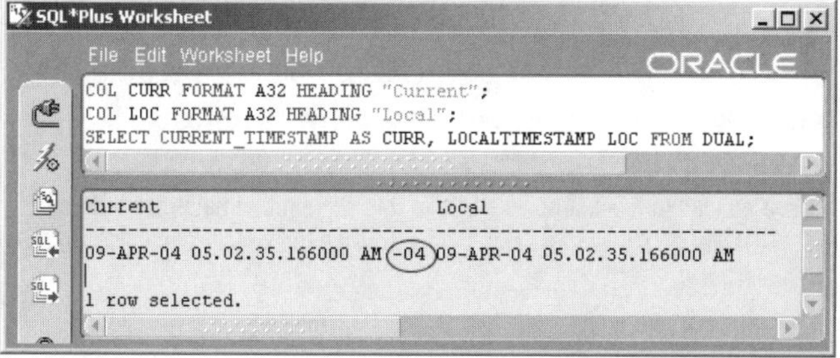

Figure 5.1 The **CURRENT_TIMESTAMP** and **LOCALTIMESTAMP** functions.

Note how the time zone of –04 is highlighted in Figure 5.1, representing the session time zone of EST, summer time adjusted for daylight savings time at –4 hours GMT.

9i The **TIMESTAMP** datatype is new to Oracle9i.

- 9i SYSTIMESTAMP—This function returns a timestamp and time zone based on the database time-zone setting (see the DBTIMEZONE function in the "Time Zones" section).

Parts of Dates

The functions listed here can be used to find pieces within a given date, such as the last day in a month. For example, LAST_DAY('01-JAN-04') will reply with 31-JAN-04. Here is the list of date part functions:

- NEXT_DAY(<date>, <weekday>)—Returns the date of the first <weekday> occurring after <date>. NEXT_DAY('01-JAN-2005','SUNDAY') returns the first Sunday of the month of January 2005. The 1st of January is a Saturday.

  In NEXT_DAY('02-JAN-2005','SUNDAY') the starting date is a Sunday, and thus the second Sunday in January is returned: the 9th of January.
- LAST_DAY(<date>)—This function simply returns the last day of the month specified by <date>.
- ADD_MONTHS(<date>, <months>)—Simply add a number of months to <date>. This function adds in months and not days. Thus, ADD_MONTHS('01-JAN-2005', 5) returns the 1st of June, whereas ADD_MONTHS('31-JAN-2005', 5) returns the 30th of June, even though the starting date is the 31st of January.
- MONTHS_BETWEEN(<date>, <date>)—This function returns the number of months between two dates. Thus, MONTHS_BETWEEN('01-JAN-05', '01-JAN-04') returns 12, representing the 12 months between the two dates. Note in the preceding example that the higher date is listed first. Switching the two dates as in MONTHS_BETWEEN('01-JAN-04', '01-JAN-05') returns -12.

You may have noticed in the examples so far in this section that dates are entered as DD-MON-YY. DD-MON-YY is the default date format for Oracle Database and is implicitly converted.

- 9i EXTRACT(<format> FROM { <date> | <timestamp> }—The EXTRACT function can be used to extract a single subset part of <date> or <timestamp>, depending on what is extracted. Figure 5.2 shows what can be extracted and how it is extracted.

Format	Example	Result
YEAR	EXTRACT(YEAR FROM DATE '2004-03-25')	2004
MONTH	EXTRACT(MONTH FROM DATE '2004-03-25')	3
DAY	EXTRACT(DAY FROM SYSDATE)	25
HOUR	EXTRACT(HOUR FROM TIME '12:24"01')	12
MINUTE	EXTRACT(MINUTE FROM LOCAL TIMESTAMP)	1
SECOND	EXTRACT(SECOND FROM LOCAL TIMESTAMP)	9.*nn*
TIMEZONE_HOUR	EXTRACT(TIMEZONE_HOUR FROM CURRANT_TIMESTAMP)	-4
TIMEZONE_MINUTE	EXTRACT(TIMEZONE_MINUTE FROM CURRENT_TIMESTAMP)	0
TIME_ZONE REGION	EXTRACT(TIMEZONE_REGION FROM CURRENT_TIMESTAMP)	US/EASTERN
TIMEZONE_ABBR	EXTRACT(TIMEZONE_ABBR FROM CURRENT_TIMESTAMP)	EST

Figure 5.2 The **EXTRACT** function.

Figure 5.2 contains various formatting and extraction options.

- ROUND(<date> [, <format>]) and TRUNC(<date> [, <format>])—These functions, as their names imply, round off and truncate date values. As with numbers, rounding implies rounding up or down, and truncation simply chops things off. Figure 5.3 clearly shows the differences between dates rounded up to years and months and dates truncated to years and months, truncating effectively rounding down.

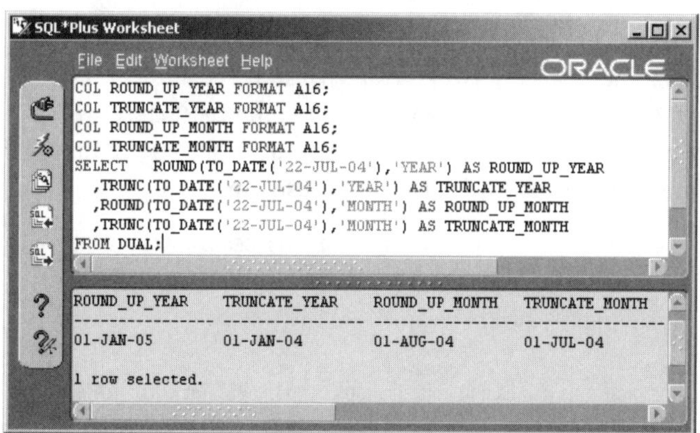

Figure 5.3 The difference between rounding up and truncating of dates.

Figure 5.4 shows format parameters for rounding and truncating of dates using the ROUND and TRUNC functions.

Format	Description
CC SCC	Century
SYYYY YYYY YEAR SYEAR YYY YY Y IYYY IYI	Years round up on July 1st
Q	Quarters round up in the 16th day of the second month
MONTH MON MM RM	Months round up on the sixteenth day
WW IW	The day of week of the first day of the year
W	The day of week of the first day of the month
DDD DD J	Day
DAY DY D	The first day of the week
HH HH12 HH24	Hour
MI	Minute

Figure 5.4 Format strings for **ROUND(<date>)** and **TRUNC(<date>)**.

Time Zones

The following functions deal with time zones and relative time zones. For example, New York is Eastern Standard Time (EST), and London, England, is on Greenwich Mean Time (GMT). Here is the list of time-zone functions:

- 9i `DBTIMEZONE` and 9i `SESSIONTIMEZONE`—These functions return time zones for the database and the current session. `-04:00` represents EST, or `-4` hours GMT.
- 9i `FROM_TZ(<timestamp>, <time zone>)`—This function creates a timestamp with a time zone from the two `<timestamp>` and `<time zone>` parameters specified. In `FROM_TZ(LOCALTIMESTAMP,'-04:00')` the `LOCALTIMESTAMP` function returns a timestamp excluding a time zone. The `FROM_TZ` function adds the time zone `-04:00` GMT to the timestamp.
- 9i `TZ_OFFSET(<time zone> | '{+|-} <HH>:<MI>' | {DB|SESSION}TIMEZONE)`—This function returns the time zone offset such as `-04:00` for EST summer time daylight savings, 4 hours west of GMT.

You can find time zone names and abbreviations from the **V$TIMEZONE_NAMES** view containing columns **TZNAME** and **TZABBREV**.

- `NEW_TIME(<date>, <zone>, <zone>)`—This function converts from one zone to another.

Use of the **NEW_TIME** function requires setting of the **NLS_DATE_FORMAT** Oracle Database configuration parameter in the configuration parameter file. Ask your database administrator to do this because changing it may cause serious unexpected problems.

- SYS_EXTRACT_UTC(<datetime time-zone>)—This function finds the GMT equivalent of a datetime including a time zone.

GMT, or Greenwich Mean Time, has been changed to UTC, or Coordinated Universal Time, or just Universal Time. GMT or UTC is at 0[dg] of longitude, running directly through the town of Greenwich, in London, England.

Datatype Conversion Functions

Datatype conversion functions are used to change values from one datatype to another. For example, TO_CHAR(SYSDATE) will convert a date datatype value into a string containing a date. Datatype conversion functions can be divided into string conversions, number conversions, datetime conversions, things with ROWIDs or hexadecimals, and character set conversions, and finally there are also some obscure datatype conversion functions.

String Conversions

String conversion functions convert datatypes such as CLOB objects into string objects. A CLOB object is a special datatype used to store extremely large text objects into binary objects (see Chapter 11). The following items will give you a better idea of how string conversions work:

- 9i TO_[N]CHAR(<string>)—Converts the string content value of a CLOB object to a string, making it accessible with regular Oracle SQL functions. Because a CLOB object is stored as binary, 0s and 1s, normal string functions such as SUBSTR cannot be applied to a CLOB object.
- 9i TO_[N]CLOB(<string>)—Converts a string to a CLOB object value. This function simply does the opposite of the TO_CHAR(<string>) listed in the preceding bullet entry.

Number Conversions

Number conversion functions convert datatypes between strings and numbers, and vice versa. For example, the string containing a number is best converted to an internal Oracle Database number being passed into a numeric function such as ABS (absolute value). Sometimes Oracle SQL will convert automatically between numbers and strings, but not always. Additionally, it is bad programming practice to assume automatic datatype conversions because this leads to bugs in software that can be very difficult to find. The following items show how number conversions work:

- TO_NUMBER(<n> [, <format>])—Converts from a string to a number. For example, TO_NUMBER('1234.56758') returns a number datatype containing the number 1234.56758. Consequently, TO_NUMBER('this is a string') returns an error because the string is not a number. Also, TO_NUMBER('1234.56758', '99999') returns an error because the input value is incorrectly formatted, seeking four digits left of the decimal, not five.
- TO_[N]CHAR(<string> [, <format>])—Converts from a number to a string. For example, TO_CHAR(54632.9439, '9,999,990.99') returns 54,632.94. 9i TO_NCHAR(<string>) is new to Oracle9i.

The preceding two functions show a <format> parameter. Formatting models for number conversions are shown in Figure 5.5. For example, TO_CHAR(9023887.99230, '$9,999,990.99') returns $9,023,887,99, and TO_CHAR(0, '$9,999,990.99') returns $0.00.

Format	Description
"$9,999,990.90"	Thousands separated with commas, with two decimals where "0.00" causes 0 to appear as "0.00" not ".00". $ adds a leading $ sign. Commas can be replaced with a group separator [$9G999G990.99]. $ can be altered to a local currency symbol using L9G999G990.99.
0999 9990	Leading and trailing 0s
B999 9D99	B replaces 0s with blanks, D allows changing the decimal character from a period [.] to something else [NLS]
EEEE	Exponential number conversion ["scientific notation"]
FM999	Leading and trailing blanks are removed
RN rn	Upper case and lower case Roman numerals
999MI 999PR	If negative: 999- and <999>
S999 999S	Leading or trailing + or - signs
TM	Minimize number of characters used by numeric output (can change to exponential format)
U999	Dual currency symbols such as Euros
99V99 99V999	10 returned as 10^2 (99V99) and 10^3 (99V999)
X	Hexadecimal conversion

Figure 5.5 Number format modeling.

Figure 5.5 shows that many variations are available for formatting of numbers.

Datetime Conversions

Datetime conversion functions convert datatypes between dates, strings, and some unusual interval datetime representations. For example, TO_CHAR(SYSDATE, 'J') will return the Julian number representation of the date value retrieved by the SYSDATE function. The following items show how datetime conversions work:

- TO_DATE(<string>, <format>)—This function converts string valued dates to DATE or equivalent datatypes. For example, TO_DATE('11-NOV-04') will return a date-formatted datatype containing the specified date.
- TO_[N]CHAR(<datetime>, <format>)—This function converts from DATE or equivalent datatypes to string values. For example, TO_CHAR(SYSDATE, 'YYYY/MM/DD') returns the internal Oracle system date for November 11, 2004, as the string 2004/11/04. 9i TO_NCHAR(<datetime>) is new to Oracle9i.
- NUMTODSINTERVAL(<n>, { 'day' | 'hour' | 'minute' | 'second' }) and NUMTOYMINTERVAL(<n>, { 'year' | 'month' })—These two functions convert from a number to an INTERVAL_DAY_TO_SECOND and INTERVAL_YEAR_TO_MONTH literal value, respectively. For example:
  - NUMTODSINTERVAL(100, 'hour') returns 100 hours: +000000004 04:00:00.000000000, or 4 days (24 hours * 4) and 4 hours.
  - NUMTODSINTERVAL(100, 'minute') returns 100 minutes: +000000000 01:40:00.000000000, or 1 hour (60 minutes) and 40 minutes.
  - NUMTOYMINTERVAL(100, 'month') returns 100 months: +000000008-04, or 8 years and 4 months.
- 9i TO_DSINTERVAL(<string>) and 9i TO_YMINTERVAL(<string>)—These two functions convert strings to INTERVAL DAY TO SECOND and INTERVAL YEAR TO MONTH values, respectively.
- 9i TO_TIMESTAMP(<string>, <format>) and 9i TO_TIMESTAMP_TZ(<string>, <format>)—These functions convert strings to TIMESTAMP and TIMESTAMP WITH TIME ZONE datatypes, respectively. The <format> parameter contains standard date formatting parameters.

Various date conversion functions show a <format> parameter. Formatting models for date conversions are shown in Figure 5.6. For example, TO_CHAR(LOCALTIMESTAMP, 'DY DD MON, YYYY HH24:MI:SS.FF3') returns a string in the format SAT 10 APR, 2004 05:34:18.772.

Format	Description
“-/ ,.;:”	Punctuation
BC AD	Before Christ and Anno Domini (after the birth of christ)
CC SCC	BC dates are negative
AM PM	Morning and afternoon
D DAY DD DDD DY	1-7, name of day, 1-31, 1-366 , name of day (abbreviated)
E EE	Era names
SS.FF1 to SS.FF9	Decimal precision for seconds
HH HH12 HH24 MI SS SSSSS	Hours, minutes, and seconds.
IW WW W	WW = 1-52 weeks in a year, W = 1-4 weeks in a month
Y, YYY YEAR SYEAR YYYY SYYYY YYY YY Y IYYY IYY IY I RR RRRR	Year
J	Julian day
MM MON MONTH RM	Month, RM is in Roman numerals
Q	Quarter
TZD TZH TZM TZR	Time zone information

Figure 5.6 Date format modeling.

Figure 5.6 shows that many variations are available for formatting of dates.

ROWIDs and Hexadecimals

These functions convert odd things such as ROWID and hexadecimal values. The following list gives you some more clues as to how these functions work:

- CHARTOROWID(<string>)—String to ROWID datatype conversion. <string> has to have the structure of a ROWID.
- ROWIDTOCHAR(<ROWID>) and 9i ROWIDTONCHAR(<ROWID>)—Converts a ROWID datatype into a string.
- HEXTORAW(<string>), RAWTOHEX(<raw>) and 9i RAWTONHEX(<raw>)—Converts between strings and raw binary values.

You are not required to understand these functions, but only to memorize them for syntax and be aware that they exist.

Character Set Conversion Functions

These functions are used to convert between different national character sets. You need to use these functions only if you use a non-US character set:

- 9i COMPOSE(<string>) and 9i DECOMPOSE(<string>)—Both functions convert between Unicode and standard ASCII character sets.

- 9i UNISTR(<string>)—Converts strings to Unicode for any character set.
- CONVERT(<string>, <target>, <source>)—Converts between two character sets.
- TRANSLATE (<string> USING [N]CHAR_CS)—Translates between database and national character sets.

You are not required to understand these functions, but only to memorize them for syntax and be aware that they exist.

Obscure Conversion Functions

Here are some obscure and rarely used conversion functions you may encounter in the exam:

- 9i ASCIISTR(<string>)—Converts an ASCII string into the database character set from any other character set.
- 9i BIN_TO_NUM(<expression>)—Bit vector or binary number to number conversion.
- CAST({<expression> | (subquery) | MULTISET (subquery)}) AS <type>—CAST is a type casting function, allowing conversions between compatible datatypes or object collection datatypes.

The **MULTISET** parameter creates a collection of rows returned by a subquery. See Chapter 8, "Subqueries and Other Specialized Queries," for an explanation of subqueries.

- TO_LOB(<long> | <long raw>)—Converts LONG or LONG RAW values to LOB value datatypes.
- TO_SINGLE_BYTE(<string>) and TO_MULTI_BYTE(<string>)—Convert between multi-byte and single-byte representations.

You are not required to understand these functions, but only to memorize them for syntax and be aware that they exist.

Miscellaneous Functions

Functions not classifiable as string, number, date, or conversion functions fall into the category of miscellaneous functions. These can be loosely divided into general functions, NLS functions, XML functions, and once again some other difficult-to-categorize obscure functions. The following list describes miscellaneous functions:

- BFILENAME(<'directory'>, <'filename'>)—Returns a BFILE pointer to a binary object filename stored in a directory on a hard drive.
- 9i COALESCE(<expression> [, <expression> ...])—Returns the first non-NULL result from a list of elements. COALESCE(NULL, NULL, 'String-1', 'String-2') returns String-1 because the first two elements are NULL.
- DECODE(<expression>, <search>, <replace> [,<search>, <replace> ...], <default>)—The DECODE function searches an expression for multiple different <search> values, returning equivalent <replace> replacement values. If no <search> is matched, <default> is returned. <search>, <replace> pairs behave like conditions in an IF-THEN or CASE statement, and the <default> option behaves like the ELSE option for IF and CASE statements. The following example returns Male or Female when gender is M or F, respectively, and an undefined default value when gender is not found:

```
SELECT DECODE(GENDER, 'M', 'Male', 'F', 'Female', 'Undefined')
    FROM ACTOR;
```

Using the **DECODE** function can hurt performance. Also note that **CASE** statement expressions and the **COALESCE** and **NULLIF** functions can substitute for a **DECODE** function.

The **DECODE** function is often included in the exam.

- DUMP(<expression> [, <format> [, <position> [, <length>]]])—This function literally dumps internal information for an expression. <format> values can be set to 8 (octal), 10 (decimal), 16 (hexadecimal), or 17 (single characters).
- EMPTY_BLOB and EMPTY_CLOB—These return empty binary object pointers. These functions are a little like object constructors in that they define or instantiate new objects.

- 9i NULLIF(<expression>, <expression>)—NULL is returned when two expressions are equal; otherwise, the first expression is returned.
- NVL(<expression>, <expression>) and NVL2(<expression>, <expression>, <expression>)—For the NVL function, if the first expression is NULL then the second is returned; otherwise, the first expression is returned. So NVL(NULL, 2) returns 2 and NVL(1, 2) returns 1.

  The NVL2 function differs in that if the first expression is not NULL, the second expression is returned; otherwise, the third expression is returned. Thus, NVL2(NULL, 1, 2) returns 2.
- UID, USER, and USERENV(<parameter>)—All these functions return specifics of the currently connected session. UID returns a unique user identifier; USER, the username; and USERENV, a specified parameter such as ISDBA. If a connection was logged in as SYSDBA, then USERENV('ISDBA') will return TRUE.
- VSIZE(<expression>)—Returns a count of the internal representation of the number of bytes in a column. For example, VSIZE('This is a string') returns 16.
- GREATEST(<expression> [, <expression> ...]) and LEAST(<expression> [, <expression> ...])—These functions simply return the greatest or least values within a list of expressions.
- NLS_CHARSET_DECL_LEN(<bytes>, <character set id>)—Returns the width of an NCHAR column.
- NLS_CHARSET_ID(<character set>)—The character set identifier.
- NLS_CHARSET_NAME(<character set id >)—The name of the character set.

XML and Other Obscure Functions

As mentioned earlier in the chapter, XML functions you might see in Oracle documentation are out scope for this book and are not included in the exam. These functions are DEPTH, EXISTSNODE, EXTRACT(XML), EXTRACTVALUE, PATH, SYS_DBURIGEN, SYS_XMLAGG, SYS_XMLGEN, UPDATEXML, XMLAGG, XMLCOLATTVAL, XMLCONCAT, XMLFOREST, XMLSEQUENCE, and XMLTRANSFORM. Other miscellaneous functions are 9i SYS_CONNECT_BY_PATH, SYS_CONTEXT, SYS_EXTRACT_UTC, SYS_GUID, and SYS_TYPEID.

Memorize the syntax of all functions and conversion formatting characters presented in this chapter. I have seen questions in Oracle certification exams on some fairly obscure functions and formatting parameters.

User-Defined Functions

A user-defined function is a function created by a user in addition to the Oracle built-in functions. Believe it or not, sometimes the plethora of available Oracle built-in functions will not suffice. Creating your own functions can be done using PL/SQL. PL/SQL is out of the scope of this book.

That's it! The next chapter examines queries for joining tables together.

Exam Prep Questions

1. What does this expression return?

   ```
   ASCII(' ')
   ```

   The answer is `32`, which is the ASCII code for a space character. The `CHR` function executed as `CHR(32)` would do the opposite and would return a single space character.

2. What does this expression return?

   ```
   INSTR('This world is not flat it is round.', 'is', 5, 2)
   ```

   The answer is `27`. The `INSTR` function finds the starting position of a string within a string. Searching begins at position `5`, ignoring the first occurrence of `is` (occurrence 0), ignoring the second occurrence of `is` (occurrence 1) and selecting the third (occurrence 2), after position `5`. The result will be the position of the substring `is` toward the end of the string in `it is round`.

3. What does this expression return?

   ```
   LPAD('This is a string', 20, 'xy')
   ```

   The answer is `xyxyThis is a string`. The `LPAD` function pads or fills a string from the left, up to the length with the specified string. Thus, because the original string is 16 characters long, the return value will add the string `xy` twice, yielding `xyxyThis is a string`.

4. What does this expression return?

   ```
   SUBSTR('This is a string', -3, 2)
   ```

   The string `in` is returned. The negative starting position dictates the search to begin at the end of the string, counting backward three characters (-3). From the end of the string, count back three characters and extract two characters, the last two characters in the string.

5. What is the difference between the `SIN` function and the `ASIN` function?

   `SIN` performs a completely opposite calculation to that of `ASIN`, mathematically known as the inverse function. `SIN` is a Sine function and `ASIN` is an ArcSine function. In trigonometry the inverse function is always prefixed with the term Arc, abbreviated in Oracle SQL with the letter *A*.

6. What is the difference between `LOCALTIMESTAMP` and `CURRENT_TIMESTAMP`?

   `CURRENT_TIMESTAMP` includes a time zone and `LOCALTIMESTAMP` does not.

7. Resolve this expression and select one answer:

```
ROUND(MONTHS_BETWEEN(LAST_DAY('04-FEB-04')
,ADD_MONTHS(NEXT_DAY('25-MAY-04','SUNDAY'),3)),0).
```

- ❑ A. **0**
- ❑ B. **4**
- ❑ C. **-6**
- ❑ D. **6**

The answer is C, or **-6**. The expression evaluates as shown by the comments in the following script:

```
ROUND
(
    MONTHS_BETWEEN
    (
        LAST_DAY('04-FEB-04')
        ,ADD_MONTHS
        (
            NEXT_DAY('25-MAY-04','SUNDAY')      — 30-MAY-04
        ,3)                               — 30-AUG-04
    )                                  — -6.032
,0)
```

8. Is there a difference between the abbreviations UTC and GMT?

   The answer is no, there is no difference between UTC and GMT. Both abbreviations represent the time at 0° longitude. UTC is the new term for GMT, Coordinated Universal Time versus Greenwich Mean Time.

9. What does **TO_CHAR(188 * 0, '$9,999,990.99')** return?

- ❑ A. **188.99**
- ❑ B. **$188.00**
- ❑ C. **$0.00**
- ❑ D. **$0.99**
- ❑ E. None of the above

The answer is C (**$0.00**). **188 * 0** yields **0**. Applying the format, the **0.99** section forces the **0** before the decimal point to be displayed as **0**. The **$** formatting character is a floating $ sign, and thus is placed up against the most significant digit. **.99** (the part after the decimals) specifies two decimal places with rounding on the third decimal place; for value of **0** the **9**s are replaced with **0**s.

10. Select the most likely response for this expression:

```
TO_CHAR(LOCALTIMESTAMP, 'DD-MM-YYYY'):
```

- ❑ A. **2004-30-10**
- ❑ B. **10-30-2004**
- ❑ C. **30-OCT-04 11.55.22.474000 PM**
- ❑ D. **10-30-TWO THOUSAND FOUR**
- ❑ E. None of the above

Answer E is correct because none of the answers are even remotely likely. A correct answer would be, for example, `30-10-2004` (October 30, 2004). Month numbers are 1 to 12 and cannot be 30. Also, years are all listed as four digits when vaguely related to the required format of DD-MM-YYYY.

11. Which of the following expressions returns the highest value?

- ❑ A. `NVL(NULL, 1)`
- ❑ B. `NVL(NULL, 2)`
- ❑ C. `NVL2(NULL, 1, 3)`
- ❑ D. `NVL2(4, 4, 2)`

Answer D is correct. The `NVL` function replaces `NULL` with a replacement value, and thus A returns `1` and `B` returns 2. The `NVL2` function replaces a non-`NULL` value with the first replacement value option, and a `NULL` value with the second replacement option. Thus C returns `3` and D returns `4`, making D return the highest value.

Joining Tables

Terms You Need to Understand

- ✓ Join
- ✓ 9i ANSI join format
- ✓ 9i Cross join
- ✓ 9i Inner join
- ✓ Intersection
- ✓ 9i Outer join
- ✓ 9i Left, right, and full outer join
- ✓ 9i Natural join
- ✓ Self join
- ✓ Deficient in information
- ✓ Equi join
- ✓ Anti join
- ✓ Range join
- ✓ Semi join
- ✓ 9i The **USING** clause
- ✓ 9i The **ON** clause

Concepts You Need to Master

- ✓ ANSI join format syntax
- ✓ Oracle join format syntax
- ✓ Natural joins and the **NATURAL** keyword
- ✓ Outer joins have tables deficient in information
- ✓ When to use the **USING** clause
- ✓ When to use the **ON** clause
- ✓ How to use aliases with joins

This chapter shows all the numerous methods of joining tables and row sets into merged output results.

What Is a Join?

What is a join? A *join* in Oracle SQL is a term used to describe retrieval of rows from more than one table in the same query. Rows from different tables, or even the same table, can be joined in various ways. We can even use two different syntactical formats for join queries. The two different syntax formats are the *Oracle format* and the ANSI (American National Standards Institute) format.

ANSI and Oracle Join Syntax

Both Oracle and ANSI join syntax formats are understood by the Oracle SQL query engine. The Oracle format may eventually be deprecated. There are a few points to note:

It is likely that both ANSI and Oracle syntax join formats will be included in the exam.

- ANSI join syntax joins tables in the FROM clause of a query. Oracle join syntax joins tables using both the FROM clause and the WHERE clause of a query.
- So far I have seen no apparent performance difference between the two join formats.
- Oracle join syntax may sometimes be easier to code for joins with many tables.
- ANSI join syntax can perform full outer joins, and Oracle join syntax cannot.

9i ANSI Join Syntax

ANSI join syntax is included in Oracle SQL for ANSI compliance. Figure 6.1 shows the basics of the ANSI join syntax where tables are joined in the FROM clause.

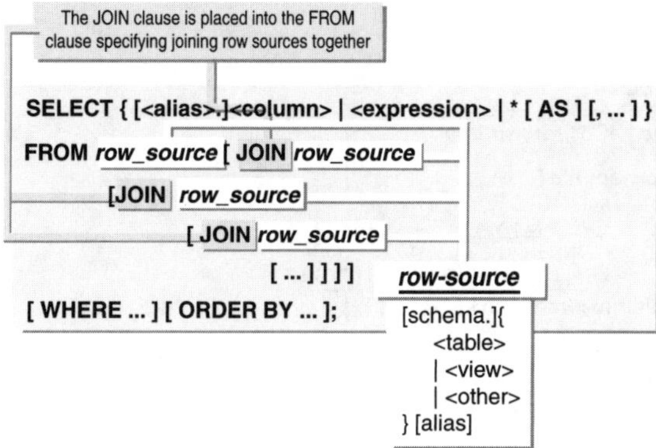

Figure 6.1 Basic ANSI join syntax.

Following is a synopsis of the syntax diagram shown in Figure 6.1:

➤ A row source is essentially where rows are retrieved from, be it a table, a view, or some other type of appropriate database object.

➤ Tables are joined for the ANSI format using a `JOIN` clause. The `JOIN` clause is embedded into the `FROM` clause of a join query:

```
FROM <table> JOIN <table>
```

Multiple tables can be joined by adding further `JOIN` clauses:

```
FROM <table> JOIN <table> JOIN <table> JOIN <table> ...
```

➤ The `SELECT`, `WHERE`, `ORDER BY`, and other clauses are unaffected.

Expanding on ANSI join syntax shown in Figure 6.1, Figure 6.2 shows the different types of joins available for ANSI join syntax.

Following is a synopsis of the syntax diagram shown in Figure 6.2:

➤ The `NATURAL` keyword creates a natural or assumed join. A natural join will use one or more columns, named the same between two tables, and join on those column names. Consider the following three tables:

```
CREATE TABLE DIRECTOR(DIRECTOR VARCHAR2(32));
CREATE TABLE MOVIE(DIRECTOR VARCHAR2(32)
    , TITLE VARCHAR2(32));
CREATE TABLE ACTOR(DIRECTOR VARCHAR2(32)
    , TITLE VARCHAR2(32), ACTOR VARCHAR2(32));
```

When the `NATURAL` keyword is used to join the `MOVIE` and `ACTOR` tables, the join will occur using the `DIRECTOR` and `TITLE` columns together:

```
SELECT * FROM MOVIE NATURAL JOIN ACTOR;
```

The `NATURAL` keyword is discussed in detail later in this chapter.

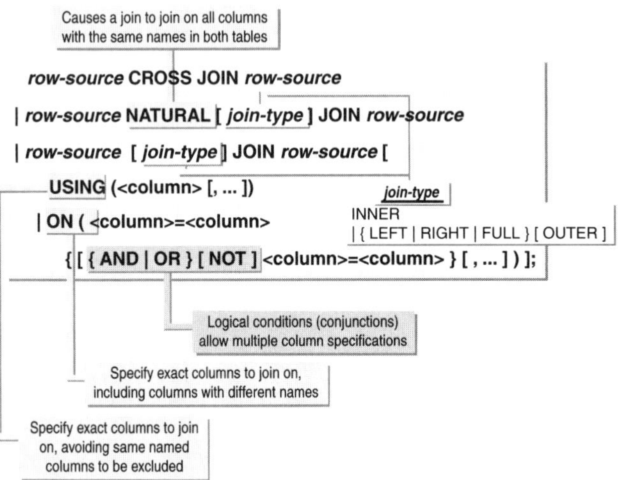

Figure 6.2 Different types of joins using ANSI join syntax.

➤ Join types can be inner or outer joins. An inner join is an intersection, and an outer join is an intersection plus rows outside the intersection. A left outer join includes rows on the left, missing on the right of the join. A right outer join includes rows on the right, missing on the left of the join. A full outer join includes rows missing on both the left and the right of the join.

➤ The USING clause allows forcing of one or more columns to be joined on, avoiding same-named columns containing different data to be excluded from a join. Consider the following two tables:

```
CREATE TABLE DIRECTOR(DIRECTOR VARCHAR2(32), COMMENTS CLOB);
CREATE TABLE MOVIE(DIRECTOR VARCHAR2(32)
    , TITLE VARCHAR2(32), COMMENTS CLOB);
```

A natural join would join on the DIRECTOR and COMMENTS columns. You do not want to join on the COMMENTS columns. Applying the USING clause and removing the NATURAL keyword resolves this issue:

```
SELECT * FROM DIRECTOR JOIN MOVIE USING(DIRECTOR);
```

➤ The ON clause allows exact column join specification when you want to include one or more columns in a join that have different names in different tables. Consider the following two tables:

```
CREATE TABLE DIRECTOR(NAME VARCHAR2(32));
CREATE TABLE MOVIE(DIRECTOR VARCHAR2(32)
    , TITLE VARCHAR2(32));
```

A natural join would not work because there are no common column names between the two tables. The ON clause allows you to specify which columns to join the two tables with:

```
SELECT * FROM DIRECTOR JOIN MOVIE
    ON(MOVIE.DIRECTOR = DIRECTOR.NAME);
```

Using aliases:

```
SELECT * FROM DIRECTOR D JOIN MOVIE M ON(M.DIRECTOR = D.NAME);
```

Oracle Join Syntax

Figure 6.3 shows the Oracle join syntax. The only addition to Oracle syntax for joins is the use of the (+) operator, sometimes called the outer join operator.

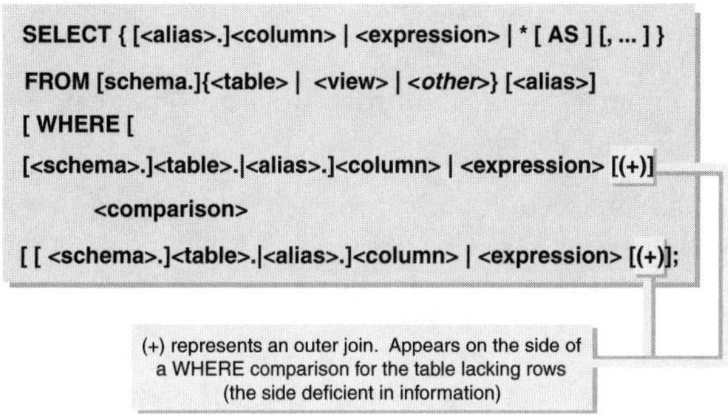

```
SELECT { [<alias>.]<column> | <expression> | * [ AS ] [, ... ] }
FROM [schema.]{<table> | <view> | <other>} [<alias>]
[ WHERE [
[<schema>.]<table>.|<alias>.]<column> | <expression> [(+)]
        <comparison>
[ [ <schema>.]<table>.|<alias>.]<column> | <expression> [(+)];
```

(+) represents an outer join. Appears on the side of a WHERE comparison for the table lacking rows (the side deficient in information)

Figure 6.3 An Oracle join syntax.

Following is a synopsis of the syntax diagram shown in Figure 6.3:

- The Oracle join syntax uses what is called the join operator, denoted by a plus sign in parentheses: (+).
- The join operator is placed on either side of a comparison of two expressions in the WHERE clause of a query, never on both sides. As a result, a full outer join is not possible using the Oracle join syntax but only using the ANSI join syntax.
- The join operator is placed on the side of the join deficient in information. The side deficient in information is the side of the join containing rows outside the intersection that are to be included in a left or right outer join.

Types of Joins

Now let's examine the various types of available joins. The following list describes them:

- *Cross Join*—A cross join merges rows from two tables into a single set of rows. A cross join is mathematically the same as a Cartesian Product.
- *Inner Join*—Combines only matching rows from two tables based on column values to form an intersection between the two tables.
- *Outer Join*—Selects rows from two tables as an inner join does, except that it includes rows present in one table and not the other. A full outer join is an obscure form of outer join including the intersection plus rows present in either table but not present in the other.

  Outer joins occur in three forms:

  - *Left Outer Join*—The intersection plus all rows from the left-side table but not in the right-side table.
  - *Right Outer Join*—The intersection plus all rows in the right-side table but not in the left-side table.
  - *Full Outer Join*—A full merge comprising all rows from both tables.

Missing rows in either table in an outer join are returned as **NULL** rows.

Full outer joins are available only when using ANSI join syntax.

- *Self Join*—A self join is, as the term implies, joining rows from a table to other rows in the same table.

Here are some other more vaguely classifiable join types:

- *Natural Join*—A join is created "naturally" using the ANSI join syntax NATURAL keyword, matching same column names between two joined tables. As you already know, a natural join using the NATURAL keyword can be either an inner join or an outer join.
- *Equi Join, Anti Join, Range Join, and Semi Join*—Equi joins combine rows using equality (=). Anti joins combine rows using inequality (!=, <>, or NOT).

Range joins combine rows using a range of values (<, >, <=, >=, or BETWEEN). Set membership or semi joins combine rows based on subset membership. They are called semi joins because they join only for the purposes of validation and do not return a joined set of column values.

- *Mutable and Complex Join*—Mutable joins contain joins with more than two tables, and a complex join is a mutable join including WHERE clause filtering.

It is unlikely that the exam will contain specific questions regarding any of the more vaguely classifiable join types apart from inner and outer joins.

Now let's examine the types of primary joins in detail.

Cross Join

A *cross join* effectively joins every row in one table with every row in another table. The net effect is that each row in one table is matched with all rows in the other table, also known as a Cartesian Product. For example, this is an ANSI cross join between the MOVIE and DIRECTOR tables:

```
SELECT TITLE, NAME FROM MOVIE CROSS JOIN DIRECTOR ORDER BY TITLE, NAME;
```

A partial result of the preceding query is shown in Figure 6.4. The cross join in Figure 6.4 tells us that the movie *Young Frankenstein* was directed by 17 directors, all the directors in my MOVIES schema. This is obviously untrue.

The Oracle equivalent is this:

```
SELECT TITLE, NAME FROM MOVIE, DIRECTOR ORDER BY TITLE, NAME;
```

Notice how the Oracle join query does not have a WHERE clause. The preceding cross join does not match any columns using a WHERE clause, and thus every movie is returned for every director, regardless of who directed a particular movie.

Inner Join

As we have seen, a cross join is a fairly pointless exercise and rarely required. An *inner join*, on the other hand, finds the intersection between two tables. In the following example each movie is matched with each director, returning all movies with their respective directors:

```
SELECT TITLE, NAME FROM MOVIE JOIN DIRECTOR USING(DIRECTOR_ID)
ORDER BY TITLE, NAME;
```

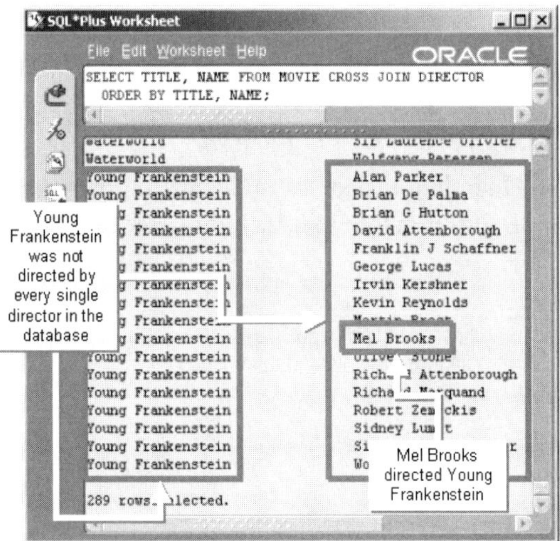

Figure 6.4 A cross join.

You can see in the partial result of the preceding query shown in Figure 6.5 that movies are now shown with their respective directors and that fewer rows are retrieved.

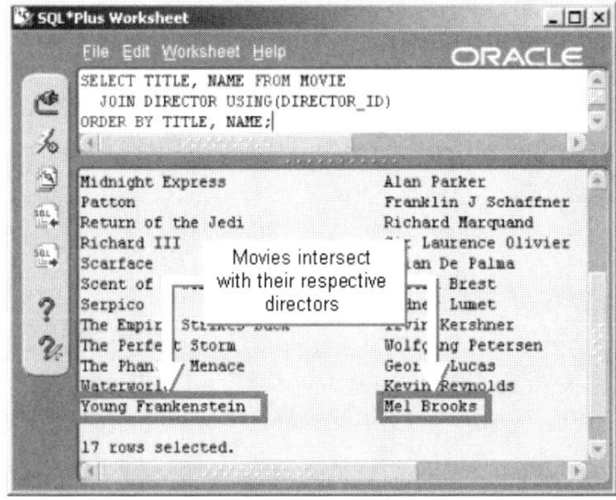

Figure 6.5 An inner join.

The Oracle equivalent is as follows:

```
SELECT TITLE, NAME FROM MOVIE M, DIRECTOR D
WHERE D.DIRECTOR_ID = M.DIRECTOR_ID ORDER BY TITLE, NAME;
```

Note a number of points with respect to the preceding Oracle join query:

➤ It has a WHERE clause.

➤ Both FROM and WHERE clauses contain join instructions.

- Aliases are not used in the ANSI join. The ANSI join syntax is "more intelligent."
- Aliases are not strictly necessary even for Oracle join syntax. Aliases are not used for the SELECT list and the ORDER BY clause in the preceding example. If the two tables had columns retrieved from or sorted by, of the same name, then aliases would be required. The following two queries are ANSI and Oracle syntax joins, respectively. The ACTOR and DIRECTOR tables both have NAME columns. The only way to distinguish between ACTOR.NAME and DIRECTOR.NAME is by using aliases.

Aliases are not necessary; qualifications are. For instance, when joining the **ACTOR** and **DIRECTOR** tables, both containing a column called **NAME**, you could use **ACTOR.NAME = DIRECTOR.NAME** syntax. In this column, names are qualified by table names and not aliases. Aliases can be used for convenience but they are not absolutely necessary.

```
SELECT A.NAME, D.NAME FROM ACTOR A
    JOIN RECOGNITION R ON(R.ACTOR_ID = A.ACTOR_ID)
        JOIN DIRECTOR D ON(D.DIRECTOR_ID = R.ACTOR_ID);
```

```
SELECT A.NAME, D.NAME FROM ACTOR A, RECOGNITION R, DIRECTOR D
WHERE R.ACTOR_ID = A.ACTOR_ID
AND D.DIRECTOR_ID = R.ACTOR_ID;
```

Inner joins are much more useful than cross joins because they produce sensible results.

Outer Join

An *outer join* retrieves the intersection of the two tables (the inner join) plus rows not in either (left or right outer join), or rows not in both tables (full outer join). An outer join can be a left outer join, a right outer join, or a full outer join.

Left Outer Join

A left outer join retrieves intersecting rows plus all rows on the left side and not on the right side of the join. This example, as shown in Figure 6.6, is a left outer join in which the intersection of the RATING and MOVIE tables is retrieved, plus all unused ratings:

```
SELECT MPAA, RATING, TITLE FROM RATING LEFT JOIN MOVIE USING (RATING_ID)
ORDER BY TITLE;
```

The keyword OUTER is optional, and thus the query could also be coded as such:

```
SELECT MPAA, RATING, TITLE FROM RATING LEFT OUTER JOIN MOVIE USING
(RATING_ID) ORDER BY TITLE;
```

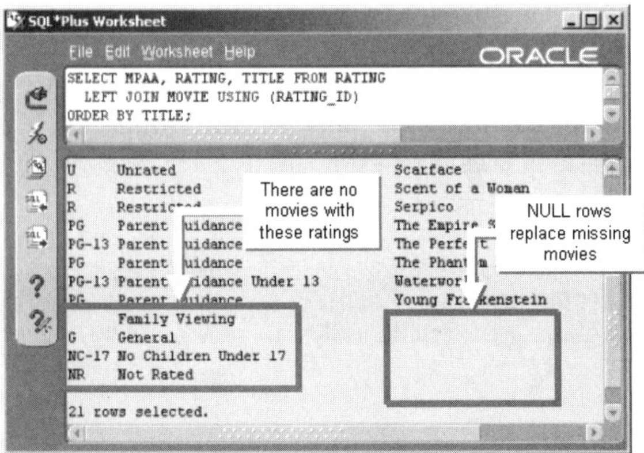

Figure 6.6 A left outer join.

Note in Figure 6.6 how ratings not assigned to any movies appear at the end of the query with NULL movie titles. Ratings with no allocated movies could be found with a query such as this:

```
SELECT MPAA, RATING FROM RATING WHERE RATING_ID NOT IN
(SELECT RATING_ID FROM MOVIE);
```

The Oracle equivalent of the left outer join is this:

```
SELECT MPAA, RATING, TITLE FROM RATING R, MOVIE M
WHERE R.RATING_ID = M.RATING_ID(+) ORDER BY TITLE;
```

In the preceding Oracle outer join query, the (+) outer join operator appears in the WHERE clause on the side referencing the table with fewer or missing rows.

The Oracle term for the side of an outer join missing rows is called the *table deficient in information.*

Right Outer Join

A right outer join is simply the opposite of a left outer join. A right outer join retrieves intersecting rows plus all non-intersecting rows on the right side of the join. Using the same query as for the left outer join, simply reverse the tables as shown in the following query. The order of the columns has also been reversed to provide clarity.

```
SELECT TITLE, MPAA, RATING FROM MOVIE RIGHT JOIN RATING USING
(RATING_ID) ORDER BY TITLE;
```

Figure 6.7 shows a partial result.

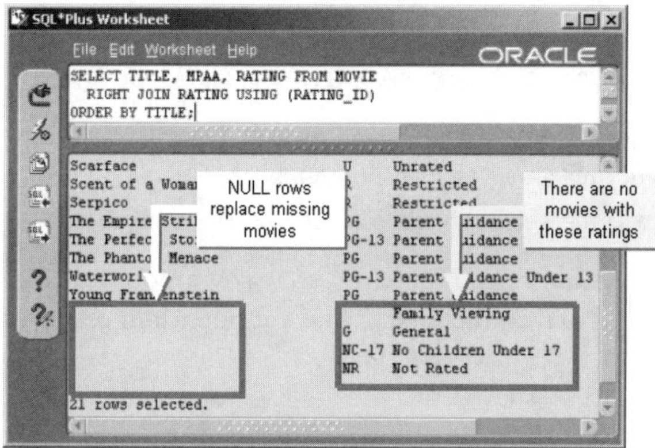

Figure 6.7 A right outer join.

The Oracle equivalent is this:

```
SELECT TITLE, MPAA, RATING FROM MOVIE M, RATING R
WHERE M.RATING_ID(+) = R.RATING_ID ORDER BY TITLE;
```

Once again, for Oracle, the join syntax of the join uses the `(+)` outer join operator, appearing on the side of the join missing rows, namely the `MOVIE` table.

Full Outer Join

A full outer join combines both a left and a right outer join, retrieving intersecting rows plus non-intersecting rows from both sides of the join.

A full outer join is not a Cartesian Product or cross join because it does not join every row on one side of the join with every row on the other side of the join. A full outer join retrieves rows intersecting from both tables plus those not in both tables.

Let's demonstrate using the `ACTOR`, `RECOGNITION`, and `AWARD` tables in the `MOVIES` schema. This first query finds the intersection between the `ACTOR` and `RECOGNITION` tables, namely all actors who have received awards:

```
SELECT NAME, AWARD_ID FROM ACTOR JOIN RECOGNITION USING(ACTOR_ID);
```

Next we create a left outer join between the ACTOR and the RECOGNITION tables, finding all actors regardless of whether they have an award but still retrieving any existing awards:

```
SELECT NAME, AWARD_ID FROM ACTOR LEFT JOIN RECOGNITION USING(ACTOR_ID);
```

The next logical step is a right outer join between the ACTOR and RECOGNITION tables, finding all awards regardless of whether an award is allocated to an actor:

```
SELECT NAME, AWARD_ID FROM ACTOR RIGHT JOIN RECOGNITION USING(ACTOR_ID);
```

Therefore, the full outer join finds all actors and awards regardless of how awards are allocated or whether an actor even has an award:

```
SELECT NAME, AWARD_ID FROM ACTOR FULL JOIN RECOGNITION USING(ACTOR_ID);
```

You can beautify the query, as shown in Figure 6.8, to make it more readable by adding a further left outer join to the query. The left outer join retrieves the name for each award:

```
SELECT NAME, AWARD FROM ACTOR
    FULL JOIN RECOGNITION USING(ACTOR_ID)
        LEFT JOIN AWARD USING(AWARD_ID)
ORDER BY ACTOR_ID, AWARD_ID;
```

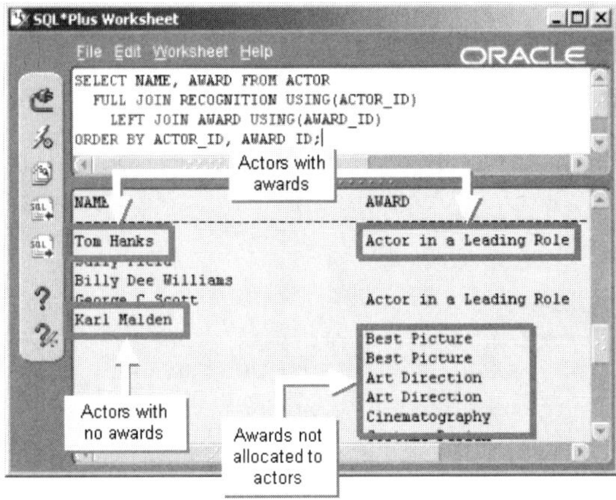

Figure 6.8 A full outer join.

There is no Oracle syntax available for full outer joins because the **(+)** outer join operator cannot appear on both sides of a **WHERE** clause join specification.

Self Join

A self join is a join that joins a table to itself. The GENRE table in the MOVIES schema is an example of a table with a self join:

```
SELECT PARENT.GENRE "Parent", CHILD.GENRE "Child" FROM GENRE PARENT
    JOIN GENRE CHILD ON (PARENT.GENRE_ID = CHILD.PARENT_ID)
ORDER BY PARENT.GENRE, CHILD.GENRE;
```

The Oracle equivalent is as follows:

```
SELECT PARENT.GENRE "Parent", CHILD.GENRE "Child" FROM GENRE PARENT
     , GENRE CHILD
WHERE PARENT.GENRE_ID = CHILD.PARENT_ID
ORDER BY PARENT.GENRE, CHILD.GENRE;
```

The self join on the GENRE table is possible partly due to the structure of the GENRE table:

```
CREATE TABLE GENRE(
     GENRE_ID NUMBER NOT NULL
    ,STYLE_ID NUMBER
    ,GENRE VARCHAR2(32)
    ,CONSTRAINT XPKGENRE PRIMARY KEY (GENRE_ID)
    ,CONSTRAINT FKG_1 FOREIGN KEY (STYLE_ID) REFERENCES GENRE);
```

And it is partly due to the nature of the data in the GENRE table, as shown in Figure 6.9.

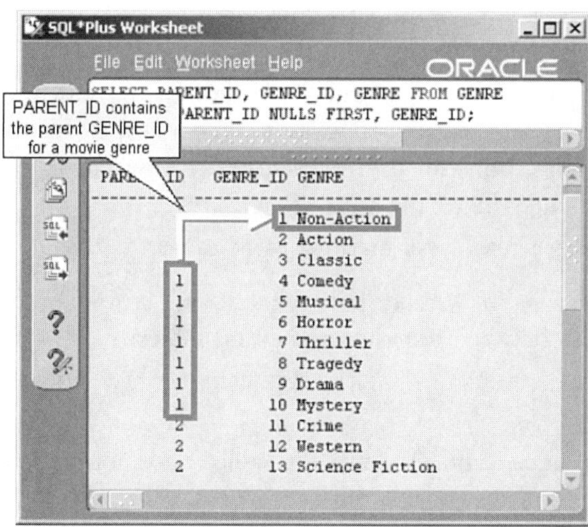

Figure 6.9 The **GENRE** table.

Figure 6.9 shows that the PARENT_ID column in the GENRE table contains the GENRE_ID value of the parent movie genre. Thus, the movie genres Classic, Comedy, and Musical are all classified as Non-Action genre movies.

A self join is sometimes known as a *fishhook join*.

Natural Joins Using ANSI Join Syntax

This section applies to ANSI join syntax: the NATURAL keyword, the USING clause, and the ON clause. The NATURAL keyword allows a join to be performed using all columns in two tables with the same column names. The USING clause allows removing some of those same named columns from the join. The ON clause allows inclusion into the join of columns with different names.

The **NATURAL** Keyword

As you already know, the NATURAL keyword finds all matching column names between two tables in a join, and joins based on those column names. This query, shown earlier in the section "Inner Join," executes an intersection between the MOVIE and DIRECTOR tables with the USING clause:

```
SELECT TITLE, NAME FROM MOVIE JOIN DIRECTOR USING(DIRECTOR_ID)
ORDER BY TITLE, NAME;
```

In the preceding query the USING clause instructs Oracle SQL to join the MOVIE and DIRECTOR tables using the DIRECTOR_ID column. The DIRECTOR_ID column is present in both tables. You can use the NATURAL keyword to allow removal of the USING clause and still get the same result:

```
SELECT TITLE, NAME FROM MOVIE NATURAL JOIN DIRECTOR ORDER BY TITLE, NAME;
```

Similarly, we can do the same for Oracle join syntax using a previously detailed left outer join query between the MOVIE and RATING tables:

```
SELECT MPAA, RATING, TITLE FROM RATING LEFT JOIN MOVIE USING (RATING_ID)
ORDER BY TITLE;
```

Using the NATURAL keyword once again produces the same result, joining on the MOVIE.RATING_ID and RATING.RATING_ID columns:

```
SELECT MPAA, RATING, TITLE FROM RATING NATURAL LEFT JOIN MOVIE
ORDER BY TITLE;
```

You could even look at a join with more than two tables, a previously used full outer join:

```
SELECT NAME, AWARD FROM ACTOR
    FULL JOIN RECOGNITION USING(ACTOR_ID)
        LEFT JOIN AWARD USING(AWARD_ID)
ORDER BY ACTOR_ID, AWARD_ID;
```

Once again, replace the USING clause with the NATURAL keyword and the same result ensues:

```
SELECT NAME, AWARD FROM ACTOR
    NATURAL FULL JOIN RECOGNITION
        NATURAL LEFT JOIN AWARD
ORDER BY ACTOR_ID, AWARD_ID;
```

On the contrary, if we used aliases, the NATURAL keyword would not be available because the aliased columns have different names. In the following query AT.ACTOR_ID has a different column name than that of R.ACTOR_ID due to the use of aliases. The same applies to the R.AWARD_ID and AW.AWARD_ID columns.

```
SELECT AT.NAME, AW.AWARD FROM ACTOR AT
    FULL JOIN RECOGNITION R ON(R.ACTOR_ID = AT.ACTOR_ID)
        LEFT JOIN AWARD AW ON(AW.AWARD_ID = R.AWARD_ID)
ORDER BY AT.ACTOR_ID, AW.AWARD_ID;
```

The **USING** Clause

The USING clause allows precise specification of columns to join tables with. The USING clause is often used where the same column name exists in two tables but the column is not the same thing in those two tables (not a primary to foreign key relationship).

For example, let's assume that both the DIRECTOR and the MOVIE tables have a REVIEW column of CLOB datatype. We probably would not want to join these two tables with the following query using the NATURAL keyword:

```
SELECT TITLE, NAME FROM MOVIE NATURAL JOIN DIRECTOR ORDER BY TITLE, NAME;
```

The NATURAL keyword will force a multiple column join. The code using the NATURAL keyword looks like this:

```
SELECT TITLE, NAME FROM MOVIE JOIN DIRECTOR USING(DIRECTOR_ID, REVIEW)
ORDER BY TITLE, NAME;
```

The USING clause can be used to restrict a join to occur on a specific column or columns common to both tables:

```
SELECT TITLE, NAME FROM MOVIE JOIN DIRECTOR USING(DIRECTOR_ID)
ORDER BY TITLE, NAME;
```

The **ON** Clause

The USING clause allows limiting of common column names when joining two tables. The ON clause allows the opposite such that differently named columns can be used to join between two tables.

For example, if my STUDIO.STUDIO_ID column was mistakenly created as STUDIO.STUD_ID, you would not be able to use the following queries:

```
SELECT STUDIO, TITLE FROM STUDIO NATURAL JOIN MOVIE;
```

or

```
SELECT STUDIO, TITLE FROM STUDIO JOIN MOVIE USING(STUDIO_ID);
```

You would have to use the ON clause to force a join between STUDIO.STUD_ID and MOVIE.STUDIO_ID (two different column names containing the same values):

```
SELECT STUDIO, TITLE FROM STUDIO S JOIN MOVIE M ON
(M.STUDIO_ID = S.STUD_ID);
```

Equi Joins (Equality), Anti Joins (Inequality), Range Joins, and Semi Joins

So far in this chapter, you have effectively covered Oracle SQL join syntax. Equi, anti, range, and semi joins are not exactly a part of join syntax, but perhaps, moreover, methods by which joins can be constructed, based on the use of different types of operators. Here is a list describing equi, anti, range, and semi joins:

- *Equi Join*—An equi join uses equality or an equals sign (=):

  ```
  SELECT TITLE, NAME FROM MOVIE M, DIRECTOR D
  WHERE D.DIRECTOR_ID = M.DIRECTOR_ID ORDER BY TITLE, NAME;
  ```

  In the preceding query a join is made between the DIRECTOR and MOVIE tables using the Oracle format with an equi join in the WHERE clause. The equi join dictates that rows are joined between the two tables whenever the DIRECTOR_ID column values match.

- *Anti Join*—An anti join does the opposite of an equi join using inequality:

  ```
  SELECT TITLE, NAME FROM MOVIE M, DIRECTOR D
  WHERE D.DIRECTOR_ID <> M.DIRECTOR_ID ORDER BY TITLE, NAME;
  ```

  This query is the same example as the one before it except that the equals sign (=) is replaced with an inequality operator (<>). In this case the anti join joins rows together between the two tables whenever DIRECTOR_ID column values do not match between the two tables. An anti join is therefore the opposite of an equi join.

- *Range Join*—A range join attempts to join ranges of values using >, <, >=, <=, or BETWEEN:

  ```
  SELECT TITLE, NAME FROM MOVIE M, DIRECTOR D
  WHERE D.DIRECTOR_ID >= M.DIRECTOR_ID ORDER BY TITLE, NAME;
  ```

  Once again, the same query is used, but the join operator is now a range join operator (>=). In this case rows are joined between the two tables when the DIRECTOR_ID column value for the DIRECTOR table is greater than or equal to the same column in the MOVIE table.

Anti joins and range joins are unusual due to the odd and somewhat nonsensical results they produce.

- *Semi Join*—Semi joins use the [NOT] IN and [NOT] EXISTS set membership operators to join tables. They are called semi joins because they are often executed as subqueries and they do not return values to the calling query. Thus, one table in a join is in a calling query and another is in a subquery. Because the subquery does not return any values, columns from two different tables are not actually physically joined. The result is the term *semi join* because it is only a partial join. For example, the following query finds all ratings used by movies, but no movie columns such as the movie title are returned:

  ```
  SELECT MPAA, RATING FROM RATING WHERE RATING_ID IN
  (SELECT RATING_ID FROM MOVIE);
  ```

Mutable and Complex Joins

What are mutable and complex joins? A *mutable join* is a multiple table join, joining more than two tables. A complex join is a term used to describe a multiple table join that includes WHERE clause filtering in addition to join specifications.

You will not be asked what a mutable or complex join is. However, the exam will very likely include joins with more than two tables, and perhaps even many more than two tables.

This is a mutable join with four tables:

```
SELECT M.TITLE "Movie", A.NAME "Actor", D.NAME "Director"
FROM MOVIE M JOIN PART P ON (P.MOVIE_ID = M.MOVIE_ID)
    JOIN ACTOR A ON (A.ACTOR_ID = P.ACTOR_ID)
        JOIN DIRECTOR D ON (D.DIRECTOR_ID = M.DIRECTOR_ID)
ORDER BY 1, 2;
```

The Oracle equivalent is shown here:

```
SELECT TITLE "Movie", A.NAME "Actor", D.NAME "Director"
FROM MOVIE M, PART P, DIRECTOR D, ACTOR A
WHERE P.MOVIE_ID = M.MOVIE_ID
AND P.ACTOR_ID = A.ACTOR_ID
AND M.DIRECTOR_ID = D.DIRECTOR_ID
ORDER BY 1, 2;
```

And this is the same mutable join but with added filtering, making it a complex mutable join:

```
SELECT TITLE "Movie", NAME "Actor", NAME "Director"
FROM MOVIE JOIN PART USING (MOVIE_ID)
    JOIN ACTOR USING (ACTOR_ID)
        JOIN DIRECTOR USING (DIRECTOR_ID)
WHERE TITLE LIKE '%a%'
ORDER BY 1, 2;
```

The Oracle equivalent is this:

```
SELECT TITLE "Movie", A.NAME "Actor", D.NAME "Director"
FROM MOVIE M, PART P, DIRECTOR D, ACTOR A
WHERE TITLE LIKE '%a%'
AND P.MOVIE_ID = M.MOVIE_ID
AND P.ACTOR_ID = A.ACTOR_ID
AND M.DIRECTOR_ID = D.DIRECTOR_ID
ORDER BY 1, 2;
```

In the preceding query the filtering part of the `WHERE` clause (`WHERE TITLE LIKE '%a%'`) is placed before the join specification. This is important in creating efficient filtering because the filter is applied before joining, reducing the size of row sets to be joined.

Exam Prep Questions

1. What type of a join is this, assuming that both tables have a common column name linked as primary and foreign key?

   ```
   SELECT NAME, ADDRESS FROM CUSTOMER NATURAL JOIN ADDRESSES;
   ```

   - ❑ A. A natural join
   - ❑ B. A left outer join
   - ❑ C. A left join
   - ❑ D. A simple join
   - ❑ E. None of the above

   Answer E is correct because none of the answers are correct. This query is an inner join or intersection between the two tables. There is no such thing as a natural join. A left and a left outer join are one and the same, which this join is not. There is no such thing as a simple join.

2. Which of these queries will cause an error?

   - ❑ A. **SELECT TITLE, NAME FROM MOVIE JOIN DIRECTOR USING(DIRECTOR_ID);**
   - ❑ B. **SELECT TITLE, NAME FROM MOVIE JOIN DIRECTOR ON(MOVIE.DIRECTOR_ID = DIRECTOR.DIRECTOR_ID);**
   - ❑ C. **SELECT TITLE, NAME FROM MOVIE NATURAL JOIN DIRECTOR;**
   - ❑ D. **SELECT TITLE, NAME FROM MOVIE, DIRECTOR WHERE MOVIE.DIRECTOR_ID = DIRECTOR.DIRECTOR_ID;**
   - ❑ E. **SELECT TITLE, NAME FROM MOVIE JOIN DIRECTOR ON(DIRECTOR_ID);**

   Answer E is the correct answer because the **ON** clause is used to specify exact column names in both tables as in answer B. All other queries are syntactically correct and will not cause an error.

3. Which of these queries is most likely to produce the fewest number of rows?

   - ❑ A. **SELECT *FROM MOVIE JOIN DIRECTOR USING(DIRECTOR_ID);**
   - ❑ B. **SELECT * FROM MOVIE M, DIRECTOR D WHERE M.DIRECTOR_ID >= D.DIRECTOR_ID;**
   - ❑ C. **SELECT * FROM MOVIE M, DIRECTOR D WHERE M.DIRECTOR_ID <> D.DIRECTOR_ID;**
   - ❑ D. **SELECT * FROM MOVIE M, DIRECTOR D WHERE M.DIRECTOR_ID != D.DIRECTOR_ID;**

   The answer is A because A produces an intersection. B is a range join in which intersecting rows plus those greater than are joined. C and D both produce the opposite of intersection because they are both anti joins.

4. What is `(+)` called?
   - ❑ A. The inner join operator
   - ❑ B. The self join operator
   - ❑ C. The outer join operator
   - ❑ D. All of the above
   - ❑ E. None of the above

   Answer C is correct. `(+)` is the outer join operator used in Oracle join syntax. There is no such thing as an inner join operator or a self join operator.

5. What is wrong with this query?

```
SELECT TITLE "Movie", A.NAME "Actor", D.NAME "Director"
FROM MOVIE M, PART P, DIRECTOR D, ACTOR A
WHERE P.MOVIE_ID = M.MOVIE_ID
AND P.ACTOR_ID = A.ACTOR_ID
AND M.DIRECTOR_ID = D.DIRECTOR_ID
AND TITLE LIKE '%a%'
ORDER BY 1, 2;
```

   - ❑ A. The **ORDER BY** clause is invalid.
   - ❑ B. The **WHERE** clause is invalid.
   - ❑ C. The **SELECT** column list does not allow column headers to be renamed in this manner.
   - ❑ D. None of the above.

   Answer D is correct. Syntactically there is nothing wrong with this query. However, from the perspective of good SQL programming practice, the **WHERE** clause filter (**TITLE LIKE '%a%'**) should be the first item in the **WHERE** clause.

6. Assume that you have two tables containing 10 movies and 10 directors, respectively. All directors direct one or more movies. How many rows will this query produce?

```
SELECT * FROM MOVIE, DIRECTOR;
```

   - ❑ A. 10 rows
   - ❑ B. 1 row
   - ❑ C. 100 rows
   - ❑ D. 0 rows
   - ❑ E. None of the above

   Answer C is correct. All directors directing one or more movies implies strict referential integrity between the two tables. In this case referential integrity makes no difference to the resulting row count. This query is a cross join, or Cartesian Product. The number of rows is equal to the product of the number of rows in both tables, or 10 * 10 = 100 rows.

7. Assume that you have two tables containing 15 movies and 10 directors. Eight movies have no director as of yet, and 3 directors have never directed a movie. A movie can have only a single director. You can also assume a one-to-one non-identifiable relationship between the two tables with a **DIRECTOR_ID** foreign key placed in the **MOVIE** table. Non-identifying implies that a movie does not have to have a director and that a director does not have to have directed any movies. How many rows will be returned by this query?

```
SELECT * FROM MOVIE JOIN DIRECTOR USING(DIRECTOR_ID);
```

- ❑ A. 7 rows
- ❑ B. 15 rows
- ❑ C. 10 rows
- ❑ D. 3 rows
- ❑ E. 8 rows
- ❑ F. None of the above

Answer A is correct. This join is an inner join. Only matching rows will be returned. There are seven movies with directors, and thus seven rows will be returned.

8. Assume that you have two tables containing 15 movies and 10 directors. Eight movies have no director as of yet, and 3 directors have never directed a movie. A movie can have only a single director but directors can direct many movies. How many rows will be returned by this query?

```
SELECT * FROM MOVIE FULL JOIN DIRECTOR USING(DIRECTOR_ID);
```

- ❑ A. 15 rows
- ❑ B. 10 rows
- ❑ C. 8 rows
- ❑ D. 3 rows
- ❑ E. None of the above

Answer E is correct. This query is a full outer join. A full outer join returns the intersection plus rows in both tables not in the other. The intersection is seven movies. Eight movies have no director, which is the left outer join. Three directors have not as of yet directed a movie, which is the right outer join. The full outer join is the sum of all three of the aforementioned: 7 + 8 + 3 rows = 18 rows.

9. How do these two queries differ?

```
SELECT TITLE "Movie", NAME "Actor", NAME "Director"
FROM MOVIE JOIN PART USING (MOVIE_ID)
    JOIN ACTOR USING (ACTOR_ID)
        JOIN DIRECTOR USING (DIRECTOR_ID)
ORDER BY 1, 2;
```

```
SELECT TITLE "Movie", A.NAME "Actor", D.NAME "Director"
FROM MOVIE M, PART P, DIRECTOR D, ACTOR A
WHERE P.MOVIE_ID = M.MOVIE_ID
AND P.ACTOR_ID = A.ACTOR_ID
AND M.DIRECTOR_ID = D.DIRECTOR_ID
ORDER BY 1, 2;
```

- ❑ A. Both queries are the same.
- ❑ B. One is ANSI format and the other is not.
- ❑ C. One works and the other does not.
- ❑ D. There is no difference.

Answer B is correct. Both queries produce the same result except that one is ANSI standard join syntax and the other is Oracle format syntax. Both queries perform an intersection or inner join among four tables.

10. What type of join is this? Select more than one answer.

```
SELECT TITLE, NAME FROM MOVIE M, DIRECTOR D
WHERE D.DIRECTOR_ID = M.DIRECTOR_ID ORDER BY TITLE, NAME;
```

- ❑ A. An inner join
- ❑ B. A self join
- ❑ C. A left outer join
- ❑ D. An equi join
- ❑ E. A range join
- ❑ F. A natural join
- ❑ G. A **USING** clause join using Oracle join syntax
- ❑ H. A natural inner join

Answers A and D are correct. The query is both an inner join and an equi join. Answers B, C, and E are incorrect and answers F, G, and H do not exist as join types.

Groups and Summaries (GROUP BY)

Terms You Need to Understand

- ✓ The **GROUP BY** clause
- ✓ Grouping functions
- ✓ Aggregation functions
- ✓ Analytical functions
- ✓ The **HAVING** clause
- ✓ 9i The **ROLLUP** clause
- ✓ 9i The **CUBE** clause
- ✓ 9i **GROUPING SETS** clauses
- ✓ The **OVER** clause
- ✓ OLAP

Concepts You Need to Master

- ✓ **SELECT** statement sequence of **WHERE**, **GROUP BY**, and **ORDER BY** clauses
- ✓ **DISTINCT** versus **ALL**
- ✓ The difference between aggregation and analytical functions
- ✓ Filtering using the **HAVING** clause
- ✓ Differences between **ROLLUP** and **CUBE** clause results
- ✓ Filtering **ROLLUP** and **CUBE** results with **GROUPING SETS**

This chapter covers grouping of output row sets. Grouping of data includes simple aggregation summaries and more complex analysis. Some advanced topics are introduced but not analyzed in depth because they are somewhat out of scope.

Additionally, this chapter contains an expansion of the MOVIES schema with a simple set of data warehouse dimension and fact tables to accommodate for GROUP BY clause examples and to keep everything interesting.

What Is GROUP BY?

GROUP BY is a SELECT statement extension clause allowing grouping and aggregating of repetitions into summary values. The GROUP BY clause can be used in conjunction with a multitude of Oracle built-in functions, even user-defined functionality written in PL/SQL. PL/SQL is out of scope for this exam and this book.

The GROUP BY clause itself can also be extended with filtering using the HAVING clause and various Online Analytical Processing (OLAP) type modifications using the ROLLUP, CUBE, and GROUPING SETS clauses. In addition, the OVER clause can be applied, transforming aggregate functions into analytical functions.

Basic GROUP BY Clause Syntax

So far in this book, we have examined numerous syntactical elements of the SELECT statement, including the SELECT list, the FROM clause, the WHERE clause, and the ORDER BY clause. Figure 7.1 shows the very basics of the GROUP BY clause syntax, expanding on the SELECT statement syntax you have learned so far.

Following is a synopsis of the syntax diagram shown in Figure 7.1:

- The GROUP BY clause is used to aggregate or group together.
- GROUP BY clause elements can refer to columns (optionally aliased) and expressions. GROUP BY clause elements cannot be positional as for the ORDER BY clause (see the section in Chapter 3 titled "Sorting Methods").

As shown in Figure 7.1, it is important to remember that the WHERE, GROUP BY, and ORDER BY clauses are optional. Additionally, the WHERE clause always appears before the GROUP BY clause, and the ORDER BY clause is always last, regardless of whether each is included.

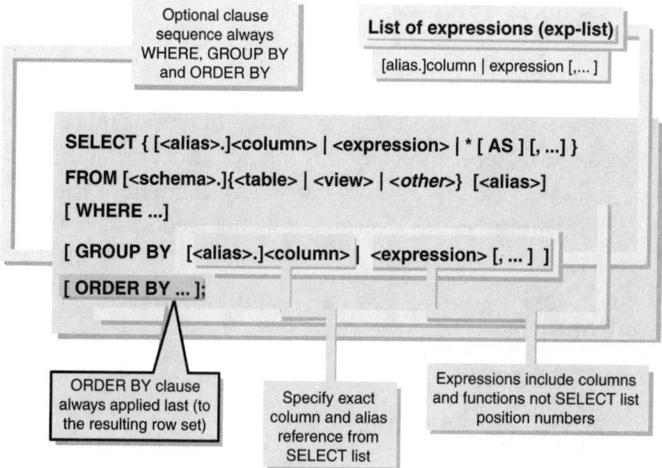

Figure 7.1 Basic **GROUP BY** clause syntax.

Remember the sequence for **WHERE**, **GROUP BY**, and **ORDER BY** clauses. The **WHERE** clause is always first and the **ORDER BY** clause is always last.

Figure 7.2 shows a simple sample query containing a GROUP BY clause.

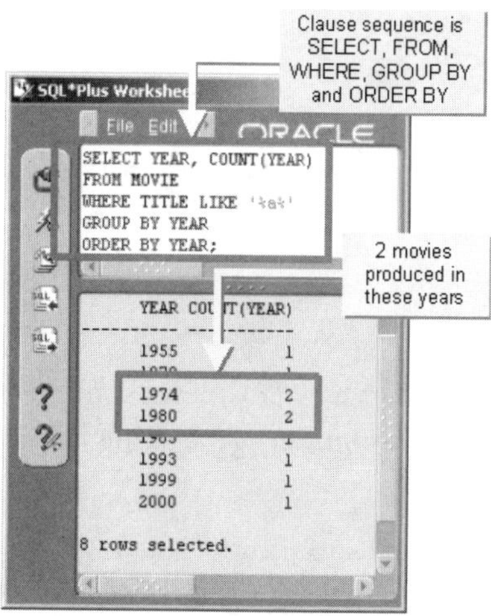

Figure 7.2 A simple **GROUP BY** clause query.

In Figure 7.2, the COUNT function is used as an aggregation for the GROUP BY clause, summarizing all movies into the years in which they were produced.

GROUP BY Clause Rules

There are a few rules to remember with respect to the GROUP BY clause:

- Any SELECT list elements not included in aggregation functions must be included in the GROUP BY list of elements. This includes both columns and expressions. The following example shows how every element in the SELECT list except the SUM(LIST_PRICE) expression is included in the GROUP BY elements list:

```
SELECT STUDIO, GENRE, NAME, DECODE(GENDER,'M','Male','F','Female')
, RATING, SUM(LIST_PRICE)
FROM MOVIE JOIN RATING USING(RATING_ID)
    JOIN STUDIO USING(STUDIO_ID)
        JOIN GENRE USING(GENRE_ID)
            JOIN DIRECTOR USING(DIRECTOR_ID)
GROUP BY STUDIO, GENRE, NAME, DECODE(GENDER,'M','Male','F','Female')
, RATING;
```

  Anything else in the GROUP BY clause will produce an error. Even the following alteration to the preceding example will produce an error, with the DECODE function expression renamed using the AS modifier in the SELECT list. This is because the GROUP BY clause is executed during query execution:

```
SELECT STUDIO, GENRE, NAME, DECODE(GENDER,'M','Male','F','Female')
AS SEX, RATING
    ,  SUM(LIST_PRICE)
FROM MOVIE JOIN RATING USING(RATING_ID)
    JOIN STUDIO USING(STUDIO_ID)
        JOIN GENRE USING(GENRE_ID)
            JOIN DIRECTOR USING(DIRECTOR_ID)
GROUP BY STUDIO, GENRE, NAME, SEX, RATING;
```

Even though the **DECODE** function result was passed into a renamed column called **SEX**, the **GENDER** column could still be used in the **GROUP BY** clause and get the same result.

- There must be at least one element of the SELECT list of elements subjected to an aggregation function. There is not much point in aggregating with GROUP BY and not aggregating anything.
- The GROUP BY element list cannot use positional specifications as with the ORDER BY clause. The ORDER BY clause is the only part of a query executed on a resulting row set.

Now let's expand the MOVIES schema.

Expanding the MOVIES Schema

The MOVIES schema is expanded as shown in Figure 7.3. In the MOVIES schema, data warehouse tables are referentially connected to the transactional tables with the MOVIE_ID primary key column in the MOVIE table.

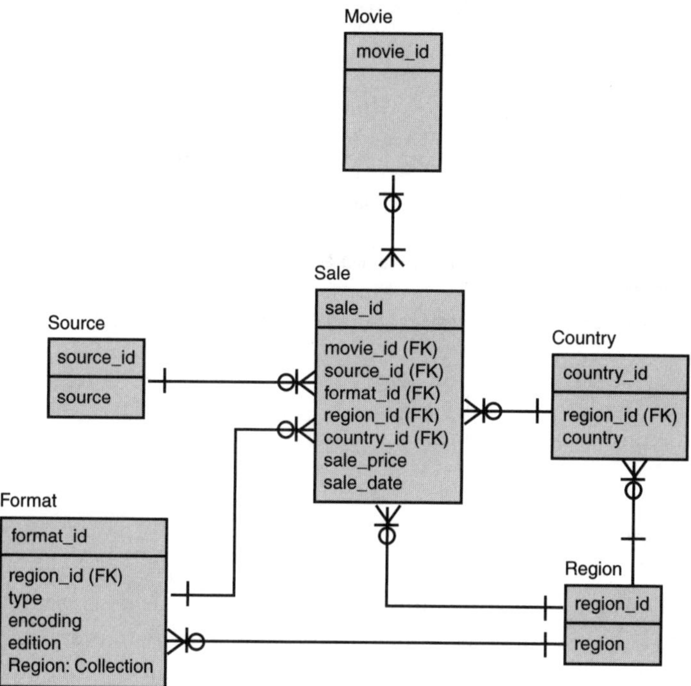

Figure 7.3 The **MOVIES** schema data warehouse tables.

The **MOVIES** schema may be expanded and altered throughout this book to accommodate different types of examples.

Here is a description of the data warehouse dimension and fact tables:

- *Dimension Tables*—Dimension tables are the dimensions of the facts, describing transactions. Dimensions contain static data or data that does not change often. Typically in data warehouse tables, static tables are affected only when static data is altered in a transactional database.

Here is a list of the dimensional tables:

- ➤ SOURCE—Gives the source point of a sale such as a retailer or a rental.
- ➤ FORMAT—Specifies the format. DVDs and VHS tapes are sold in different countries according to formats used in those countries. For instance, in Europe VHS tapes use the PAL system, different from the NTSC format used in North America.
- ➤ REGION—Lists different regions in the world.
- ➤ COUNTRY—Lists different countries, which are part of regions.

➤ *Fact Tables* (SALE)—Fact tables contain a transactional history of sales of movies in various formats.

Scripts to create the **MOVIES** schema and add data to tables can be found on my website at the following URL:

http://www.oracledbaexpert.com/oracle/OracleSQLExamCram2/index.html.

Now let's look at grouping functions.

Grouping Functions

Grouping functions are different from single row functions as described in Chapter 5, "Single Row Functions." Single row functions apply to every row of a SQL statement not affecting the number of rows returned. Grouping functions, on the other hand, do apply aggregation and analysis and thus produce groupings of rows, resulting in fewer rows returned by a query.

Numerous Oracle built-in aggregation functions are available for use in the GROUP BY clause. Custom-built functions can also be used in the GROUP BY clause, but that is PL/SQL and is out of the scope of this book.

Aggregation functions can be broken down as shown here:

➤ *Aggregates*—Aggregation is another term used to describe grouping functions. An aggregation is a process of grouping rows from their individual rows into fewer groups. Aggregation functions fall into several categories:

- ➤ *Simple Summaries*—These are basic summaries such as MAX and SUM, which find a maximum and sum of, respectively.
- ➤ *Simple Statistics*—These include statistical functions such as variance and standard deviation.

- *Statistical Distributions*—These include sophisticated statistical functions such as cumulative and percent point distributions.
- *Rankings*—There are a number of ranking functions. A ranking function defines the rank or importance of something among other things.
- *Groupings*—These functions are used in conjunction with 9i ROLLUP and 9i CUBE extensions to the GROUP BY clause.

- *Analytics*—Analytical functions can utilize most of the various aggregation functions, applying an OVER clause. Some functions are used exclusively with the OVER clause and not for aggregation.

Analytical functions and the **OVER** clause do not appear to be included in the exam except perhaps vaguely.

Aggregate Functions

An aggregation function operates on a group of rows, returning a single value for each group returned. In the example in Figure 7.2, the count of movies made for each year was returned. Now let's examine the different types of aggregation functions in detail.

Simple Summaries

Simple summary functions perform basic tasks such as counting, averaging, or summing up:

- COUNT(* | [DISTINCT|ALL] <expression>)—Makes a count of all rows or values found. For example, the following query counts all the rows in the MOVIE table:

  ```
  SELECT COUNT(*) FROM MOVIE;
  ```

  This next query returns a count of all years in which at least one movie was made, as stored in the MOVIE table:

  ```
  SELECT COUNT(DISTINCT(YEAR)) FROM MOVIE;
  ```

- AVG([DISTINCT|ALL] <expression>)—Finds an average. The following example finds the average LIST_PRICE value for all movies in the MOVIE table:

  ```
  SELECT AVG(LIST_PRICE) FROM MOVIE;
  ```

- `MIN([DISTINCT|ALL] <expression>)`—Finds the minimum of all values. This example finds the earliest produced movie in the `MOVIE` table:

  ```
  SELECT MIN(YEAR) FROM MOVIE;
  ```

- `MAX([DISTINCT|ALL] <expression>)`—Finds the maximum of all values. This example finds the most recent movie in the `MOVIE` table:

  ```
  SELECT MAX(YEAR) FROM MOVIE;
  ```

- `SUM([DISTINCT|ALL] <expression>)`—Finds the sum of all values. The following example finds the sum of all `LIST_PRICE` values for all movies in the `MOVIE` table:

  ```
  SELECT SUM(LIST_PRICE) FROM MOVIE;
  ```

Simple Statistics

Simple statistical functions perform basic tasks such as calculations of standard deviations and variances:

- `STDDEV([DISTINCT|ALL] <expression>)`—Standard deviation is the average distance from the mean of a set of values.
- `VARIANCE([DISTINCT|ALL] <expression>)`—Square of standard deviation from the mean or the average deviation around the mean.
- `CORR(<expression>, <expression>)`—Correlation coefficient of two expressions, or, in other words, the quality of a least squares fit to a set of values.
- `STDDEV_{POP|SAMP}(<expression>)`—Standard deviation as applied to a population or a sample.
- `VAR_{POP|SAMP}(<expression>)`—Variance as applied to a population or a sample.
- `COVAR_{POP|SAMP}(<expression>)`—Covariance as applied to a population or sample. Covariance is the average product of the difference between two population or sample means, or two sets of data in other words.
- `REGR_{<linear regression>} (<expression>, <expression>)`—These functions are all linear regression least squares, regression fit functions. Linear regression functions are `SLOPE`, `INTERCEPT`, `COUNT`, `R2`, `AVGX`, `AVGY`, `SXX`, `SYY`, and `SXY`.

Some functions include the **[DISTINCT | ALL]** option and others do not. This could evoke trick questions.

Statistical Distributions

Statistical distribution functions help to assess where values are within a distribution of a set of values:

- CUME_DIST(<expression> [, ...]) WITHIN GROUP (ORDER BY <expression> [, ...])—A cumulative frequency distribution plots the probability of values being within a histogram interval.

For all functions containing an option for an **ORDER BY** clause, general **ORDER BY** clause syntax applies, as in **ASC** or **DESC** and **NULLS FIRST** or **NULLS LAST** (see Chapter 3, "Filtering [**WHERE**] and Sorting Data [**ORDER BY**]").

- 9i PERCENTILE_{CONT|DIST}(<expression>) WITHIN GROUP (ORDER BY <expression>)—The inverse distribution for continuous or discrete distributions. This function is the inverse of the CUME_DIST function, and thus probabilities found by a cumulative distribution function can be found by this function.

Rankings

A ranking function is used to assess the ranking or the importance of a value within a set of values:

- RANK(<expression> [, ...] WITHIN GROUP(ORDER BY <expression> [, ...])—Finds the rank of a value within a group.
- PERCENT_RANK((<expression> [, ...] WITHIN GROUP(ORDER BY <expression> [, ...])—A cumulative distribution function as applied to rankings.
- DENSE_RANK((<expression> [, ...] WITHIN GROUP(ORDER BY <expression> [, ...])—Finds the rank of a row inside a sorted set of rows.
- {MIN|MAX|SUM|AVG|COUNT|VARIANCE|STDDEV} KEEP (DENSE_RANK {FIRST|LAST} ORDER BY <expression> [, ...]—Finds the first or last row inside a sorted set of rows.

Groupings

Grouping functions consist of the GROUP_ID, GROUPING, and GROUPING_ID functions. These three functions all apply to aggregates and super aggregates when using the ROLLUP and CUBE extensions to the GROUP BY clause.

- 9i GROUP_ID()—Removes duplicate groups from ROLLUP and CUBE clause GROUP BY extensions.
- GROUPING(<expression>)—Separates super aggregated and aggregated groups from ROLLUP and CUBE clause GROUP BY extensions.

➤ 9i GROUPING_ID(<expression> [, ...])—Returns a hierarchical level value for multiple level aggregated groups when using ROLLUP and CUBE clause GROUP BY extensions.

Analytics

Analysis allows more extensive examination of groups and subgroups within groups. Analytical aggregations can be cumulative, centered, moving, or summary in nature. This type of SQL function is most applicable to reporting and data warehouse databases because it is OLAP in nature. Analytical functions effectively create a window over ranges of rows. The window can be moved, varied in size, or determined by a measure such as time. Analytics are implemented using the OVER clause, whose syntax is shown in Figure 7.4.

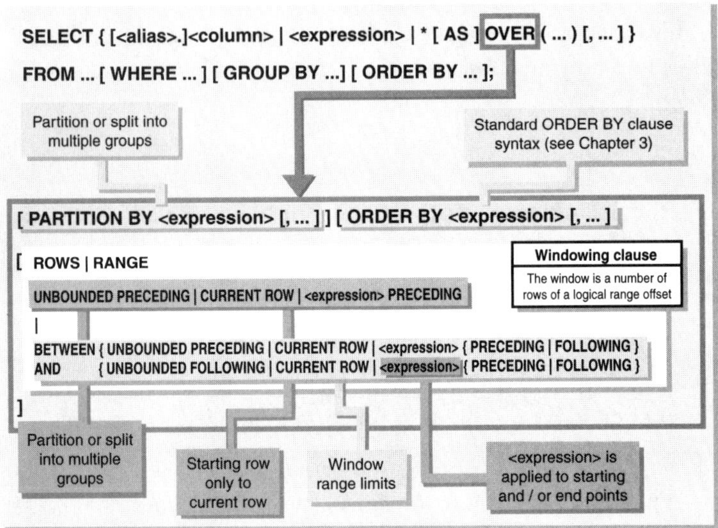

Figure 7.4 Analytic function **OVER** clause syntax.

Following is a synopsis of the syntax diagram shown in Figure 7.4:

➤ The OVER clause allows a function to execute on the results of a query.

➤ The PARTITION BY clause partitions or breaks up a query result into groups.

➤ The ORDER BY clause sorts rows within a partition and has the same syntax as the ORDER BY clause for a query (see Chapter 3).

- The windowing clause applies to a starting row or a range between two rows, within a row set returned by a query. The window can effectively slide through the range of rows or a partition among a group of partitions. Window start and end points can be specified as unbounded (start or finish), as the current row, or with an expression:
  - The UNBOUNDED PRECEDING and UNBOUNDED FOLLOWING clauses set a window to start and end at the beginning and end of a partition, respectively.
  - The CURRENT ROW clause starts or ends a window at the current row.
  - An expression can be applied to determine starting and ending row window boundaries where PRECEDING and FOLLOWING clauses apply to the beginning and ending of a partition, respectively.

Aggregate functions allowed to be used as analytical functions are **COUNT**, **AVG**, **SUM**, **MIN**, **MAX**, and all the standard deviation, variance, and covariance functions. Not all functions allow full **OVER** clause syntax.

Analytical-Only Functions

Some functions can be applied only as analytical functions using the OVER clause. The following list describes these types of functions:

- 9i {FIRST|LAST}_VALUE(<expression>) OVER(...)—The FIRST_VALUE and LAST_VALUE functions return first and last values, respectively, from a row set.
- {LAG|LEAD}(<expression> [, <offset>] [, <default]) OVER(...)—The LAG and LEAD functions allow access to more than one row in a table at once, effectively creating a self join. LAG allows a relative row offset prior to the current row; LEAD, a relative row offset to a subsequent row.
- ROW_NUMBER() OVER(...)—A unique sequential row number value is allocated to each returned row for the entire query, or counting within each partition.
- NTILE(<expression>) OVER(...)—This function divides rows into histogram bucket allocations.
- RATIO_TO_REPORT(<expression>) OVER(...)—This function provides a ratio between a current row value and the sum of all values returned by the query, for all rows returned.

The following sample query uses the `OVER` clause joining `MOVIE`, `REGION`, `COUNTRY`, and `SALE` tables, giving summed-up revenue values for each movie in each country, in each region:

```
COL MOVIE FORMAT A24
COL REGION FORMAT A16
COL COUNTRY FORMAT A16
COL SALES FORMAT $9,990
SELECT M.TITLE AS MOVIE, R.REGION, C.COUNTRY,SUM(S.SALE_PRICE) AS SALES
FROM REGION R JOIN COUNTRY C USING(REGION_ID)
        JOIN SALE S USING(COUNTRY_ID)
        JOIN MOVIE M USING(MOVIE_ID)
WHERE R.REGION IN ('Asia', 'North America')
GROUP BY M.TITLE, R.REGION, C.COUNTRY ORDER BY M.TITLE, R.REGION,
C.COUNTRY;
```

The preceding query is adjusted using an `OVER` clause, as shown in Figure 7.5, now including the cumulative column. Row-by-row accumulation is a very simple use of the `OVER` clause, potentially much more in depth and complex.

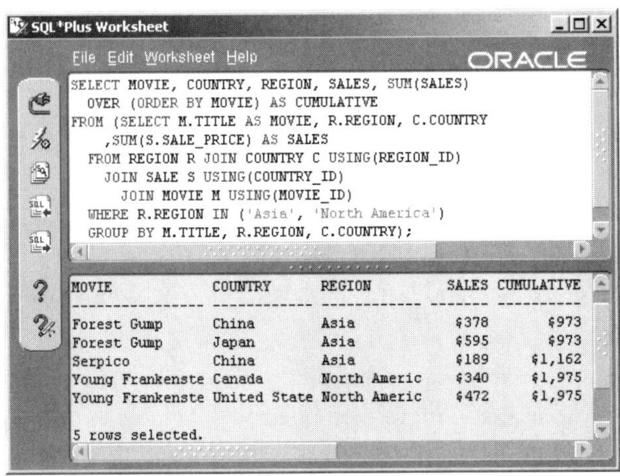

Figure 7.5 Using the analytic **OVER** clause.

Now let's examine the `HAVING` clause.

Filtering with the HAVING Clause

The `HAVING` clause is used to filter out unwanted groups and is thus applied to the `GROUP BY` clause, as shown in Figure 7.6.

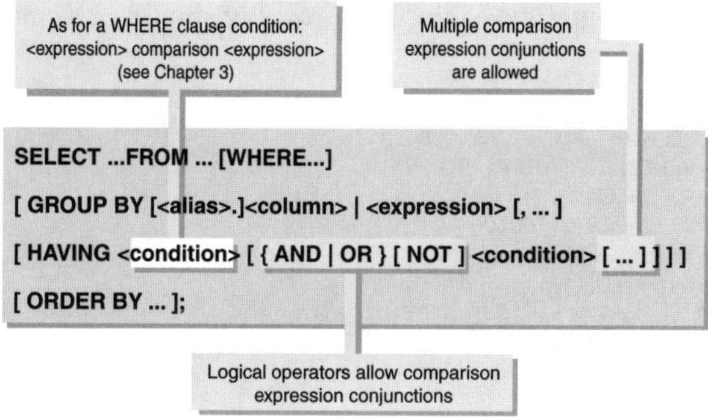

Figure 7.6 Filtering **GROUP BY** groups with the **HAVING** clause.

Following is a synopsis of the syntax diagram shown in Figure 7.6:

- The `WHERE` clause is used to filter rows from a query as they are read from the database (see Chapter 3). The `HAVING` clause is used to filter grouped rows created by the `GROUP BY` clause, after all rows have been retrieved from the database.
- The `HAVING` clause has more or less the same syntax as the `WHERE` clause, including conditional expressions:

  ```
  <expression> <condition> <expression>
  ```

  Or:

  ```
  YEAR > 2000
  ```

  And conjunctions of conditional expressions:

  ```
  (YEAR = 2000 OR YEAR = 2001) AND REVIEW < 500
  ```

Do not use the **HAVING** clause to filter if the **WHERE** clause can be used. **WHERE** clause filtering performs better.

The following query is an appropriate use for the `HAVING` clause such that resulting groups are filtered with the `HAVING` clause. The level of filtering required for this query cannot be performed using the `WHERE` clause because the `WHERE` clause is executed before the `GROUP BY` clause. The `HAVING` clause filters the results of the `GROUP BY` clause. As already stated, this is because the `WHERE` clause operates on all rows retrieved and the `HAVING` clause on the results of the `GROUP BY` clause. The `WHERE` clause therefore cannot possibly filter out groups created by the `GROUP BY` clause. Therefore, unless you are filtering the resulting groups created by a GROUP BY clause, you probably should be using the WHERE clause.

```
SELECT MOVIE, COUNTRY, REGION, SALES
    , SUM(SALES) OVER (ORDER BY MOVIE) AS CUMULATIVE
FROM (SELECT M.TITLE AS MOVIE, R.REGION, C.COUNTRY
    , SUM(S.SALE_PRICE) AS SALES
FROM REGION R JOIN COUNTRY C USING(REGION_ID)
    JOIN SALE S USING(COUNTRY_ID)
        JOIN MOVIE M USING(MOVIE_ID)
WHERE R.REGION IN ('Asia', 'Europe', 'North America')
GROUP BY M.TITLE, R.REGION, C.COUNTRY
HAVING SUM(S.SALE_PRICE) > 500);
```

9i Extending GROUP BY: ROLLUP and CUBE

The GROUP BY clause can be extended with OLAP functionality using the ROLLUP and CUBE clauses. The results of ROLLUP and CUBE clauses can be filtered with the GROUPING SETS clause. Figure 7.7 shows the syntax for the ROLLUP, CUBE, and GROUPING SETS clauses. In their most simplistic forms, the ROLLUP and CUBE clauses can be used to produce super-aggregates, aggregates of aggregates. In other words, the ROLLUP clause can be used to produce subtotals and grand totals for groups within a query. The CUBE clause extends the ROLLUP clause by producing cross-tabulation reports, generating combinations of all possible values.

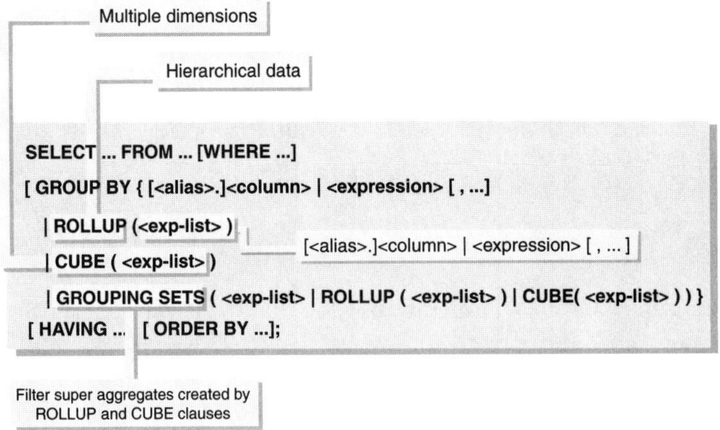

Figure 7.7 **ROLLUP**, **CUBE**, and **GROUPING SETS** clause syntax.

Understanding the inner workings and output of **ROLLUP**, **CUBE**, and **GROUPING SETS** clauses is not really required for this exam. However, you need to know how to build these clauses from a purely syntactical perspective.

Following is a synopsis of the syntax diagram shown in Figure 7.7:

- The ROLLUP clause can be used to produce hierarchical data, effectively providing subtotals and grand totals for subset groups within aggregations produced by a GROUP BY clause.
- The CUBE clause goes a little further and deeper than the ROLLUP clause by allowing creation of cross-tabulations in multiple dimensions—in other words, subtotals for groups within a set of groups, plus subtotals between different groups, followed by grand totals.
- The GROUPING SETS clause can be used to filter out the results of ROLLUP and CUBE clauses.

Figure 7.8 shows an application of the ROLLUP clause.

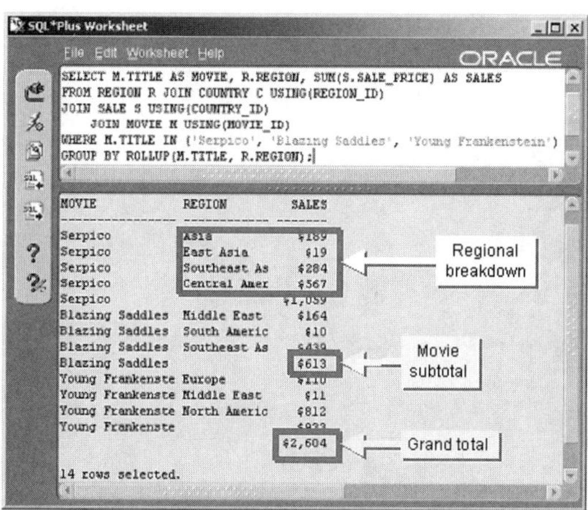

Figure 7.8 The **ROLLUP** clause.

In Figure 7.8 the ROLLUP clause produces totals on the combination of movie title by region. Thus, there are subtotals for each movie and a grand total at the end of the query.

Figure 7.9 shows an application of the CUBE clause.

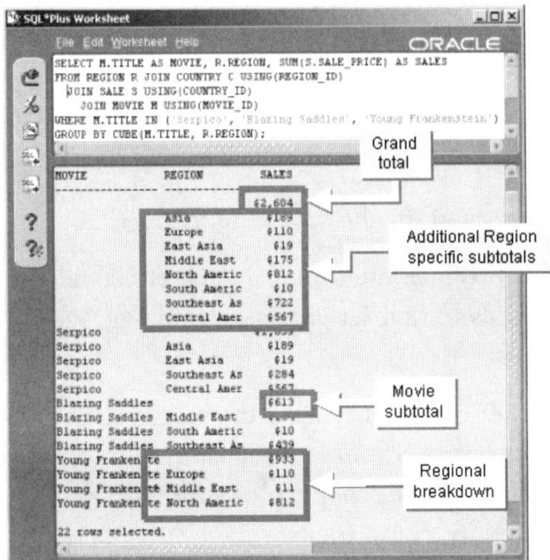

Figure 7.9 The **CUBE** clause.

In Figure 7.9, the `CUBE` clause produces totals on the combination of movie titles by region, as for the `ROLLUP` clause, but adding regional totals.

Figure 7.10 shows filtering of super aggregates using the `GROUPING SETS` clause.

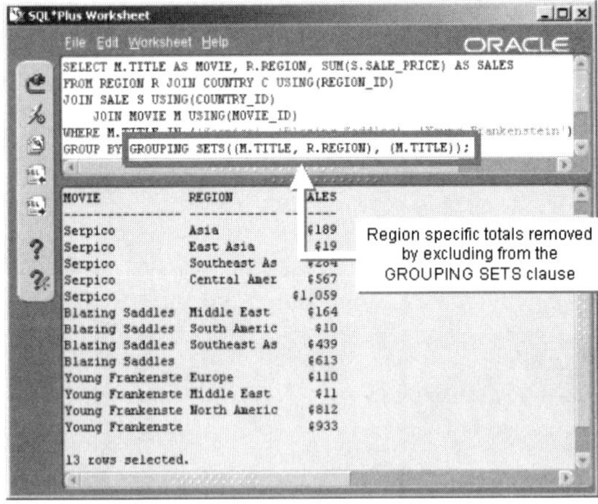

Figure 7.10 The **GROUPING SETS** clause.

In Figure 7.10, only movie titles by region and movie title totals are shown. Regional subtotals are filtered out of the grouped results using the `GROUPING SETS` clause.

Exam Prep Questions

1. Place these clauses in the correct sequence.

   - ❑ A. **ORDER BY**
   - ❑ B. **FROM**
   - ❑ C. **WHERE**
   - ❑ D. **SELECT**
   - ❑ E. **GROUP BY**
   - ❑ F. **HAVING**

   The correct sequence is D, B, C, E, F, A. **SELECT** comes first, followed by **FROM** and **WHERE**. The **HAVING** clause always comes after the **GROUP BY** clause because it filters the results of the **GROUP BY** clause. The **ORDER BY** clause always comes last.

2. Which of these clauses are optional? Pick more than one.

   - ❑ A. **SELECT**
   - ❑ B. **FROM**
   - ❑ C. **WHERE**
   - ❑ D. **GROUP BY**
   - ❑ E. **ROLLUP**
   - ❑ F. **HAVING**
   - ❑ G. **ORDER BY**
   - ❑ H. All of the above

   Answers C, D, E, F, and G should be selected. The **WHERE**, **GROUP BY**, and **ORDER BY** clauses are optional. The **HAVING** clause is an optional filter for **GROUP BY** results, and the **ROLLUP** clause is an optional extension to the **GROUP BY** clause. **SELECT** and **FROM** clauses are mandatory.

3. Which line is wrong in this query?

   ```
   1. SELECT TITLE, NAME
   2.     , DECODE(GENDER,'M','Male','F','Female') AS SEX
   3.     , SUM(LIST_PRICE)
   4. FROM MOVIE JOIN DIRECTOR USING(DIRECTOR_ID)
   5. GROUP BY TITLE, NAME, SEX;
   ```

   - ❑ A. 1
   - ❑ B. 2
   - ❑ C. 3
   - ❑ D. 4
   - ❑ E. 5

   Answer E is correct. Line 2 defines the **DECODE** function column as being renamed to **SEX**. The **GROUP BY** clause cannot use renamed columns, only the original column names or an expression.

A better form of the query is as follows, such that the **DECODE** function expression is copied into the **GROUP BY** clause:

```
SELECT TITLE, NAME
    , DECODE(GENDER,'M','Male','F','Female')
    , SUM(LIST_PRICE)
FROM MOVIE JOIN DIRECTOR USING(DIRECTOR_ID)
GROUP BY TITLE, NAME, DECODE(GENDER,'M','Male','F','Female');
```

4. Which of these clauses are used for filtering rows in a query? Select two answers.

- ❑ A. **FROM** clause
- ❑ B. **WHERE** clause
- ❑ C. **GROUP BY** with **ROLLUP** clause
- ❑ D. **HAVING** clause
- ❑ E. **ORDER BY** clause

Answers B and D are correct. The **WHERE** clause filters rows from the query, and the **HAVING** clause filters group rows produced by the **GROUP BY** clause. The **FROM** clause accesses tables, **GROUPBY** with **ROLLUP** aggregates and super-aggregates, and the **ORDER BY** clause sorts.

5. Which of these are true?

- ❑ A. The **ROLLUP** clause is best applied to hierarchical data.
- ❑ B. The **CUBE** clause is best applied to multiple dimensional data.
- ❑ C. The **GROUPING SETS** clause can be used to filter out aggregations produced by the **GROUP BY** clause.
- ❑ D. The **GROUPING SETS** clause can be used to filter out aggregations produced by the **ROLLUP** and **CUBE** clauses.
- ❑ E. All of the above.

Answers A, B, and D are correct. C is wrong because D provides a more concise description. Therefore, E is wrong as well.

6. Which line is incorrect in this query?

```
1. SELECT D.NAME, D.GENDER, MIN(M.YEAR)
2.      , AVG((M.RANK*M.REVIEWS)/100) AS RANKING
3. FROM DIRECTOR D JOIN MOVIE M USING(DIRECTOR_ID)
4. WHERE M.TITLE LIKE '%a%'
5. GROUP BY D.NAME, D.GENDER
6. ORDER BY D.NAME;
```

- ❑ A. 1
- ❑ B. 2
- ❑ C. 3
- ❑ D. 4
- ❑ E. 5
- ❑ F. 6
- ❑ G. None of the above

Answer G is correct. There is nothing wrong with this query.

7. Which of these is true? Select one answer.

   ❑ A. Single row functions do something to every row of a query.

   ❑ B. Grouping functions create fewer rows as summaries, from every row of a query.

   ❑ C. None of the above.

   ❑ D. Both A and B.

   Answer D is correct. The statements in both A and B are correct.

8. This query finds 34 rows from 12 regions, 34 countries, and 17 movie titles, which is the join of the three tables, grouped by country within region, for all movie titles with **SALE** entries. The result is a total number of groups equal to the number of rows in the **COUNTRY** table:

```
SELECT REGION, COUNTRY, COUNT(TITLE)
FROM REGION
    JOIN COUNTRY USING (REGION_ID)
        JOIN SALE USING(COUNTRY_ID)
            JOIN MOVIE USING(MOVIE_ID)
GROUP BY REGION, COUNTRY ORDER BY 1, 2;
```

   This next query rolls up on the region and country, returning how many rows?

```
SELECT REGION, COUNTRY, COUNT(TITLE)
FROM REGION
    JOIN COUNTRY USING (REGION_ID)
        JOIN SALE USING(COUNTRY_ID)
            JOIN MOVIE USING(MOVIE_ID)
GROUP BY ROLLUP(REGION, COUNTRY)
ORDER BY 1, 2;
```

   ❑ A. 47 rows

   ❑ B. 50 rows

   ❑ C. 34 rows

   ❑ D. 12 rows

   ❑ E. 46 rows

   Answer A is correct. In the basic **GROUP BY** query, 34 country groupings are returned. All the **ROLLUP** clause does is to add appropriate subtotals and a grand total. Because there are already existing totals for the country based on the **COUNT** function, all you need to do is add subtotals for each region with sales, and a grand total, to find the answer. Thus, 34 countries + 12 regions + 1 grand total is the total row count returned, 47 rows.

9. How many rows will be returned with this query, assuming that the **MOVIE** table contains 17 rows?

```
SELECT DISTINCT(COUNT(YEAR)) FROM MOVIE;
```

   ❑ A. 0 rows

   ❑ B. 1 row

   ❑ C. 34 rows

- ❑ D. 17 rows
- ❑ E. None of the above

Answer B is correct. The **COUNT** function returns a count of all rows in the **MOVIE** table on a single row. Because **DISTINCT** is acting on a single row and a single value, it does not do anything.

10. Which line contains an error?

```
1. SELECT TITLE, RATING
2. , AVG(LIST_PRICE)
3. FROM MOVIE
4. GROUP BY TITLE;
```

- ❑ A. 1
- ❑ B. 2
- ❑ C. 3
- ❑ D. 4

Answer D is correct. Because the aggregate function is applied to **LIST_PRICE** and both **TITLE** and **RATING** are retrieved individually, the **GROUP BY** clause should include both **TITLE** and **RATING** columns. The query should look like this:

```
SELECT TITLE, RATING
, AVG(LIST_PRICE)
FROM MOVIE
GROUP BY TITLE, RATING;
```

Subqueries and Other Specialized Queries

Terms You Need to Understand

- ✓ Subquery
- ✓ Scalar subquery
- ✓ Single row subquery
- ✓ Multiple row subquery
- ✓ Multiple column subquery
- ✓ Correlated subquery
- ✓ Regular subquery
- ✓ Inline view
- ✓ Nested subquery
- ✓ Composite query
- ✓ Hierarchical query
- ✓ Parallel query
- ✓ 9i Flashback query
- ✓ 9i The **WITH** clause

Concepts You Need to Master

- ✓ Different types of subqueries
- ✓ Where subqueries can be used
- ✓ Set operators
- ✓ Hierarchical query operators
- ✓ Subquery comparison conditions

This chapter covers all the aspects of subquery processing, including how subqueries are constructed and where they can be used. Additionally, other specialized, more obscure query types are introduced.

What Is a Subquery?

A *subquery* is a query contained within another query, a *calling query*. The subquery is effectively a temporary cursor or chunk of memory created and allocated during the life of the subquery. Subquery details are then accessible from the calling query by the subquery cursor.

Subqueries can sometimes be used to assist with performance and are often used to reduce the complexity of large cumbersome SELECT statements.

Where Can Subqueries Be Located?

Subqueries can be located in place of an expression in a SQL command. A subquery is nearly always enclosed in parentheses. Thus, (<subquery>) is equivalent to (<expression>). The following SQL statements allow use of subqueries:

- The SELECT clause elements list:

```
SELECT M.TITLE, (SELECT MPAA FROM RATING WHERE RATING_ID = M.RATING_ID)
FROM MOVIE M;
```

- The FROM clause (an inline view):

```
SELECT M.TITLE, R.MPAA
FROM MOVIE M, (SELECT RATING_ID, MPAA FROM RATING) R
WHERE M.RATING_ID = R.RATING_ID;
```

- The WHERE clause:

```
SELECT TITLE FROM MOVIE WHERE RATING_ID IN
(SELECT RATING_ID FROM RATING);
```

- The ORDER BY clause:

```
SELECT M.TITLE, (SELECT MPAA FROM RATING WHERE RATING_ID = M.RATING_ID)
FROM MOVIE M
ORDER BY (SELECT MPAA FROM RATING WHERE RATING_ID = M.RATING_ID);
```

- An INSERT statement VALUES clause:

```
INSERT INTO STUDIO(STUDIO_ID, STUDIO)
VALUES((SELECT MAX(STUDIO_ID)+1 FROM STUDIO)
    , 'This should be a sequence');
```

- An UPDATE statement set clause:

```
UPDATE STUDIO SET STUDIO = 'Sony produced ' ||
    (SELECT TITLE FROM MOVIE WHERE MOVIE_ID=1)
WHERE STUDIO = 'This should be a sequence';
```

- A CASE statement expression:

```
SELECT NAME
    , CASE (SELECT GENDER FROM ACTOR WHERE ACTOR_ID = A.ACTOR_ID)
      WHEN 'F' THEN 'Female'
      WHEN 'M' THEN 'Male'
      ELSE 'Unknown'
      END
FROM ACTOR A;
```

- Tables and views can be created using subqueries:

```
CREATE TABLE STUDIOS AS SELECT * FROM STUDIO;

CREATE VIEW MOVIES AS SELECT * FROM MOVIE;
```

- A table can have rows inserted into it with a subquery. First I create a copy of the STUDIO table with no rows using ROWNUM < 1. This copies the structure of the table only and not the data:

```
CREATE TABLE STUDIOCOPY AS SELECT * FROM STUDIO WHERE ROWNUM < 1;
```

  Now I add the rows to the new table using an INSERT statement containing a subquery:

```
INSERT INTO STUDIOCOPY SELECT * FROM STUDIO;
```

Subqueries creating tables and views for running mass insertions do not require parentheses. Thus, **<subquery>** applies as opposed to **(<subquery>)**.

  Table and view creation are covered in Chapter 12 and Chapter 13, respectively.

- A function parameter (built in or PL/SQL):

```
SELECT LENGTH((SELECT TITLE FROM MOVIE WHERE MOVIE_ID=1)) FROM DUAL;
```

Now that you know where you can use queries, the next step is to briefly examine the inclusion of subqueries into comparison conditions (see Chapter 4, "Operators, Conditions, Pseudocolumns, and Expressions," for more information).

Comparison Condition Subquery Syntax

Figure 8.1 presents a simple picture of how comparison condition syntax is altered by subqueries. In short, `<expression>` can be replaced with `(<subquery>)`.

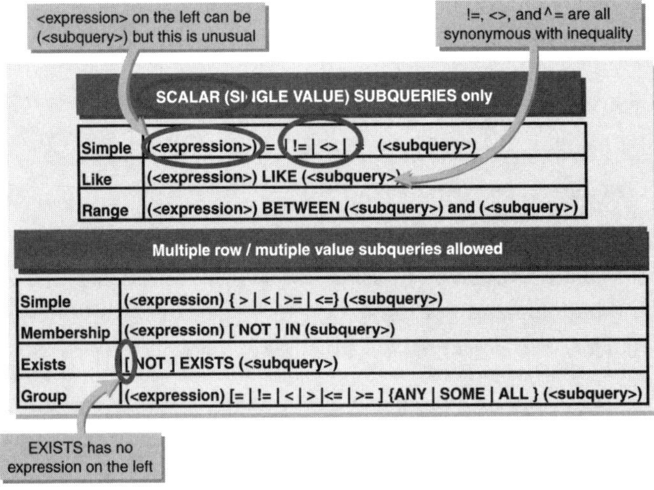

Figure 8.1 Comparison condition syntax for subqueries.

Following is a synopsis of the syntax details shown in Figure 8.1:

- Here we see extensions and modifications to conditions described in Chapter 4. The modifications are simple in that `(<subquery>)` is exchanged for `<expression>`.
- A subquery is an expression by definition. Therefore, `(<subquery>)` is equal to `<expression>`.
- Syntactically, subqueries usually are enclosed in parentheses, as in `(<subquery>)`, but not always!
- Examine the Simple condition under Scalar subqueries in Figure 8.1. Note that `<expression> = (<subquery>)` can also be `(<subquery>) = (<subquery>)`. Therefore, this query is syntactically correct:

```
SELECT * FROM DIRECTOR WHERE DIRECTOR_ID IN
    (SELECT DIRECTOR_ID FROM DIRECTOR);
```

And this query also is syntactically correct:

```
SELECT * FROM PART WHERE (SELECT MOVIE_ID FROM MOVIE_ID)
    IN (SELECT MOVIE_ID FROM RECOGNITION);
```

- The operators `!=`, `<>`, and `^=` all represent inequality or not equal to.
- The `EXISTS` condition does not have an expression on the left, but only on the right, as in this example:

```
SELECT * FROM DIRECTOR D WHERE EXISTS
    (SELECT * FROM MOVIE WHERE DIRECTOR_ID = D.MOVIE_ID);
```

In Figure 8.1 we can see that subqueries have been broken into scalar and multiple row subqueries. A scalar subquery returns a single value, and a multiple row subquery returns one or more rows or values. Let's examine the different types of subqueries in detail.

Types of Subquery

Subqueries can be classified into categories as given in the following list. It should become clear as you read through this chapter that some of these categories are intertwined. In other words, a subquery can fall into more than one category. Here is the first set of subquery categories:

- Scalar (single column or value)
- Single row (scalar if a single column)
- Multiple row (single or multiple column)
- Multiple column (single or multiple row)

Here is the second set of subquery categories:

- Correlated (connection passed from calling to subquery)
- Inline view (can be correlated)
- Nested (can be correlated)

The first and second sets of categories can be combined in any manner. For example, a single row subquery can also be a correlated subquery, or an inline view can also be a multiple column subquery.

The categories for many of the subquery types previously listed describe what each subquery type does.

Scalar Subquery

A scalar subquery simply returns a single value, a scalar value. In SQL statements in which only a single value is required, an error will be returned when more than one item is returned to a calling query from a subquery. More than one item implies more than one column, more than one row, or both.

This query uses a scalar subquery to validate against a single movie:

```
SELECT MPAA, RATING FROM RATING WHERE RATING_ID =
    (SELECT RATING_ID FROM MOVIE WHERE MOVIE_ID = 1);
```

This query does the same as the preceding one, but the finding is based on a string rather than a number:

```
SELECT * FROM STUDIO WHERE STUDIO_ID =
    (SELECT STUDIO_ID FROM MOVIE WHERE TITLE = 'Young Frankenstein');
```

This query uses a SELECT statement element to find a single studio for each movie:

```
SELECT M.TITLE, (SELECT STUDIO FROM STUDIO WHERE STUDIO_ID = M.STUDIO_ID)
FROM MOVIE M;
```

This query is the opposite of the preceding one and will return an error. This is because it is possible for the subquery to find more than a single movie per studio:

```
SELECT S.STUDIO, (SELECT TITLE FROM MOVIE WHERE STUDIO_ID = S.STUDIO_ID)
FROM STUDIO S;
```

Single Row Subquery

A single row subquery returns an entire row or a single iteration of a set of columns to a calling query. If a single column is returned, a single row subquery is also a scalar subquery. For example, in the following the subquery returns a single row with a single column (RATING_ID) because the RATING_ID column is a primary key and is thus unique:

```
SELECT TITLE FROM MOVIE WHERE RATING_ID =
    (SELECT RATING_ID FROM RATING WHERE RATING_ID = 1);
```

Multiple Row Subquery

A multiple row subquery simply returns more than one row, containing one or more columns. Thus, a multiple row subquery can also be a multiple column subquery. The next two examples use IN and EXISTS to find all movie titles assigned a valid rating. Both subqueries potentially find more than a single row:

```
SELECT TITLE FROM MOVIE WHERE RATING_ID IN (SELECT RATING_ID FROM RATING);

SELECT M.TITLE FROM MOVIE M WHERE EXISTS (SELECT RATING_ID FROM RATING
WHERE RATING_ID = M.RATING_ID);
```

Because the preceding two queries access multiple rows, but return a Boolean value, they could also conceivably be called scalar value returning subqueries because they return only `true`, `false`, or `NULL`: a single, and thus, scalar value.

Multiple Column Subquery

A multiple column subquery returns more than a single value, in one or more rows. The following subqueries process two columns for the two parenthesized, comma-delimited columns on the left side of the `WHERE` clause:

```
SELECT TITLE FROM MOVIE WHERE (RATING_ID, STUDIO_ID) IN
    (SELECT RATING_ID, STUDIO_ID FROM RATING NATURAL JOIN
    MOVIE NATURAL JOIN STUDIO);
```

The following examples also contain multiple column subqueries:

```
CREATE TABLE STUDIOS AS SELECT * FROM STUDIO;

CREATE VIEW MOVIES AS SELECT * FROM MOVIE;

INSERT INTO STUDIOS SELECT * FROM STUDIO;

SELECT M.TITLE, R.MPAA FROM MOVIE M
    , (SELECT RATING_ID, MPAA FROM RATING) R
    WHERE M.RATING_ID = R.RATING_ID;
```

Correlated Subquery

A correlated subquery simply allows the passing of a referential value to a subquery such that the subquery is able to reference each row of the calling query. We have already seen the following query in this chapter, passing a `RATING_ID` for each row found in the `MOVIE` table into the subquery in both the `SELECT` list and the `ORDER BY` clause:

```
SELECT M.TITLE, (SELECT MPAA FROM RATING WHERE RATING_ID = M.RATING_ID)
FROM MOVIE M
ORDER BY (SELECT MPAA FROM RATING WHERE RATING_ID = M.RATING_ID);
```

Correlated subqueries have been traditionally used with `EXISTS`. In the following example the `RATING_ID` column value is passed down into the subquery:

```
SELECT * FROM MOVIE M WHERE EXISTS
    (SELECT RATING_ID FROM RATING WHERE RATING_ID = M.RATING_ID);
```

Using `IN`, we could change the preceding query as shown here:

```
SELECT * FROM MOVIE M WHERE M.RATING_ID IN
    (SELECT RATING_ID FROM RATING WHERE RATING_ID = M.RATING_ID);
```

In general, **EXISTS** is best suited to queries in which the most selective filter is in the calling query. **IN** is usually best suited to queries with the most selective filter in the subquery.

The following two queries use IN rather than EXISTS because they do not pass correlating referential values into their respective subqueries:

```
SELECT * FROM MOVIE WHERE RATING_ID IN (SELECT RATING_ID FROM RATING);

SELECT * FROM MOVIE WHERE RATING_ID IN (1, 2, 3, 4, 5);
```

A *noncorrelated query* is sometimes called a *regular subquery.*

Inline View

An inline view is a subquery nested in the FROM clause of a calling query. Values are retrieved from the subquery by assigning an alias to the subquery as a whole. In the following example we are pulling the MPAA and RATING columns from the RATING table into the calling query. The RATING_ID column is then used to join between the RATING (the inline view aliased as R) and the MOVIE tables:

```
SELECT M.TITLE, R.MPAA, R.RATING
FROM MOVIE M ,(SELECT RATING_ID, MPAA, RATING FROM RATING) R
WHERE M.RATING_ID = R.RATING_ID;
```

An inline view is a little like a temporary table. A temporary table is a table created to contain data temporarily. For instance, a report might require data from multiple tables in an order completely contrary to underlying table structure. A temporary table could be used to make this type of processing more efficient. An inline view is a little like a temporary table in that the results of a query are created in memory temporarily within the subquery (the inline view), the results of which are passed on to a calling query.

Nested Subquery

In general, a nested subquery is a subquery nested down to multiple levels. In effect, a nested query can contain multiples of other types of subqueries in multiple nested layers of subqueries. In the following example there are two nested layers in the FROM clause:

```
SELECT TITLE, AC.ACTOR, AC.AWARD
FROM MOVIE NATURAL JOIN PART
    ,(SELECT NAME AS ACTOR, AW.ACTOR_ID, AW.AWARD FROM ACTOR AC
        ,(SELECT ACTOR_ID, AWARD FROM AWARD NATURAL JOIN RECOGNITION) AW
     WHERE AC.ACTOR_ID = AW.ACTOR_ID) AC
WHERE AC.ACTOR_ID = PART.ACTOR_ID;
```

In this next example there are five nested layers. This shows the power of subqueries. Mixing different subquery types in different layers where appropriate can help to filter out rows precisely when tuning complex queries, particularly joins.

For the purposes of simplicity, the following query can be thought of as executing from the inside out. In other words, you would look at the query from the perspective of reading the tables in the order of ACTOR, AWARD, RECOGNITION, DIRECTOR, and MOVIE.

```
SELECT M.TITLE FROM MOVIE M
WHERE EXISTS
(
    SELECT * FROM DIRECTOR D
    WHERE D.DIRECTOR_ID = M.DIRECTOR_ID
    AND EXISTS
    (
        SELECT * FROM RECOGNITION R
        WHERE R.DIRECTOR_ID = D.DIRECTOR_ID
        AND EXISTS
        (
            SELECT * FROM AWARD A
            WHERE A.AWARD_ID = R.AWARD_ID
            AND EXISTS
            (
                SELECT * FROM ACTOR ACT
                WHERE ACT.ACTOR_ID = R.ACTOR_ID
            )
        )
    )
);
```

Contrary to the previous comment, the preceding query might not read tables in the order of ACTOR, AWARD, RECOGNITION, DIRECTOR, and MOVIE. In fact, the Optimizer may think differently and change this order of execution depending on what the tables are, how large they are, and indexes present, among many other possible factors. This topic is a little out of the scope of this book, but the following is a query plan for the preceding query in a schema with no statistics:

```
Position  Level Query
   0        1   SELECT STATEMENT  on
   1        2    FILTER  on
   1        3     TABLE ACCESS FULL on MOVIE
   2        3     NESTED LOOPS  on
   1        4      NESTED LOOPS  on
   1        5       NESTED LOOPS  on
   1        6        INDEX UNIQUE SCAN on XPK_DIRECTOR
   2        6        TABLE ACCESS BY INDEX ROWID on RECOGNITION
   1        7         INDEX RANGE SCAN on XFK_RECOGNITION
   2        5       INDEX UNIQUE SCAN on XPK_AWARD
   2        4      INDEX UNIQUE SCAN on XPK_ACTOR
```

The position column is part of the query plan and a point in the execution process in reverse. The LEVEL psuedocolumn is used to display the level of a node in a tree structure and provides a little more detail than the position column. Also, the greater the amount of indentation in the output shows what is executed first. For this query the Optimizer has decided that tables should be executed in the order of RECOGNITION, DIRECTOR, AWARD, ACTOR, MOVIE.

9i The WITH Clause

The WITH clause allows creation of named subqueries. The results can be accessed by subsequent queries using the name generated by the WITH clause, much like an inline view accessed from a calling query through the alias of the inline view. Figure 8.2 shows the syntax for the WITH clause.

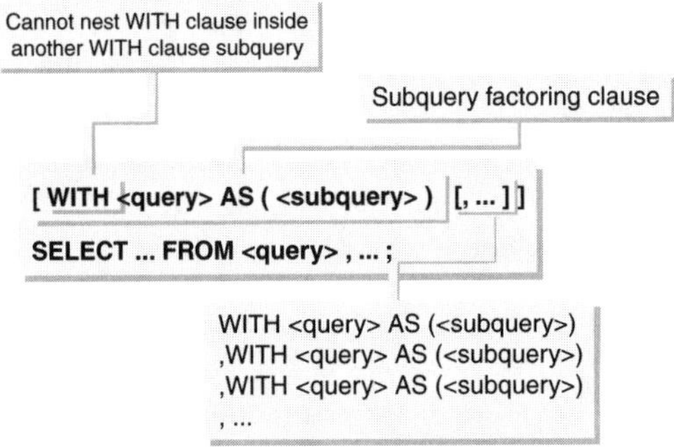

Figure 8.2 Subquery **WITH** clause syntax.

Following is a synopsis of the syntax diagram shown in Figure 8.2:

- The subquery factoring or WITH clause creates a named subquery that can be accessed later by a calling query.
- There can be multiple named subqueries defined for each WITH clause. The calling query can access all WITH clause defined subqueries.

The **WITH** clause is also known as the *subquery factoring clause.*

Here's a step-by-step example of what can be done when the WITH clause is used:

1. Join the RATING and MOVIE tables:

```
SELECT MOVIE_ID, MPAA, RATING FROM RATING NATURAL JOIN MOVIE;
```

2. Join the MOVIE, RECOGNITION, and AWARD tables:

```
SELECT M.MOVIE_ID, AW.AWARD
FROM MOVIE M JOIN RECOGNITION R ON(R.MOVIE_ID = M.MOVIE_ID)
    JOIN AWARD AW ON(AW.AWARD_ID = R.AWARD_ID);
```

3. Plug the first two joins above into WITH clauses called RATINGS and AWARDS. Join the new names RATINGS and AWARDS together:

```
WITH RATINGS AS
    (SELECT MOVIE_ID, MPAA, RATING FROM RATING NATURAL JOIN MOVIE),
    AWARDS AS (
SELECT M.MOVIE_ID, AW.AWARD
      FROM MOVIE M JOIN RECOGNITION R ON(R.MOVIE_ID = M.MOVIE_ID)
         JOIN AWARD AW ON(AW.AWARD_ID = R.AWARD_ID)
)
SELECT * FROM AWARDS JOIN RATINGS ON(RATINGS.MOVIE_ID =
AWARDS.MOVIE_ID);
```

4. Join the new RATINGS query to the SALE and REGION table join, plus semi-join the new AWARDS query in a WHERE filter EXISTS clause:

```
COL SALES FORMAT 9,990
COL NET FORMAT $9,990.99
COL REGION FORMAT A16
WITH RATINGS AS (SELECT MOVIE_ID, MPAA, RATING FROM RATING
NATURAL JOIN MOVIE)
    , AWARDS AS (
        SELECT M.MOVIE_ID, AW.AWARD
        FROM MOVIE M JOIN RECOGNITION R ON(R.MOVIE_ID = M.MOVIE_ID)
           JOIN AWARD AW ON(AW.AWARD_ID = R.AWARD_ID))
SELECT R.REGION, RATINGS.MPAA, COUNT(S.SALE_ID) AS SALES,
SUM(S.SALE_PRICE) AS NET
FROM SALE S JOIN REGION R ON(R.REGION_ID = S.REGION_ID)
    JOIN RATINGS ON(RATINGS.MOVIE_ID = S.MOVIE_ID)
WHERE EXISTS (SELECT AWARD FROM AWARDS WHERE MOVIE_ID = S.MOVIE_ID)
GROUP BY R.REGION, RATINGS.MPAA;
```

The result of the preceding query is shown in Figure 8.3. This simply goes to show the kind of complexity that can be managed when using the WITH clause.

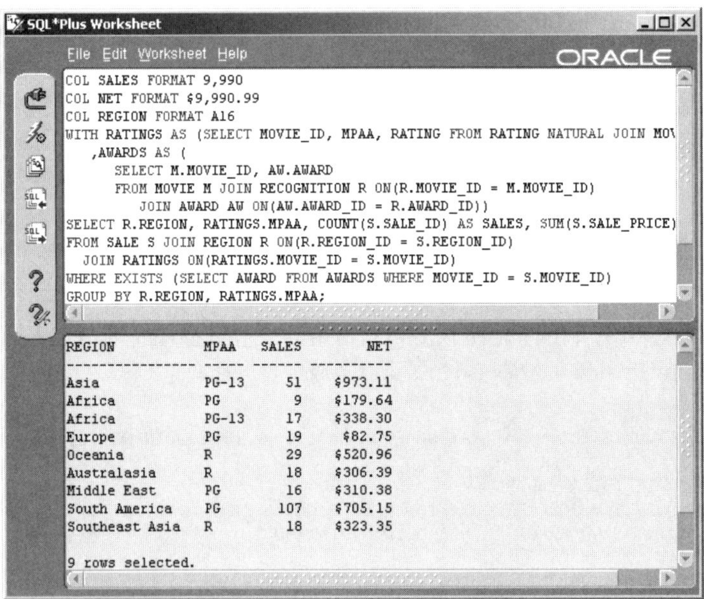

Figure 8.3 Using the **WITH** clause.

The query in Figure 8.3 is effectively grouping sales numbers and net dollar values into regions by ratings (ratings within regions).

Granularity in coding usually leads to simplification in coding. However, granularity can lead to poor performance.

Specialized Queries

There are various types of specialized queries, doing some obscure and perhaps rather odd things. Specialized query types can be categorized this way:

- Composite
- Hierarchical
- Parallel
- 9i Flashback

Composite Query

A composite query concatenates the rows from two queries in which column numbers retrieved (SELECT list elements) and datatypes match. So you can do this:

```
SELECT MOVIE_ID, TITLE FROM MOVIE
UNION
SELECT MOVIE_ID, NULL FROM RECOGNITION;
```

But you cannot do what is in the next query because the datatypes for the TO_CHAR(MOVIE_ID) and MOVIE_ID are different:

```
SELECT TO_CHAR(MOVIE_ID), TITLE FROM MOVIE
UNION
SELECT MOVIE_ID, NULL FROM RECOGNITION;
```

Notice that the preceding two queries replaced the second column retrieved from the RECOGNITION table with NULL.

Composite queries use set operators to concatenate queries together. The set operators are listed here:

- UNION—Returns unique or distinct rows from two queries. If rows have identical values for all columns, only the first occurrence of each will be returned. The GENRE table contains multiple levels of hierarchical data. You will use the two top levels of the GENRE table to demonstrate composite queries. Here, you are creating a view called CATEGORY by copying out only the highest-level rows:

  ```
  CREATE OR REPLACE VIEW CATEGORY AS
      SELECT GENRE_ID AS CATEGORY_ID, GENRE AS CATEGORY FROM
          GENRE WHERE PARENT_ID IS NULL;
  ```

  The next query will concatenate the GENRE table and the CATEGORY view using UNION. The result is all distinct rows from both the view and the table, effectively the same as retrieving from the GENRE table alone:

  ```
  SELECT GENRE_ID, GENRE FROM GENRE
  UNION
  SELECT * FROM CATEGORY
  ORDER BY 1;
  ```

An **ORDER BY** clause always sorts the result of a concatenated query as a whole, not each query separately. Remember, the **ORDER BY** clause sorts the result of a processed query row set, as the last execution step.

- UNION ALL—Returns all rows from two queries including duplications.

  The next example using UNION ALL will retrieve all rows from both table and view without stripping duplicate rows. Therefore, the highest-level rows will be retrieved twice because they exist in both GENRE table and CATEGORY view:

```
SELECT GENRE_ID, GENRE FROM GENRE
UNION ALL
SELECT * FROM CATEGORY
ORDER BY 2;
```

- INTERSECT—Returns distinct rows common to both queries; an intersection. This example will return only one row for each of the highest-level rows, the rows in the view:

```
SELECT GENRE_ID, GENRE FROM GENRE
INTERSECT
SELECT * FROM CATEGORY;
```

- MINUS—Returns all distinct rows in the first query not in the second query. MINUS returns the opposite of an intersection. This query returns every row not at the highest level (not in the view, the row source on the right):

```
SELECT GENRE_ID, GENRE FROM GENRE
MINUS
SELECT * FROM CATEGORY;
```

  This second query returns no rows at all because all rows in the CATEGORY view exist in the GENRE table. Subtracting the rows in the GENRE table from the CATEGORY view results in nothing left to retrieve from the CATEGORY view:

```
SELECT * FROM CATEGORY
MINUS
SELECT GENRE_ID, GENRE FROM GENRE;
```

Hierarchical Query

Hierarchical queries can be used to retrieve data from hierarchical row sets and organize results in a hierarchy. What is a hierarchy? A *hierarchy* is like an inverted tree with branches containing finer detail as you progress farther toward the leaves of the tree. Hierarchical query syntax is shown in Figure 8.4.

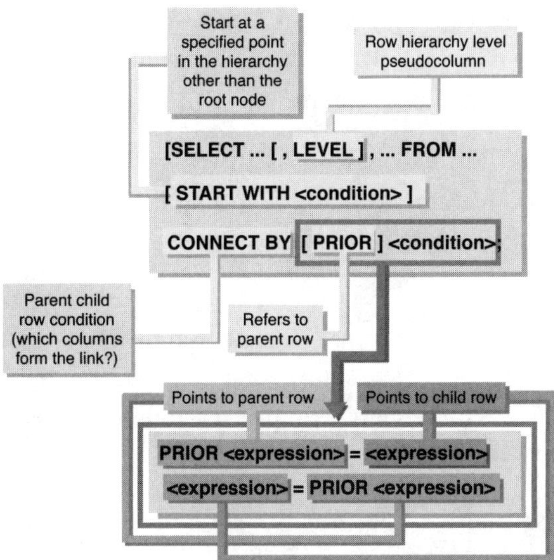

Figure 8.4 Hierarchical query syntax.

Following is a synopsis of the syntax diagram shown in Figure 8.4:

- The START WITH clause forces the query to begin returning the hierarchy from the node specified.
- The LEVEL pseudocolumn returns the level of each node within the hierarchy produced.
- The CONNECT BY clause defines columns to link parent and child rows together.
- The parent row is referred to using the PRIOR operator. In the MOVIES schema GENRE table, there is a column for the current genre (GENRE_ID) and a column for the parent of that current genre (PARENT_ID). For example, a War movie is an Action movie, and thus the row for War movies would have the GENRE_ID for Action movies in its PARENT_ID column. In the following code snippet the GENRE_ID is in the parent row, denoted as PRIOR, and the PARENT_ID column is in the current row:

  ```
  CONNECT BY PARENT_ID = PRIOR GENRE_ID
  ```

  The PRIOR operator always refers to a parent row of the curent row.

As shown in Figure 8.4, hierarchical queries are constructed using the CONNECT BY clause, the PRIOR operator, and the START WITH clause. The LEVEL pseudocolumn can be used to return the level of a row in the hierarchy. In the following query the CONNECT BY clause must use the PRIOR operator to connect a genre (PARENT_ID) to its parent row (PRIOR GENRE_ID). The parent row exists in the child row as the value in the `PARENT_ID` column. This example finds all Action movie genres, including all genres within the Action genre:

```
SELECT GENRE_ID, GENRE, LEVEL, PARENT_ID FROM GENRE
START WITH GENRE = 'Action' CONNECT BY PRIOR GENRE_ID = PARENT_ID
ORDER BY 1, 2;
```

If you were to switch the `PRIOR` operator, as in the following query, because Action is a top-level genre (has no parent genre) the following query will return only one row:

```
SELECT GENRE_ID, GENRE, LEVEL, PARENT_ID FROM GENRE
START WITH GENRE = 'Action' CONNECT BY GENRE_ID = PRIOR PARENT_ID
ORDER BY 1, 2;
```

The results for both of the hierarchical query examples listed previously are shown in Figure 8.5.

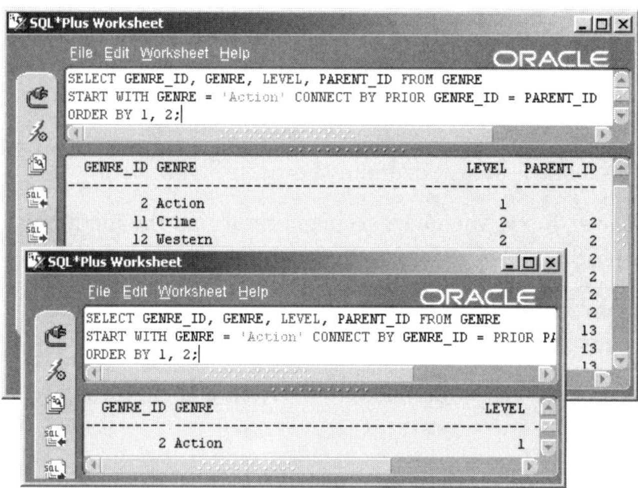

Figure 8.5 Hierarchical query examples.

Parallel Query

Parallel queries are most effective when used on multiple CPU platforms, including Oracle Partitioning with partitions on separate spindles. RAID arrays are an appropriate substitute. These types of DML and DDL statements can be executed in parallel:

- Queries containing at least one full table scan containing a `SELECT`, `INSERT`, `UPDATE`, or `DELETE` command (see my other book *Oracle High Performance Tuning for 9i and 10g*, ISBN: 1555583059).

- Queries against partitions, preferably using local indexes stored in the relevant partitions (*Oracle High Performance Tuning for 9i and 10g*, ISBN: 1555583059).
- `CREATE TABLE AS SELECT...` commands (see Chapter 11).
- `CREATE INDEX` and `ALTER INDEX REBUILD` commands (see Chapter 12).

Multiple examples for parallel queries are well beyond the scope of this book. The easiest method of executing a parallel query is by using a hint as in the example shown next:

```
SELECT /*+ PARALLEL(SALE, 4) */ * FROM SALE;
```

In the preceding example, the hint is suggesting to the Optimizer that the query should be executed in parallel. Parallel execution can be on multiple CPUs, multiple I/O spindles, or even shared server processes and a single CPU.

Hints are tuning and thus are out of scope for this book. However, you need to remember that hints make suggestions, they do not command. In other words, if a server platform does not have multiple CPUs, the Optimizer may simply ignore the hint in the preceding example.

9i Flashback Query

Flashback queries allow querying of data in a database at a specified point in time or at a specific data change point in the past. Effectively, this is known as a consistent data snapshot. Flashback query syntax is shown in Figure 8.6.

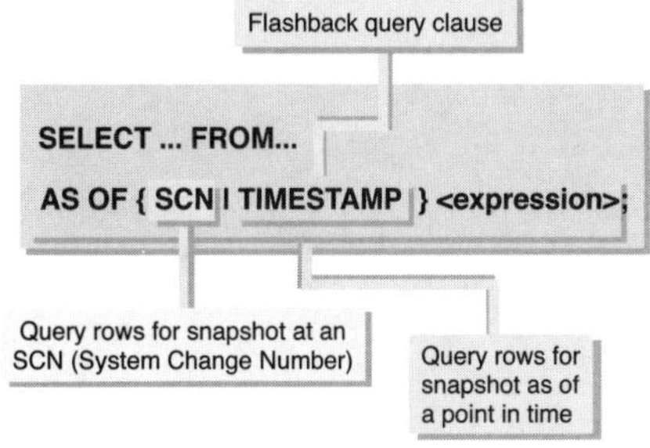

Figure 8.6 Flashback query syntax.

Following is a synopsis of the syntax diagram shown in Figure 8.6:

- A flashback query allows possible access to data as it was at a specified point in time.

- Flashback queries can be executed back to a point in time using a TIMESTAMP or back to an SCN (System Change Number). An SCN is a sequential number automatically allocated to and stamped onto each database change as it is made.

For more information on Flashback Queries, refer to *Oracle SQL Jumpstart with Examples*, ISBN: 1555583237. Authors: Gavin Powell and Carol McCullough-Dieter.

For example, the following query will read the MOVIE table as of 10 days ago. If the table definition has been altered, an error will be returned:

```
SELECT * FROM MOVIE AS OF TIMESTAMP(SYSTIMESTAMP - INTERVAL '10' DAY);
```

Flashback queries require automatic undo configuration and will not function if your database uses manual rollback.

Some specialized queries shown here are out of scope, but you might want to be sure to remember some detail for composite and hierarchical queries.

Exam Prep Questions

1. Where is the **LEVEL** pseudocolumn used? Select the best answer.

   ❑ A. In subqueries

   ❑ B. In the **WITH** clause

   ❑ C. In the **GROUP BY** clause

   ❑ D. In hierarchical queries

   ❑ E. None of the above

   The answer is D. The **LEVEL** pseudocolumn is not used anywhere but in hierarchical queries.

2. What does the **START WITH** clause in a hierarchical query do?

   ❑ A. Forces return of the hierarchy from the root node

   ❑ B. Forces return of the hierarchy from a specified node

   ❑ C. Connects parent and child rows

   ❑ D. Connects child and parent rows

   ❑ E. All of the above

   B is correct. **START WITH** allows the hierarchy to be created from a node within the hierarchical tree to begin a depth-first search from. A hierarchical data structure creates an upside-down treelike structure with multiple branches and leaves. A depth-first search traverses the tree from the root downward to the deepest level first, then proceeding back upward to the next branch and searching downward again, until the entire tree is traversed. A breadth-first search finds all nodes on a given level within the hierarchy before proceeding down to the next level in the tree. Answer A is correct only if the root node is specified. The root node is not '' or **NULL**. C and D relate to the **CONNECT BY** clause and the **PRIOR** operator. As a result, E is most certainly incorrect.

3. What is the difference between these two queries?

   ```
   SELECT GENRE_ID, GENRE, LEVEL, PARENT_ID FROM GENRE
   START WITH GENRE = 'Action' CONNECT BY PRIOR GENRE_ID = PARENT_ID
   ORDER BY 1, 2;

   SELECT GENRE_ID, GENRE, LEVEL, PARENT_ID FROM GENRE
   START WITH GENRE = 'Action' CONNECT BY PARENT_ID = PRIOR GENRE_ID
   ORDER BY 1, 2;
   ```

   ❑ A. There is a difference between the code of the two queries and the result will be different.

   ❑ B. There is a difference between the code of the two queries but the result will be the same.

   ❑ C. The **CONNECT BY** clauses are identical.

- ❑ D. A and C.
- ❑ E. B and C.

Answer E is correct. There is a coding difference between the two queries, but the result will be the same. The **CONNECT BY** clause in both queries is the same except that the expressions on either side of the equality operator are reversed. The **PRIOR** operator still applies to the **GENRE_ID** column: the parent row.

4. Which of these are types of subqueries?
   - ❑ A. Scalar subquery
   - ❑ B. Single row subquery
   - ❑ C. Multiple row subquery
   - ❑ D. Multiple column subquery
   - ❑ E. Correlated subquery
   - ❑ F. Regular subquery
   - ❑ G. Inline view
   - ❑ H. Nested subquery
   - ❑ I. Composite query
   - ❑ J. Hierarchical query
   - ❑ K. Parallel query
   - ❑ L. Flashback query

   All answers are correct. All of these are valid subquery types.

5. Which of these clauses or SQL code statements cannot contain subqueries?
   - ❑ A. **SELECT**
   - ❑ B. **FROM**
   - ❑ C. **WHERE**
   - ❑ D. **ORDER BY**
   - ❑ E. **INSERT**
   - ❑ F. **UPDATE**
   - ❑ G. **GROUP BY**
   - ❑ H. **CASE** expression
   - ❑ I. **CREATE TABLE**
   - ❑ J. **CREATE VIEW**

   The answer is G. The only clause or statement unable to contain subqueries is the **GROUP BY** clause. All other options allow subqueries. A **SELECT** clause can contain a subquery in the elements-retrieved list. A **FROM** clause subquery is an inline view. An **INSERT VALUES** clause can contain a subquery. An **UPDATE SET** clause can contain a subquery, and so on.

6. What is wrong with this **INSERT** statement, if anything?

```
INSERT INTO STUDIO(STUDIO_ID, STUDIO)
VALUES((SELECT MAX(STUDIO_ID)+1 FROM STUDIO), 'This is a new studio');
```

- ❑ A. The two columns on the first line should be reversed.
- ❑ B. **MAX** should be changed to **MIN**.
- ❑ C. The string should be enclosed in " (double quotes) instead of ' (single quotes).
- ❑ D. **MAX(STUDIO_ID)+1** should be changed to **MAX(STUDIO_ID)-1**.
- ❑ E. None of the above.

The answer has to be E. Reversing the two columns will cause two datatype errors. Using **MIN** instead of **MAX** will probably cause a duplication error on a unique primary key, and the same applies to D. There is an aesthetic error in that **MAX(STUDIO_ID)+1** should be replaced with a sequence such as **STUDIO_SEQ.NEXTVAL**.

7. The **MOVIE_ID** column is of datatype **NUMBER**. How could this query be repaired?

```
SELECT TO_CHAR(MOVIE_ID), TITLE FROM MOVIE
UNION
SELECT MOVIE_ID, NULL FROM RECOGNITION;
```

- ❑ A. Change the **UNION** set operator to a **UNION ALL** set operator.
- ❑ B. Change the **UNION** set operator to an **INTERSECT OR MINUS** set operator.
- ❑ C. The **TO_CHAR** function can be removed.
- ❑ D. The **NULL** command can be removed.
- ❑ E. The **MOVIE_ID** column in the second query should be of the form **TO_NUMBER(MOVIE_ID)**.

Answer C is correct. The **UNION** set operator expects columns retrieved to be of identical datatypes, with the same column order between the two concatenated queries. **TO_CHAR(MOVIE_ID)** is a string datatype (**CHAR** or **VARCHAR2**), and **MOVIE_ID** is a **NUMBER** datatype. C will resolve the datatype compatibility error.

8. Two tables are concatenated using a set operator. Both tables have rows. Some rows exist in both tables, and both tables have rows not present in the other. Which set operator will retrieve the most rows when concatenating all rows in both tables?

- ❑ A. **UNION**
- ❑ B. **DISTINCT**
- ❑ C. **UNION ALL**
- ❑ D. **INTERSECT**
- ❑ E. **MINUS**

C is correct. Why? **UNION** finds all distinct rows in both, certainly more than **INTERSECT** (some rows, not all) or **MINUS** (some rows, not all). Regardless of those facts, because some rows exist in both tables, there are duplicates. Thus, nothing will retrieve more rows than **UNION ALL**. **UNION ALL** does the same as **UNION** except that it also returns additional duplicate rows. B is incorrect because it is not a set operator. Answer A will find all **DISTINCT** rows in both (some rows exist in both tables). D will find rows in both (some rows exist in both tables). E will find rows only in either table (both tables have rows not present in the other). A, B, and D are also incorrect.

9. Why will this query produce an error? Assume that there is more than one row in the **MOVIE** table.

```
SELECT MPAA, RATING FROM RATING WHERE RATING_ID =
    (SELECT RATING_ID FROM MOVIE);
```

- ❑ A. Equality allows more than one row to be returned from a subquery.
- ❑ B. The subquery will return many rows containing a single value.
- ❑ C. The subquery will return a single value in a single row.
- ❑ D. All of the above.
- ❑ E. None of the above.

Answer B is correct. The subquery returns more than a single row. Equality can only be validated against a single scalar value. You cannot ask whether something is equal to more than one different thing at the same—it is mathematically impossible. The **WHERE** clause using an equality operator (=) can validate against only one row; otherwise, an error results. The **MOVIE** table has more than one row and thus the calling query fails. The subquery on the **MOVIE** table must be a scalar subquery. It is not; it is a multiple row subquery (retrieves more than single value).

10. How many columns will this query retrieve, given the fact that the **MOVIE** table has 13 columns and the **RATING** table has 4 columns?

```
SELECT *
FROM MOVIE M ,(SELECT RATING_ID, MPAA, RATING FROM RATING) R
WHERE M.RATING_ID = R.RATING_ID;
```

The answer is 17, the sum of the columns in the two tables. **SELECT *** retrieves rows for all available columns from both the **MOVIE** table and the inline view created from the **RATING** table.

SQL*Plus Formatting

Terms You Need to Understand

- ✓ Environmental settings
- ✓ Scripting
- ✓ Variable substitution
- ✓ Session
- ✓ **&**, **&&**, **DEFINE**, and **UNDEFINE**
- ✓ **@**, **@@**, **RUN**, and **START**
- ✓ **COLUMN**

Concepts You Need to Master

- ✓ Environmental settings are set for each execution of a SQL*Plus program
- ✓ Reconnecting within SQL*Plus does not reinitialize environmental settings
- ✓ Set environment variables with the **SET** command
- ✓ Creating scripts in SQL*Plus
- ✓ Editing scripts in SQL*Plus
- ✓ Executing scripts in SQL*Plus
- ✓ Variable substitution in SQL*Plus
- ✓ Formatting using the **COLUMN** command
- ✓ Differences between SQL*Plus and iSQL*Plus

This chapter covers advanced formatting using SQL*Plus tools for database administrators, developers, and report writers. There are several SQL*Plus tools, as seen in the following list:

- SQL*Plus (for Windows)
- SQL*Plus Worksheet (part of Oracle Enterprise Manager)
- A command-line version of SQL*Plus
- 9i iSQL*Plus or "Internet SQL*Plus" allowing execution of SQL commands from within a browser

The various aspects of using the SQL*Plus tools include environmental settings, scripting, variable substitution, formatting, and finally a discussion of the 9i iSQL*Plus tool.

Environmental Settings

An environmental setting allows a connected SQL*Plus instance to be formatted in a specific manner. SQL*Plus environmental settings are set for each instantiation of a SQL*Plus execution and not the duration of a session, unless otherwise altered within that session. The following subsections will give you more detail on the SQL*Plus environmental settings you should be familiar with for the exam.

An *instance* or *instantiation* of SQL*Plus is an execution of the SQL*Plus executable program. Disconnecting from a session within a running instance of SQL*Plus and reconnecting to the same username or even a different username will not reinitialize environmental settings.

A default environment can be built for any SQL*Plus session on a specific computer by adding SQL*Plus **SET** commands to the **GLOGIN.SQL** configuration file in the **$ORACLE_HOME/sqlplus/admin** directory.

The SHOW Command

First, if you need to see the environmental settings of a current session, use the SHOW command, and this will display any environmental settings currently in use. The following snippet shows you the syntax for the SHOW command:

```
SHOW { <variable> | ALL }
```

To display all environmental settings for a session, type the following command into SQL*Plus:

```
SHOW ALL
```

There also may be instances in which you want to see only one or two variables rather than all. For example, to display a single environmental variable, such as the number of lines on a page, you can use something like the following commands:

```
SHOW LINESIZE
SHOW LINES PAGES
```

Remember that environmental settings can be displayed on the screen using the SHOW command. The SET command is used to set or change these same environmental settings. This leads us into the next section covering the SET command and more detail on environmental settings.

The SET Command

If you want to change an environmental setting, use the SET command, as in the following syntax:

```
SET { <variable> <value> }
```

The following example will set the LINESIZE value or line width to 132 characters:

```
SET LINESIZE 132
```

Some environmental settings contain multiple settings and can be fairly complex. Additionally, there are around 60 environmental settings available within SQL*Plus.

Most of the environmental settings have shorthand versions, which are sometimes as little as three characters. For example, the syntax for the number of lines on a single page can be any of the following:

```
SET LINESIZE <n>

SET LIN <n>

SET LINES <n>
```

It is not necessary to end a SQL*Plus environmental setting or other command with a semicolon.

The Syntax of Environmental Settings

Many of the SQL*Plus environmental settings are useful for general DBA and development work. However, with the advent of sophisticated graphical reporting tools, many of the more sophisticated settings are seldom used on a day-to-day basis. Some of the more useful environmental settings are given in the following bulleted list. These settings are listed in descending order of usefulness, in relation to what I have used often, working as both a DBA and a developer.

Many of these environmental settings may appear in an exam. There are many more environmental settings available. It is advisable to read up on details on environmental settings in Oracle documentation before taking the exam.

All SQL*Plus environmental settings are initially set to default values. Environmental setting default values can be overridden using the **SET** command or by entries made in the **GLOGIN.SQL** SQL*Plus configuration file.

- `SET WRA[P] { ON | OFF }`—Text can be wrapped to a new line when exceeding the `LINESIZE` specification. Multiple lines of text on the screen can be difficult to read, so I prefer to use `SET WRAP OFF`.
- `SET LIN[ESIZE] <n>`—This setting changes the width of lines across the page. The default value for SQL*Plus is 80 characters and for SQL*Plus Worksheet is 1024 characters. I usually set this value along with `SET WRAP OFF` in my `GLOGIN.SQL` SQL*Plus configuration file. There are a multitude of default installation settings in the `GLOGIN.SQL` SQL*Plus configuration file. For the purpose of making my use of SQL*Plus easier, I usually add the following line to the end of my `GLOGIN.SQL` file:

  ```
  set wrap off linesize 132
  ```

  Uppercase is most commonly used, but the case of letters is irrelevant to function.

GLOGIN.SQL settings are instantiated with every new execution of SQL*Plus and not for each new session creation from within an already-running SQL*Plus program. Session creation is connecting to a database. You can connect to a database from within an already existing SQL*Plus executable program without shutting down and restarting the SQL*Plus executable. In this case **GLOGIN.SQL** settings will not be re-instantiated. For example, your **GLOGIN.SQL** file contains an entry **SET LINESIZE 132**. When you start SQL*Plus for the first time, **LINESIZE** (width of the line) is set to 132 characters by the entry in the **GLOGIN.SQL** file. You change the line size to 80 characters by executing the command **SET LINESIZE 80**. The line size will subsequently be set to 80 characters as long as that SQL*Plus executable program is not shut down. Even if you reconnect inside the same SQL*Plus program using **CONNECT <anotheruser>/<password>**, the **SET LINESIZE 132** command in the **GLOGIN.SQL** file is not re-executed. Thus, the line size still remains 80 characters, not 132 characters—unless, of course, another manual change is made, such as **SET LINESIZE 40**. This will change the line size to 40 characters.

Arbitrarily changing environmental settings in **GLOGIN.SQL** SQL*Plus configuration can cause problems if the client machine is shared or on a server utilized by multiple administrators.

- `SET PAGES[IZE] <n>`—The size of a page determines the number of lines between page breaks. Headers are included in the page line count. The default value is 14 lines.

Be aware that the **SET PAGES <n>** command cannot be entered as **SET PAG <n>.**

- `SET TIMI[NG] { ON | OFF }`—This setting displays an elapsed time for the execution of an executed command such as a query. `SET TIMING ON` is useful when you're doing timing tests for performance tuning of SQL code.
- `SET SERVEROUT[PUT] { ON | OFF } <other beyond scope elements>`—The `SET SERVEROUTPUT ON` command allows echoing to the screen of output from the `DBMS_OUTPUT.PUT_LINE` procedure, useful for tracing of PL/SQL procedures. There is a buffer limit or default size limitation of 2000 characters over which an error will be returned. Use the`DBMS_OUTPUT.ENABLE(1000000)` procedure to set the buffer to maximum value. Executing `DBMS_OUTPUT.DISABLE` after completion of testing frees the 1,000,000-byte buffer for other use. The syntax `<other beyond scope elements>` implies that there are other options for this command but they are out of the scope of this book. This clause simply tells you that there are other options and that they were not simply ignored.
- `SET HEA[DING] { ON | OFF }`—This setting switches display of column headings on and off.

Setting the page length to **0** using **SET PAGES 0** also executes the command **SET HEADING OFF**. A zero-sized page returns rows with no headings.

- `SET FEED[BACK] { ON | OFF }`—The command `SET FEEDBACK OFF` suppresses the *n* `Rows Returned` message at the end of the execution of a query. This can be useful when executing scripts that execute other embedded scripts, reducing error output generated by non-executable lines. In other words, the line `55 Rows Returned` is not an executable command in SQL*Plus and will throw an error if generated into an executable script.
- `SET NULL <string>`—This setting replaces any `NULL`s returned by queries with a specified string, for instance when executing outer join queries (see Chapter 6). The following `SET NULL <string>` variations are worth remembering:
  - `SET NULL`—Causes an error.
  - `SET NULL ''`—Resets the replacement value with `NULL`.
  - `SET NULL <string>`—Replaces any `NULL` column values in a query with the word `<string>`.
  - `SET NULL 'this is a string'`—Replaces any `NULL` column values with the string `this is a string`.
  - `SET NULL this is a string`—This setting command causes an error because there are multiple values.

  The `NVL` and `NVL2` functions can be used to replace `NULL` values with queries for specific columns (see Chapter 5). The `SET NULL <string>` command in SQL*Plus applies to entire queries.
- `SET ESC[APE] { ON | OFF | \<c> }`—Various characters such as the backslash character (`\`, the default) are used to execute commands in SQL*Plus. As for many programming or scripting languages, an escape character is sometimes required to allow non-interpretation of those specific characters.
- `SET SQLP[ROMPT] { <string> | SQL> }`—This setting will change the prompt in SQL*Plus. This command is useful when writing scripts executing other scripts.
- `SET NUMW[IDTH] <width>` and `SET NUMF[ORMAT] <format>`—These settings will apply default width and formatting (see Chapter 5) settings.

- SET CMDS[EP] { ON | OFF | <c>} and SET COLSEP { <string> | }—CMDSEP can be used to change the command separator, defaulted to a semicolon (;). COLSEP is defaulted to a space character and can be used to change to a different character between output columns for every row in a query.
- SET RECSEP {WR[APPED]|EA[CH]|OFF} and SET RECSEPCHAR { <c> | }—RECSEP places a separator character between each output line of queries. WRAPPED applies to wrapped lines only and EACH to every line, generating the record separator between every line of output. RECSEPCHAR can be used to replace the default space character.
- SET TERM[OUT] { ON | OFF }—SET TERMOUT OFF will not echo executed commands when executing those SQL*Plus commands within a script.
- SET PAU[SE] { ON | OFF | <string> }—A pause halts execution of SQL*Plus on page breaks and awaits user response, much like an operating system MORE command.
- SET LONG <n>—This command is essential for displaying output stored in LONG and CLOB datatypes, often useful for displaying XML documents stored in the database. XML is out of scope for this book, but without setting this value to something such as SET LONG 2000, XML document display is useless in SQL*Plus. For XML in Oracle SQL, see my book *Oracle SQL Jumpstart with Examples*, ISBN: 1555583237. Authors: Gavin Powell and Carol McCullough-Dieter.

Here is a sample script using various SET command settings. This script can be executed from within SQL*Plus, executing a contained generated script:

```
SET TERMOUT OFF ECHO OFF FEED OFF TRIMSPOOL ON HEAD OFF PAGES 0;
SPOOL C:\TEMP\COUNT.LOG;
COLUMN TABLE_NAME FORMAT A16;
SELECT 'SELECT '''||TABLE_NAME||''','', TRIM(COUNT(*)) FROM '
    ||TABLE_NAME||';'
FROM   USER_TABLES;
SPOOL OFF;
SET TERMOUT ON;
@C:\TEMP\COUNT.LOG;
SET TERMOUT ON ECHO ON FEED ON TRIMSPOOL OFF HEAD ON PAGES 40;
```

Instantiating the default editor from SQL*Plus using the EDIT command allows entry and storing of this script using the SQL*Plus SAVE command. However, most editors allow saving of scripts from within the editor.

The command **SPOOL ON** will open an output spool file, and the command **SPOOL OFF** will close the currently open output spool file.

The output of the intermediate script is as follows:

```
SELECT 'ACTOR,', TRIM(COUNT(*)) FROM ACTOR;
SELECT 'AWARD,', TRIM(COUNT(*)) FROM AWARD;
SELECT 'COUNTRY,', TRIM(COUNT(*)) FROM COUNTRY;
...
SELECT 'SOURCE,', TRIM(COUNT(*)) FROM SOURCE;
SELECT 'STUDIO,', TRIM(COUNT(*)) FROM STUDIO;
```

Figure 9.1 shows part of the final output for the preceding table rows counting script.

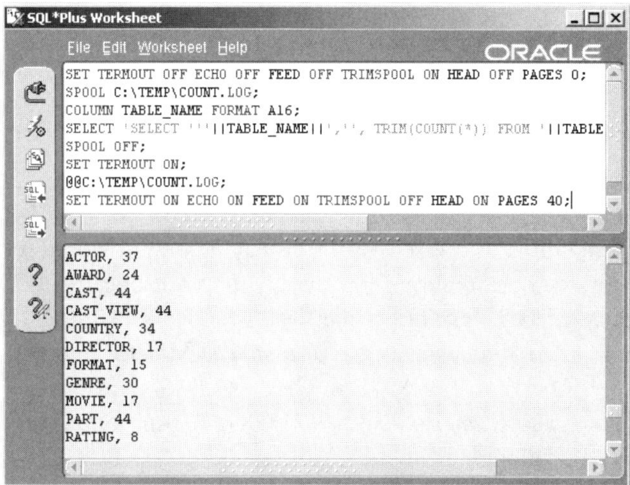

Figure 9.1 Using SQL*Plus environmental settings.

The script that generated the output shown in Figure 9.1 used various SQL*Plus environmental settings.

Scripts and Variable Substitution

This section examines scripting, namely editing and executing scripts in SQL*Plus, and then provides details on variable substitution. Variable substitution is quite literally as the term describes. Variables are used as substitutes for literal values, expecting values to be plugged into those variables.

Scripting in SQL*Plus

As you saw in the preceding section, the `SPOOL` command was used to open and close an output file. You can also edit commands currently contained in the SQL*Plus buffer using the `EDIT` command or editing menu options in the various SQL*Plus tools. You can edit a script using the EDIT command as shown here:

```
EDIT [ <script> ][;]
```

Both the <script> variable and the semicolon are optional, and the default filename is afiedt.buf. When executing SQL*Plus for Windows on a Windows box, the SQL*Plus program is usually executed from an icon. The default icon created during Oracle installation has its working directory set to the $ORACLE_HOME\bin directory. In a Unix environment the SQL*Plus Windows executable file may be initiated from a shell, and could be initiated (executed) from any path. The afiedt.buf file will be stored in the path from which the SQL*Plus tool was executed, if not the $ORACLE_HOME/bin directory.

There is a line editor built into SQL*Plus. Line editors allow editing of individual lines. Some simple commands are shown here:

- LIST { <n> | ALL } —Lists a single line or all lines in the buffer. For ALL the last line will be the current line; otherwise, line <n> is current.
- DEL { <n> | <n> <n> | * }—Deletes a single line (<n>), a range of lines (<n> <n>), or all lines in the buffer (*).
- INPUT <string>—Adds a line after the current line.

Scripting will be on the exam.

You also need to know how to execute scripts. Scripts can be executed using the START, RUN, @, and @@ commands. The @ command can be used to execute a script. The @@ searches for scripts within the path in which the calling script is located, executing those contained scripts if found within the same path as the initial calling script. The @@ command does not require an explicit path to be specified. The START [<script>] and RUN [<script>] commands also execute scripts. The differences between the @ and @@ commands are best explained by example.

On a Windows box let's say you have two scripts in the C:\TEMP directory:

```
--This file is C:\TEMP\PARENT.SQL
SET SERVEROUTPUT ON FEEDBACK OFF;
EXEC DBMS_OUTPUT.PUT_LINE('Executing PARENT.SQL');
@C:\TEMP\CHILD.SQL
SET SERVEROUTPUT OFF;

--This file is CHILD.SQL.
EXEC DBMS_OUTPUT.PUT_LINE('Executing CHILD.SQL');
```

The preceding scripts will both execute and produce the output shown here:

```
SQL> SET FEEDBACK OFF
SQL>  @C:\TEMP\PARENT.SQL
Executing PARENT.SQL
Executing CHILD.SQL
```

The `PARENT.SQL` script can be changed as shown next to produce the same result, substituting the `@` command and explicit path setting `C:\TEMP\` with the `@@` command:

```
--This file is C:\TEMP\PARENT.SQL
SET SERVEROUTPUT ON;
EXEC DBMS_OUTPUT.PUT_LINE('Executing PARENT.SQL');
@@CHILD.SQL
SET SERVEROUTPUT OFF;
```

Variable Substitution in SQL*Plus

Variables can be created in SQL*Plus and later filled, typically in scripts. As in many other scripting languages, the `&` character (ampersand) is used to represent a variable such that `&1` represents the first variable, `&2` the second, and so on. When parameters are passed into the script, such as in the example shown next, the values are substituted for the variables. Let's break this example down. Let's say you execute SQL*Plus in command-line form, on a Windows box, with a command typed into a shell of the following form:

```
SQLPLUS MOVIES/MOVIES@OLTP @C:\TEMP\GETMOVIES.SQL 10 a
```

The preceding command is passing two parameters, `10` and `a`, into a script called `GETMOVIES.SQL`. Additionally, in a Unix or Linux environment the same command might be something like this (Unix and Linux are case sensitive, Windows is not in this respect):

```
sqlplus MOVIES/MOVIES@OLTP /tmp/GETMOVIES.SQL 10 a
```

This is the content of the `GETMOVIES.SQL` script:

```
SELECT MOVIE_ID, TITLE FROM MOVIES
WHERE MOVIE_ID < &1 AND TITLE LIKE '%&2%';
EXIT;
```

The previously shown shell executed `SQLPLUS` command would replace `&1`, the first parameter, with the value `10`, and `&2`, the second parameter, with the value `a`. The execution process and result are shown in Figure 9.2. The `EXIT` command exits the execution from the command line of the `sqlplus` executable program.

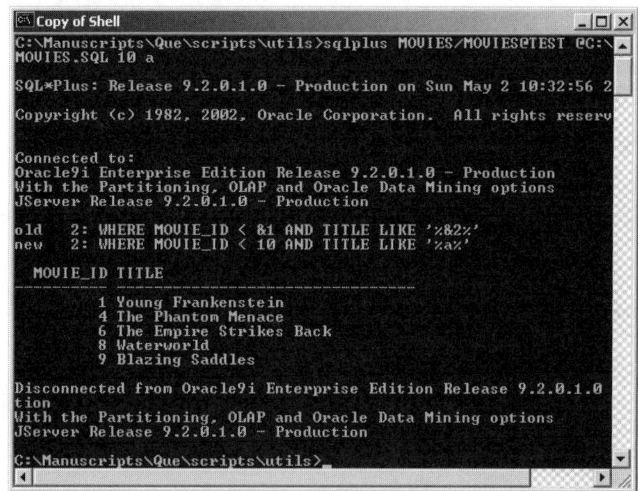

Figure 9.2 Variable substitution in SQL*Plus.

Figure 9.2 shows that the parameters `10` and `a` are substituted into the variables `&1` and `&2`, respectively.

The DEFINE Command

The DEFINE [<variable>[=<string>]] command is another variable substitution command that can be used within a script to create a named variable and even assign a value to it, as shown in the following script:

```
DEFINE MOVIE=10
SELECT MOVIE_ID, TITLE FROM MOVIES
WHERE MOVIE_ID < &MOVIE AND TITLE LIKE '%&2%';
```

Executing the command `DEFINE` without any parameters displays all current variables created using the `DEFINE` command. Examine Figure 9.3.

In Figure 9.3 the `&MOVIE` variable is substituted with the defined value `10`, and the variable `&2` in `'%$2%'` is substituted with the user entry of the letter *i*. The following command is not included in the script in Figure 9.3 but could be used in that script to change the prompt:

```
ACCEPT MOVIE PROMPT 'Movie ID Range?'
```

The UNDEFINE Command

The UNDEFINE <variable> [, ...] command can be used to remove one or more defined variables from the buffer. The command `UNDEFINE` does nothing.

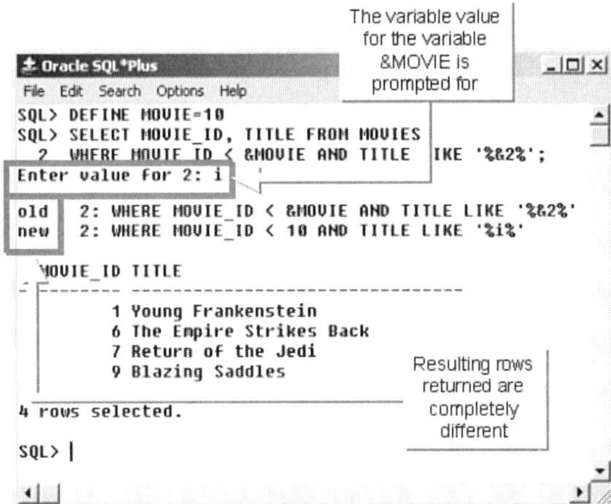

Figure 9.3 Variable substitution in SQL*Plus on-the-fly.

Variable substitution will be on the exam.

Formatting for Readability

Other than formatting of individual column values (see Chapter 5, "Single Row Functions"), entire queries can have specific formats applied to them on a query-by-query basis. Various SQL*Plus commands can be included in this section. You will briefly examine the `COLUMN`, `REPHEADER`, `REPFOOTER`, `TTITLE`, `BTITLE`, `BREAK`, and `COMPUTE` commands.

The COLUMN command will be on the exam. Other commands discussed in this section may be on the exam, but it is unlikely because modern reporting tools are sophisticated to the point of making report generation in SQL*Plus unusual.

Column Formatting and Headings

The `COLUMN` command allows alteration of the output format for columns returned by a query. Figure 9.4 shows the syntax for the `COLUMN` formatting command.

Remember that the **COLUMN** command can apply to all values in a column within a query, and any other column with the same name. The exceptions are the **COLUMN HEADING** command and related options.

Figure 9.4 shows numerous options available for formatting columns and column headings.

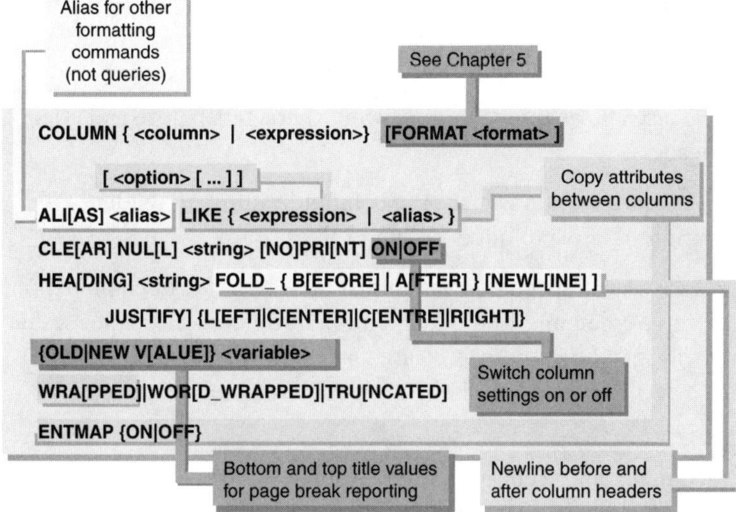

Figure 9.4 Formatting columns with the **COLUMN** command.

Following is a synopsis of the syntax diagram shown in Figure 9.4:

- The FORMAT clause applies a format to a column, named

  ```
  COLUMN FEATURE FORMAT A32
  SELECT TITLE AS FEATURE FROM MOVIE;
  ```

  or otherwise:

  ```
  COLUMN TITLE FORMAT A16
  SELECT TITLE FROM MOVIE;
  ```

  See Chapter 5, “Single Row Functions,” for more details on formatting for different datatypes.

- The ALIAS clause is used to assign an alias to a column. The alias can be referred to by other COLUMN commands, plus the BREAK and COMPUTE commands.

- The LIKE clause repeats settings for another COLUMN command into the current COLUMN command.

- The `CLEAR` clause sets column settings back to default values. The command `CLEAR COLUMNS` clears all current `COLUMN` command settings back to default values.
- Executing the command `COLUMN <column> NOPRINT` removes the column from subsequent query row results. The `PRINT` clause includes the column again.
- `COLUMN <column> HEADING ["]<string>["]` changes the column heading for subsequent queries. The `"` (double quotes) are optional, only to be used for column headings containing spaces (more than a single word, for example, `"Discount %"` in Figure 9.5).
- The `FOLD` clause allows insertion of newline characters before and after column headers.
- The various `JUSTIFY` options place the column heading on the left, center, or right relative to query column values.
- The `NEW_VALUE` clause specifies a variable in page headers, in combination with the `TTITLE` command (top of page title); in other words, a new value for the new page. The `OLD_VALUE` clause applies to the bottom of the page, the `BTITLE` command, and obviously the last value on the current page.
- Various wrapping and truncation options apply by wrapping and truncation to various types of characters and datatypes.
- The `ENTMAP` clause allows for HTML and not literal interpretation of special HTML characters such as the tag delimiters `<` and `>`. Refer to the following URL for details on HTML:

  http://www.oracledbaexpert.com/menu/HTML.html

Figure 9.5 shows various examples of the use of the `COLUMN` command. This is the query in Figure 9.5:

```
COLUMN MOVIE FORMAT A24 HEADING Movie JUSTIFY CENTER
COLUMN REGION FORMAT A16 HEADING Region
COLUMN COUNTRY FORMAT A16 HEADING Country
COLUMN SUM(S.SALE_PRICE) FORMAT $9,990 HEADING Revenue
COLUMN DISCOUNT FORMAT 990.0 HEADING "Discount %"
SELECT M.TITLE AS MOVIE, R.REGION, C.COUNTRY, SUM(S.SALE_PRICE)
    ,AVG(((M.LIST_PRICE-S.SALE_PRICE)/M.LIST_PRICE)*100) AS DISCOUNT
FROM REGION R JOIN COUNTRY C USING(REGION_ID)
    JOIN SALE S USING(COUNTRY_ID)
        JOIN MOVIE M USING(MOVIE_ID)
WHERE R.REGION IN ('Asia', 'North America')
GROUP BY M.TITLE, R.REGION, C.COUNTRY
ORDER BY M.TITLE, R.REGION, C.COUNTRY;
```

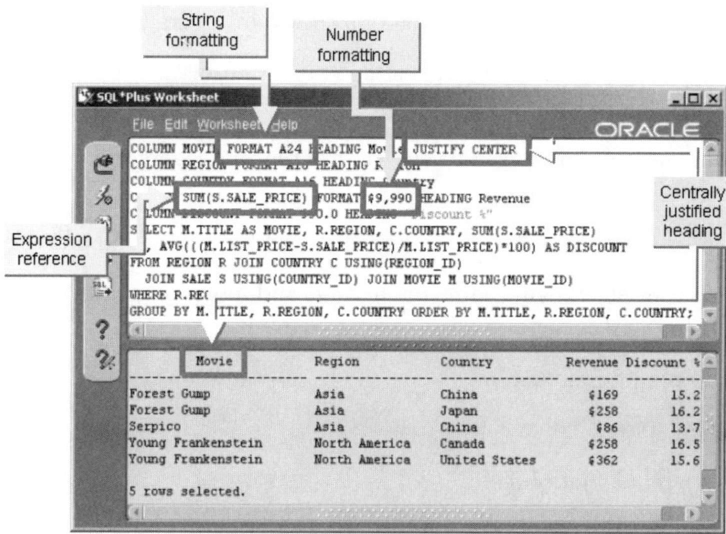

Figure 9.5 The **COLUMN** command in action.

Headers and Footers

Headers and footers can be either report headers and footers or page headers and footers. A page header is repeated for every page of a report. A report header appears once at the start of a report. Similarly, the same applies to page footers and report footers.

Report Headers and Footers

Report headers and footers are controlled by the REPHEADER and REPFOOTER commands. Figure 9.6 shows the syntax for the REPHEADER and REPFOOTER formatting commands.

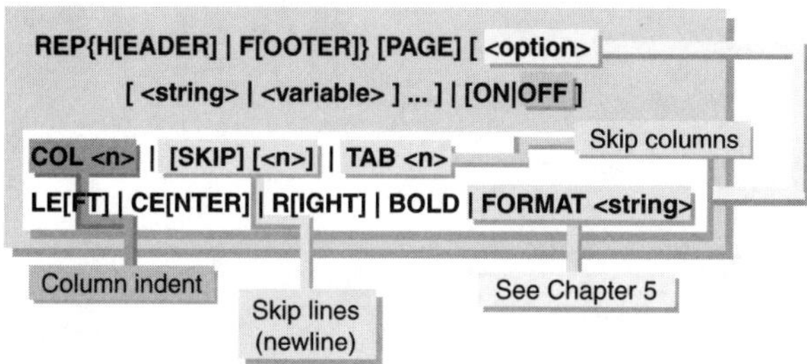

Figure 9.6 Report headers and footers with the **REPHEADER** and **REPFOOTER** commands.

Following is a synopsis of the syntax diagram shown in Figure 9.6:

- The PAGE option ejects an extra page after a report header and before a report footer.
- Strings and variable values can be copied into report headers and footers.
- The ON and OFF options switch report headers and footers on and off.
- Various options all applying to report headers and footers are listed here:
  - COL is a column indentation.
  - SKIP skips lines.
  - TAB is a tab indentation.
  - LEFT, CENTER, and RIGHT are justification rules.
  - BOLD prints in bold font.
  - FORMAT applies formatting parameters and models to text. See Chapter 5 for details on formatting specifications.

Figure 9.7 shows an example of the use of the REPHEADER and REPFOOTER commands. Note the use of the line continuation character in Figure 9.7 when a single-line command is extended onto a following line.

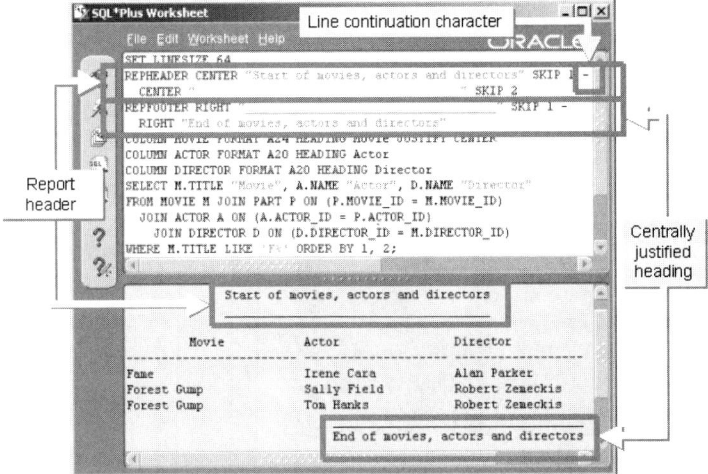

Figure 9.7 The **REPHEADER** and **REPFOOTER** commands in action.

Page Headers and Footers

The TTITLE command creates a title at the top of a page, and the BTITLE command creates a title at the bottom of a page. Unlike the REPHEADER and REPFOOTER commands, which create headings at the start and end of an entire report, the TTITLE and BTITLE commands repeat headers and footers on every page of a report.

Figure 9.8 shows the syntax for the TTITLE and BTITLE formatting commands.

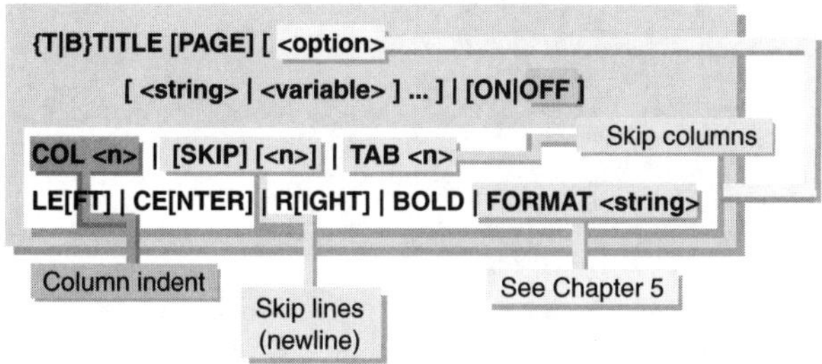

Figure 9.8 Page headers and footers with the **TTITLE** (top of page title) and **BTITLE** (bottom of page title) commands.

A synopsis of the syntax diagram shown in Figure 9.8 is not necessary because the syntactical structure of the TTITLE and BTITLE commands is identical to that of the REPHEADER and REPFOOTER commands. See the synopsis for Figure 9.6 for further details.

Figure 9.9 shows a sample use of the REPHEADER, REPFOOTER, TTITLE, and BTITLE commands. The example in Figure 9.9 is a little abstract but serves to explain the distinct purpose of each of these formatting commands.

Page Breaks and Grouping Computations

Reports or SQL*Plus output can be broken into groups using breaks and subset calculations with the BREAK and COMPUTE commands. Remember that the COMPUTE command is dependent on the use of the BREAK command, establishing break points in a report at which computations are performed.

Figure 9.10 shows the syntax for the BREAK formatting command.

Following is a synopsis of the syntax diagram shown in Figure 9.10:

- The BREAK ON clause specifies a column name or expression on which a repetitive report break point is to be made. Other options are BREAK ROW, executing a break point for every row returned, and BREAK REPORT, allowing the COMPUTE command to control where break points occur.

SQL*Plus Worksheet

File Edit Worksheet Help ORACLE

```
SET LINESIZE 64 PAGESIZE 15
REPHEADER CENTER "Report Header" SKIP 1 CENTER "_______________" SK
TTITLE "Page header"
REPFOOTER RIGHT "_______________" SKIP 1 RIGHT "Report Footer"
BTITLE SKIP 1 CENTER "Page footer"
COLUMN MOVIE FORMAT A24 HEADING Movie JUSTIFY CENTER
COLUMN ACTOR FORMAT A20 HEADING Actor
COLUMN DIRECTOR FORMAT A20 HEADING Director
SELECT M.TITLE "Movie", A.NAME "Actor", D.NAME "Director"
FROM MOVIE M JOIN PART P ON (P.MOVIE_ID = M.MOVIE_ID)
  JOIN ACTOR A ON (A.ACTOR_ID = P.ACTOR_ID)
    JOIN DIRECTOR D ON (D.DIRECTOR_ID = M.DIRECTOR_ID)
WHERE M.TITLE LIKE 'The %' ORDER BY 1, 2;
```

```
Tue May 04                                             page    1
                          Page header

                          Report Header
                          _____________
        Movie            Actor                Director
------------------------ -------------------- ------------------
The Empire Strikes Back  Billy Dee Williams   Irvin Kershner
The Empire Strikes Back  Carrie Fisher        Irvin Kershner
The Empire Strikes Back  Harrison Ford        Irvin Kershner
The Empire Strikes Back  Mark Hamill          Irvin Kershner
The Perfect Storm        Diane Lane           Wolfgang Petersen

                           Page footer

Tue May 04                                             page    2
                          Page header

        Movie            Actor                Director
------------------------ -------------------- ------------------
The Perfect Storm        George Clooney       Wolfgang Petersen
The Perfect Storm        Mark Wahlberg        Wolfgang Petersen
The Phantom Menace       Ewan McGregor        George Lucas
The Phantom Menace       Liam Neeson          George Lucas
                                                  _____________
                                                  Report Footer

                           Page footer
```

Figure 9.9 Report- and page-level header and footer commands in action.

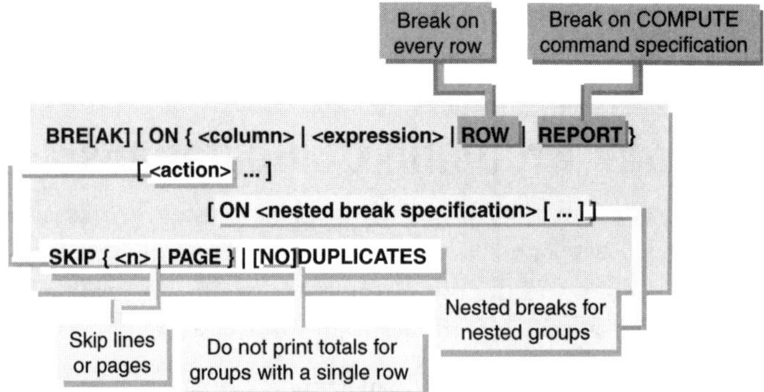

Figure 9.10 Creating explicit reporting subtotals using the **BREAK** command.

➤ Possible actions when a break point occurs are SKIP, allowing skipping of lines or a page, and suppression of duplicate values, for instance, exclusion of subtotals for groups with a single row returned.

➤ BREAK command specifications can be nested depending on the number of available groupings:

```
BREAK ON ... ON ... ON ...
```

Figure 9.11 shows an example of the use of the BREAK command to insert a break into the report whenever the title of the movie changes. Note how movie titles are printed only once. Also note that previous header and footer specifications have been switched off using the REPHEADER OFF, TTITLE OFF, REPFOOTER OFF, and BTITLE OFF commands.

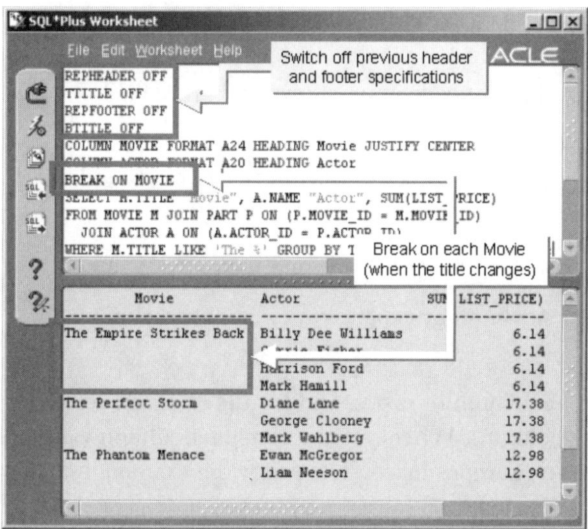

Figure 9.11 The **BREAK** command in action.

Figure 9.12 shows the syntax for the COMPUTE formatting command. The COMPUTE command is used in tandem with the BREAK command because the COMPUTE command requires report break points to function, break points created by the BREAK command.

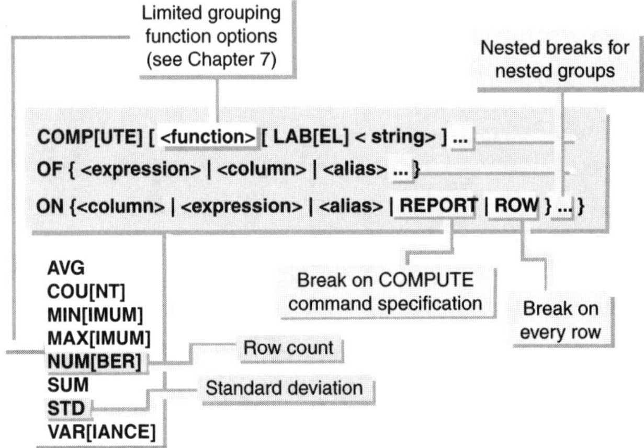

Figure 9.12 Controlling break content using the **COMPUTE** command.

Following is a synopsis of the syntax diagram shown in Figure 9.12:

- Specific functions can be used with the COMPUTE command. These functions are AVG, COUNT, MIN, MAX, NUM (row count), SUM STD (standard deviation), and VAR (variance).
- The LABEL clause prints a text string or label for a computed value.
- The OF clause refers to a column or expression to compute, sum up, average, and so on.
- The ON clause refers to a column or expression for the OF clause to compute by (the grouping column). Whenever the grouping column value changes, the computation is reproduced. The following example returns all SALE table entries with a subtotal for each country:

```
BREAK ON COUNTRY SKIP 1;
COMPUTE SUM LABEL 'Movie Sales' OF SALE_PRICE ON COUNTRY;
SELECT COUNTRY, TITLE, SALE_PRICE FROM COUNTRY
    JOIN SALE USING(COUNTRY_ID)
        JOIN MOVIE USING(MOVIE_ID)
ORDER BY COUNTRY;
```

- Computations with the COMPUTE command can be specified for all nested break points specified with nested breaks declared with the BREAK command.

Figure 9.13 shows a sample use of the BREAK and COMPUTE commands together, including both input query and output results.

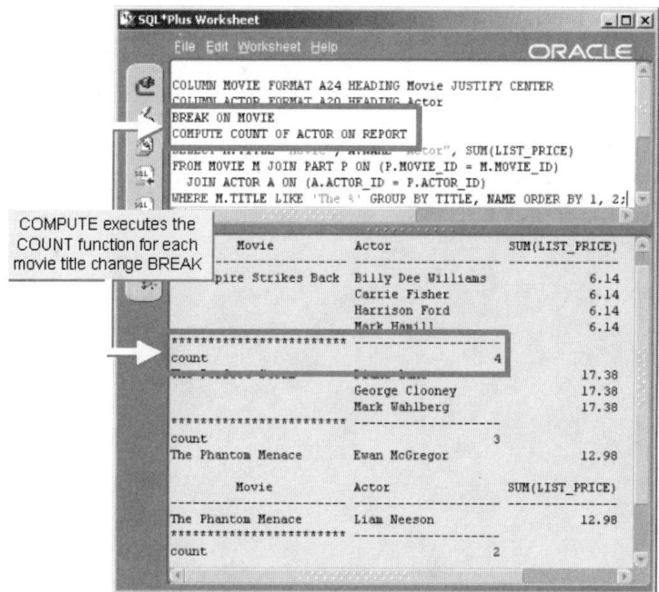

Figure 9.13 The **COMPUTE** and **BREAK** commands in action.

9i iSQL*Plus

iSQL*Plus is a browser executable version of the SQL*Plus tool, namely Internet SQL*Plus. This section is divided into distinct areas covering the differences between SQL*Plus and iSQL*Plus, embedding of SQL*Plus scripts into HTML browser pages, and finally customization of iSQL*Plus display.

Examine the details of the differences between SQL*Plus and iSQL*Plus carefully. Read this information in Oracle documentation as well. It is likely these differences will be questioned in the exam.

Differences Between SQL*Plus and iSQL*Plus

The primary difference between SQL*Plus and iSQL*Plus is basically simple. iSQL*Plus not only runs in a browser but also provides full access into all SQL*Plus engine environmental settings and command structures.

iSQL*Plus is far more user-friendly and graphical in nature than SQL*Plus. Numerous SQL*Plus commands and environmental settings simply do not apply in iSQL*Plus. Additionally, there are some specific SQL*Plus commands excluded from iSQL*Plus due to Internet security issues, or commands used as script editing commands in SQL*Plus. The following list describes some of these commands:

- Environmental settings not applying in iSQL*Plus (`SET <command>`):
  - `EDITFILE`
  - `FLUSH`
  - `NEWPAGE`
  - `PAUSE`
  - `SHIFTINOUT`
  - `SHOWMODE`
  - `SQLBLANKLINES`
  - `SQLCONTINUE`
  - `SQLNUMBER`
  - `SQLPREFIX`
  - `SQLPROMPT`
  - `SUFFIX`
  - `TAB`
  - `TERMOUT`
  - `TIME`
  - `TRIMOUT`
  - `TRIMSPOOL`
- SQL*Plus commands not applying to or not available in iSQL*Plus:
  - `ACCEPT`—This command is simply not available.
  - `CLEAR SCREEN`—iSQL*Plus has a button for this.
  - `PASSWORD`—iSQL*Plus has a password screen.
  - `PAUSE`—This command is simply not available.
- SQL*Plus commands excluded from iSQL*Plus due to security issues:
  - `GET`—iSQL*Plus uses a special script-loading button.

- HOST—The HOST command allows execution of a command in the host machine operating system. You would not want unknown people from remote locations "doing stuff" in your operating system, a serious security issue!
- SPOOL—iSQL*Plus has a preference setting for this option, which is restrictive for security reasons. The SPOOL command allows writing of files to a database server. As with the HOST command, this can be a serious security issue. You simply do not want unknown persons writing "stuff" to your I/O system—viruses and hacking tools and other such nasty little bugs!
- STORE—The STORE command writes session-altered SQL*Plus configurations to a file in the operating system. Any type of writing from a browser to the operating system of a server is a serious breach of security.

Various commands, such as **SET SQLPROMPT,** do not apply in SQL*Plus Worksheet, as well as in iSQL*Plus. SQL*Plus Worksheet does not have a command-line prompt.

HTML Embedded Scripts

iSQL*Plus can execute a SQL script that is embedded in an HTML file. Both the HTML file and the SQL script must be stored on a database or Apache web server machine in the `$ORACLE_HOME/Apache/Apache/htdocs` directory.

This is a simple script placed on the server called `movies.sql`:

```
SELECT MOVIE_ID, TITLE FROM MOVIE WHERE TITLE LIKE '%i%';
```

This is a simple HTML file using a JavaScript function to change the URL as the HTML file loads, instantly loading the iSQL*Plus report into the browser:

```
<HTML>
<HEAD>
<TITLE>Movies</TITLE>
<SCRIPT LANGUAGE="JavaScript">
function loadWin()
{
window.location.href =
"http://2000server:7778/isqlplus?userid=movies/movies@test&script=
➥http://2000server:7778/movies.sql";
}
</SCRIPT>
</HEAD>
<BODY onLoad="loadWin()">
</BODY></HTML>
```

The result of the preceding script is shown in Figure 9.14.

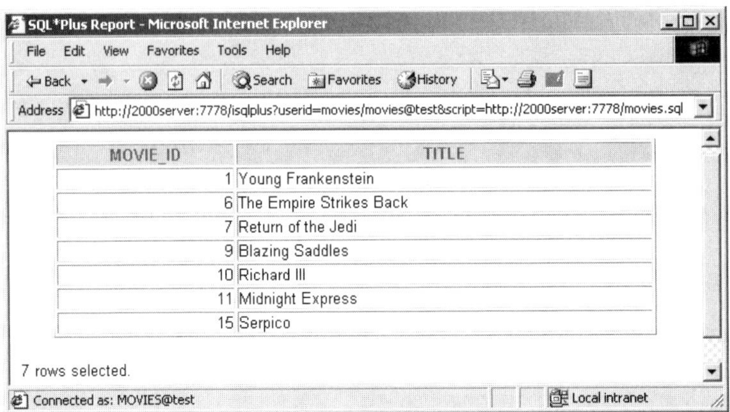

Figure 9.14 Running a query in iSQL*Plus.

With respect to security, it is best to request a username and password when executing iSQL*Plus reports.

Customizing Display

Preferences can be changed to alter the appearance of iSQL*Plus reports from within the GUI. Additionally, there is a Cascading Style Sheet (CSS), which can be used to change the default appearance configuration for all iSQL*Plus query output. Change the CSS file on the server. CSS is part of Dynamic Hypertext Markup Language (DHTML). See the following URL for further detail on the use of DHTML:

http://www.oracledbaexpert.com/menu/DHTML.html

The CSS file is called `iplus.css` and is placed in the `$ORACLE_HOME/sqlplus/admin/iplus` directory on a server machine. I have altered my server CSS file in the following way, and the altered result of the iSQL*Plus in Figure 9.14 is shown in Figure 9.15. The HTML table heading tag (TH) has foreground and background colors changed to white and black, respectively:

```
TH {
        font : bold 10pt Arial, Helvetica, sans-serif;
        color : white;
        background : black;
        padding : 0px 0px 0px 0px;
}
```

I also changed the multiple TABLE, table row (TR), and table cell (TD) tag:

```
TABLE, TR, TD {
        font : 10pt Arial, Helvetica, sans-serif;
        color : Black;
        background : #F0F0F0;
        border : 1
        padding : 1px 1px 1px 1px;
        margin : 1px 1px 1px 1px;
}
```

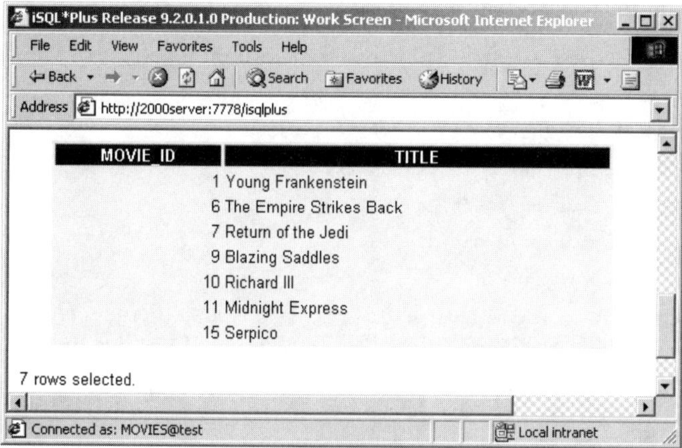

Figure 9.15 Customizing the display of iSQL*Plus queries by changing the CSS configuration.

Exam Prep Questions

1. You execute the SQL*Plus program and connect to a user. Executing the **SHOW LINES** command returns **linesize 80**. You then execute the command **SET LINESIZE 132**, disconnect, and reconnect to a different username. What is **LINESIZE** now?

   There is only one answer and that is 132, because disconnecting and reconnecting will not reset the **LINESIZE** value. Only reexecuting the SQL*Plus program will reset the value of **LINESIZE** to the default value.

2. Where and what is the default SQL*Plus environmental settings configuration file?

   - ❑ A. **$ORACLE_HOME/sqlplus/admin/iplus/iplus.css**
   - ❑ B. **$ORACLE_HOME/sqlplus/admin/glogin.txt**
   - ❑ C. **$ORACLE_HOME/sqlplus/admin/env.sql**
   - ❑ D. **$ORACLE_HOME/sqlplus/admin/glogin.sql**
   - ❑ E. None of the above

   D is the correct answer and thus E is incorrect. A is also incorrect because it is a CSS file for iSQL*Plus display settings. The files listed for B and C do not exist.

3. Which one of these is the odd one out?

   - ❑ A. **SET LINES 80**
   - ❑ B. **SET LIN 85**
   - ❑ C. **SET LINE 94**
   - ❑ D. **SET LINESIZE 132**
   - ❑ E. **SET L 85**

   E is the odd one out and thus E is the correct answer. A, B, C, and D will all change the **LINESIZE** environmental setting for a SQL*Plus session. E will produce an error because **LINESIZE** is entered as only a single character, **L**. In general, environmental settings require entry of at least three characters to set the correct value, as in B.

4. Which methods can be used to switch off column headings in SQL*Plus? Select more than one.

   - ❑ A. **SET HEAD OFF**
   - ❑ B. **SET HEADING OFF**
   - ❑ C. **SET HEADING ON**
   - ❑ D. **SET PAGES 0**
   - ❑ E. A and B

   A, B, D, and E are all correct answers. **SET PAGES 0** removes the page count and removes headers, returning all rows without any pages breaks. C switches headings on so it is incorrect. E is correct as well, because both A and B are the same command.

5. Select the valid methods for executing a SQL*Plus script.
   - ❑ A. **@script.sql**
   - ❑ B. **@@script.sql**
   - ❑ C. **START script**
   - ❑ D. **RUN script.sql**
   - ❑ E. All of the above

   All answers are correct and thus E is the correct answer. Even C is correct because the **.sql** file extension is the default and does not have to be specified.

6. How can a variable be declared in a SQL*Plus script? Select valid answers.
   - ❑ A. **&movie_id**
   - ❑ B. **&&title**
   - ❑ C. ***movie_id**
   - ❑ D. **DEFINE MOVIE_ID**
   - ❑ E. **UNDEFINE MOVIE_ID**

   A, B, and D are correct. Values can be dereferenced from variables in scripts using the **&** and **&&**. The **DEFINE** command allows declaration of a named variable within a script. C is incorrect because an asterisk (*****) is meaningless in SQL*Plus. E is also incorrect because the **UNDEFINE** command is to do the opposite of the **DEFINE** command, uninstantiate or "undeclare" a variable.

7. If I have set headers using the **REPHEADER**, **TTITLE**, **REPFOOTER**, and **BTITLE** commands, how do I switch off those headers?
   - ❑ A. Disconnect and reconnect to the same username
   - ❑ B. Disconnect and reconnect to a different username
   - ❑ C. **REPHEADER OFF**
   - ❑ D. None of the above
   - ❑ E. All of the above

   The correct answer is D. A and B are incorrect because disconnecting and reconnecting changes nothing with respect to headers and footers, both for pages and for an entire query report. C is correct but will turn off only report headers. Switching off other headers and footers requires other commands: **REPFOOTER OFF**, **TTITLE OFF**, and **BTITLE OFF**, all on separate lines. Therefore C is incorrect. E cannot be correct because D is correct.

8. Which of these are valid SQL*Plus commands?
   - ❑ A. **SET NULL**
   - ❑ B. **SET NULL ''**
   - ❑ C. **SET NULL hi there**
   - ❑ D. **SET NULL 'hi there'**
   - ❑ E. All of the above

B and D are correct. A and C are invalid because **SET NULL** requires a setting and the string **hi there** must be enclosed in single quotes (**'hi there'**) as in D in order to be interpreted by the SQL*Plus engine correctly. B is valid, resetting any previous setting to **NULL**. D is correct as already discussed. E is obviously incorrect, because A and C are incorrect.

9. Which of these are valid **COLUMN** commands in SQL*Plus? Select the correct answer.

- ❑ A. **COLUMN MOVIE FORMAT A24 HEADING Movie - JUSTIFY CENTER**
- ❑ B. **COLUMN REGION FORMAT A16 HEADING Region**
- ❑ C. **COLUMN COUNTRY FORMAT A16 HEADING Country**
- ❑ D. **COLUMN SUM(S.SALE_PRICE) FORMAT $9,990 - HEADING Revenue**
- ❑ E. **COLUMN DISCOUNT FORMAT 990.0 HEADING - "Discount %"**
- ❑ F. All of the above

F is the correct answer because A, B, C, D, and E are all valid SQL*Plus commands. The hyphen is a SQL*Plus line continuation character. All answers are syntactically correct.

10. Why are the SQL*Plus **GET**, **HOST**, **SPOOL**, and **STORE** commands excluded from iSQL*Plus command syntax? Answer with a single word.

The answer is *security*. iSQL*Plus executes reports in a browser, potentially over the Internet. Unknown users, anywhere in the world, cannot be allowed to write to the disks of server machines. All these commands communicate directly with the operating system on a server.

Changing Data (DML)

Terms You Need to Understand

- ✓ Data Manipulation Language (DML)
- ✓ Data Definition Language (DDL)
- ✓ **DEFAULT**
- ✓ **INSERT**
- ✓ **UPDATE**
- ✓ **DELETE**
- ✓ **TRUNCATE**
- ✓ **MERGE**
- ✓ Transaction
- ✓ **COMMIT**
- ✓ **ROLLBACK**
- ✓ **SAVEPOINT**

Concepts You Need to Master

- ✓ Single table **INSERT**
- ✓ Multiple table **INSERT**
- ✓ Default values
- ✓ Transactional control
- ✓ Transactions and consistency of data
- ✓ Transactions and DDL commands

This chapter describes how to change data in an Oracle database, concluding with details on transactional control. Transactional control is most important to user concurrency and maintaining consistency of data in a database.

What Is the Difference Between DML and DDL?

Data Manipulation Language (DML) implies manipulation of and changes to data in a database. Changes to a database encompass adding new data plus changing or removing existing data.

New data is added using the INSERT command, changed using the UPDATE command, and removed from the database using the DELETE command. Other similar commands include MERGE (a new command found in 9i) and TRUNCATE. MERGE is a DML command used to both add new data and change existing data in a single table. TRUNCATE is actually a Data Definition Language (DDL) command used to delete all rows from a table at once.

9i A **MERGE** command is sometimes known as an *upsert command* because it updates and inserts rows in a single table concurrently.

Whereas DML commands change data in tables, DDL commands change metadata. *Metadata* is the data about the data or the structures used to contain the data. In other words, whereas DML commands alter data within tables, DDL commands change the structure of the table itself. Whereas DML commands change column and row values, DDL commands change column attributes such as datatype.

One crucial difference between DML and DDL commands is that DDL commands cannot be undone (rolled back). After a DDL command is executed, a ROLLBACK command does not apply. A DML command, once executed, can be undone until a COMMIT command is executed.

The INSERT Command

Recall that the INSERT command is used to add new data to a table. There are three syntactical forms of the INSERT command:

- Insert into a single table, as shown in Figure 10.1.

➤ Insert into one or many tables using a conditional multiple table INSERT command. Conditions determine which of multiple single INSERT commands are executed. Conditional multiple table INSERT commands are shown later in Figure 10.3.

➤ Insert into many tables using a non-conditional multiple table INSERT command. In this case, there are no conditions applied and thus all tables are inserted into, as shown later in Figure 10.4.

Single Table INSERT

A single table INSERT command allows insertion of new rows into a single table. Figure 10.1 shows the syntax for a single table INSERT command.

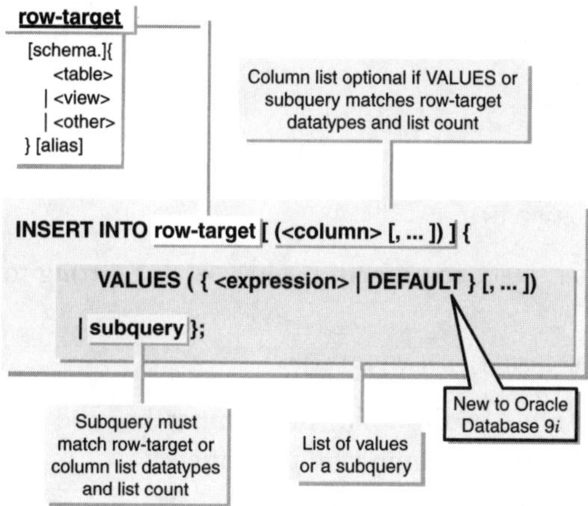

Figure 10.1 Single table **INSERT** command syntax.

Following is a synopsis of the syntax diagram shown in Figure 10.1:

➤ The target object of an INSERT command can be a table or a view, in any schema allowing appropriate access.

➤ The column list is optional if all columns in the table are included in the VALUES clause.

➤ The VALUES clause specifies values to be placed into columns as defined by the column list order. If a column list is not defined, all columns must be placed into the VALUES clause in the order in which they are declared for the table.

➤ 9i Default expressions can be used to replace VALUES clause entries.

- A subquery can replace the VALUES clause as long as the column entry datatypes match those defined by the column list or, if no column list is defined, all columns in the declared order for the table.

9i DEFAULT

As shown in Figure 10.1, new version 9i syntax allows for column DEFAULT value settings. Following are examples of the different forms of the single table INSERT command. This first example does not need to include column names because all columns in the table are included:

```
INSERT INTO ACTOR VALUES(100, 'Mel Gibson', 'M', 'Tough Guy');
```

Specifying the column names allows you to exclude nullable column names or those having default values, or both:

```
INSERT INTO ACTOR(ACTOR_ID,NAME,GENDER) VALUES(101,'Susan Sarandon','F');
```

From there, the ACTOR table looks like this using the DESC ACTOR command:

```
SQL> DESC ACTOR;
 Name                 Null?    Type
 -------------------- -------- ------------
 ACTOR_ID             NOT NULL NUMBER
 NAME                 NOT NULL VARCHAR2(32)
 GENDER               NOT NULL CHAR(1)
 TYPECAST                      VARCHAR2(64)
```

Next, execute the following ALTER TABLE command to add a DEFAULT setting to the GENDER column:

```
ALTER TABLE ACTOR MODIFY (GENDER CHAR(1) DEFAULT 'M');
```

You can now add to the ACTOR table in the following manner because the DEFAULT setting is triggered if the GENDER column is not specified:

```
INSERT INTO ACTOR(ACTOR_ID, NAME) VALUES(102, 'Sean Connery');
```

Figure 10.2 shows the rows added to the ACTOR table with Sean Connery added as being Male and Mel Gibson typecasted as a tough guy.

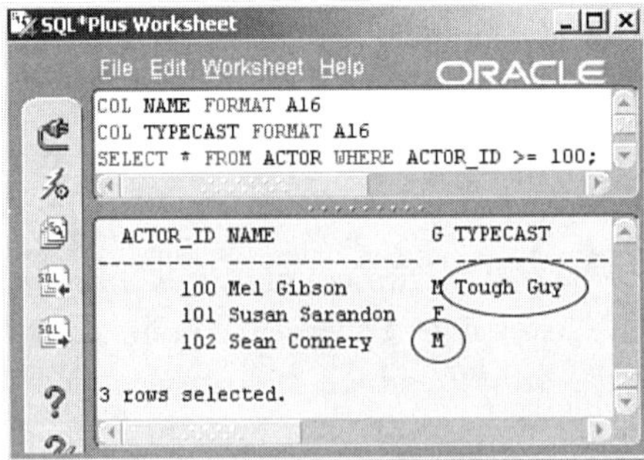

Figure 10.2 Different single table **INSERT** command results.

Multiple Table INSERT

A multiple table `INSERT` command allows insertion into more than a single table with the same `INSERT` command. Multiple table `INSERT` commands fall into two categories. The first is a *conditional multiple table* `INSERT` command, as shown in the syntax diagram in Figure 10.3. The second is a *non-conditional multiple table* `INSERT` command, as shown later in the syntax diagram in Figure 10.4.

Conditional Multiple Table INSERT Command

As described earlier, a conditional multiple table `INSERT` command includes conditions determining which of many single `INSERT` commands are executed. Let's begin with a conditional multiple table `INSERT` command, as shown by the syntax in Figure 10.3.

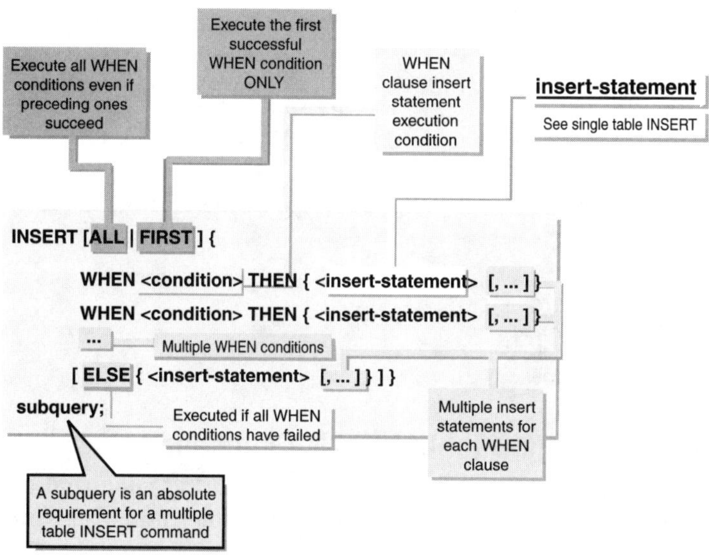

Figure 10.3 Conditional multiple table **INSERT** command syntax.

Following is a synopsis of the syntax diagram shown in Figure 10.3:

- A conditional multiple table `INSERT` command operates on `WHEN` clause conditions. The `ALL` option will execute an `INSERT` command for all successful `WHEN` clause conditions. The `FIRST` option will `INSERT` only for the first successful `WHEN` condition encountered, bypassing all following `WHEN` conditions for a particular row.
- There can be multiple `WHEN` conditions for a given multiple `INSERT` command.

- If all WHEN conditions fail, the ELSE condition will be executed.
- Each WHEN condition and the ELSE clause can have multiple INSERT commands.
- A subquery is required for a multiple INSERT command in order to access rows to be inserted.

Begin by creating three separate sales tables representing sales made in three different years (WHERE ROWNUM < 1 copies the table structure only with no rows copied):

```
CREATE TABLE SALE2003 AS SELECT * FROM SALE WHERE ROWNUM < 1;
CREATE TABLE SALE2004 AS SELECT * FROM SALE WHERE ROWNUM < 1;
CREATE TABLE SALE2005 AS SELECT * FROM SALE WHERE ROWNUM < 1;
```

Now, you distribute the annual rows to the three separate annualized tables. You do not need to specify ALL or FIRST because the nature of the data ensures no duplication across the three separate tables:

```
INSERT
    WHEN TO_CHAR(SALE_DATE, 'YYYY') = '2003' THEN INTO SALE2003
    WHEN TO_CHAR(SALE_DATE, 'YYYY') = '2004' THEN INTO SALE2004
    WHEN TO_CHAR(SALE_DATE, 'YYYY') = '2005' THEN INTO SALE2005
SELECT * FROM SALE;
```

You could verify rows in the source table (SALE) against the separate tables by using queries such as this:

```
SELECT TO_CHAR(SALE_DATE, 'YYYY'), COUNT(TO_CHAR(SALE_DATE, 'YYYY'))
FROM SALE GROUP BY TO_CHAR(SALE_DATE, 'YYYY');
SELECT COUNT(*) FROM SALE2003;
SELECT COUNT(*) FROM SALE2004;
SELECT COUNT(*) FROM SALE2005;
```

Non-Conditional Multiple Table INSERT Command

As you already know, a non-conditional multiple table INSERT command has no conditions and simply inserts rows into multiple tables using the same INSERT command. Now you will examine a non-conditional multiple table INSERT command as shown by the syntax in Figure 10.4.

Following is a synopsis of the syntax diagram shown in Figure 10.4:

- A non-conditional multiple INSERT command will execute all contained INSERT commands.
- A subquery is required for a multiple INSERT command in order to access rows to be inserted.

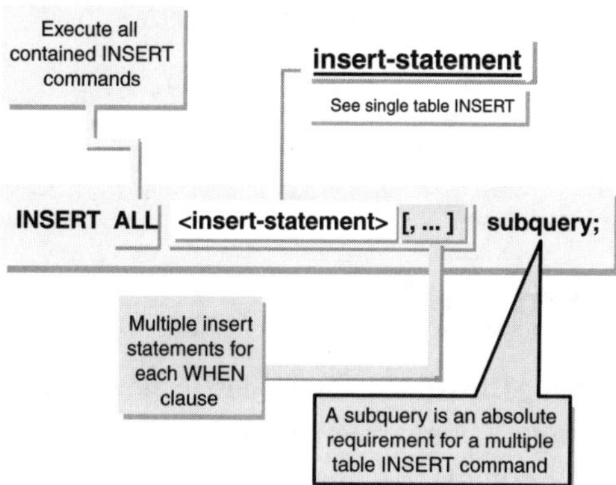

Figure 10.4 Non-conditional multiple table **INSERT** command syntax.

A conditional multiple table INSERT command can be used to spread data into multiple separate tables. On the other hand, a non-conditional multiple table INSERT command can be used to summarize data from multiple tables into a single table. First, you will create a new form of sales table. This new table will contain multiple amount value columns for the three separate years, similar in nature to the conditional multiple table example but in a single table:

```
CREATE TABLE SALES AS SELECT * FROM SALE;
ALTER TABLE SALES ADD (SALE2003 FLOAT, SALE2004 FLOAT, SALE2005 FLOAT);
```

Now you can spread the data from the SALE table into the three separate year columns in the new table:

```
UPDATE SALES SET SALE2003 = SALE_PRICE
WHERE TO_CHAR (SALE_DATE, 'YYYY') = 2003;
UPDATE SALES SET SALE2004 = SALE_PRICE
WHERE TO_CHAR(SALE_DATE, 'YYYY') = 2004;
UPDATE SALES SET SALE2005 = SALE_PRICE
WHERE TO_CHAR(SALE_DATE, 'YYYY') = 2005;
```

Finally, remove the SALE_PRICE column from the new SALES table and remove all the rows from the original SALE dimension table:

```
ALTER TABLE SALES DROP COLUMN SALE_PRICE;
TRUNCATE TABLE SALE;
```

Now you can use a non-conditional INSERT command to put the SALES entries back into the SALE table:

```
INSERT ALL
    INTO SALE(SALE_ID,MOVIE_ID,SOURCE_ID,FORMAT_ID,REGION_ID,COUNTRY_ID
        ,SALE_DATE,SALE_PRICE)
    VALUES(SALE_ID,MOVIE_ID,SOURCE_ID,FORMAT_ID,REGION_ID,COUNTRY_ID
        ,SALE_DATE,SALE2003)
    INTO SALE(SALE_ID,MOVIE_ID,SOURCE_ID,FORMAT_ID,REGION_ID,COUNTRY_ID
        ,SALE_DATE,SALE_PRICE)
    VALUES(SALE_ID,MOVIE_ID,SOURCE_ID,FORMAT_ID,REGION_ID,COUNTRY_ID
        ,SALE_DATE,SALE2004)
```

```
    INTO SALE(SALE_ID,MOVIE_ID,SOURCE_ID,FORMAT_ID,REGION_ID,COUNTRY_ID
        ,SALE_DATE,SALE_PRICE)
    VALUES(SALE_ID,MOVIE_ID,SOURCE_ID,FORMAT_ID,REGION_ID,COUNTRY_ID
        ,SALE_DATE,SALE2005)
SELECT SALE_ID,MOVIE_ID,SOURCE_ID,FORMAT_ID,REGION_ID,COUNTRY_ID
    ,SALE_DATE,SALE2003,SALE2004,SALE2005 FROM SALES;
```

The UPDATE Command

The UPDATE command is used to change existing row values in tables. The UPDATE command can be used to change a single row, multiple rows, or even all the rows in a table with a single command. The syntax for the UPDATE command is shown in Figure 10.5.

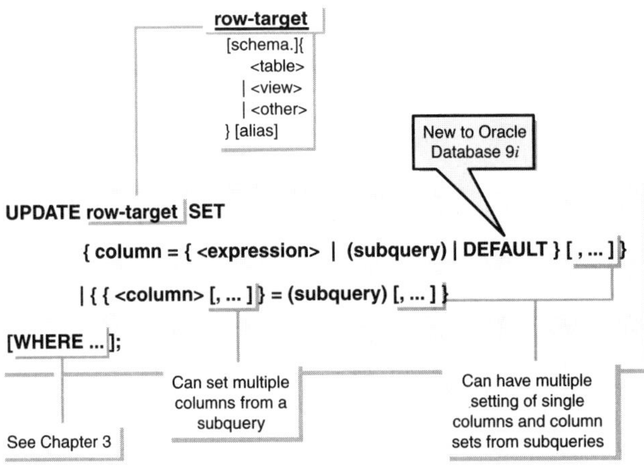

Figure 10.5 **UPDATE** command syntax.

Following is a synopsis of the syntax diagram shown in Figure 10.5:

- The target object of an UPDATE command can be a table or a view, in any schema allowing appropriate access.
- The UPDATE SET clause can consist of one or more column value pair settings.
- Each column value pair sets a column in the target table to an expression. An expression can be a value or even a subquery.
- When subqueries are used, multiple columns can be set at once using a multiple column returning subquery.
- 9i Default expressions can be used to replace column value settings.
- A WHERE clause can be applied to an UPDATE command in order to filter rows being updated, updating some rows and not others.

The INSERT command shown in Figure 10.1 shows new column default syntax (the 9i DEFAULT clause). Similarly, the syntax for the UPDATE command in Figure 10.5 shows that there is new syntax allowing for column DEFAULT value settings with the UPDATE command.

Here are some sample table UPDATE commands. This first example changes a single value in a single row in the STUDIO table:

```
UPDATE STUDIO SET STUDIO = 'Miramax Studios Incorporated'

WHERE STUDIO = 'Miramax Studios';
```

The next example changes some rows in the STUDIO table:

```
UPDATE STUDIO SET STUDIO = LOWER(STUDIO) WHERE STUDIO LIKE '%a%';
```

And this next example changes all rows in the STUDIO table because there is no WHERE clause:

```
UPDATE STUDIO SET STUDIO = INITCAP(STUDIO);
```

You can also do some other interesting things with the UPDATE command. First, you will create a new table by inserting all rows including only the primary key SALE_ID unique row identifier and modifying the new table to allow NULL values for the MOVIE_ID and SALE_DATE columns:

```
CREATE TABLE SALECOPY AS SELECT * FROM SALE WHERE ROWNUM < 1;
ALTER TABLE SALECOPY MODIFY(MOVIE_ID NUMBER NULL, SALE_DATE DATE NULL);
INSERT INTO SALECOPY(SALE_ID) SELECT SALE_ID FROM SALE;
```

Change a single column for all rows in the SALECOPY table using a subquery:

```
UPDATE SALECOPY SC SET SC.MOVIE_ID =
    (SELECT MOVIE_ID FROM SALE WHERE SALE_ID = SC.SALE_ID);
```

Change two columns for all rows, each with a separate subquery, using a single UPDATE command:

```
UPDATE SALECOPY SC SET
     SC.SOURCE_ID = (SELECT SOURCE_ID FROM SALE WHERE SALE_ID = SC.SALE_ID)
    ,SC.FORMAT_ID = (SELECT FORMAT_ID FROM SALE WHERE SALE_ID
            = SC.SALE_ID);
```

Set multiple columns using a single subquery (the columns being set are comma-delimited and parenthesized):

```
UPDATE SALECOPY SC SET
    (SC.REGION_ID, SC.COUNTRY_ID) =
        (SELECT REGION_ID, COUNTRY_ID FROM SALE WHERE SALE_ID = SC.SALE_ID);
```

You can even combine the previous two examples, setting multiple column sets using multiple subqueries:

```
UPDATE SALECOPY SC SET
     (SC.SOURCE_ID, SC.FORMAT_ID) =
        (SELECT SOURCE_ID, FORMAT_ID FROM SALE WHERE SALE_ID = SC.SALE_ID)
    ,(SC.REGION_ID, SC.COUNTRY_ID) =
        (SELECT REGION_ID, COUNTRY_ID FROM SALE WHERE SALE_ID = SC.SALE_ID);
```

The DELETE Command

The DELETE command can be used to remove one row, some rows, or all rows from a table. The DELETE command syntax is shown in Figure 10.6.

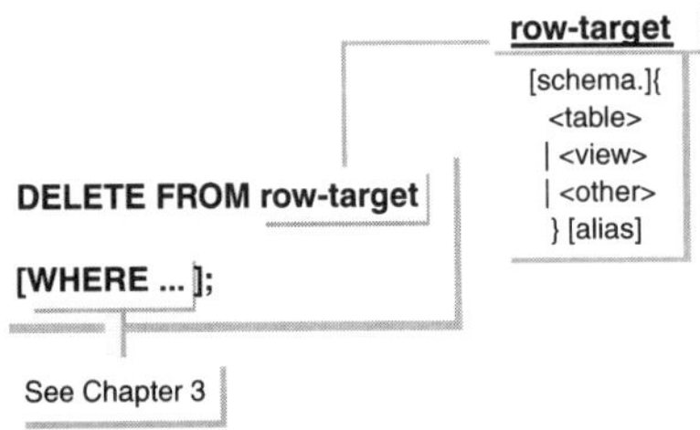

Figure 10.6 DELETE command syntax.

Following is a synopsis of the syntax diagram shown in Figure 10.6:

- The target object of a DELETE command can be a table or a view, in any schema allowing appropriate access.
- A WHERE clause can be applied to a DELETE command in order to filter rows being deleted, deleting some rows and not others.

As shown in Figure 10.6, the DELETE command syntax is extremely simple. You can delete a single row or multiple rows from a table by specifying a WHERE clause filter. When deleting a single row from a table, apply a very explicit filter, finding only a single row. This example deletes a single row from the recently created SALECOPY table:

```
DELETE FROM SALECOPY WHERE SALE_ID = 1;
```

The following command deletes multiple rows from the SALECOPY table by using a filter finding several rows:

```
DELETE FROM SALECOPY WHERE MOVIE_ID < 5;
```

This next command deletes all rows from the SALECOPY table because no WHERE clause is specified:

```
DELETE FROM SALECOPY;
```

The TRUNCATE Command

The purpose of the TRUNCATE command is similar to that of the DELETE command. The TRUNCATE command can be used to remove all rows from a table, much like using a DELETE command that does not have a WHERE clause filter. TRUNCATE command syntax is very simple:

```
TRUNCATE TABLE <table>;
```

The DELETE command is a DML command. The TRUNCATE command is a DDL command. As a result, there are several differences between the DELETE and TRUNCATE commands:

- As already stated, the TRUNCATE command removes all rows from a table, and the DELETE command has the option of removing all rows from a table. In other words, the DELETE command can remove one, many, or all rows from a table. The TRUNCATE command can *only* remove all rows from a table.
- Removal of rows from a table using the TRUNCATE command cannot be rolled back because the TRUNCATE command is a DDL command. A DELETE command removing all rows from a table can be rolled back because the DELETE command is a DML command.
- The TRUNCATE command will execute much faster than a DELETE command, most noticeably for larger tables. The TRUNCATE command is faster because it does not build up rollback entries as the DELETE command does.

Memorize differences between the **TRUNCATE** command and the **DELETE** command. This one is a favorite!

Be careful executing the **TRUNCATE** command because removal of data cannot be recovered within SQL, and not without difficulty and irritation from a DBA by other more complex methods. **DELETE** command removals can be undone, assuming that an explicit or implicit **COMMIT** command has not yet been executed.

9i The MERGE Command

In review, the MERGE command is a DML command used to both add new data and change existing data in a table. Typically, two merged tables are known as the source and target tables. Rows existing in both are updated in the target, from the source. Rows existing only in the source are added to the target table. The syntax for the MERGE command is shown in Figure 10.7.

Following is a synopsis of the syntax diagram shown in Figure 10.7:

- 9i The MERGE command allows merging of rows from two separate tables, commonly known as a source table and a target table. Rows not in the target table are inserted if present in the source table. Rows already in the target table are updated if present in the source table.

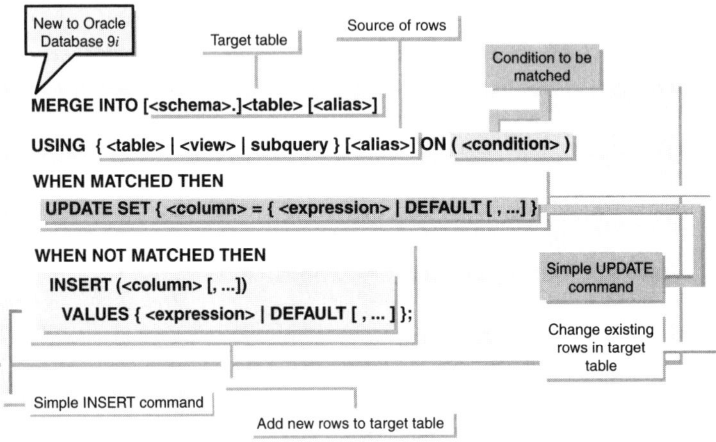

Figure 10.7 **MERGE** command syntax.

- The `USING` clause specifies the source table, view, or subquery. The source table contains changes to be merged into the target table, either insertions of new rows or updates to existing rows.
- The `ON` clause specifies a condition matching rows between source and target tables, such as equal column values in both tables.
- If the `ON` clause match succeeds between the two tables, the `WHEN MATCHED` clause is executed, updating row values from source to target table.
- If the `ON` clause match fails between the two tables then the `WHEN NOT_MATCHED` clause is executed, insert a new row into the target table from the source table.

You could use the `MERGE` command to merge the contents of our `SALE` data warehouse table with a table containing daily sales records with the structure:

```
SQL> DESC DAILYSALES
 Name                  Null?    Type
 ----------------- -------- -----------
 MOVIE_ID              NOT NULL NUMBER
 SOURCE_ID                      NUMBER
 FORMAT_ID                      NUMBER
 REGION_ID                      NUMBER
 COUNTRY_ID                     NUMBER
 AMOUNT                         FLOAT(126)
 DTE                            DATE
```

You can create the `DAILYSALES` table with the following command (the data added from the main `SALE` table is bogus because of the nature of the data, but it is functional):

```
CREATE TABLE DAILYSALES AS SELECT MOVIE_ID,SOURCE_ID,FORMAT_ID
    ,REGION_ID,COUNTRY_ID,SALE_PRICE AS AMOUNT,SALE_DATE AS DTE FROM SALE;
```

Now use the following MERGE command:

```
MERGE INTO SALE S
    USING DAILYSALES DS
    ON(DS.MOVIE_ID = S.MOVIE_ID
        AND DS.SOURCE_ID = S.SOURCE_ID
        AND DS.FORMAT_ID = S.FORMAT_ID
        AND DS.REGION_ID = S.REGION_ID
        AND DS.COUNTRY_ID = S.COUNTRY_ID
        AND DS.DTE = S.SALE_DATE)
    WHEN MATCHED THEN
        UPDATE SET SALE_PRICE = DS.AMOUNT + SALE_PRICE
    WHEN NOT MATCHED THEN
        INSERT VALUES(SALE_SEQ.NEXTVAL, DS.MOVIE_ID
            , DS.SOURCE_ID, DS.FORMAT_ID, DS.REGION_ID
            , DS.COUNTRY_ID, DS.AMOUNT, SYSDATE);
```

The following points should be noted about the MERGE command example just shown:

- The SALE table is the target table in which rows are changed or added to.
- The DAILYSALES table is the source of rows to be changed or added.
- Matching rows are rows found to be in both tables based on the condition in the USING clause of the MERGE command. These rows are updated in the target SALE table.
- Nonmatching rows are added to the SALE table as new rows.

Transactional Control

A *transaction* in Oracle SQL is a sequence of one or more commands in which changes are not yet committed permanently to the database. A transaction is completed when changes are committed or undone (rolled back).

It is important to remember that all DDL commands commit automatically and DML commands do not. By definition, a single DDL command constitutes a transaction. Multiple DML commands can constitute a single transaction as long as database changes are not committed or rolled back.

Transactional control is a term used to describe groupings of database changes, which can be either permanently stored or completely undone. Several commands are used to maintain various aspects of transactional control:

- COMMIT—Permanently stores changes to the database.

- ROLLBACK—Undoes any database changes not yet committed to the database using the COMMIT command, or an inadvertent automatic commit caused by a DDL command, or disconnecting from a session cleanly.
- SAVEPOINT—Allows for partial rollback within a transaction back to a defined label.
- SET TRANSACTION—Allows control of the way in which a transaction behaves, such as waiting for a lock to be released or aborting when a lock cannot be obtained.
- LOCK TABLE—Allows placing of a temporary lock onto a table in a specified manner. The LOCK TABLE command is very rarely used and is more of a database administrator than Oracle SQL coding function. It does not need to be covered in this book.

COMMIT, ROLLBACK, and SAVEPOINT

The COMMIT command is always faster to execute than a ROLLBACK command based on the premise that COMMIT commands *should* be executed from within applications much more frequently. When a DML change is made to a database, three things occur:

- Log entries are written.
- Changes are written to the table.
- Rollback entries allowing possible undoing of table changes are written.

When a COMMIT command is executed, the following happens:

- Rollback entries for changes made are removed (marked reusable).

When a ROLLBACK command is executed, the following things happen:

- Log entries are written, recording rollback (undo) changes to be made to tables (undone in tables).
- Rollback entries are applied to tables to undo changes previously made in tables.
- Rollback entries are removed.

From this list it is easy to understand why a COMMIT command is always faster than a ROLLBACK command.

A SAVEPOINT command can be used to establish a partial rollback point within a transaction. Executing the following sequence of commands will add the studio. The change of name for the studio will be executed and immediately rolled back to the SAVEPOINT label INSERTDONE. The change to the name of the studio will thus not be executed.

```
INSERT INTO STUDIO VALUES(500, 'A New Studio');
SAVEPOINT INSERTDONE;
UPDATE STUDIO SET STUDIO = 'A Changed Studio' WHERE STUDIO_ID = 500;
ROLLBACK TO SAVEPOINT INSERTDONE;
```

SET TRANSACTION

The SET TRANSACTION command can be used to force a specific transaction to behave in a specific manner. Figure 10.8 shows the syntax for the SET TRANSACTION command.

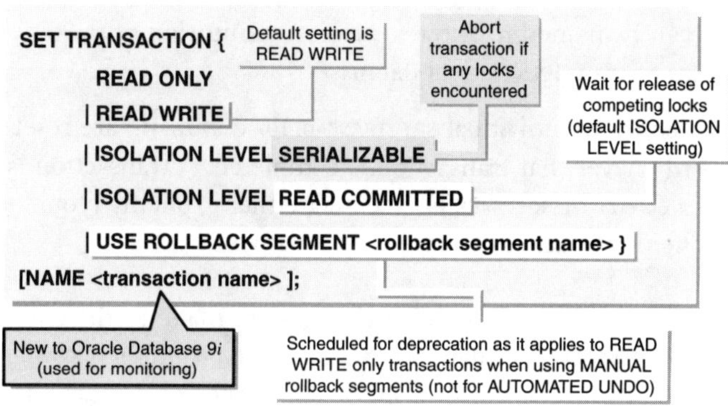

Figure 10.8 **SET TRANSACTION** command syntax.

Following is a synopsis of the syntax diagram shown in Figure 10.8:

- The SET TRANSACTION command applies to changes not yet committed to a database. Thus, a transaction consists of one or more uncommitted (not committed or rolled back) DML commands.
- Default settings for both a transaction and the SET TRANSACTION command are READ WRITE and ISOLATION LEVEL READ COMMITTED. READ WRITE sets statement level consistency, forcing all queries to see data as a snapshot before the start of each DML statement. ISOLATION LEVEL READ COMMITTED forces a transaction to wait for row lock release if any locks are causing contention with the current transaction.
- Setting a transaction to read-only sets transaction-level read consistency, forcing all queries to see data as a snapshot before the start of a transaction.

- Setting the ISOLATION LEVEL to SERIALIZABLE effectively serializes transactions, forcing the transaction to abort when locking contention is encountered. An aborted transaction is rolled back automatically (undone).
- The USE ROLLBACK SEGMENT clause allows use of a specific manual rollback segment for a transaction.

Manual rollback is deprecated in favor of automated undo and is not recommended. Understanding of manual rollback and automated undo is database administration and beyond the scope of this book and this exam.

- 9i Transactions can be named to allow for easier monitoring of the progress and status of transactions in a database.
- The settings created by an individual SET TRANSACTION command are reset to default values whenever that transaction is completed. A transaction is completed when a COMMIT or ROLLBACK is executed, either explicitly (you type it in) or implicitly (Oracle Database does it for you).

The following command will ensure that no changes are made to the database until a COMMIT or ROLLBACK command is executed, or an implicit COMMIT command is performed on execution of a DDL command, or a clean disconnection of the current session is made:

```
SET TRANSACTION READ ONLY;
```

The default settings if explicitly specified are shown in the following commands:

```
SET TRANSACTION READ WRITE;

SET TRANSACTION ISOLATION LEVEL READ COMMITTED;
```

Executing the preceding two SET TRANSACTION commands would require terminating the first transaction with, for instance, a ROLLBACK command before executing the second SET TRANSACTION command.

Exam Prep Questions

1. Select any correct answers:
   - ❑ A. DML commands execute an implicit rollback.
   - ❑ B. DML commands require an explicit **COMMIT** to be rolled back.
   - ❑ C. DDL commands can be undone.
   - ❑ D. DDL commands change data in tables.
   - ❑ E. None of the above.

   E is correct because A, B, C, and D are incorrect. DML commands execute no implicit or explicit transactional control commands, such as **COMMIT** or **ROLLBACK**. Thus, A and B are wrong. C is incorrect because DDL commands do execute an implicit **COMMIT** and committed data cannot be undone. D is incorrect because DDL commands change table structure and not data stored in tables.

2. What type of an **INSERT** command is this?

```
INSERT INTO ACTOR VALUES(100,'Mel Gibson','M','Tough Guy');
```

   - ❑ A. A multiple table conditional **INSERT** command
   - ❑ B. A single table conditional **INSERT** command
   - ❑ C. A single table **INSERT** command
   - ❑ D. A multiple table non-conditional **INSERT** command
   - ❑ E. A single table non-conditional **INSERT** command

   C is correct. This command is a single table **INSERT** command; therefore, A and D are both incorrect. Both B and E are incorrect because there is no such thing as single table conditional or non-conditional **INSERT** commands.

3. What's wrong with this command? Select two answers.

```
INSERT
 WHEN TO_CHAR(SALE_DATE, 'YYYY') = '2003' THEN INTO SALE2000
 WHEN TO_CHAR(SALE_DATE, 'YYYY') = '2003' THEN INTO SALE2001
 WHEN TO_CHAR(SALE_DATE, 'YYYY') = '2003' THEN INTO SALE2002
 WHEN TO_CHAR(SALE_DATE, 'YYYY') = '2003' THEN INTO SALE2003
 WHEN TO_CHAR(SALE_DATE, 'YYYY') = '2004' THEN INTO SALE2004
 WHEN TO_CHAR(SALE_DATE, 'YYYY') = '2005' THEN INTO SALE2005
SELECT * FROM SALE;
```

   - ❑ A. There is a syntax error.
   - ❑ B. There are too many **INSERT** commands.
   - ❑ C. There is no syntax error.
   - ❑ D. The first three rows are pointless.
   - ❑ E. None of the above.

   C and D are correct. C is correct because there are no syntax errors. D is correct because the first three rows create 2003 data in tables for other years. There is no syntax error so A is wrong. There is no documented restriction of a limitation on the number of **INSERT** commands, so B is wrong. E is obviously incorrect because D is correct.

4. Given the table shown, select the **INSERT** commands that will cause errors:

```
SQL> DESC TEST
 Name              Null?    Type
 ----------------- -------- ------------
 ID                NOT NULL NUMBER
 STR               NOT NULL VARCHAR2(32) DEFAULT 'Empty String'
```

- ❑ A. **INSERT INTO TEST(ID) VALUES(1);**
- ❑ B. **INSERT INTO TEST VALUES(2, 'This is a string');**
- ❑ C. **INSERT INTO TEST(ID, STR) VALUES(3, 'This is another string');**
- ❑ D. **INSERT INTO TEST(STR) VALUES('This is another string still');**
- ❑ E. **INSERT INTO TEST(ID) VALUES('This is yet another string');**

D and E should be selected because both will cause syntax errors. D will cause an error because the ID column is not included and it is non-nullable with no default setting. E is incorrect because of a datatype mismatch between the **NUMBER** datatype ID column and the string to be added as an ID.

5. Assume that all columns exist in both tables. Will this command cause an error, yes or no?

```
UPDATE SALECOPY SC SET
    SC.REGION_ID, SC.COUNTRY_ID =
        (SELECT REGION_ID, COUNTRY_ID FROM SALE
            WHERE SALE_ID = SC.SALE_ID);
```

The answer is yes because the second line should have the two columns parenthesized as the subquery is: **(SC.REGION_ID, SC.COUNTRY_ID)**.

6. Which commands will remove all rows from the table assuming that any filters filter out at least one row?

- ❑ A. **TRUNCATE TABLE TEST;**
- ❑ B. **DELETE FROM TEST WHERE ID = 1;**
- ❑ C. **TRUNCATE TABLE TEST WHERE ID = 1;**
- ❑ D. **REMOVE TABLE TEST;**
- ❑ E. **DELETE FROM TEST;**

A and E are correct. The **TRUNCATE** command removes all rows, and a **DELETE** command without a **WHERE** clause does the same. B is incorrect because the filter will filter out at least one row, and thus not all rows will be removed. C is incorrect because a **TRUNCATE** command cannot have a **WHERE** clause. D is incorrect because there is no **REMOVE** command in Oracle SQL.

7. Select any correct answers:

- ❑ A. MERGE joins three tables together.
- ❑ B. **MERGE** copies rows from one table to another.
- ❑ C. **MERGE** executes an upsert, updating an existing row when found.

- ❑ D. **MERGE** executes an upsert, adding a new row when not found.
- ❑ E. **MERGE** executes an upsert, which changes existing rows and adds non-existent rows.

B is correct because **MERGE** could copy rows from one table to another, assuming that there are no existing rows in the target table. Both C and D are correct because a row is updated if found and added if not found. It follows from the answers to C and D that answer E is correct as well, for both reasons. A is incorrect because **MERGE** merges two tables, not three.

8. Select the ways in which a transaction is terminated:
   - ❑ A. **SAVEPOINT**
   - ❑ B. **COMMIT**
   - ❑ C. **ROLLBACK**
   - ❑ D. **SET TRANSACTION**
   - ❑ E. A clean session disconnection with outstanding commits

   B, C, and E are correct. **COMMIT** stores permanently, **ROLLBACK** removes changes, and a clean disconnection from a session will execute a **COMMIT** on any outstanding transactions. D is incorrect because the **SET TRANSACTION** command determines the way in which transactions are handled, not controlling the instance of transaction termination. A is incorrect because **SAVEPOINT** defines a label and in no way executes transactional control.

9. Fill in the blank: **[ ] TEST SET ID=3;**

   The answer is the keyword **UPDATE**. This example is an **UPDATE** command.

10. Which command aborts a transaction if locks are encountered?
    - ❑ A. **SET TRANSACTION USE ROLLBACK SEGMENT RB1;**
    - ❑ B. **SET TRANSACTION NAME 'testing';**
    - ❑ C. **SET TRANSACTION ISOLATION LEVEL SERIALIZABLE;**
    - ❑ D. **SET TRANSACTION ISOLATION LEVEL READ COMMITTED;**
    - ❑ E. **SET TRANSACTION NAME 555;**

    C is correct as it has the appropriate option. A is incorrect because it deals with a rollback segment allocation. B is incorrect because it names a transaction. D is incorrect because the transaction will wait until a lock is released. E is incorrect because it attempts to name a transaction and is incorrect syntactically because the **NAME** parameter should be a string, not a number.

Tables, Datatypes, and Constraints (DDL)

Terms You Need to Understand

- ✓ Table
- ✓ Datatype
- ✓ Constraint
- ✓ Index
- ✓ View
- ✓ Index Organized Table (IOT)
- ✓ Cluster
- ✓ Materialized view
- ✓ Sequence
- ✓ Synonym
- ✓ Partition
- ✓ **DEFAULT**
- ✓ **VARRAY**
- ✓ Nested table
- ✓ Inline constraint
- ✓ Out-of-line constraint
- ✓ **NOT NULL** constraint
- ✓ Check constraint
- ✓ Primary key constraint
- ✓ Foreign key
- ✓ **ENABLE** or **DISABLE**
- ✓ **VALIDATE** and **NOVALIDATE**

Concepts You Need to Master

- ✓ Oracle built-in datatypes
- ✓ User-defined datatypes
- ✓ Constraint states
- ✓ Creating tables
- ✓ Altering tables
- ✓ Dropping, truncating, and renaming tables
- ✓ Tables, columns, datatypes, and constraints and how they relate to each other

This chapter examines the details of table creation and maintenance plus use of column datatypes within tables. Constraints are used to control access to, within, and between both tables and, occasionally, views. Views are covered in Chapter 12, "Views, Indexes, Sequences, and Synonyms (DDL)."

Database Objects

Before examining tables in detail, let's take a quick look at different database objects available in Oracle Database. There are 23 object types available in Oracle 9.2.0.1. You need to understand that a database is not made up of only tables but many other types of objects as well. These are some of the more significant types of objects:

- *Table*—Tables are definitional structures in which column/row data is built within that structure.
- *Index*—An index is a shortened and better-organized partial copy of a table, used for fast access to table data.
- *View*—A view is a logical overlay containing a query, executed whenever the view is accessed. Repeated query execution can make views very inefficient in busy environments.
- *Index Organized Table (IOT)*—An IOT contains all table rows and columns but is sorted and organized in the manner of an index; it is an indexed table or an index created from all the columns in a table. An IOT can be very efficient if the IOT is accessed in the sorted order.
- *Cluster*—A cluster groups frequently accessed columns, in addition to indexed columns, from one or more tables. A cluster is a form of a preconstructed data set, usually constructed for a SQL join.
- *Materialized View*—A materialized view is a physically preconstructed view of data containing data copied into the materialized view. Materialized views can be highly efficient in read-only environments and are often used for replication, for distribution, and in data warehouses.
- *Sequence*—A sequence is an internal counter often used to populate primary and foreign surrogate key columns for Referential Integrity.
- *Synonym*—A synonym provides object transparency by creating a more easily used reference to another object in the database, in the current or any other schema, or even in a different database across a database link. In other words, a synonym is a substitute or an *easier-to-use* name for an object within any accessible schema.

- *Partition*—Partitions or Oracle Partitioning allows both tables and indexes to be created as physically partitioned objects. Oracle Partitioning allows division of objects into separate physical files and layers.
- *Datatypes*—Special datatypes can be created using the `CREATE TYPE` command, allowing construction of user-defined types and structures. Also, binary objects such as BLOB binary objects can be used to store binary data such as multimedia.
- *PL/SQL Objects*—PL/SQL objects are procedures, functions, packages, triggers, and types (see the preceding bulleted entry, "Datatypes"). These objects are all out of the scope of this exam because they are part of PL/SQL.

A basic understanding of the main available Oracle Database objects is required, as described here.

Creating Tables

Tables can be created in different forms. A table can be relational or an object table, among many other forms. In general, a relational table contains relational database attributes linked to other tables using Referential Integrity rules and constraints. An object table in a relational database, such as Oracle Database, is by definition a relational table containing some type of object structure. Oracle Database has additional table structures such as temporary tables, IOTs, clusters, external tables, XML tables, and partitioned tables. Only relational tables and minimal detail on object tables are relevant to this exam.

A table is created using the `CREATE TABLE` command with the syntax shown in Figure 11.1.

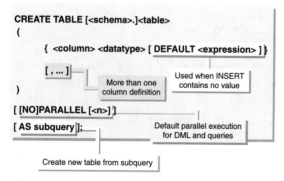

```
CREATE TABLE [<schema>.]<table>
(
    { <column> <datatype> [ DEFAULT <expression> ] }
    [ , ... ]
)
[ [NO]PARALLEL [<n>] ]
[ AS subquery ];
```

More than one column definition

Used when INSERT contains no value

Default parallel execution for DML and queries

Create new table from subquery

Figure 11.1 CREATE TABLE command syntax.

Following is a synopsis of the syntax diagram shown in Figure 11.1:

- A table can be created in any schema a user has access to.
- Columns are added to a table as `<column> <datatype>` pairs. Each column must have a valid datatype.
- The `DEFAULT <expression>` clause allows automatic setting of a column to a predetermined value.
- The syntax element `[,...]` implies that more than a single column can be specified in a single `CREATE TABLE` command.
- A table can be created to allow certain types of commands to be executed against it in parallel, usually on multiple CPU platforms.
- A table can be created using a subquery, taking all the column datatypes and rows retrieved by the subquery.

Figure 11.1 shows the very basics of the syntax of the `CREATE TABLE` command. The complete syntax of the `CREATE TABLE` command is much more involved. Specific sections of the `CREATE TABLE` command syntax are covered in this chapter. Sections omitted are not included in this particular exam. Here is a very simple `CREATE TABLE` command:

```
CREATE TABLE STUDIOS(
     STUDIO_ID NUMBER NOT NULL
    ,STUDIO VARCHAR2(32) NOT NULL);
```

In the preceding script the `STUDIO` table is created containing two columns. The first column is called `STUDIO_ID` and is of datatype `NUMBER`. The second column is called `STUDIO` and is of datatype `VARCHAR2(32)`. Both columns have a `NOT NULL` constraint. Datatypes and constraints will be dealt with shortly.

Following is another sample `CREATE TABLE` command containing a `DEFAULT` setting (see Chapter 10, "Changing Data [DML]") on the `GENDER` column:

```
CREATE TABLE ACTORS(
     ACTOR_ID     NUMBER NOT NULL
    ,NAME         VARCHAR2(32) NOT NULL
    ,GENDER       CHAR(1) DEFAULT 'M' NOT NULL
    ,TYPECAST     VARCHAR2(64) NULL);
```

A table can also be created from a subquery and allow for parallel processing, assuming that the database server has more than one central processing unit (CPU):

```
CREATE TABLE SALES PARALLEL 2 AS SELECT * FROM SALE;
```

You can create a table from any type of query, even a join, as in the following example:

```
CREATE TABLE PEOPLE AS SELECT M.TITLE "Movie", A.NAME "Actor"
    ,D.NAME "Director"FROM MOVIE M
    JOIN PART P ON (P.MOVIE_ID = M.MOVIE_ID)
        JOIN ACTOR A ON (A.ACTOR_ID = P.ACTOR_ID)
            JOIN DIRECTOR D ON (D.DIRECTOR_ID = M.DIRECTOR_ID)
ORDER BY 1, 2;
```

All that the preceding `CREATE TABLE` command has done is to create a new table called `PEOPLE` from a four-table join. The four tables in the join are the `MOVIE`, `PART`, `ACTOR`, and `DIRECTOR` tables.

Datatypes

Now let's examine the different datatypes that can be used to define columns in tables. A *datatype* is a method by which data is coerced into being of a particular format, such as an integer or a date.

Oracle Built-In Datatypes

Oracle built-in datatypes are shown in Figure 11.2.

Datatype	Description	NLS
VARCHAR2(<size>)	Variable length strings upto 4000 bytes.	NVARCHAR2(<size>)
CHAR(<size>)	Fixed length strings upto 2000 bytes.	NCHAR(<size>)
NUMBER(<precision>, <scale>)	Fixed point number upto 38 bytes where <precision> is total digits and <scale> is decimal points. <precision> = 1 to 38, <scale> = -84 to 127.	
FLOAT(precision)	Floating point number upto 126 bytes	
DATE	Stores dates from 01/01/4712 BC to 12/31/9999 AD	
TIMESTAMP(<fraction>) [WITH [LOCAL] TIME ZONE]	Timestamp value storage. Range as for DATE. <fraction> = fractions of a second.	
INTERVAL YEAR(<year>) TO MONTH	Period of time in years and months.	
INTERVAL DAY(<day>) TO SECOND	Period of time in days, hours, minutes, and seconds.	
LONG	LONG is for upto 2GB strings.	
RAW and LONG RAW	2000 bytes and 2GB of raw binary data respectively.	
BLOB	Binary object for objects such as multimedia.	
CLOB	Binary object for very large strings.	NCLOB
BFILE	Binary file pointer. Usually the most efficient storage method for large binary objects. Requires a directory object.	
ROWID and UROWID	Unique address of a row in a table, primarily stored in indexes for fast table row access. UROWID is the ROWID equivalent used for IOTs.	

Figure 11.2 Oracle Database built-in datatypes.

The **TIMESTAMP** datatype is new to Oracle9i.

Refer to Chapter 5, "Single Row Functions," in the section "Datatype Conversion Functions," for formatting specifications of some of the datatypes such as **DATE** and **NUMBER**, in addition to other examples in this chapter.

Many other datatypes are available, such as ANSI standard supported datatypes, all converting automatically to Oracle Database internal datatypes. For example, the following `CREATE TABLE` command creates two columns with `INTEGER` and `SMALLINT` datatypes:

```
CREATE TABLE TEST(ID1 INTEGER, ID2 SMALLINT);
```

These ANSI-supported datatypes are converted by Oracle Database to `NUMBER(38)` datatypes. Thirty-eight bytes is the maximum length for a `NUMBER` datatype, as shown next by the `DESC TEST` command of the table just created:

```
SQL> DESC TEST
 Name                Null?    Type
 ------------------ -------- -----------
 ID1                          NUMBER(38)
 ID2                          NUMBER(38)
```

User-Defined Datatypes

A user-defined datatype is, as the term implies, defined or created by the user (you). Various structures can be used to create these new user datatypes, such as arrays and pointers. These structures are shown in Figure 11.3.

Datatype	Description
VARRAY	Fixed length array where the number of elements is pre-determined. Creates an objects collection.
TABLE	A nested table is a variable length array where unlike a VARRAY the number of elements is not pre-determined. A nested table is a pointer, similar to a by-reference or BYREF pointer. Creates an object collection.
REF	Object table pointer type much like a relational table foreign key.

Figure 11.3 Oracle Database user-defined datatypes.

A user-defined datatype is essentially an object datatype. An object datatype has a name and at least one attribute, and it can have methods. In the object world an attribute is the equivalent of a table column, and a method is a function contained within the object. Methods can be built for Oracle Database user-defined datatypes using PL/SQL. PL/SQL is not included in this exam, so we will ignore methods.

To create a user-defined datatype, we have to utilize the CREATE TYPE command. A vastly simplified version of the syntax for the CREATE TYPE command is shown in Figure 11.4.

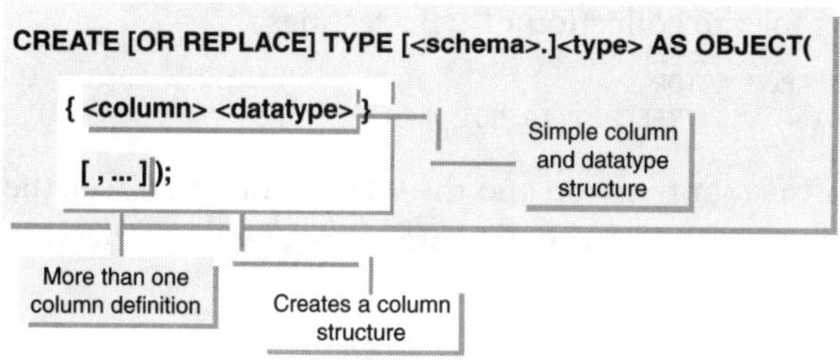

Figure 11.4 CREATE TYPE command syntax.

Following is a synopsis of the syntax diagram shown in Figure 11.4:

- A TYPE definition is created using the CREATE TYPE statement with the AS OBJECT clause.
- Each column specification must have a valid datatype.
- The syntax element [, ...] means that more than a single column can be created for a type created using the CREATE TYPE command.

Much of the syntax for the CREATE TYPE command not shown in Figure 11.4 is omitted because it is not in this exam.

As shown in Figure 11.3, VARRAY and TABLE are both array datatypes that can be used to create object collections. An array is a repetition of the same structure, much like rows are repetitions of the column structure in a table. An object collection is really an object methodology term for an array, except that a collection is completely contained within a parent object, perhaps within a hierarchy of objects. With respect to this exam, an object collection is a datatype or pointer that contains many elements all of the same datatype.

Beginning with the VARRAY datatype, you can create a datatype to contain a collection of different type castings for each actor using a VARRAY datatype. In the following, the type created is an array of 100 elements, each containing a single column of datatype VARCHAR2(64):

```
CREATE OR REPLACE TYPE TYPECASTCOLLECTION
    AS VARRAY(100) OF VARCHAR2(64);
/
```

You will now create a copy of the ACTOR table into a new table called ACTORS using the VARRAY collection for the TYPECAST column. You will create the new ACTORS table replacing all Multiple type castings from the original ACTOR table, with all possible type castings for other actors, excluding Multiple or NULL, using this query as a basis for the collection of type castings:

```
SELECT DISTINCT(TYPECAST) FROM ACTOR
WHERE TYPECAST != 'Multiple' AND TYPECAST IS NOT NULL;
```

The following query uses the CAST function and the MULTISET operator (see the section "Obscure Conversion Functions" in Chapter 5) to create a collection within a query:

```
CREATE TABLE ACTORS AS SELECT A.ACTOR_ID, A.NAME, A.GENDER
    , CAST(
        MULTISET(
            SELECT DISTINCT(TYPECAST) FROM ACTOR
            WHERE TYPECAST != 'Multiple' AND TYPECAST IS NOT NULL
        ) AS TYPECASTCOLLECTION
    ) AS TYPECAST
FROM ACTOR A;
```

In the preceding query, the MULTISET operator creates the collection. The CAST function typecasts (programming terminology, not actor typecasting) the MULTISET created VARRAY collection into the TYPECAST collection column in the new ACTORS table. To retrieve the TYPECAST collection from the new ACTORS table, use a query such as this:

```
SELECT TYPECAST FROM ACTORS;
```

Using nested tables is similar to using VARRAYS, with some differences. A nested table is really a table within a table accessing the child table using the TABLE keyword. First we create a new type structure to contain addresses:

```
CREATE OR REPLACE TYPE ADDRESS AS OBJECT (STREET VARCHAR2(128)
,CITY VARCHAR2(32), STATE CHAR(2), ZIP NUMBER(5));
/
```

The preceding ADDRESS type structure has multiple columns, just like a table. Now let's create a nested table, allowing for multiple ADDRESS type structure repetitions:

```
CREATE OR REPLACE TYPE ADDRESSCOLLECTION AS TABLE OF ADDRESS;
/
```

Add the nested table collection object to the new ACTORS table, specifying a table where the nested table object is to be stored:

```
ALTER TABLE ACTORS ADD(ADDRESSES ADDRESSCOLLECTION)
   NESTED TABLE ADDRESSES STORE AS ADDRESSESTABLE;
```

To change data in the nested table address collection in the new ACTORS table, assuming that actors have multiple addresses, of course, use this UPDATE command:

```
UPDATE ACTORS SET ADDRESSES = ADDRESSCOLLECTION(
     ADDRESS('Street1','City1','NY',11722)
    ,ADDRESS('Street2','City2','CA',94066)
    ,ADDRESS('Street3','City3','FL',33066)
) WHERE ACTOR_ID = 1;
```

You can retrieve address collections from the new ACTORS table using this query:

```
SELECT ADDRESSES FROM ACTORS WHERE ACTOR_ID = 1;
```

You can retrieve individual items from the collection using this query (even the COL formatting command can be used):

```
COL STREET FORMAT A16
SELECT * FROM TABLE(SELECT ADDRESSES FROM ACTORS WHERE ACTOR_ID = 1);
```

The output for the preceding two queries is shown in Figure 11.5.

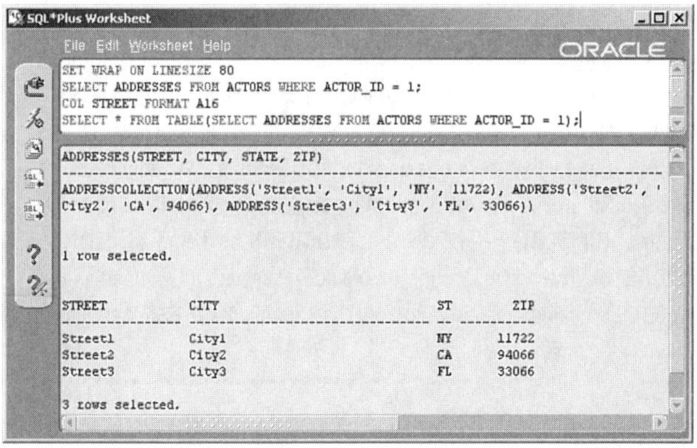

Figure 11.5 Retrieving data from nested table object user-defined datatypes.

A REF datatype is an Object Identifier (OID) or database-wide unique pointer to an object. In the previous example using the ADDRESSES collection and the ACTORS table, we assumed that actors had multiple addresses, which is probably incorrect. What you can do is to store a single address for an actor, placing a REF datatype OID pointer from the new ACTORS table into an ADDRESSES table containing addresses of all actors in a single nested table collection.

The tables and types must be altered in the correct sequence due to dependencies:

```
ALTER TABLE ACTORS DROP COLUMN ADDRESSES;
DROP TYPE ADDRESSCOLLECTION;
DROP TYPE ADDRESS;
CREATE OR REPLACE TYPE TADDRESS AS OBJECT (STREET VARCHAR2(128)
, CITY VARCHAR2(32), STATE CHAR(2), ZIP NUMBER(5));
/
CREATE TABLE ADDRESSES OF TADDRESS;
INSERT INTO ADDRESSES VALUES('Street1','City1','NY',11722);
INSERT INTO ADDRESSES VALUES('Street2','City2','CA',94066);
INSERT INTO ADDRESSES VALUES('Street3','City3','FL',33066) ;
```

Now add the REF datatype column pointer to the new ACTORS table and set three different actors to the three different addresses created by the preceding INSERT commands:

```
ALTER TABLE ACTORS ADD(ADDRESS REF TADDRESS SCOPE IS ADDRESSES);
UPDATE ACTORS SET ADDRESS = (SELECT REF(ADDY) FROM ADDRESSES ADDY
WHERE ADDY.STATE = 'NY')WHERE ACTOR_ID = 1;
UPDATE ACTORS SET ADDRESS = (SELECT REF(ADDY) FROM ADDRESSES ADDY
WHERE ADDY.STATE = 'CA')WHERE ACTOR_ID = 2;
UPDATE ACTORS SET ADDRESS = (SELECT REF(ADDY) FROM ADDRESSES ADDY
WHERE ADDY.STATE = 'FL')WHERE ACTOR_ID = 3;
```

Clarification for TYPE Naming Conventions

Just as a reminder or perhaps for clarification, you might have noticed my naming conventions for **TYPE** definitions, variables declared against those **TYPE** definitions, and collections of those variables. If you are confused by this, particularly in the preceding example with three **UPDATE** commands, perhaps this note will explain. **TADDRESS** is a **TYPE** definition denoted by the letter *T*, a **TYPE** definition representing an address of a person. **ADDRESS** is a variable declared against that **TYPE** called **TADDRESS**; effectively the same thing as declaring a variable as being of datatype **NUMBER (counter NUMBER)**, I have declared **ADDRESS** as being of datatype **TADDRESS (ADDRESS TADDRESS)**. The collection of multiple addresses is aptly named as the plural **ADDRESSES**. **ADDRESSES** contains many iterations of the variable **ADDRESS**, defined as datatype **TADDRESS**.

Retrieve the pointer from the new ACTORS table with this query:

```
SELECT NAME, ADDRESS FROM ACTORS WHERE ACTOR_ID IN (1,2,3);
```

Retrieve the actor and his address, through the pointer, using the DEREF function:

```
SELECT NAME, DEREF(ADDRESS) FROM ACTORS WHERE ACTOR_ID IN (1,2,3);
```

The DEREF function is the opposite of the REF function, simply dereferencing or retrieving the actual value the REF pointer points to: the address of the actor.

Constraints

Constraints restrict the application of rules both within and between tables. Why would you use constraints? Constraints can allow you to place rules on data to be placed into tables. For example, if you want to make sure that all actors have a name, you can place a NOT NULL constraint on the NAME column of the ACTOR table. It makes no sense to have a nameless actor. Figure 11.6 shows the syntax for the CREATE TABLE command, expanding the already-described syntax to cater for constraints.

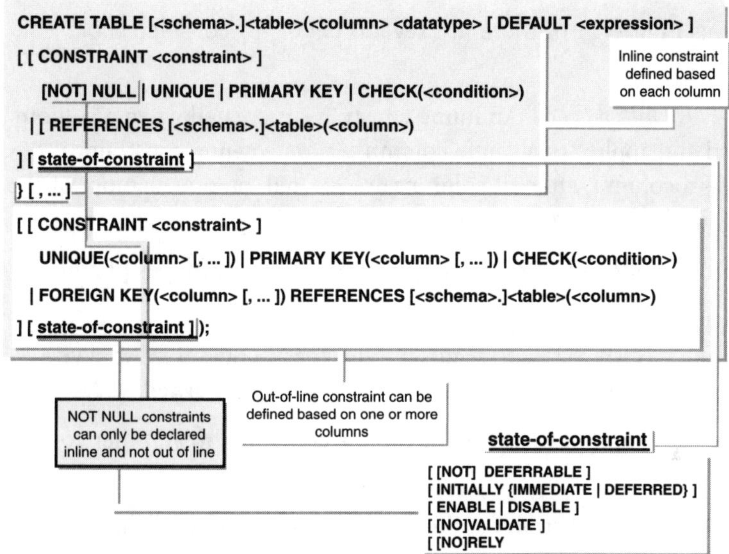

Figure 11.6 **CREATE TABLE** command syntax, including constraints.

Following is a synopsis of the syntax diagram shown in Figure 11.6:

- Constraints can be declared as inline or out-of-line.
- Constraints can be optionally named using the CONSTRAINT <constraint> syntax. Constraints not named are given internally Oracle Database–generated names.
- An inline constraint is declared on a single specific column.
- Out-of-line constraints are declared after all column definitions and can be declared for more than a single column. Constraints referencing more than a single column must be declared as out-of-line.
- The NOT NULL constraint is single column specific and must be declared inline.

- Inline constraints can be NOT NULL, UNIQUE, PRIMARY KEY, CHECK, or REFERENCES (a foreign key).
- Out-of-line constraints can be UNIQUE, PRIMARY KEY, CHECK or FOREIGN KEY ... REFERENCES.
- Constraint states can be applied either inline or out-of-line, determining behavior for a constraint that a state is specified for.
- Constraint states can be DEFERRABLLE, NOT DEFERRABLE, INITIALLY IMMEDIATE, INITIALLY DEFERRED, ENABLE, DISABLE, VALIDATE, NOVALIDATE, RELY, or NORELY.

In examining Figure 11.6, there are several details to consider about constraints:

- *Inline Versus Out-of-Line*—An inline constraint is created when a column is created and applies to a single column. An out-of-line constraint is created as a column, after all columns are created, on one or more of the columns in the CREATE TABLE command.
- *Types of Constraints*—The following four sub-bullets are types of constraints you should be familiar with for the exam:
    - [NOT]NULL—A NOT NULL constraint implies that a column must have a value placed into it or otherwise an error will be returned.
    - UNIQUE—A column value must be unique compared to all other rows in a table.
    - CHECK—A check constraint validates a value setting for a column, such that the column value in every row must conform to the specified condition.
    - PRIMARY KEY *and* FOREIGN KEY REFERENCES—These constraints apply to Referential Integrity. Referential Integrity is not on this exam. Briefly, a primary key uniquely identifies a row in a table, and a foreign key identifies a row against a primary key in a different table or, rarely, even the same table. Primary and foreign keys establish relations (dependent relationships) between entities.
- *Constraint State*—Constraint states set a constraint as having a specific type of behavior. For example, a really obvious constraint state is DISABLE. Setting a constraint state to DISABLE means that the constraint is created but will not be verified. Here is a list of constraint states:
    - ENABLE | DISABLE—ENABLE and DISABLE switch a constraint on or off, respectively.

- [NO]VALIDATE—NOVALIDATE does not require that existing rows comply with an enabled constraint, but requires only that new rows do so. VALIDATE requires that all rows comply. If a constraint is enabled on a table with existing data, VALIDATE will cause all existing rows to be validated against the constraint.
- [NOT] DEFERRABLE—Constraint checking is delayed until a transaction is completed, such as on the execution of a COMMIT or ROLLBACK command.
- INITIALLY {IMMEDIATE | DEFERRED}—This state applies to DEFERRABLE constraints only. The IMMEDIATE option executes constraint checking at the end of subsequent SQL commands. DEFERRED executes constraint checking after the end of subsequent transactions.
- [NO]RELY—The RELY constraint state applies to materialized views and query rewrite.

The **RELY** constraint state is way out of scope for this exam, but be aware that it exists. You do not have to know what the **RELY** constraint state is or what it means for this exam.

Only factual questions may be asked about constraint states; thus, examples are not necessary. A favorite is often **ENABLE NOVALIDATE**, implying that a constraint is applied to newly inserted rows and not to existing rows.

Here is a CREATE TABLE command for a table called MOVIES. All constraints are inline, including both primary keys and foreign keys (REFERENCES ...). Additionally, there is a UNIQUE constraint on the TITLE column, and there are two CHECK constraints on the YEAR and STATE columns:

```
CREATE TABLE MOVIES(
     MOVIE_ID      NUMBER NOT NULL PRIMARY KEY
    ,SAGA_ID       NUMBER NOT NULL REFERENCES SAGA
    ,GENRE_ID      NUMBER NOT NULL REFERENCES GENRE
    ,DIRECTOR_ID   NUMBER NOT NULL REFERENCES DIRECTOR
    ,STUDIO_ID     NUMBER NOT NULL REFERENCES STUDIO
    ,RATING_ID     NUMBER NOT NULL REFERENCES RATING
    ,TITLE         VARCHAR2(32) NOT NULL UNIQUE
    ,YEAR          NUMBER NOT NULL CHECK(YEAR > 1910)
    ,STATE         CHAR(2) CHECK(STATE IN ('NY','CA','FL'))
    ,RELEASE       DATE NULL
    ,RANK          NUMBER NULL
    ,REVIEW_RANK   NUMBER(2,1) NULL);
```

Here is another MOVIES table with fewer columns than the preceding CREATE TABLE command but using both inline and out-of-line constraints, including some multiple-column constraints. Out-of-line constraints can operate on more than a single column:

```
CREATE TABLE MOVIES(
     SAGA_ID         NUMBER NOT NULL
    ,GENRE_ID        NUMBER NOT NULL REFERENCES GENRE
    ,STUDIO_ID       NUMBER NOT NULL REFERENCES STUDIO
    ,TITLE           VARCHAR2(32) NOT NULL UNIQUE
    ,YEAR            NUMBER NOT NULL CHECK(YEAR > 1910)
    ,RELEASE         DATE NULL
    ,STATE           CHAR(2) CHECK(STATE IN('NY','CA','FL'))
    ,RANK            NUMBER NULL
    ,REVIEW_RANK     NUMBER(2,1) NULL
    ,OVERALL_RANK    NUMBER NOT NULL
    ,CONSTRAINT      PK_MOVIE PRIMARY KEY(SAGA_ID, GENRE_ID, STUDIO_ID)
    ,CONSTRAINT      FK_MOVIE_SAGA FOREIGN KEY(SAGA_ID) REFERENCES SAGA
        ,CHECK(RELEASE IS NULL OR TO_CHAR(RELEASE, 'YYYY') > YEAR)
        ,CHECK(((NVL(RANK,0)/(NVL(RANK,1)*NVL(REVIEW_RANK,1)))*100)>25));
```

In the preceding CREATE TABLE command, the following constraints and constraint states are evident:

- Inline constraints are those placed against each column individually:
    - NOT NULL constraints force entry of a value into the column and are placed on the following columns: SAGA_ID, GENRE_ID, STUDIO_ID, TITLE, YEAR, and OVERALL_RANK.
    - NULL constraints are practically not a constraint by definition, because they place no restriction. However, the following columns are allowed to be NULL: RELEASE, RANK, and REVIEW_RANK. Note that the STATE column has neither NOT NULL nor NULL declared. However, the CHECK constraint will not allow a NULL entry.
    - Two foreign key constraints are declared on the GENRE_ID and STUDIO_ID columns, referencing the GENRE and STUDIO tables respectively.
    - The TITLE column has a UNIQUE constraint, meaning that no two movies can have the same name.
    - The YEAR and STATE columns have CHECK constraints. The YEAR must always be greater than the year 1910 (YEAR > 1910) and the STATE can only be New York, California, or Florida (STATE IN ('NY','CA','FL')).
- Out-of-line constraints are placed after all column definitions, applying to the table as a whole, as opposed to individual columns as for inline constraints:
    - The primary key PK_MOVIE is declared on three columns and thus cannot possibly be declared on a single column. The primary key forces uniqueness across the concatenation of all three values SAGA_ID, GENRE_ID, and STUDIO_ID.

- A single foreign key is declared on the SAGA_ID column as an out-of-line constraint. This constraint can be done at the column level as an inline constraint, but that is not essential—it can be inline or out-of-line.
- Two out-of-line CHECK constraints are declared. Both of the out-of-line CHECK constraints validate against more than a single column and thus cannot be declared inline. An inline constraint can be declared for only a single column at a time.

9i Altering Tables

The structure of a table can be changed using the ALTER TABLE command. In this section we will examine changing the table in general; changing column datatypes; and adding, changing, and dropping constraints using the ALTER TABLE command. Figure 11.7 shows the basics of the ALTER TABLE command relevant to this exam.

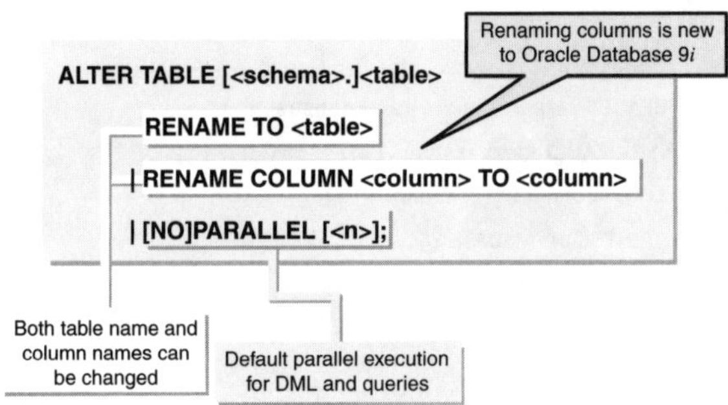

Figure 11.7 Basic **ALTER TABLE** command syntax for this exam.

Following is a synopsis of the syntax diagram shown in Figure 11.7:

- The ALTER TABLE command can be used to change the structure and behavior of a table in any accessible schema.
- A table can be renamed.
- 9i A single column in a table can be renamed.
- A table can be altered to allow for parallel execution against the table.

9i As shown in Figure 11.7, columns within tables can now be renamed:

```
ALTER TABLE STUDIO RENAME COLUMN STUDIO TO STUDIO_NAME;
```

We can also rename a table:

```
ALTER TABLE STUDIO RENAME TO STUDIOS;
```

And we can set default parallelism for a table:

```
ALTER TABLE SALE NOPARALLEL;
```

Columns

Figure 11.8 shows another version of the `ALTER TABLE` command showing options to add, modify, and drop columns within an existing table. The syntax diagram in Figure 11.8 also includes use of inline constraints at the column level.

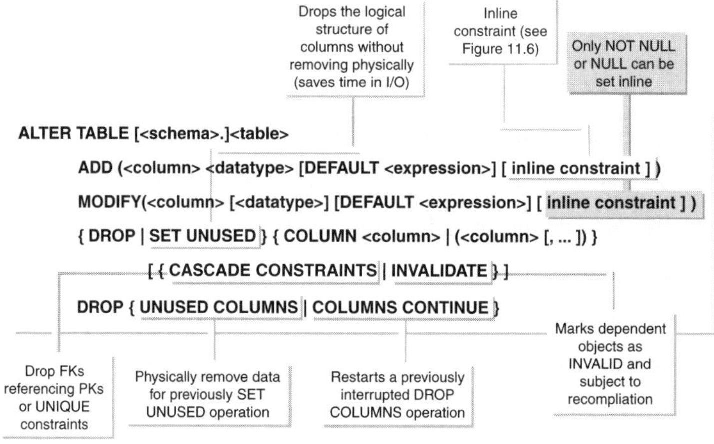

Figure 11.8 **ALTER TABLE** command syntax for dealing with inline constraints.

Following is a synopsis of the syntax diagram shown in Figure 11.8:

- The `ALTER TABLE` command can be used to add new columns, or change or drop existing columns.
- When a column is being added or modified, an inline constraint can be created for a column.
- A column cannot be added as having a `NOT NULL` constraint when there are already rows in the table.
- A column can be dropped altogether or set as unused. An unused column drops the column reference in metadata, making the column

inaccessible to the general user population, retaining physical column values. This can help performance substantially for very large tables at times of high activity, removing the need for physical restructuring.

- Unused columns previously dropped as set unused can subsequently be dropped using the DROP UNUSED COLUMNS option.
- A previously interrupted drop column operation can be restarted from the point where it left off using the COLUMNS CONTINUE clause.
- If a primary or unique key column is dropped using the CASCADE CONSTRAINTS option, any foreign key constraints referring to the primary or unique keys will be dropped as well.
- The INVALIDATE option will mark as INVALID any objects, such as PL/SQL procedures or TYPE definitions, referring to the dropped column.

The syntax diagram for the ALTER TABLE command in Figure 11.8 expands on the syntax in Figure 11.7. First, create a clean copy of the MOVIE table with no constraints, some missing columns, and some incorrect datatypes:

```
CREATE TABLE MOVIES(
     SAGA_ID     FLOAT
    ,GENRE_ID    FLOAT
    ,RATING_ID   NUMBER
    ,DIRECTOR_ID NUMBER
    ,STUDIO_ID   NUMBER
    ,TITLE       VARCHAR2(32)
    ,YEAR        NUMBER
    ,RELEASE     DATE
    ,LIST_PRICE  FLOAT
    ,RANK        NUMBER
    ,REVIEWS     NUMBER
    ,REVIEW_RANK NUMBER(2,1));
```

This command adds a column to the MOVIE table with a NULL inline constraint:

```
ALTER TABLE MOVIES ADD (MOVIE_ID FLOAT NULL);
```

Now let's modify the added and existing columns to have the correct datatypes and constraints (only NULL or NOT NULL can be set inline):

```
ALTER TABLE MOVIES MODIFY(MOVIE_ID NUMBER NOT NULL
    , SAGA_ID NUMBER NOT NULL, GENRE_ID NUMBER NOT NULL);
```

Drop an unwanted column:

```
ALTER TABLE MOVIES DROP COLUMN RELEASE;
```

And now drop two unwanted columns at once:

```
ALTER TABLE MOVIES DROP(REVIEWS, REVIEW_RANK);
```

Now set a column as unused and thus inaccessible to general query access:

```
ALTER TABLE MOVIES SET UNUSED COLUMN TITLE;
```

Now drop all unused columns:

```
ALTER TABLE MOVIES DROP UNUSED COLUMNS;
```

Constraints

Figure 11.9 shows yet another version of the `ALTER TABLE` command, showing options to add, modify, rename, and drop constraints within an existing table. As you might recall from earlier in this chapter, constraints restrict values that can be placed into columns in tables.

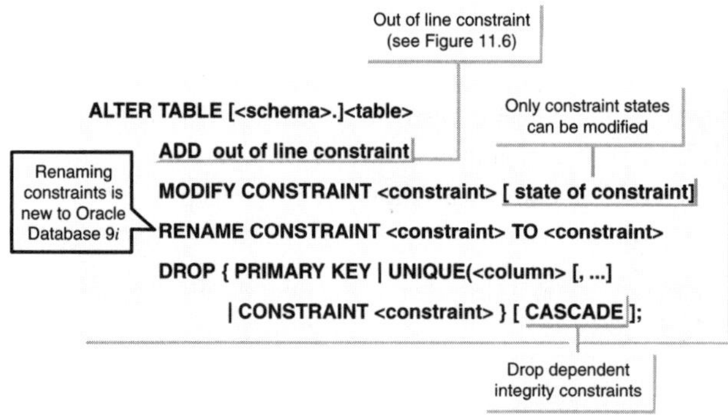

Figure 11.9 ALTER TABLE command syntax for dealing with out-of-line constraints.

Following is a synopsis of the syntax diagram shown in Figure 11.9:

- An out-of-line constraint can be added to a table using the `ALTER TABLE` command.
- Only out-of-line constraint states can be modified using the `ALTER TABLE` command.
- 9i A constraint can be renamed.
- `PRIMARY KEY` and `UNIQUE` key out-of-line constraints can be dropped.
- An out-of-line constraint can be dropped by name.
- The `CASCADE` option will drop dependent integrity constraints, as well as foreign keys dependent on primary or unique key constraints.

As shown in Figure 11.9, the `ALTER TABLE` command can be used to change constraints and constraint states from an out-of-line perspective.

Add a constraint this way:

```
ALTER TABLE MOVIES ADD CONSTRAINT UK_MOVIES PRIMARY KEY(MOVIE_ID);
```

When modifying, you can only change the state of a constraint:

```
ALTER TABLE MOVIES MODIFY CONSTRAINT UK_MOVIES ENABLE;
```

9i Now we can rename the constraint:

```
ALTER TABLE MOVIES RENAME CONSTRAINT UK_MOVIES TO PK_MOVIES;
```

Now let's drop the constraint:

```
ALTER TABLE MOVIES DROP CONSTRAINT PK_MOVIES;
```

Dropping and Truncating Tables

The DROP TABLE command is used to drop tables. The TRUNCATE command, as discussed in Chapter 10, is an alternative to a DELETE command removing all rows from a table. Thus, a TRUNCATE command is the same as a DELETE command without a WHERE clause. The TRUNCATE command is also an alternative to the DROP TABLE command except that the table structure is retained where all the data rows are destroyed.

The **TRUNCATE** command is a DDL command and thus implicitly executes a **COMMIT** command. In other words, a **TRUNCATE** command cannot be undone using a **ROLLBACK** command.

The DROP TABLE command destroys both the table structure and its data. The syntax for the DROP TABLE command is shown in Figure 11.10.

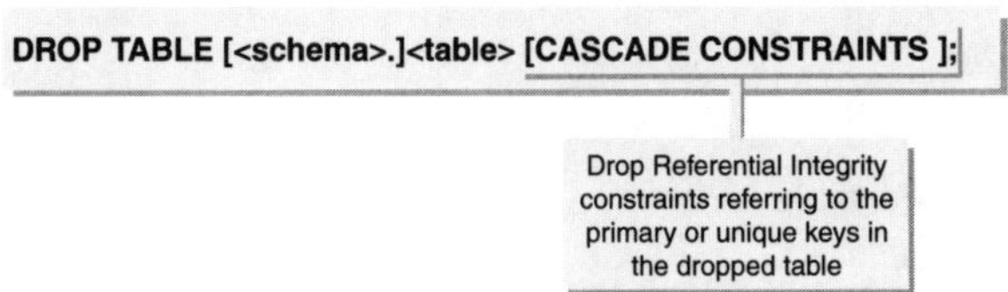

Figure 11.10 DROP TABLE command syntax.

Following is a synopsis of the syntax diagram shown in Figure 11.10:

- The DROP TABLE command can be used to drop a table in any accessible schema.
- The CASCADE CONSTRAINTS option will drop foreign key constraints referring to primary or unique key constraints present on the dropped table.

Using the DROP TABLE command syntax shown in Figure 11.10, this command destroys the MOVIES table created in the preceding section:

```
DROP TABLE MOVIES;
```

Metadata Views

This section lists the Oracle Database metadata views for database objects covered in this chapter.

Metadata (Oracle Data Dictionary) views are not required for this exam, but they can be extremely useful. Utilize an active Oracle Database you have access to, or read Oracle documentation, regarding the contents of the table metadata views mentioned here. Get a general idea of column names and data content from the documentation. You may find the metadata views extremely useful!

Tables

These metadata views describe the structure of tables created within the current user (schema):

- USER_TABLES—High-level table information.
- USER_TAB_COLUMNS—Column definitions in tables.
- USER_UNUSED_COL_TABS—Table columns marked as unused by an ALTER TABLE <table> SET UNUSED command.

Datatypes

These metadata views describe user-defined type structures such as TYPE definitions created with the CREATE TYPE command, nested tables, and VARRAY arrays:

- USER_TYPES—User-defined types.
- USER_NESTED_TABLES—Nested table objects.
- USER_NESTED_TABLE_COLS—The columns in nested table objects.
- USER_VARRAYS—VARRAY array object structures.

Constraints

These metadata views describe the structure of constraints created in tables:

- USER_CONSTRAINTS—High-level detail covering constraint table allocation, ownership, constraint types, and current states.
- USER_CONS_COLUMNS—Constraint column level detail.

Exam Prep Questions

1. Which of these are valid Oracle Database objects?

   ❑ A. Table

   ❑ B. Materialized cluster

   ❑ C. Table organized index

   ❑ D. View

   ❑ E. All of the above

   A and D are correct and thus E is incorrect. B is incorrect because there is no such thing as a materialized cluster. There is such a thing as a materialized view. C is also incorrect because there is no such thing as a table organized index. There is such a thing as an index organized table (an IOT).

2. Which line is incorrect in this query?

   ```
   1. CREATE TABLE ACTORS(
   2. ACTOR_ID NUMBER NOT NULL
   3. ,NAME VARCHAR2(32) NOT NULL
   4. GENDER NUMBER DEFAULT 'M' NOT NULL
   5. ,TYPECAST VARCHAR2(64) NULL);
   ```

   Line number 4 is incorrect because the **DEFAULT** clause will attempt to place a character into a **NUMBER** field, causing a syntax error. All other lines are syntactically correct.

3. What is the maximum length of a **VARCHAR2** datatype?

   The answer is 4000 characters (bytes). No explanation is required. This is just a fact.

4. Select the option for the largest and smallest positive numbers that can be set into a **NUMBER(5,2)** datatype.

   ❑ A. 999.99 and 0.01

   ❑ B. 999.99 and 0

   ❑ C. 99999 and 0.01

   ❑ D. 99999 and 0

   ❑ E. None of the above

   D is the correct answer so E is obviously wrong. The values must be positive and thus negative values are irrelevant. The largest value is 99999, five digits, because the precision of the number is 5. The smallest value is 0 because 0 is the smallest possible positive number. Therefore, D is correct. As a result, A, B, and C are incorrect.

5. What will the datatypes in the following **CREATE TABLE** command be?

   ```
   CREATE TABLE TEST(ID1 INTEGER, ID2 SMALLINT);
   ```

   ❑ A. **INTEGER** and **SMALLINT**

   ❑ B. **INTEGER** and **INTEGER**

- ❑ C. **NUMBER** and **NUMBER**
- ❑ D. Both **NUMBER(38)**
- ❑ E. None of the above

INTEGER and **SMALLINT** are ANSI standard datatypes and will be automatically converted to internal Oracle Database datatypes: **NUMBER(38)** or 38-byte **NUMBER** datatypes. Therefore, D is the correct answer and answers A, B, C, and E are incorrect.

6. Select the correct answer:
   - ❑ A. A **VARRAY** is a fixed-length array and a nested table is a dynamic array.
   - ❑ B. A **VARRAY** is a dynamic array and a nested table is a fixed-length array.
   - ❑ C. A **REF** datatype is a fixed-length array.
   - ❑ D. All of the above
   - ❑ E. None of the above

   A is the correct answer. For C **REF** is an object pointer datatype, not an array. Therefore, answers B, C, D, and E are all incorrect.

7. Which of these are valid constraints? Select all correct answers.
   - ❑ A. **NOT NULL**
   - ❑ B. **CHECK**
   - ❑ C. **UNIQUE**
   - ❑ D. **PRIMARY KEY**
   - ❑ E. **FOREIGN KEY**

   All of these answers are correct. **NOT NULL** prohibits a column from having no value. A **CHECK** constraint executes a validity check on a column value. A **UNIQUE** constraint forces a column value to be unique against the same column value across all rows of the table. **PRIMARY KEY** and **FOREIGN KEY** constraints are used to enforce Referential Integrity.

8. What does this command do? Select the best answer.

   ```
   ALTER TABLE MODIFY CONSTRAINT PK_STUDIO ENABLE NOVALIDATE;
   ```

   - ❑ A. Enables the **PK_STUDIO** constraint
   - ❑ B. Enables the **PK_STUDIO** primary key constraint
   - ❑ C. Disables a constraint
   - ❑ D. Allows existing rows to not comply with the constraint
   - ❑ E. Allows existing rows to not comply with the constraint but enforces the constraint for newly added rows

   E is the correct answer. **ENABLE** activates the constraint, and **NOVALIDATE** does not require validation against the constraint for already existing rows, only enforcing against newly added rows. As a result, answers A, B, C, and D are all either incorrect or partially correct. A is correct but accounts only for the **ENABLE** constraint state. B is correct as well but is the incorrect answer for the same reason that answer A is incorrect. C is totally wrong. D, like answers A and B, is only partially correct.

9. Which of these commands will not cause an error?

- ❑ A. `ALTER TABLE MOVIES MODIFY`
  `(MOVIE_ID NUMBER PRIMARY KEY);`
- ❑ B. `ALTER TABLE MOVIES MODIFY`
  `(MOVIE_ID NUMBER CHECK(MOVIE_ID > 1);`
- ❑ C. `ALTER TABLE MOVIES MODIFY`
  `(MOVIE_ID NUMBER NOT NULL);`
- ❑ D. `ALTER TABLE MOVIES MODIFY`
  `(MOVIE_ID NUMBER NULL);`
- ❑ E. `ALTER TABLE MOVIES MODIFY`
  `(MOVIE_ID NUMBER UNIQUE);`

Answers C and D are correct and answers A, B, and E are all incorrect. Why? Only the **NULL** constraint can be set within an **ALTER TABLE** command when constraints are being set inline. Other constraints must be set as out-of-line constraints in this situation.

10. Which metadata view can be used to examine table column structure for the currently logged-in user?

- ❑ A. **USER_TABLES**
- ❑ B. **USER_CONSTRAINTS**
- ❑ C. **USER_TAB_ATTRIBUTES**
- ❑ D. **USER_TABLE_COLUMNS**
- ❑ E. None of the above

Answer E is correct because none of those answers are correct. The correct answer would be **USER_TAB_COLUMNS**. For A and B both **USER_TABLES** and **USER_CONSTRAINTS** exist but neither access table column details. The metadata views listed under C and D do not exist.

Views, Indexes, Sequences, and Synonyms (DDL)

Terms You Need to Understand

- ✓ View
- ✓ Index
- ✓ Sequence
- ✓ Public synonym
- ✓ Private synonym
- ✓ Virtual column

Concepts You Need to Master

- ✓ Updatable views
- ✓ Constraint views
- ✓ Updating join subquery views
- ✓ Changing table data using updatable views
- ✓ The **WITH CHECK OPTION** for updatable views
- ✓ Changing views must account for all required (**NOT NULL**) columns in the underlying table (unless **NOT NULL** columns have **DEFAULT** settings)
- ✓ What virtual columns are and what causes them to be created
- ✓ Creating, altering, and dropping views
- ✓ Creating, altering, and dropping indexes
- ✓ Creating, altering, and dropping sequences
- ✓ Creating and dropping synonyms

This chapter describes views, indexes, sequences, and synonyms. Views are an overlay or logical window onto data in underlying tables. Indexes provide fast access to data in tables. Sequences are automated counters, and synonyms provide transparent access to objects.

Views

A *view* is a logical overlay over other database objects. An overlay is a nonpermanent and nonphysical abstraction of data. Put simply, a view does not contain any data but contains a query. This query is executed every time a view is accessed.

Views are often used to simplify for software development purposes. This is often a mistake if a database becomes large. Views are also used for security purposes. Specific groups of users can have privileged or restricted access to specific columns or rows within tables, or both.

A materialized view is not a view. A materialized view physically stores the result of a query and is normally used in data warehouse environments. Materialized views are not in the scope of this exam.

Creating Views

Figure 12.1 shows the syntax for the `CREATE VIEW` command.

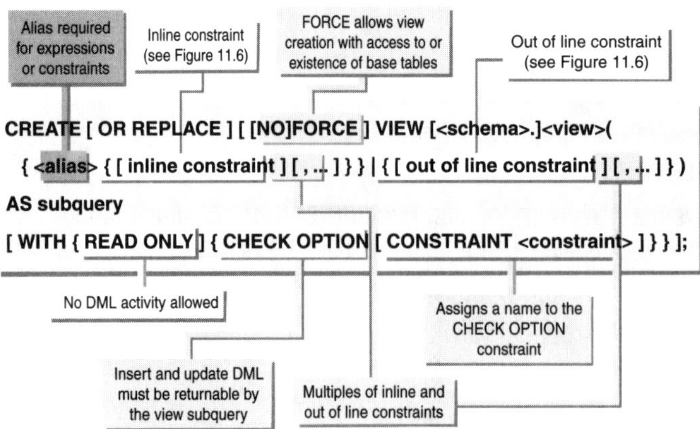

Figure 12.1 **CREATE VIEW** command syntax.

Following is a synopsis of the syntax diagram shown in Figure 12.1:

- The CREATE VIEW command will allow view creation in any accessible schema.
- A view is created using a subquery.
- Creating a view with the FORCE option will allow the creation of the view when underlying tables do not exist. A compilation error for the view will be returned.
- Both inline and out-of-line constraints can be created on views, but constraints are limited to those on underlying tables.
- A view created with the READ ONLY option prohibits DML activity on the view.
- When the CHECK OPTION is used, any INSERT or UPDATE commands applied with the view must match any restrictions for the view subquery.
- The CONSTRAINT <constraint> syntax element simply assigns a name to an updatable view CHECK CONSTRAINT.

There are numerous annotations in Figure 12.1, all best explained by example. This is a simple view retrieving rows from one table:

```
CREATE VIEW STUDIOS AS SELECT * FROM STUDIO;
```

This next example creates a view from a join, a join between a table and the view just created:

```
CREATE VIEW STUDIOMOVIES AS SELECT * FROM STUDIOS NATURAL JOIN MOVIE;
```

You could add some filtering and sorting to a query in a view. The OR REPLACE option is used to replace the existing STUDIOMOVIES view created previously:

```
CREATE OR REPLACE VIEW STUDIOMOVIES AS SELECT * FROM STUDIOS
NATURAL JOIN MOVIE WHERE TITLE LIKE '%a' ORDER BY TITLE;
```

The next view will not be created because one of the underlying tables, the STARS table, does not exist:

```
CREATE VIEW MOVIESTARS AS SELECT * FROM STARS NATURAL JOIN MOVIE;
```

You can force the view creation by using the FORCE option. The view creation will succeed but with an error message returned. Additionally, selecting from the view will return an error unless the missing STARS table is created:

```
CREATE FORCE VIEW MOVIESTARS AS SELECT * FROM STARS NATURAL JOIN MOVIE;
```

Changing Data from Views

Using DML with views implies using a view to execute INSERT, UPDATE, and DELETE commands against tables underlying a view. Those underlying tables can be a single table or even multiple tables in a join query, allowing changes to one of the tables underlying a view. The DML command adds a new row to the STUDIO table through the STUDIOS view:

```
INSERT INTO STUDIOS VALUES(101, 'Independent Films Incorporated');
```

Next, update the row just created:

```
UPDATE STUDIOS SET STUDIO = 'Independent Films Inc.'
WHERE STUDIO_ID = 101;
```

It follows that we can also remove a row from an underlying table through a view:

```
DELETE FROM STUDIOS WHERE STUDIO_ID = 101;
```

There are restrictions and some little quirks with respect to executing DML commands to change tables through views:

- Any DML created or altered rows must generally fit in with restrictions applied by the query in the view. For instance, change the STUDIOS view, adding a WHERE clause:

  ```
  CREATE OR REPLACE VIEW STUDIOS AS SELECT * FROM STUDIO
  WHERE STUDIO_ID < 100;
  ```

  Guess what? The UPDATE and DELETE DML commands previously executed against the STUDIOS view will not fail but will reply with `0 rows updated` and `0 rows deleted`, respectively. The INSERT command will succeed even though the WHERE clause is invalid for the view. However, selecting from the view will not return the row for `STUDIO.STUDIO_ID = 101` because the WHERE clause in the view subquery is not satisfied. To ensure that rows added conform to filtering requirements for the view, use `WITH CHECK OPTION`:

  ```
  CREATE OR REPLACE VIEW STUDIOS AS SELECT * FROM STUDIO
  WHERE STUDIO_ID < 100 WITH CHECK OPTION;
  ```

  A similar INSERT command against the STUDIOS view will now fail, returning a `view WITH CHECK OPTION where-clause violation` error:

  ```
  INSERT INTO STUDIOS VALUES(102, 'Independent Films Inc.');
  ```

- A view does not have to contain all columns in an underlying table to allow insertion through the view. However, any missing columns must be accounted for at the table level as nullable columns, or NOT NULL columns with DEFAULT value settings. For example, the DIRECTOR table contains three NOT NULL constrained columns and no DEFAULT settings. The view shown in Figure 12.2 is allowed. The subsequent INSERT command is not, because the GENDER column is not included. Setting a DEFAULT value for the GENDER column in the underlying DIRECTOR table solves the problem, as shown by the result in Figure 12.2.

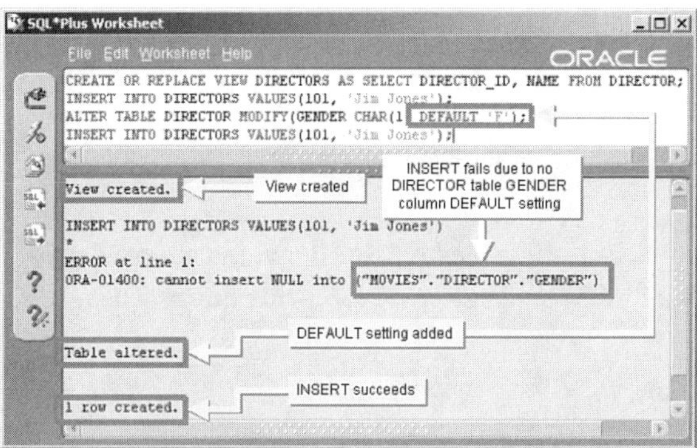

Figure 12.2 **NOT NULL** constraints and **DEFAULT** settings in underlying tables.

- As you can see in the syntax diagram in Figure 12.1, the STUDIOS view could have been created using the READ ONLY option, thereby prohibiting DML activity on underlying tables through a view:

  ```
  CREATE OR REPLACE VIEW STUDIOS AS SELECT * FROM STUDIO WITH READ ONLY;
  ```

  Executing the same three INSERT, UPDATE, and DELETE DML commands discussed previously will cause errors.

- All NOT NULL constraints must be included. For a single table view, the primary key constraint is included automatically. For a join table view, at least one of the primary keys or a unique key must be included. The reason is that individual rows must be locatable. The STUDIOS view created previously in this chapter is simple and thus by default includes all the necessary constraints, including all NOT NULL constraints and the primary key constraint. Join views can cause problems. The obvious reason is that updating rows through the view must be uniquely findable in the underlying tables. The following view allows DML table changes to both tables because both primary keys are included:

  ```
  CREATE OR REPLACE VIEW STUDIOMOVIES AS SELECT *
  FROM STUDIO NATURAL JOIN MOVIE;
  ```

  Here is a join view on two existing MOVIE schema tables:

  ```
  CREATE OR REPLACE VIEW GEOGRAPHY AS SELECT REGION_ID, COUNTRY_ID
  , REGION, COUNTRY FROM REGION NATURAL JOIN COUNTRY;
  ```

  There is a one-to-many relationship between the REGION and COUNTRY tables. The COUNTRY table can be updated through the view as a single row:

  ```
  UPDATE GEOGRAPHY SET COUNTRY = 'North Korean Republic'
  WHERE COUNTRY_ID = 29;
  ```

A single row in the REGION table cannot be updated through the view because many COUNTRY rows must be updated as well, so this query will not work:

```
UPDATE GEOGRAPHY SET REGION_ID = 105, REGION = 'EEC'
WHERE REGION_ID = 2;
```

Attempting to update rows in both tables is also illegal because we cannot change more than one table through a view, so this query will not work either:

```
UPDATE GEOGRAPHY SET REGION_ID = 105, COUNTRY_ID = 1
WHERE REGION_ID = 2;
```

Due to underlying table restrictions, both tables would need to be updated. All the following three INSERT commands will cause errors:

```
INSERT INTO GEOGRPAHY(REGION_ID, COUNTRY_ID, REGION, COUNTRY)
VALUES(101, 102, 'Southern Africa', 'Zimbabwe');
INSERT INTO GEOGRPAHY(REGION_ID, COUNTRY_ID, REGION)
VALUES(101, 102, 'Southern Africa');
INSERT INTO GEOGRPAHY(COUNTRY_ID, COUNTRY)
VALUES(102, 'Zimbabwe');
```

On the same basis as using INSERT and UPDATE commands, deletions through join query views will not work either:

```
DELETE FROM GEOGRAPHY WHERE COUNTRY_ID = 3;
DELETE FROM GEOGRAPHY WHERE REGION_ID = 2;
DELETE FROM GEOGRAPHY WHERE REGION_ID = 2 AND COUNTRY_ID = 3;
```

➤ Subqueries in views prohibit DML activity because there is no way to interpret where to place a new row into a semi-join. Semi-joins other than inline views do not return columns, so columns cannot be found. Inline views change column names using an alias, creating virtual columns. For the same reason, anything in a view query not precisely matching a column name in an underlying table can cause a problem for DML commands executed against the view. For instance, if a view query contains a function against a column from an underlying table, the resulting functional expression will not be able to update any columns in the underlying table. The following example will not allow DML table changes to the DIRECTOR.NAME column because the view creates the column as an expression. The expression cannot be executed in reverse from the view back into the table, causing the subsequent INSERT command to fail:

```
CREATE OR REPLACE VIEW DIRECTORS AS
SELECT DIRECTOR_ID, INITCAP(NAME) AS DIRECTOR FROM DIRECTOR;
INSERT INTO DIRECTORS(DIRECTOR_ID, DIRECTOR)
VALUES(102, 'Clint Eastwood');
```

The phrase INITCAP(NAME) AS DIRECTOR assigns an alias to the expression INITCAP(NAME) because the view requires a virtual column name.

- A view containing a query including a GROUP BY clause, an ORDER BY clause, or a DISTINCT clause will not allow DML activity on underlying tables. Both the GROUP BY clause and the DISTINCT clause create summary groups, thus returning potentially fewer rows than all rows in the table. Therefore, underlying table rows would be impossible to find. The ORDER BY clause sorts the results of a query. Therefore, updating a view with an ORDER BY clause in its subquery is not allowed because rows to be updated cannot be found.

Updatable Table Columns Through Views

When you want to verify whether view columns can be subjected to DML commands, you can check the USER_UPDATABLE_COLUMNS metadata view, as shown in Figure 12.3.

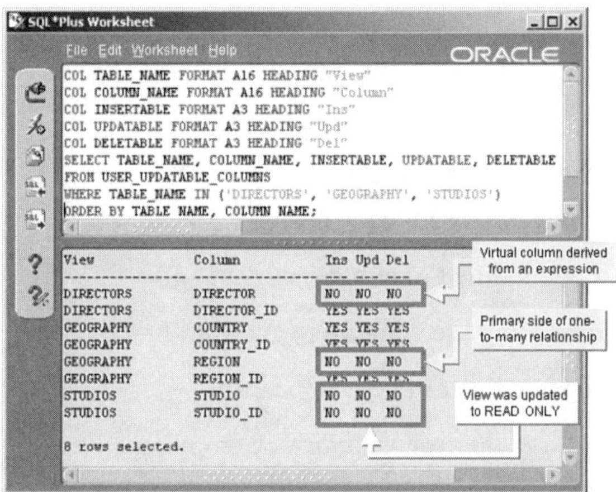

Figure 12.3 Updatable columns through views (**USER_UPDATABLE_COLUMNS**).

Adding Constraints to Views

9i Figure 12.1 shows that inline and out-of-line constraints can be added to views. Constraints are not enforced in views but are enforced from underlying tables. Thus, view constraints are specifiable only in the states DISABLE and NOVALIDATE and must mirror underlying tables. View constraints can be only one of UNIQUE, PRIMARY KEY, or FOREIGN KEY constraints. This example mirrors the MOVIE.TITLE column unique constraint into the MOVIES view:

```
CREATE OR REPLACE VIEW MOVIES (TITLE UNIQUE DISABLE NOVALIDATE, YEAR
, RELEASE, LIST_PRICE, RANK, REVIEWS, REVIEW_RANK)
AS SELECT TITLE, YEAR, RELEASE
,LIST_PRICE, RANK, REVIEWS, REVIEW_RANK FROM MOVIE;
```

Altering and Dropping Views

This section examines the ALTER VIEW and DROP VIEW commands. The ALTER VIEW command is limited to changes on constraints. Figure 12.4 shows the syntax for the ALTER VIEW command.

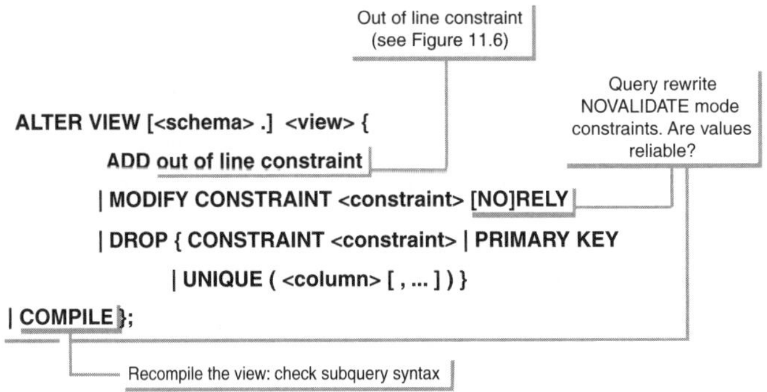

Figure 12.4 **ALTER VIEW** command syntax.

Following is a synopsis of the syntax diagram shown in Figure 12.4:

- An new out-of-line constraint can be added.
- The constraint states can be modified only between RELY and NORELY.
- A constraint can be dropped using the name of the constraint.
- PRIMARY KEY or UNIQUE KEY constraints can be dropped.
- A view can be recompiled using the COMPILE option. Compiling a view simply resubmits the contained subquery to the SQL engine for reparsing, checking syntax.

For an updatable view, only the constraints of underlying tables can be created, altered, or dropped using the ALTER VIEW command. In other words, view constraints must match underlying tables or must not be created at all. The net effect is to mimic constraint behavior of underlying tables in the updatable view. Otherwise, the ALTER VIEW command can be used to recompile a view. Recompiling a view simply reparses the syntax of the SQL code in a view subquery. The MOVIESTARS view was created earlier in this chapter using the FORCE option because the STARS table did not exist:

```
CREATE TABLE STARS(MOVIE_ID NUMBER NOT NULL REFERENCES MOVIE(MOVIE_ID)
,POPULARITY NUMBER NOT NULL);
```

Now use the ALTER VIEW command to recompile the MOVIESTARS view, and no error will be returned:

```
ALTER VIEW MOVIESTARS COMPILE;
```

The syntax for the DROP VIEW command is shown in Figure 12.5.

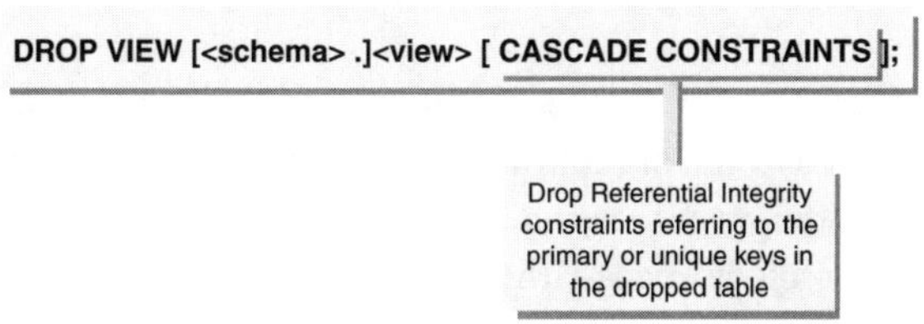

Figure 12.5 **DROP VIEW** command syntax.

In Figure 12.5, the CASCADE CONSTRAINTS option will drop any Referential Integrity constraints (foreign keys on other tables) referring to primary or unique key constraints built in the view. The following DROP VIEW commands destroy all the views created in this chapter thus far:

```
DROP VIEW DIRECTORS;
DROP VIEW GEOGRAPHY;
DROP VIEW MOVIES;
DROP VIEW MOVIESTARS;
DROP VIEW STUDIOMOVIES;
DROP VIEW STUDIOS;
```

Inline Views and Top-N Analysis

The topics of Top-N analysis and inline views are grouped in discussions on views in many Oracle texts. I prefer to classify Top-N analysis as WHERE clause filtering; see Chapter 3, "Filtering (WHERE) and Sorting Data (ORDER BY)," specifically the section "Top-N Queries."

Indexes

Much of the detail with respect to indexes is out of scope for this exam. This exam simply requires syntactical knowledge as to how to create and maintain indexes. Indexing topics covering index types, uses, reorganization dropping, and monitoring are in the next Oracle Certification exam. However, brief coverage of indexing is warranted here.

What is an index? In simplest terms, an index is a very small physical columnar portion of a table, sorted in a preferred order. In other words, if a table has 50 columns and 1 million rows, I could create an index on a single column. It follows that physical I/O reading the single column index will be much faster than reading all 50 columns 1 million times. Additionally, an index is created in sorted order, and thus reading the index in the sorted order removes any resorting processing. There are also other factors to consider with respect to reading indexes and performance. For instance, an Oracle Database BTree index has a maximum of three branch levels and one leaf node level. Therefore, reading a BTree index for an exact match (single row) requires at the most four block reads—that's three branch blocks and one leaf block. Therefore, if our 1 million row times 50 column table hypothetically occupies a single block for every row, it thus occupies 50 million blocks. That is an enormous row size but it will demonstrate a point. Fifty million blocks in a standard 8KB block size database is 39GB. Finding an exact row using an index requires five block reads: up to four blocks to find the table `ROWID` pointer in the index, followed by reading a single table block to find the actual row in the table. The `ROWID` stored in the index points to the exact address location of the row in the table on disk (or in memory). Therefore, a single row match scans five blocks; that's 40KB, a great deal less than 39GB. That is why we use indexes!

Creating Indexes

The `CREATE INDEX` command is used to create indexes. Indexes are used to allow fast access into data in tables. Figure 12.6 shows the syntax for the `CREATE INDEX` command.

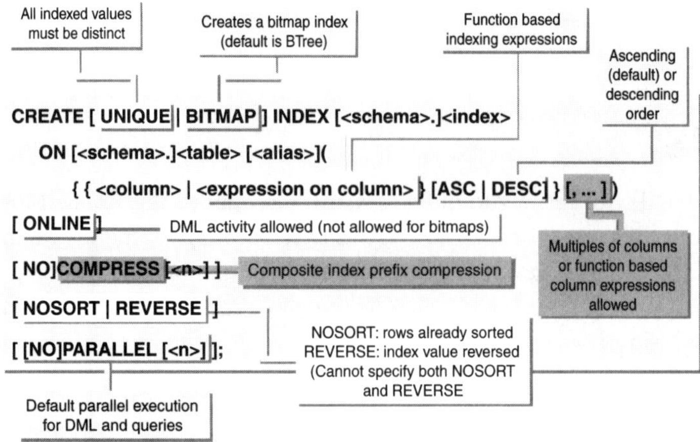

Figure 12.6 CREATE INDEX command syntax.

Following is a synopsis of the syntax diagram shown in Figure 12.6:

- An index can be created for an accessible table.
- The `UNIQUE` option creates an index with distinct values only. Attempting to create a unique index on values that are not unique will return an error.
- The default for the `CREATE INDEX` command is a BTree index. A BTree index is an index created in the structure of an upside-down tree with layers of branches and leaves. The leaves contain the indexed values, and the branches allow a rapid search path through to specific leaves.
- The `BITMAP` option creates a special type of index best used for low cardinality data. Low cardinality data is data with very few unique values. A bitmap index assigns 0s and 1s to values representing on or off.
- Function-based indexes can be created using an expression on a column or multiple columns. A function-based index stores the result of the functional expression. Resulting index searches search for the result of the function.
- `ASC` or `DESC` implies that an index can be created in ascending or descending sorted order.
- The syntax element `[, ...]` means that an index can be one or more columns or expressions, or a combination thereof.
- Creating an index using the `ONLINE` option only rewrites the actual index file after the index has already been created in temporary space. The net effect is minimal interference with concurrent DML activity.
- The `COMPRESS` option removes duplications of values in composite indexes. A composite index is an index consisting of more than a single column. Compression is performed up to a factor of one fewer than all columns in a composite index.
- The `NOSORT` option assumes that rows are already sorted in the table, and thus when the index is being generated, no sorting is required.
- A `REVERSE` index is a reverse key index. The values in each column of the index are reversed. In other words, indexing the value `abcdef` into reverse order would be `fedcba`.

Do not confuse a reverse key (**REVERSE**) index with a descending sort. A descending (**DESC**) sort index sorts rows in descending order (reverse ascending) between rows, not reversing column values.

- Indexes can be created allowing for parallel execution against them using the PARALLEL option.

This command creates an index on the MOVIE.RANK column:

```
CREATE INDEX AK_MOVIE_1 ON MOVIE(RANK) ONLINE;
```

The preceding command creates the index ONLINE, allowing DML activity on the table during the index creation process. What ONLINE effectively does is to retain any existing index during the index rebuild, only temporarily halting DML activity on the table when copying index entries in from the newly built index.

This command creates a composite index on three columns such that the first and second columns are compressed:

```
CREATE INDEX AK_MOVIE_2 ON MOVIE(TITLE, YEAR, RANK) COMPRESS 2;
```

The preceding command will remove duplicate values for prefix columns: TITLE and YEAR. This next command creates the same index but with the YEAR sorted in descending order:

```
CREATE INDEX AK_MOVIE_2 ON MOVIE(TITLE, YEAR DESC, RANK) COMPRESS 2;
```

A function-based index is created with an expression as in the following example:

```
CREATE INDEX FB_MOVIE_1 ON MOVIE
    ( ( REVIEWS / ( REVIEWS * REVIEW_RANK ) ) * 100) ONLINE;
```

Certain requirements are explicit for function-based index creation and use:

- Cost-based optimization must be in use.
- The connected user must have the QUERY_REWRITE privilege and have execution privileges on any user-defined functions.
- Oracle Database configuration parameter settings QUERY_REWRITE_ENABLED = TRUE and QUERY REWRITE_INTEGRITY = TRUSTED must be set.
- It is essential to generate statistics for a function-based index. If statistics are not generated for a function-based index, the Optimizer will not use it. Statistics can be generated in three ways: (1) using the COMPUTE STATISTICS option in the CREATE INDEX command, (2) using the ANALYZE command, and (3) using the DBMS_STATS package.

Generation of statistics is not included in this exam.

Altering and Dropping Indexes

Figure 12.7 shows the syntax for the `ALTER INDEX` and `DROP INDEX` commands.

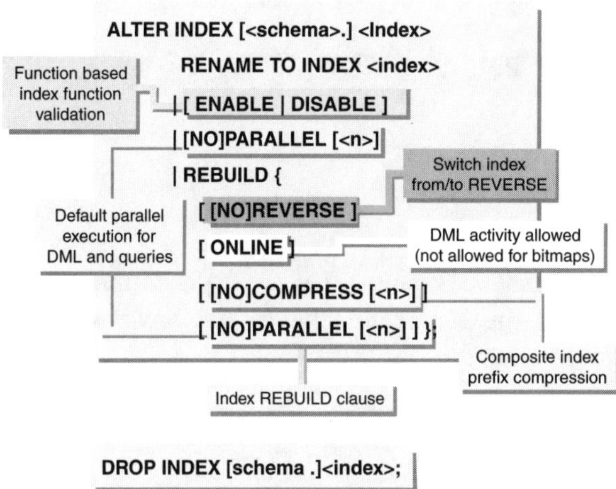

Figure 12.7 **ALTER INDEX** and **DROP INDEX** command syntax.

Following is a synopsis of the syntax diagram shown in Figure 12.7:

- The `RENAME` option allows an index to be renamed.
- The `ENABLE` and `DISABLE` options switch on or off the availability of a function-based index, perhaps after a block of PL/SQL code within the function was altered and a PL/SQL compilation error resulted.
- The `PARALLEL` option allows specification of parallel execution on an index.
- The `REBUILD` option contains various factors, all of which are optional. Executing a command such as the following simply rebuilds the index with existing parameters:

  ```
  ALTER INDEX ThisIndex REBUILD;
  ```

  `ALTER INDEX` command `REBUILD` options are as listed here:

  - The `REVERSE` option rebuilds the index as a reverse key or normal index (`NOREVERSE`).
  - The `ONLINE` option rebuilds the index online.

- The COMPRESS option compresses columns in an index.
- The PARALLEL option allows or prohibits parallel processing for an index.

Figure 12.7 describes the ALTER INDEX and DROP INDEX commands more than adequately using annotations. The most frequently used version of the ALTER INDEX command involves the REBUILD option, allowing reconstruction of an index from the ground up. Rebuilding indexes can help performance significantly:

```
ALTER INDEX AK_MOVIE_1 REBUILD ONLINE;
```

The preceding index can be dropped as shown here:

```
DROP INDEX AK_MOVIE_1;
```

Sequences

A sequence is an automatic sequence counter that can be used for various purposes. Figure 12.8 shows the syntax for the CREATE SEQUENCE, ALTER SEQUENCE, and DROP SEQUENCE commands.

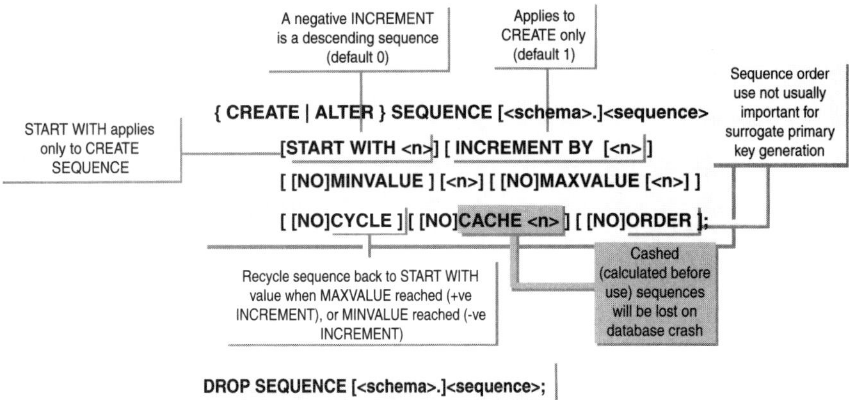

Figure 12.8 **CREATE**, **ALTER**, and **DROP SEQUENCE** command syntax.

Following is a synopsis of the syntax diagram shown in Figure 12.8:

- Create a new sequence using the CREATE SEQUENCE command, and change an existing sequence using the ALTER SEQUENCE command.
- The START WITH clause determines the first value of a sequence with the first execution of the NEXTVAL pseudocolumn on the sequence. The default value is set to 0 (START WITH not specified). The START WITH value can also be both negative or positive.

- The INCREMENT value is defaulted to 1 and can be any value but 0.
- The MINVALUE and MAXVALUE settings must be consistent with the increment. In other words, if INCREMENT is -1, a MINVALUE of 0 will cause an error. The same rule applies to the setting for START WITH. Obviously, the same applies for setting NOMINVALUE and NOMAXVALUE. All the parameters have to make sense, in relation to other settings.
- The CYCLE option will recycle sequences when the CYCLE value is reached. For example, setting CYCLE to 10 will recycle back to the value of START WITH after CYCLE is reached.
- The CACHE option will store pre-calculated values for a sequence into memory.
- The ORDER option forces a sequence to always be generated in sequential order.

This command creates a sequence for a surrogate primary key in the STUDIO table:

```
CREATE SEQUENCE STUDIO_SEQ START WITH 1 INCREMENT BY 1 NOMAXVALUE NOCYCLE;
```

The preceding STUDIO_SEQ sequence begins counting at 1, in steps of 1 (the second sequence value will be 2), has no maximum value and does not recycle back to the START WITH value of 1.

When rows are inserted into the STUDIO table, the sequence is accessed this way:

```
INSERT INTO STUDIO(STUDIO_ID,STUDIO) VALUES(STUDIO_SEQ.NEXTVAL
,'Columbia/TriStar Studios');
```

The STUDIO_SEQ sequence can be dropped using the DROP SEQUENCE command as shown here:

```
DROP SEQUENCE STUDIO_SEQ;
```

Sequences can be accessed using the NEXTVAL and CURRVAL pseudocolumns (see Chapter 4, "Operators, Conditions, Pseudocolumns, and Expressions").

Sequences can be accessed in the following commands:

- The column list of a SELECT command:

  ```
  SELECT STUDIO_SEQ.NEXTVAL, STUDIO_ID, STUDIO FROM STUDIO;
  ```

- An INSERT command VALUES list (the same as the preceding example):

  ```
  INSERT INTO STUDIO(STUDIO_ID,STUDIO) VALUES
  (STUDIO_SEQ.NEXTVAL,'Columbia/TriStar Studios');
  ```

- The column list of a subquery contained within the VALUES list of an INSERT command:

```
INSERT INTO RATING(RATING_ID,GROUP_ID,MPAA,RATING)
VALUES(RATING_SEQ.NEXTVAL,
    (SELECT RATING_ID FROM RATING
    WHERE RATING='Family Viewing'),'G','General');
```

- An UPDATE command SET clause:

```
UPDATE RATING SET GROUP_ID = STUDIO_SEQ.NEXTVAL WHERE MPAA IS NULL;
```

- In a MERGE DML command (this example is copied from Chapter 10):

```
MERGE INTO SALE S USING DAILYSALES DS
    ON(DS.MOVIE_ID = S.MOVIE_ID
        AND DS.SOURCE_ID = S.SOURCE_ID
        AND DS.FORMAT_ID = S.FORMAT_ID
        AND DS.REGION_ID = S.REGION_ID
        AND DS.COUNTRY_ID = S.COUNTRY_ID
        AND DS.DTE = S.SALE_DATE)
WHEN MATCHED THEN
    UPDATE SET SALE_PRICE = DS.AMOUNT + SALE_PRICE
WHEN NOT MATCHED THEN
    INSERT VALUES(SALE_SEQ.NEXTVAL, DS.MOVIE_ID, DS.SOURCE_ID
    , DS.FORMAT_ID, DS.REGION_ID
    , DS.COUNTRY_ID, SYSDATE, DS.AMOUNT);
```

Synonyms

Synonyms in general terms can be public or private. A synonym is created as private by default (no keyword required) and is accessible only to the user creating the synonym or any user receiving privileges on the synonym. A private synonym can link to an object in a different schema, assuming that appropriate privileges are available. A public synonym is available to all users. Both private and public synonyms, whomever granted to, still require granting of access privileges to underlying objects.

Figure 12.9 shows the syntax for the CREATE SYNONYM and DROP SYNONYM commands. There is no ALTER SYNONYM command. If a synonym must be changed, it has to be dropped and re-created.

Following is a synopsis of the syntax diagram shown in Figure 12.9:

- The CREATE SYNONYM command can be used to create a new synonym in any accessible schema.
- Using REPLACE allows for the replacement of an existing synonym. There is no ALTER SYNONYM command.
- A synonym created with the PUBLIC option creates a synonym available to all users, assuming, of course, that those grantee users have access to underlying tables.

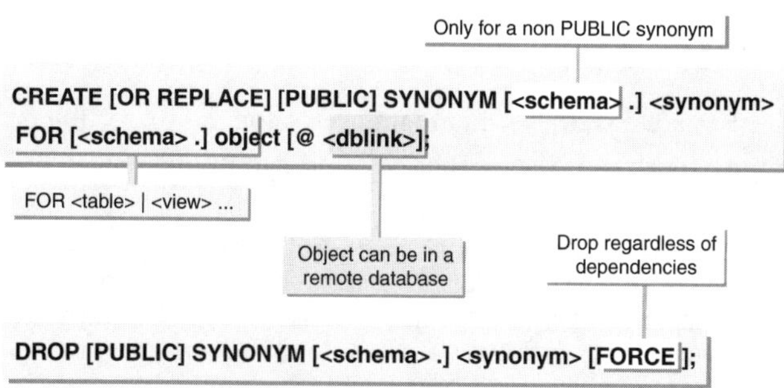

Figure 12.9 **CREATE** and **DROP SYNONYM** command syntax.

- Creating or replacing a synonym as `PUBLIC` can only be performed by an object for the currently connected user, not for other `[<schema>.]` referenced schemas.
- A synonym can be created for an object in a remote database, across a database link.
- The `DROP` synonym command allows dropping of synonyms. Dropping a `PUBLIC` synonym requires the `DROP PUBLIC SYNONYM` syntax form of the command.
- Dropping a synonym using the `FORCE` option drops a synonym regardless of any existing dependencies.

As shown in Figure 12.9, a synonym can even access an object in a different and perhaps even remote database, across a network using a database link, specified by the option `[ @dblink ]`.

Synonyms provide transparency and are generally beneficial to development processes and distributed environments such as in replicated databases.

A public synonym accessible to all database users could be created as shown next, allowing access to the `MOVIES` schema `MOVIE` table for all users in my database:

```
CREATE PUBLIC SYNONYM MYMOVIES FOR MOVIE;
```

The `MYMOVIES` synonym is then accessed just like a table:

```
SELECT * FROM MYMOVIES;
```

The `CREATE SYNONYM` and `CREATE PUBLIC SYNONYM` privileges are required for creation of private and public synonyms, respectively.

Metadata Views

This section lists the Oracle Database metadata views for database objects covered in this chapter: views, indexes, sequences, and synonyms.

Metadata (Oracle Data Dictionary) views are not required for this exam, but they can be extremely useful. Utilize an active Oracle Database you have access to, or read Oracle documentation, regarding the contents of the table metadata views mentioned here. Get a general idea of column names and data content from the documentation. You may find the metadata views extremely useful!

Views

These metadata views describe the structure of views created within the current user (schema):

- `USER_VIEWS`—View structure and columns.
- `USER_UPDATABLE_COLUMNS`—All columns in all views plus indication of potential underlying table DML activity for `INSERT`, `UPDATE`, and `DELETE` commands.

Indexes

These metadata views describe the structure of indexes created within the current user (schema):

- `USER_INDEXES`—General index structure.
- `USER_IND_COLUMNS`—Structure of columns and tables within indexes.
- `USER_IND_EXPRESSIONS`—Expressions for function-based indexes.

Sequences and Synonyms

These metadata views describe the structure of sequences and synonyms created within the current user (schema):

- `USER_SEQUENCES`—Shows all sequence metadata details.
- `USER_SYNONYMS`—Shows all synonym metadata details.

Finding the Right Metadata Views

Metadata views in Oracle Database are divided into metadata views and performance views. The names of most of the standard performance views are prefixed with the string `V$`. Thus, the performance view `V$SQL` contains SQL code for parsed SQL commands. V$ performance views are out of scope for this exam. To find the names of all V$ performance, execute the following query while logged in as the SYS user:

```
SELECT TABLE_NAME FROM DICTIONARY
WHERE TABLE_NAME LIKE 'V$%' ORDER BY 1;
```

A small fraction of the database metadata views are in scope for this exam. Metadata views can be divided into three separate sections named by different prefixes: ALL_, DBA_, and USER_. For example, (1) ALL_TABLES finds all tables for all users in the database, (2) DBA_TABLES finds all tables for all users with DBA privileges, and (3) USER_TABLES finds all tables for the currently connected user. The most obvious difference among the ALL_TABLES, DBA_TABLES, and USER_TABLES metadata views is that ALL_TABLES and DBA_TABLES both have an OWNER column. The OWNER column contains the name of the schema owner of the table. Thus, the USER_TABLES metadata view does not require an owner because it lists only tables belonging to the current owner (user or schema).

Exam Prep Questions

1. Which of these are Oracle Database objects?
   - ❑ A. Index
   - ❑ B. Materialized index
   - ❑ C. Private table
   - ❑ D. Public synonym
   - ❑ E. All of the above

   Correct answers are A and D. B is incorrect because there is no such thing as a materialized index, but there is a materialized view. C is also incorrect because there is no such thing as a private table. Because B and C are wrong, E is incorrect.

2. For the following **CREATE VIEW** command, only the **MOVIE** table exists. Which commands will create a new view?
   - ❑ A.
   ```
   CREATE VIEW BOXOFFICEMOVIES
      AS SELECT * FROM BOXRECEIPTS
      NATURAL JOIN MOVIE WHERE RANK > 100;
   ```
   - ❑ B.
   ```
   CREATE VIEW BOXOFFICEMOVIES
      AS SELECT * FROM BOXRECEIPTS
      NATURAL JOIN MOVIE;
   ```
   - ❑ C.
   ```
   CREATE FORCE VIEW BOXOFFICEMOVIES
      AS SELECT * FROM BOXRECEIPTS
      NATURAL JOIN MOVIE WHERE RANK > 100;
   ```
   - ❑ D.
   ```
   CREATE FORCE VIEW BOXOFFICEMOVIES
      SELECT * FROM BOXRECEIPT
      NATURAL JOIN MOVIE;
   ```
   - ❑ E. None of the above

   C is correct because it accesses a non-existent table using the **FORCE** option, and the **WHERE** clause does not affect the query. D is incorrect because the **AS** keyword is missing between the view name and the **SELECT** command. E is incorrect because both A and B are wrong. Both A and B are wrong because if a table does not exist in a view subquery, the **FORCE** option is required.

3. Which of these elements in view subqueries allow a view to be used to change data in underlying tables with DML commands?
   - ❑ A. Contains one or more subqueries
   - ❑ B. Contains an **ORDER BY** clause
   - ❑ C. Contains an **ORDER** clause and a **GROUP BY** clause
   - ❑ D. Contains a **WHERE** clause and a **DISTINCT** clause
   - ❑ E. None of the above

   E is the correct answer. A view is not updatable if the view subquery contains a subquery, a function, a **GROUP BY** clause, an **ORDER BY** clause, or a **DISTINCT** clause.

4. Which of these constraints can be applied to a view?

- ❑ A. **CHECK**
- ❑ B. **NOT NULL**
- ❑ C. **UNIQUE**
- ❑ D. **FOREIGN KEY**
- ❑ E. **PRIMARY KEY**

Only **UNIQUE**, **FOREIGN KEY**, and **PRIMARY KEY** constraints can be applied to a view. Thus, A and B are incorrect and C, D, and E are correct.

5. Which set of constraint states applies to all view constraints?

- ❑ A. **ENABLE NOVALIDATE**
- ❑ B. **ENABLE VALIDATE**
- ❑ C. **RELY VALIDATE**
- ❑ D. **DISABLE VALIDATE**
- ❑ E. **DISABLE NOVALIDATE**

E is the correct answer because view constraints are applied by underlying table constraints and not by a view. Additionally, view constraints must mirror underlying table constraints. Thus, **ENABLE** and **VALIDATE** are incorrect and therefore A, B, C, and D are all incorrect.

6. Can columns be altered with the **ALTER VIEW** command?

The answer is no, they cannot. Only constraints can be changed and the view can be recompiled.

7. What is the maximum number of reads of a unique BTree index and a table the index is built from, to find a single row in the table? Assume that a single row for a table does not exceed storage space of one block.

- ❑ A. 4
- ❑ B. 2
- ❑ C. 0
- ❑ D. 3
- ❑ E. 5

E is the correct answer. An Oracle Database can have up to three branch nodes and one leaf node, each occupying a block, making four blocks at most. The row in the table occupies less than one block. Thus, between two and five blocks are read, the maximum being five blocks.

8. This command creates a sequence. What will the seventh value be?

```
CREATE SEQUENCE TEST_SEQ START WITH 5 INCREMENT BY -3
    MINVALUE -10 MAXVALUE 5 CYCLE ORDER CACHE 3;
```

- ❑ A. 5
- ❑ B. 2
- ❑ C. −1

- ❑ D. −10
- ❑ E. −7

The sequence numbers are generated in seven steps. The values for those seven steps are **5**, **2**, **-1**, **-4**, **-7**, **-10**, and **5**. Thus, A is correct at 5. All other answers are incorrect.

9. Which query shows table names of all tables for the currently connected user?

- ❑ A. **SELECT TABLE FROM USER_TAB_COLS;**
- ❑ B. **SELECT TABLE FROM USER_TABLES;**
- ❑ C. **SELECT TABLE_NAME FROM DBA_TABLES;**
- ❑ D. **SELECT TABLE_NAME FROM ALL_TABLES;**
- ❑ E. None of the above

The correct query is **SELECT TABLE_NAME FROM USER_TABLES;**. Therefore, answer E is correct and it follows that answers A, B, C, and D are incorrect.

10. Which users can access the table through the synonym created by this DDL command?

```
CREATE PUBLIC SYNONYM MYMOVIES FOR MOVIE;
```

- ❑ A. All users
- ❑ B. All users with read access to the **MOVIE** table
- ❑ C. Only the user who created the table and the synonym
- ❑ D. The user who created the table and another user who created the synonym, even if the user who created the synonym does not have access to the other user's table
- ❑ E. None of the above

B is the best answer. Answer A might be incorrect if any users do not have access to the **MOVIE** table. C is incorrect because the synonym is created publicly and super users have access automatically. D is incorrect because both users must have access to the table. Because B is correct, E is incorrect.

Security (DDL)

Terms You Need to Understand

- ✓ User
- ✓ Schema
- ✓ **CREATE USER**
- ✓ Default tablespaces
- ✓ Role
- ✓ **CREATE ROLE**
- ✓ Grant privilege
- ✓ Revoke privilege
- ✓ Object privilege
- ✓ System privilege
- ✓ **SYS** user
- ✓ **SYSTEM** user
- ✓ **CONNECT** role
- ✓ **RESOURCE** role

Concepts You Need to Master

- ✓ Creating users
- ✓ Access privileges between the **SYS** and **SYSTEM** users
- ✓ The difference between object and system privileges
- ✓ The importance of the **CREATE SESSION** system privilege
- ✓ Object privilege cascade revokes
- ✓ System privilege cascade revokes
- ✓ Roles group privileges for easy security maintenance
- ✓ **CONNECT** and **RESOURCE** roles and who gets them

This chapter deals with Oracle database security issues. Details included are schemas (users), roles for grouping privileges, and finally granting and revoking of privileges.

Schemas and Users

A *schema* is by dictionary definition a diagrammatic representation of a model. In Oracle Database the terms *schema* and *user* are used loosely, but they are synonymous and are used interchangeably. In other words, when a user connects to a database, that user can contain schema objects such as tables. Thus, there is a CREATE USER command but no CREATE SCHEMA command.

Types of Users

Various types of users can be created in an Oracle Database. On an abstract level a user can be an administrator, a developer, or an end user. An administrator is a person who maintains the database itself. A developer builds structures in a database, such as tables, and writes applications software to access data in those tables. An end user is the type of user who uses the applications, usually creating and changing data indirectly through front-end applications. A front-end application often makes data access and maintenance transparent to application end users.

Different types of users must therefore have different levels of access, authorization, and privileges, allowing completion of only their assigned tasks. The privileges required for administrators are omnipotent in some respects. Developers are allowed to create new objects such as tables. Application end users are usually allowed only to create and change data in tables without being able to change the structure of the tables themselves.

With respect to database administration, there are a few default users created by an Oracle installation and database creation process that you need to be aware of:

- SYS—This user is the most powerful user in an Oracle Database and is a database administration super-user. The SYS user is generally used to perform the most high-level administration tasks, such as shutting down and starting up a database.
- SYSTEM—The SYSTEM user is intended as a less powerful version of the SYS user. The SYSTEM user is used to perform less drastic tasks than the SYS user, such as creation of new users.

➤ *Other Oracle Provided Users*—Other users (schemas) are provided by Oracle installations for specific options and functions.

Only database administration users such as the **SYS** and **SYSTEM** user, or any user assigned specific privileges such as a user assigned administration roles, can create new database users.

Creating Users

Users are required in an Oracle Database to allow different types of people to connect to a database and perform specific functions. The syntax for the `CREATE USER` command is shown in Figure 13.1.

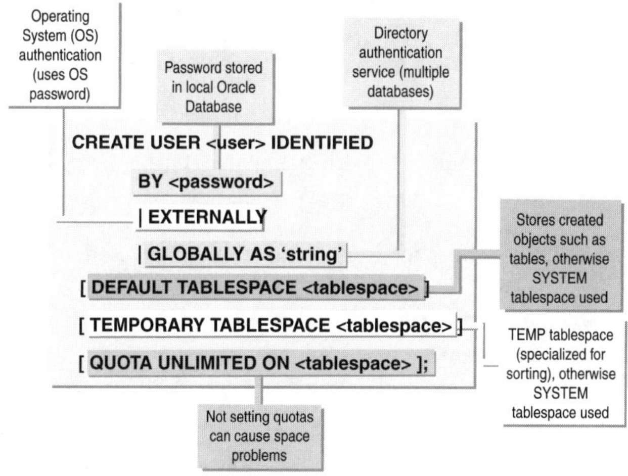

Figure 13.1 **CREATE USER** command syntax.

The following is a synopsis of the syntax diagram shown in Figure 13.1:

➤ The `BY <password>` option stores an encrypted form of a user password into your database.

➤ The `EXTERNALLY` option uses the operating system user logon for authentication.

➤ The `GLOBALLY AS 'string'` requires the use of a directory service for user authentication.

➤ Setting a default tablespace creates all objects created by the user in the default tablespace, unless otherwise specified when creating objects such as tables or indexes. The default tablespace will be set as the `SYSTEM` tablespace if the `DEFAULT TABLESPACE` option is not specified in the CREATE USER command. This will allow users to create objects such as tables and indexes in the SYSTEM tablespace. The SYSTEM tablespace contains metadata (table definitions). Mixing metadata and general user tables in the SYSTEM tablespace can cause serious performance issues.

- In earlier versions of Oracle, it was essential to define a temporary tablespace when creating a user to avoid sorting using the SYSTEM tablespace. This is no longer an issue if a database is created using the DEFAULT TEMPORARY TABLESPACE option in the CREATE DATABASE command (defaulted in the Database Configuration Assistant).
- Quotas are required for specified tablespaces; otherwise, objects cannot be created in a user.

The **CREATE USER** command is usually the prerogative of a database administrator. To be able to create a user, you may need to have the **CREATE USER** system privilege or administrative privileges. Ask your administrator if there is a problem creating users. The **MOVIES** schema already has appropriate privileges assigned to it.

This first example creates a user called JIM with password JIM:

```
CREATE USER JIM IDENTIFIED BY JIM;
```

This next example sets default tablespace, temporary tablespace, and quotas on specific tablespaces:

```
CREATE USER JOE IDENTIFIED BY JOE
    DEFAULT TABLESPACE DATA TEMPORARY TABLESPACE TEMP
    QUOTA UNLIMITED ON DATA QUOTA UNLIMITED ON TEMP;
```

In the preceding example, the default tablespace is changed to DATA; the temporary sort space (temporary tablespace), to the TEMP tablespace. With the SYS user logged in, the query shown in Figure 13.2 reveals assigned default tablespaces:

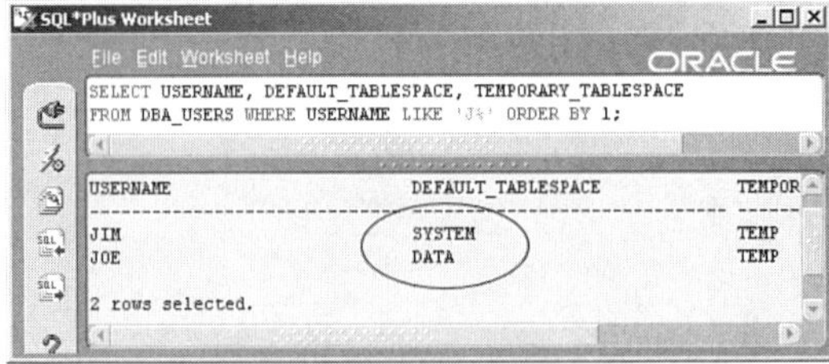

Figure 13.2 Viewing default user tablespaces.

As you may recall from the synopsis for Figure 13.1, allowing a user to use the SYSTEM tablespace for data storage is inefficient because it absolutely will create contention between metadata structures (table definitions) and the data in those tables. This will affect overall database performance.

Remember to specify the **DEFAULT TABLESPACE** and **TEMPORARY TABLESPACE** options when executing the **CREATE USER** command.

The **ALTER USER** and **DROP USER** commands are not covered in this exam but are in the next Oracle certification exam.

Grouping Privileges Using Roles

Both system and object privileges can be grouped together into what is called a *role*. A role applies a set of privileges to a user or group of users performing a specific function. For example, a user requiring read-only reporting on MOVIES schema data warehouse tables would require the following privileges:

```
GRANT SELECT ON COUNTRY TO JIM;
GRANT SELECT ON FORMAT TO JIM;
GRANT SELECT ON REGION TO JIM;
GRANT SELECT ON SALE TO JIM;
GRANT SELECT ON SOURCE TO JIM;
```

Figure 13.3 shows the syntax for the CREATE ROLE command.

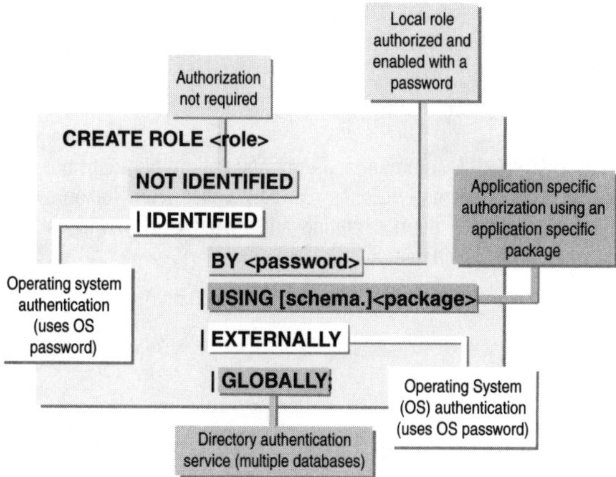

Figure 13.3 **CREATE ROLE** command syntax.

The following is a synopsis of the syntax diagram shown in Figure 13.3:

- A role is created as not identified by default. A non-identified role does not require password authentication.
- Using the `IDENTIFIED` option for a role simply requires that a user seeking to enable a role with the `SET ROLE` command, requires authentication to enable the role using the `SET ROLE` command.
- Role authentication is allowed by a password stored locally in the database, externally from the operating system, globally using a directory service, or by an application-specific package.

Examining Figure 13.3, we can create a role in the simplest form:

```
CREATE ROLE DWUSER;
```

Creation of a role may require administrative privileges such as the **CREATE ROLE** privilege. Ask your administrator for help.

To make the data warehouse user privileges easier to manage (see the previous example), we can assign the privileges to a role:

```
GRANT SELECT ON COUNTRY TO DWUSER;
GRANT SELECT ON FORMAT TO DWUSER;
GRANT SELECT ON REGION TO DWUSER;
GRANT SELECT ON SALE TO DWUSER;
GRANT SELECT ON SOURCE TO DWUSER;
```

Now you can make things much easier for multiple users by assigning just the role to all data warehouse users:

```
GRANT DWUSER TO JIM, JOE;
```

The **ALTER ROLE** and **DROP ROLE** commands are not covered in this exam but are in the next Oracle certification exam. Privileges can be revoked from (taken away from) roles as well as granted to them. Granting and revoking of privileges are covered in the next section of this chapter.

Privileges

Before discussing how to grant and revoke privileges syntactically, we need to make a brief examination of some of the privileges available to a user. Privileges are of two basic types:

- *Object Privileges*—These privileges provide DML-capable access to user objects, such as read and write access to tables using the `SELECT`, `INSERT`,

UPDATE, and DELETE privileges. Other possible privilege requirements are the EXECUTE privilege on objects such as procedures and TYPE objects, the ALTER and SELECT privileges on sequences, and perhaps even the INDEX privilege allowing access to the CREATE INDEX command for developers using specific tables. If you wanted to create an OLTP application role, you could use the following:

```
CREATE ROLE OLTPUSER;
```

You can use the following GRANT commands to grant DML access to the OLTPUSER role for all tables:

```
GRANT INSERT, UPDATE, DELETE, SELECT ON ACTOR TO OLTPUSER;
GRANT INSERT, UPDATE, DELETE, SELECT ON AWARD TO OLTPUSER;
GRANT INSERT, UPDATE, DELETE, SELECT ON DIRECTOR TO OLTPUSER;
GRANT INSERT, UPDATE, DELETE, SELECT ON GENRE TO OLTPUSER;
GRANT INSERT, UPDATE, DELETE, SELECT ON MOVIE TO OLTPUSER;
GRANT INSERT, UPDATE, DELETE, SELECT ON PART TO OLTPUSER;
GRANT INSERT, UPDATE, DELETE, SELECT ON RATING TO OLTPUSER;
GRANT INSERT, UPDATE, DELETE, SELECT ON RECOGNITION TO OLTPUSER;
GRANT INSERT, UPDATE, DELETE, SELECT ON SAGA TO OLTPUSER;
GRANT INSERT, UPDATE, DELETE, SELECT ON STUDIO TO OLTPUSER;
```

Then you could grant the role as a single group of privileges to multiple OLTP application users:

```
GRANT OLTPUSER TO JIM, JOE;
```

This is the basics of object privileges. The next exam covers the details of object privilege identification.

- *System Privileges*—These privileges imply access for changing metadata, such as creating tables and indexes. When privileges are allocated to developers, system privileges such as CREATE ANY TABLE, CREATE ANY INDEX, EXECUTE ANY PROCEDURE, CREATE ROLE, and CREATE SEQUENCE could be granted.

This exam covers only basic granting and revoking of simple object privileges, not system privileges. The next exam covers the details of both object and system privilege identification.

Granting Privileges

The GRANT command, as already seen in this chapter, is used to assign privileges to users. The syntax for the GRANT command is shown in Figure 13.4.

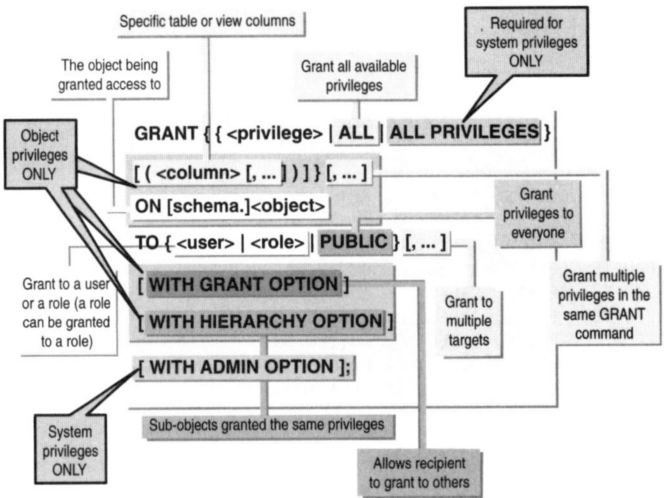

Figure 13.4 **GRANT** command syntax.

The following is a synopsis of the syntax diagram shown in Figure 13.4:

- The term applied to a user granting a privilege is the *owner* or *grantor*.
- The term applied to a user receiving a grant on a privilege is the *grantee*.
- The syntax diagram in Figure 13.4 includes syntax for granting of both system and object privileges.
- A system privilege allows a user to create metadata objects and work with objects in general, such as creation of tables and access to administration and development-level functionality.
- An object privilege allows access to data stored in objects such as allowing a user to add new rows to a table using an INSERT command.
- When granting privileges to a user, use the TO clause.
- When granting all system privileges, use the syntax GRANT ALL PRIVILEGES:

```
GRANT ALL PRIVILEGES TO JOE;
```

- When granting all object privileges, use the syntax `GRANT ALL` or `GRANT ALL PRIVILEGES`, where the clause `PRIVILEGES` is optional:

```
GRANT ALL ON CUSTOMER TO JOE;
GRANT ALL PRIVILEGES ON CUSTOMER TO JOE;
```

- The optional syntax element `[ ( <column> [, ... ] ) ] } [, ... ]` specifies that object privileges can be granted detailing no columns for an entire table, for a single column in a table, or for multiple columns in a table. The final section of the syntax element `[, ... ]` implies that multiple sets of columns can be specified.
- Object privileges are always granted `ON` a specific object in a specific schema using the syntax element `ON [schema.]<object>`.
- A privilege can be granted to a list of users, to a list of roles (roles can be granted to users), or to all users by using the `PUBLIC` option.

Remember that granting a synonym to all users using the **PUBLIC** option requires that the grantee must have direct access to the underlying object the synonym refers to.

- The `WITH GRANT OPTION` clause applies to object privileges only. This option allows a grantee who has been granted a privilege including the `WITH GRANT OPTION` clause to in turn grant privileges on that object to other users.
- The `WITH HIERARCHY OPTION` clause applies to object privileges only, granting privileges on a granted object, inclusive of any sub-object privilege grants as well.
- The `WITH ADMIN OPTION` clause applies to system privileges only. Granting a system privilege using the `WITH ADMIN OPTION` clause allows the grantee to grant those same system privileges to other users.

You have already seen the use of the `GRANT` command in this chapter. Now let's go a little further. The first thing to do is to create a new user:

```
CREATE USER JACK IDENTIFIED BY JACK;
```

Trying to connect to the new user `JACK` at this stage will cause an error, denying login due to the absence of the `CREATE SESSION` privilege. Thus, the following command is essential:

```
GRANT CREATE SESSION TO JACK;
```

Commonly, new application users are assigned the CONNECT role and new development users the CONNECT plus the RESOURCE roles:

```
GRANT CONNECT TO JACK;
CREATE USER DEVELOPER IDENTIFIED BY DEVELOPER;
GRANT CONNECT, RESOURCE TO DEVELOPER;
```

Database administrators such as the **SYS** and **SYSTEM** user usually grant administrative-level system privileges.

Previous versions of Oracle Database included a DBA role. The DBA role no longer exists as of version 9.2.0.1. **CONNECT** and **RESOURCE** roles have been discouraged as of Oracle Database 9i, and they are scheduled for deprecation in a future version. The objective of this approach is a minimal default security specification, requiring DBAs to define security parameters such as roles from scratch. This new approach is required to address past security issues.

We have already seen GRANT commands executed to allocate DML and querying capabilities to different users, when we created users JIM and JOE earlier in this chapter. Let's go over some of the finer points of the GRANT command syntax as shown in Figure 13.4.

You can grant access to specific columns within a table or view (applies to INSERT, UPDATE, and REFERENCES):

```
GRANT INSERT (ACTOR_ID, NAME, GENDER) ON ACTOR TO JACK;
```

The preceding GRANT command will allow JACK to add new rows to the MOVIES.ACTOR table using INSERT commands like the following. This is because the TYPECAST column is nullable and the GENDER column has a DEFAULT value of M for male:

```
INSERT INTO MOVIES.ACTOR(ACTOR_ID,NAME,GENDER)
    VALUES(1001,'a new actor','M');

INSERT INTO MOVIES.ACTOR(ACTOR_ID,NAME,GENDER)
    VALUES(1002,'another new actor',DEFAULT);

INSERT INTO MOVIES.ACTOR(ACTOR_ID,NAME)
    VALUES(1003,'yet another new actor');
```

This form of INSERT command will not, however, be permitted for JACK because even though the TYPECAST column is nullable, it must still be specified in the VALUES clause:

```
INSERT INTO MOVIES.ACTOR
    VALUES(1004,'and yet another new actor',DEFAULT);
```

In the preceding GRANT command, the user JACK is not granted access to the MOVIES.ACTOR.TYPECAST column. In the next GRANT command, we are allowing JACK to have all available access privileges to the MOVIE table, including INSERT, UPDATE, DELETE, SELECT, and other object-level privileges, including access to all columns on the MOVIES.ACTOR table:

```
GRANT ALL ON MOVIE TO JACK;
```

Now let's create yet another user:

```
CREATE USER JANET IDENTIFIED BY JANET;
GRANT CONNECT TO JANET;
```

Connecting back to the MOVIES schema, we can allow access for JACK to the ACTOR table and also allow JACK to give those permissions to other users:

```
GRANT ALL ON MOVIES.ACTOR TO JACK WITH GRANT OPTION;
```

Notice in the preceding GRANT command how the ACTOR table is still in the MOVIES schema. Now you would connect to the user JACK:

```
GRANT SELECT ON MOVIES.ACTOR TO JANET WITH GRANT OPTION;
```

Now JANET can read the ACTOR table in the MOVIES schema because JACK granted her the SELECT privilege on that table.

The next few groups of commands will create yet another user called JANICE and grant the same SELECT privilege initially granted to JACK, through to JANET, and finally on to JANICE. Like JACK, JANET also has the WITH GRANT OPTION, but JANICE does not. So connected as an administrator, create a user called JANICE:

```
CREATE USER JANICE IDENTIFIED BY JANICE;
GRANT CONNECT TO JANICE;
```

And connected as JANET, grant the SELECT privilege to JANICE, this time excluding the WITH GRANT OPTION:

```
GRANT SELECT ON MOVIES.ACTOR TO JANICE;
```

Neither JANET nor JANICE can change data in the MOVIES.ACTOR table because they were granted only the SELECT privilege (read-only). If JANET or JANICE attempts to change data in the MOVIES.ACTOR table, she will be returned an insufficient privileges error.

One further thing we can do is to grant privileges to everyone. In the following example, connected as the MOVIES user, all object privileges are granted on the DIRECTOR table to all users using the PUBLIC keyword:

```
GRANT ALL ON DIRECTOR TO PUBLIC;
```

All users such as JIM, JOE, JACK, and JANET can now access the MOVIES.DIRECTOR table in all respects.

Revoking Privileges

Revoking privileges does the exact opposite of granting privileges. Whereas the `GRANT` command increases access permissions for a user, the `REVOKE` command decreases access permissions for a user. Figure 13.5 shows the syntax for the `REVOKE` command.

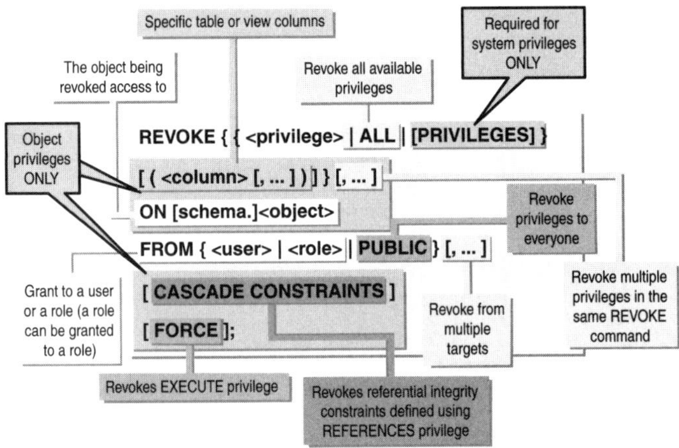

Figure 13.5 **REVOKE** command syntax.

The following is a synopsis of the syntax diagram shown in Figure 13.5:

➤ The term applied to a user revoking a privilege is the *owner* or *revoker*.

➤ The term applied to a user from whom a privilege is revoked is the *revokee* or *grantee*.

➤ The syntax diagram in Figure 13.5 includes syntax for revoking of both system and object privileges.

➤ When revoking privileges from a user, use the `FROM` clause.

➤ When revoking all system privileges, use the syntax `REVOKE ALL PRIVILEGES`:

```
REVOKE ALL PRIVILEGES FROM JOE;
```

➤ When revoking all object privileges, use the syntax `REVOKE ALL` or `REVOKE ALL PRIVILEGES`, where the clause `PRIVILEGES` is optional:

```
REVOKE ALL ON CUSTOMER FROM JOE;
REVOKE ALL PRIVILEGES ON CUSTOMER FROM JOE;
```

- The optional syntax element `[ ( <column> [, ... ] ) ] } [, ... ]` specifies that object privileges can be revoked detailing no columns for an entire table, for a single column in a table, or for multiple columns in a table. The final section of the syntax element `[, ... ]` implies that multiple sets of columns can be specified.
- Object privileges are always revoked ON a specific object in a specific schema using the syntax element `ON [schema.]<object>`.
- A privilege can be revoked from a list of users, from a list of roles (roles can be revoked from users), or from all users by using the PUBLIC option.
- The CASCADE CONSTRAINTS clause revokes Referential Integrity constraints defined by the revokee, using the REFERENCES privilege.
- The FORCE clause revokes EXECUTE privileges on dependent objects.

Connected as the MOVIES user, this command revokes all privileges granted on the MOVIES.DIRECTOR table, previously granted to PUBLIC (everyone):

```
REVOKE ALL ON DIRECTOR FROM PUBLIC;
```

Now revoke the SELECT privilege on the MOVIES.ACTOR table from JACK, who granted the same privilege to JANET, who in turn granted the same privilege to JANICE:

```
REVOKE SELECT ON ACTOR FROM JACK;
```

The WITH GRANT OPTION was used to pass the privilege from MOVIES to JANET, and on to JANICE. The REVOKE command removes the SELECT privilege from all three users. The same would not occur with system privileges. Revokes executed for system privileges do not cascade across multiple users.

Automated cascading revoking occurs on object privileges and not system privileges. This is a favorite exam question, usually put indirectly. This is important to remember so it will be repeated. System privileges previously granted will not be revoked in a cascading manner. Thus, when system privileges are being revoked, only the revokee loses system privileges, not any users granted system privileges by the revokee. On the contrary, object privileges are revoked in a cascading manner. Therefore, revoking object privileges from the revokee causes all users to whom the revokee granted those revoked object privileges to also have those privileges revoked.

Connect as an administrator, grant the system privilege GRANT ANY PRIVILEGE to all users, and grant the CREATE TABLE system privilege to the user JACK:

```
CONNECT SYS/PASSWORD@TEST AS SYSDBA;
GRANT GRANT ANY PRIVILEGE TO JACK, JANET, JANICE;
GRANT CREATE TABLE TO JACK;
```

Now connect to JACK and grant the CREATE TABLE system privilege to JANET:

```
CONNECT JACK/JACK@TEST;
GRANT CREATE TABLE TO JANET;
```

Now connect to JANET, who in turn grants the CREATE TABLE system privilege to JANICE:

```
CONNECT JANET/JANET@TEST;
GRANT CREATE TABLE TO JANICE;
```

Now if you connect to the administrator again and revoke the CREATE TABLE system privilege from JACK only, the CREATE TABLE system privilege grants from JACK to JANET and from JANET to JANICE will remain:

```
CONNECT SYS/PASSWORD@TEST AS SYSDBA;
REVOKE CREATE TABLE FROM JACK;
```

Metadata Views

This section lists the Oracle Database metadata views for database objects covered in this chapter: users, roles, and privileges. Here's a rundown:

- *Users*—The only item to include here is the USER_USERS view, containing user specifications such as default and temporary tablespace settings.
- *Roles*—These metadata views describe attributes of roles and privileges granted to those roles:
  - USER_ROLE_PRIVS—Roles granted to a user.
  - ROLE_ROLE_PRIVS—Roles granted to roles. Obviously, a role cannot be granted to itself.
  - ROLE_TAB_PRIVS—Object privileges granted to a role.
  - ROLE_SYS_PRIVS—System privileges granted to a role.
- *Privileges*—These metadata views describe system privileges made and received, and table and column-level object privileges made and received:
  - USER_TAB_PRIVS—Object privileges granted to PUBLIC or the current user.
  - USER_TAB_PRIVS_MADE—Object privileges made by the current user.
  - USER_TAB_PRIVS_RECD—Object privileges made to the current user.
  - USER_COL_PRIVS—Same as USER_TAB_PRIVS but applying to individual columns in a table or view.

- USER_COL_PRIVS_MADE—Same as USER_TAB_PRIVS_MADE but applying to individual columns in a table or view.
- USER_COL_PRIVS_RECD—Same as USER_TAB_PRIVS_RECD but applying to individual columns in a table or view.
- USER_SYS_PRIVS—Granted system privileges, assigned to both users and roles.

Utilize an active Oracle Database you have access to, or read Oracle documentation, regarding the contents of the table metadata views mentioned here. Get a general idea of column names and data content.

By far, the easiest way to view Oracle Database security details and settings is to use the Oracle Enterprise Manager Console GUI. Connect to the database in the Oracle Enterprise Manger Console and expand the Security item, searching through the Users and Roles items.

Exam Prep Questions

1. Select one of the following as the correct answer.
   - ❑ A. `CONNECT SYS/password@TEST;`
     `SHUTDOWN IMMEDIATE;`
   - ❑ B. `CONNECT SYSTEM/password@TEST;`
     `SHUTDOWN;`
   - ❑ C. `CONNECT SYSTEM/password@TEST;`
     `SHUTDOWN ABORT;`
   - ❑ D. `CONNECT JACK/jack@TEST;`
     `SHUTDOWN IMMEDIATE;`
   - ❑ E. None of the above

   Answer E is correct. Answer A is incorrect because **SYS** must be connected **AS SYSDBA** or **AS SYSOPER**. B, C, and D are all incorrect because only the **SYS** user can shut down a database, even if the **SYSTEM** user is granted the **SYSDBA** or **SYSOPER** privileges.

2. Which of these commands creates a user authenticated internally by an Oracle Database?
   - ❑ A. `CREATE USER TEST1 IDENTIFIED BY password;`
   - ❑ B. `CREATE USER TEST1 IDENTIFIED EXTERNALLY;`
   - ❑ C. `CREATE USER TEST1 IDENTIFIED BY password`
     `DEFAULT TABLESPACE DATA;`
   - ❑ D. `CREATE USER TEST1 IDENTIFIED BY password`
     `DEFAULT TABLESPACE DATA TEMPORARY TABLE TEMP;`
   - ❑ E. `CREATE USER TEST1;`

   Answers A, C, and D are all correct because they include the **IDENTFIED BY** password option. B is incorrect because the user will be authenticated by the operating system (**EXTERNALLY**). E will cause a syntax error.

3. Select all valid commands.
   - ❑ A. `CREATE ROLE ROLE1;`
   - ❑ B. `CREATE ROLE ROLE1 NOT IDENTIFIED;`
   - ❑ C. `CREATE ROLE ROLE1 IDENTIFIED BY password;`
   - ❑ D. `CREATE ROLE ROLE1 EXTERNALLY;`
   - ❑ E. `CREATE ROLE ROLE1 IDENTIFIED GLOBALLY;`
   - ❑ F. All of the above

   A, B, C, and E are all syntactically valid. D is invalid because the keyword **IDENTIFIED** is missing. Because D is incorrect, F is also incorrect.

4. What type of privileges are **SELECT**, **INSERT**, **INDEX**, and **UPDATE**?
   - ❑ A. Administration
   - ❑ B. **SYS** user

- ❑ C. Object
- ❑ D. System
- ❑ E. None of the above

These are all object privileges usually allocated to end-user application functionality in the form of direct grants or application roles. Roles are then granted to users.

5. You grant some system privileges to user A using the **WITH ADMIN OPTION** clause, and you grant some object privileges to user A using the **WITH GRANT OPTION** clause. User A in turn grants the same privileges to user B and user C. If all of both system and object privileges are then revoked from user A by an administrator, what is the result?

- ❑ A. All users lose all privileges.
- ❑ B. All users lose all system privileges.
- ❑ C. All users lose all object and system privileges.
- ❑ D. User A loses system privileges.
- ❑ E. None of the above.

E is the correct answer. Revokes on object privileges do cascade, removing all granted access to anyone else with granted permissions. Revokes on system privileges do not cascade. A, B, and C contradict the cascade rules. D would be correct only if no object privileges were involved. The final result is that only user A loses system privileges but all of users A, B, and C lose object privileges. Object privilege revokes are cascaded, whereas system privileges are not cascaded.

6. In the following **GRANT** command, who can add new rows to **TABLEA**?

```
GRANT SELECT, UPDATE, DELETE ON TABLEA TO PUBLIC;
```

- ❑ A. Everyone
- ❑ B. The user **PUBLIC**
- ❑ C. Nobody
- ❑ D. Anyone
- ❑ E. None of the above

C is the correct answer because the **INSERT** privilege is not included in the **GRANT** command. Answer A is incorrect because it completely contradicts C. B is just silly because **PUBLIC** is not a user but more of a concept. D is wrong because it implies the same answer as A.

7. What is wrong with this command? Select the best answer.

```
GRANT SELECT (ACTOR_ID, NAME, GENDER) ON ACTOR TO JACK;
```

- ❑ A. Nothing is wrong.
- ❑ B. Only **INSERT**, **UPDATE**, and **REFERENCES** privileges apply to individual columns.
- ❑ C. Only **INSERT**, **UPDATE**, and **REFERENCES** privileges apply to individual table columns.

- ❑ D. Only **INSERT**, **UPDATE**, and **REFERENCES** privileges apply to individual table and view columns.
- ❑ E. None of the above.

B, C, and D are all correct, but because D mentions both tables and views, it is a better option than B and C. Answer A is incorrect because the **SELECT** privilege cannot be granted on a column basis. E is incorrect because D is correct.

8. Which metadata views show table privileges granted to the current user?

- ❑ A. **USER_TAB_PRIVS**
- ❑ B. **USER_TAB_PRIVS_MADE**
- ❑ C. **USER_TAB_PRIVS_RECD**
- ❑ D. **USER_USERS**
- ❑ E. **DBA_USERS**

A and C are both correct answers, although A returns privileges granted to **PUBLIC** as well as those granted to the current user. B is wrong because it implies privileges granted to other users, not to the current user. D and E are both incorrect because they have nothing to do with privileges.

9. What would cause this command to produce an error?

```
GRANT SELECT ON MOVIES.ACTOR TO JANICE;
```

- ❑ A. The current user is the **SYS** user.
- ❑ B. The current user has **SELECT** but not **INSERT** access to the **MOVIES.ACTOR** table.
- ❑ C. The current user is the **MOVIES** user.
- ❑ D. The current user is not **MOVIES**, **JANICE**, or an administrator.
- ❑ E. The current user is not **MOVIES**, **JANICE**, or an administrator but has **SELECT** access to the **MOVIES.ACTOR** table, and the **WITH GRANT OPTION** allocated.

A is okay because **SYS** is a super-user and more or less omnipotent within a database. B will not cause a problem with **SELECT** but will with **INSERT**. C will certainly not cause a problem because the **MOVIES** user can allocate privileges to anyone for its own tables. E is absolutely correct and D does not detail the specifics in E, and thus D is the best answer, most likely to cause a problem.

10. How can user specifications be changed?

- ❑ A. The **DROP USER** command
- ❑ B. The **CREATE USER** command
- ❑ C. The **CHANGE USER** command
- ❑ D. The **ALTER USER** command
- ❑ E. None of the above

D is the correct answer. E is obviously wrong. A destroys users, B creates new users, and for C the **CHANGE USER** command does not exist.

Practice Test #1 (60 questions)

This exam is numbered as 1Z0-007 and named *Introduction to Oracle9i: SQL*. This Oracle certification exam is the first in a series of Oracle certification exams for various tracks. A track can certify you as a database administrator, a PL/SQL developer, or an Oracle Forms developer.

What are some effective methods for studying for this exam?

- Read this exam cram from cover to cover.
- Take all the tests at the end of each chapter and grade yourself.
- Take the two exams at the end of this book, one being the topic of this chapter. Grade yourself on these tests as well.
- This is extreme, but the method I used to study for this exam was to use various texts and type up what I had learned into web pages, published on my website (http://www.oracledbaexpert.com). This method enabled me to absorb far more facts than simply reading a book such as this. It also allowed me to later refer to what I had learned, even at client sites.
- Read and use the Oracle online documentation and software bundled documentation, at work in your Oracle DBA or development role.
- It is vaguely possible to pass this exam simply by committing all facts to short-term memory and learning everything by heart. However, there is a lot of material to cover and you risk failing. To get a good result, well over the pass mark, a good understanding of the material is required. Simple memorization does not necessarily provide an in-depth understanding.

- One of the best ways to learn is by practice. Use the examples in this book to practice executing SQL code against a test database, even to the point of typing every SQL statement into the database and executing it.

This first practice exam will not only test your knowledge of Oracle SQL syntax, usability, and functionality, but also attempt to verify your level of understanding of the material. You might find some of the questions in this first practice test extremely difficult to answer correctly. In general, Oracle certification exams do have some very tricky questions. You need to able to answer at least some of the more difficult questions to pass this certification exam. The second practice test, in Chapter 16, will ease the pressure on you somewhat by focusing on memory retention and testing your knowledge of syntax for Oracle SQL, as opposed to the complexities of its application.

1. A table called **MOVIE** has the following columns:

```
MOVIE_ID          NOT NULL NUMBER PRIMARY KEY
TITLE             NOT NULL VARCHAR2(32)
YEAR              NOT NULL NUMBER
RELEASE                    DATE
LIST_PRICE                 FLOAT(126)
RANK                       NUMBER
REVIEWS                    NUMBER
REVIEW_RANK                NUMBER(2,1)
```

   Which two of these SQL code snippets are valid?

   - ❑ A. **SELECT SUM(RELEASE)**
   - ❑ B. **SELECT MAX(RELEASE)**
   - ❑ C. **WHERE SUM(YEAR) > 1999**
   - ❑ D. **FROM SUM(YEAR)**
   - ❑ E. **SELECT TITLE, SUM(REVIEWS*RANK)**
     FROM MOVIE GROUP BY TITLE;
   - ❑ F. **SELECT TITLE, SUM(MAX(REVIEWS*RANK))**

2. What is the meaning of the abbreviation DML?

   - ❑ A. Data Manipulative Language
   - ❑ B. Data Manipulation Commands
   - ❑ C. Data Manipulative Commands
   - ❑ D. Data Manipulative Statements
   - ❑ E. None of the above

3. Let's assume that a **ROLLBACK** command is executed after each of the SQL commands listed below. Which of these commands cause the **ROLLBACK** command to have no effect?

   - ❑ A. **INSERT**
   - ❑ B. **CREATE TABLE**
   - ❑ C. **CREATE SYNONYM**

- ❑ D. **MERGE**
- ❑ E. **TRUNCATE**

4. Which of these clauses will return a sorted result?

- ❑ A. **ORDER BY**
- ❑ B. **FROM**
- ❑ C. **OVER**
- ❑ D. **DISTINCT**
- ❑ E. None of the above

5. This **CREATE TABLE** command creates a table called **MOVIE**:

```
CREATE TABLE MOVIE(
    MOVIE_ID          NOT NULL NUMBER PRIMARY KEY
    TITLE             NOT NULL VARCHAR2(32)
    YEAR              NOT NULL NUMBER
    RELEASE                    DATE
    LIST_PRICE                 FLOAT(126)
    REVIEW_RANK                NUMBER(2,1));
```

Select the following commands that retrieve all data from the **MOVIE** table. The **MOVIE** table is in the **MOVIES** schema.

- ❑ A. **SELECT * FROM MOVIE;**
- ❑ B. **SELECT M.* FROM MOVIE M;**
- ❑ C. **SELECT * FROM MOVIES.MOVIE;**
- ❑ D. **SELECT MOVIE_ID, TITLE, YEAR, RELEASE**
  , LIST_PRICE, REVIEW_RANK FROM MOVIE;
- ❑ E. **SELECT * FROM MOVIE WHERE ROWNUM > 1000000;**

6. This is the structure of a table called **MOVIE**:

```
MOVIE_ID          NOT NULL NUMBER PRIMARY KEY
TITLE             NOT NULL VARCHAR2(32)
YEAR              NOT NULL NUMBER
RELEASE                    DATE
LIST_PRICE                 FLOAT(126)
RANK                       NUMBER
REVIEWS                    NUMBER
REVIEW_RANK                NUMBER(2,1));
```

Which lines contain syntax errors?

```
1. SELECT MOVIE_ID, TITLE, YEAR, RELEASE
2. LIST_PRICE, REVIEW_RANK
3. FROM MOVIE
4. WHERE MOVIE_ID > '5'
5. ORDER BY YEAR / NVL(RANK, 1);
```

- ❑ A. 1 and 2
- ❑ B. 1 or 2, and 5
- ❑ C. 4 and 5
- ❑ D. 1 or 2, and 4
- ❑ E. None of the above

7. You create a new user identified by an Oracle internally stored password. This user is a development user who can create tables, views, and indexes in his schema. Which is the best option?

   ❑ A.
   ```
   CREATE USER DEV IDENTIFIED EXTERNALLY
   DEFAULT TABLESPACE DATA TEMPORARY TABLESPACE TEMP;
   GRANT CREATE SESSION, CREATE TABLE
        , CREATE VIEW TO DEV;
   ```
   ❑ B.
   ```
   CREATE USER DEV IDENTIFIED BY dev
   DEFAULT TABLESPACE SYSTEM TEMPORARY TABLESPACE TEMP;
   GRANT CREATE SESSION, CREATE TABLE
        , CREATE VIEW TO DEV;
   ```
   ❑ C.
   ```
   CREATE USER DEV IDENTIFIED BY dev
   DEFAULT TABLESPACE DATA TEMPORARY TABLESPACE TEMP;
   GRANT CREATE SESSION, CREATE VIEW TO DEV;
   ```
   ❑ D.
   ```
   CREATE USER DEV IDENTIFIED BY dev
   DEFAULT TABLESPACE DATA TEMPORARY TABLESPACE TEMP;
   GRANT CREATE TABLE, CREATE VIEW TO DEV;
   ```
   ❑ E.
   ```
   CREATE USER DEV IDENTIFIED BY dev
   DEFAULT TABLESPACE DATA TEMPORARY TABLESPACE TEMP;
   GRANT CREATE SESSION, CREATE TABLE
        , CREATE VIEW TO DEV;
   ```

8. Which line should be changed to remove the syntax error in this query?

   ```
   1. SELECT A.*
   2. FROM DIRECTOR
   3. NATURAL JOIN MOVIE
   4. WHERE ROWNUM < 10;
   ```

   ❑ A. 1
   ❑ B. 2
   ❑ C. 3
   ❑ D. 4
   ❑ E. There is no syntax error

9. Which of these queries are valid?

   ❑ A. `SELECT * FROM DUAL;`
   ❑ B. `SELECT SYSDATE FROM DUAL;`
   ❑ C. `SELECT ROWNUM FROM DUAL;`
   ❑ D. `SELECT COUNT(*) FROM DUAL;`
   ❑ E.
   ```
   SELECT (SELECT * FROM DUAL), D1.*, D2.*
   FROM DUAL D1, (SELECT * FROM DUAL) D2;
   ```

10. What will the following expression return when the **PRICE** is **NULL**?

    ```
    POWER((NVL(PRICE, 0) / NVL(PRICE, 1)) * 5, 2)
    ```

    ❑ A. 25
    ❑ B. 5

- ❑ C. 2
- ❑ D. 1
- ❑ E. None of the above

11. This is the structure of a table called **MOVIE**:

```
MOVIE_ID            NOT NULL NUMBER PRIMARY KEY
TITLE               NOT NULL VARCHAR2(32)
YEAR                NOT NULL NUMBER
RELEASE                      DATE
LIST_PRICE                   FLOAT(126)
RANK                         NUMBER
REVIEWS                      NUMBER
REVIEW_RANK                  NUMBER(2,1));
```

Which lines contain syntax errors?

```
1. SELECT MOVIE_ID, TITLE, YEAR, RELEASE
2. LIST_PRICE, REVIEW_RANK
3. FROM MOVIE
4. WHERE MOVIE_ID > '5'
5. ORDER BY LIST_PRICE / NVL(RANK, 1);
```

- ❑ A. 1 and 2
- ❑ B. 1 or 2, and 5
- ❑ C. 4 and 5
- ❑ D. 1 or 2, and 4
- ❑ E. None of the above

12. This is the structure of a table called **MOVIE**:

```
MOVIE_ID            NOT NULL NUMBER PRIMARY KEY
TITLE               NOT NULL VARCHAR2(32)
YEAR                NOT NULL NUMBER
RELEASE                      DATE
LIST_PRICE                   FLOAT(126)
RANK                         NUMBER
REVIEWS                      NUMBER
REVIEW_RANK                  NUMBER(2,1));
```

The following query will retrieve **NULL** values from the **RELEASE** column in the **MOVIE** table. Where are **NULL** values sorted by default, and where will they be sorted using the following query?

```
SELECT RELEASE FROM MOVIE ORDER BY RELEASE DESC NULLS LAST;
```

- ❑ A. First and first
- ❑ B. First and last
- ❑ C. Last and first
- ❑ D. Last and last
- ❑ E. None of the above

13. Which three of these statements are correct?

- ❑ A. The **SUM** function adds multiple values together.
- ❑ B. The **ADD_MONTHS** function adds up to 12 months to a date.
- ❑ C. **LPAD** returns a left padded (filled) string.

- ❑ D. `LTRIM` removes all occurrences of a set of characters in a string.
- ❑ E. `SIGN` returns a positive number if passed a number greater than or equal to 0.

14. Assuming that all `CONNECT` commands are valid and that user `MOVIES` contains a sequence called `MOVIE_SEQ`, which of these command groups will not cause an error?

    ❑ A.
    ```
    CONNECT MOVIES/MOVIES@TEST
    SELECT MOVIE_SEQ.CURRVAL FROM DUAL;
    ```
    ❑ B.
    ```
    CONNECT MOVIES/MOVIES@TEST
    SELECT MOVIE_SEQ+1 FROM DUAL;
    ```
    ❑ C.
    ```
    CONNECT MOVIES/MOVIES@TEST
    SELECT MOVIE_SEQ.CURRVAL FROM DUAL;
    SELECT MOVIE_SEQ.NEXTVAL FROM DUAL;
    ```
    ❑ D.
    ```
    CONNECT MOVIES/MOVIES@TEST
    SELECT MOVIE_SEQ.NEXTVAL FROM DUAL;
    SELECT MOVIE_SEQ.CURRVAL FROM DUAL;
    ```
    ❑ E. None of the above

15. There are various methods of turning off column headings when retrieving data using SQL*Plus. Which of these apply?

    ❑ A. `SET PAGESIZE 0`
    ❑ B. `SET HEA OFF`
    ❑ C. `SET PAGES 0`
    ❑ D. `SET HEADING OFF`
    ❑ E. `SET HEAD OFF`

16. Will an error be caused by this `CREATE TABLE` command? If so, what will cause the error?

    ```
    CREATE TABLE TEST(A FLOAT, B CHAR, C VARCHAR2, D NUMBER
        , E DATE);
    ```

    ❑ A. No error will be returned.
    ❑ B. Yes. The table name `TEST` is invalid.
    ❑ C. Yes. The `CHAR` column must have a declared size.
    ❑ D. Yes. All columns but the date column must have declared sizes.
    ❑ E. Yes. The length of the `VARCHAR2` variable must be defined.

17. This is the definition for the `ACTOR` table in the `MOVIES` schema:

    ```
    ACTOR_ID          NOT NULL NUMBER Primary key
    NAME              NOT NULL VARCHAR2(32)
    GENDER            NOT NULL CHAR(1)
    TYPECAST                   VARCHAR2(64)
    ```

The **ACTOR** table contains this data in the **NAME**, **GENDER**, and **TYPECAST** columns:

```
Michelle Pfeiffer          F Multiple
Tom Hanks                  M Action Drama
Sally Field                F Multiple
Billy Dee Williams         M Science Fiction
George C Scott             M Multiple
```

Assume that there are no indexes on the **ACTOR** table other than the primary key on the **ACTOR_ID** column. Which commands will cause an error?

- ❑ A. **CREATE BITMAP INDEX AK_TYPECAST_BM1**
  ON ACTOR(GENDER);
- ❑ B. **CREATE UNIQUE INDEX AK_TYPECAST_BTU1**
  ON ACTOR(NAME);
- ❑ C. **CREATE UNIQUE INDEX AK_TYPECAST_BTU2**
  ON ACTOR(TYPECAST);
- ❑ D. **CREATE UNIQUE INDEX AK_TYPECAST_BTU3**
  ON ACTOR(NAME) OFFLINE;
- ❑ E. **CREATE UNIQUE INDEX AK_TYPECAST_BTU4**
  ON ACTOR(TYPECAST) ONLINE;

18. Assume you are logged in as **SYS** (**SYSDBA**) and that any database links (**dblink**) exist error free. The synonym called **TEST_SYN** exists as **PUBLIC**. Which of these commands will not cause an error?

- ❑ A. **CREATE PUBLIC SYNONYM TEST_SYN FOR MOVIES.MOVIE;**
- ❑ B. **CREATE PUBLIC SYNONYM TEST_SYN**
  FOR MOVIES.MOVIE@DBLINK1;
- ❑ C. **DROP PUBLIC SYNONYM TEST_SYN FORCE;**
- ❑ D. **CREATE OR REPLACE SYNONYM TEST_SYN FOR MOVIES.MOVIE;**
- ❑ E. **CREATE OR REPLACE PUBLIC SYNONYM TEST_SYN**
  FOR MOVIES.MOVIE;

19. The user **SYS**, connected as **SYSDBA**, wants to create a synonym for the **MOVIES.MOVIE** table. There are other users in the database, two of which are **JIM** and **JOE**. Both **JIM** and **JOE** have only the **CREATE SESSION** privilege, allowing them to connect to the database. **JIM** can see movies and **JOE** cannot. **JOE** needs to see movies as well. Which command is the most appropriate? Select one answer best suiting tight security.

- ❑ A. **CREATE PUBLIC SYNONYM SMOVIE FOR MOVIES.MOVIE;**
- ❑ B. **CREATE PUBLIC SYNONYM SMOVIE FOR MOVIES.MOVIE;**
  GRANT SELECT ON MOVIES.MOVIE TO JIM, JOE;
- ❑ C. **CREATE PUBLIC SYNONYM SMOVIE FOR MOVIES.MOVIE;**
  GRANT SELECT ON MOVIES.MOVIE TO JIM;
- ❑ D. **CREATE SYNONYM MOVIES.SMOVIE FOR MOVIES.MOVIE;**
  GRANT SELECT ON MOVIES.SMOVIE TO JOE;
- ❑ E. None of the above

20. Which of these statements are true with respect to datatypes?

- ❑ A. **NUMBER** and **FLOAT** can be a maximum of 38 bytes.
- ❑ B. The **DATE** datatype stores date values with a timestamp.
- ❑ C. **CHAR** and **VARCHAR2** default to 1 byte if no length is defined.
- ❑ D. Both **VARCHAR2** and **CHAR** can exceed 2,000 bytes.
- ❑ E. **VARCHAR2** can be a maximum size of 4,000 bytes; **CHAR**, 2,000 bytes.

21. For which **CREATE VIEW** definitions will the **INSERT** command return an error? Assume that before the **INSERT** command is executed, the row added does not yet exist in the underlying **STUDIO** table:

```
INSERT INTO STUDIOS VALUES(45, 'A new studio');
```

- ❑ A.
```
CREATE OR REPLACE VIEW STUDIOS AS
     SELECT STUDIO_ID, STUDIO FROM STUDIO
     WHERE STUDIO_ID < 10;
```
- ❑ B.
```
CREATE OR REPLACE VIEW STUDIOS AS
     SELECT STUDIO_ID, STUDIO FROM STUDIO
     WHERE STUDIO_ID > 10 WITH CHECK OPTION;
```
- ❑ C.
```
CREATE OR REPLACE VIEW STUDIOS AS
     SELECT STUDIO_ID, STUDIO FROM STUDIO
     WHERE STUDIO_ID < 10 WITH CHECK OPTION;
```

22. What is wrong with these commands?

```
CREATE TABLE STUDIO(
     STUDIO_ID    NUMBER NOT NULL
    ,STUDIO        VARCHAR2(32) NOT NULL
    ,CONSTRAINT    XPK_STUDIO PRIMARY KEY(STUDIO_ID));
CREATE UNIQUE INDEX XAK_STUDIO_1 ON STUDIO(STUDIO);
CREATE UNIQUE INDEX XAK_STUDIO_2 ON STUDIO(STUDIO_ID);
```

- ❑ A. The first index command has a syntax error.
- ❑ B. The **CONSTRAINT** in the **CREATE TABLE** command has a syntax error.
- ❑ C. The second **CREATE INDEX** command has a syntax error.
- ❑ D. Not enough columns are defined for the **STUDIO** table.
- ❑ E. None of the above.

23. Which of these statements are correct?

- ❑ A. Nested tables (**TABLE**) store fixed-length arrays.
- ❑ B. **VARRAY** objects store large character strings.
- ❑ C. The smallest **VARCHAR2** allowed is **1**: **VARCHAR2(1)**.
- ❑ D. **VARRAY** objects store dynamic arrays.
- ❑ E. The largest **CHAR** allowed is 2,000 bytes: **CHAR(2000)**.

24. Which of these statements are not true?

- ❑ A. Tables can be renamed using the **ALTER TABLE** command.
- ❑ B. Columns in tables can be renamed using the **ALTER TABLE** command.
- ❑ C. Constraints can be renamed using the **ALTER TABLE** and **ALTER VIEW** commands.

- ❑ D. Indexes can be renamed using the **ALTER INDEX** command.
- ❑ E. Views can be renamed using the **ALTER VIEW** command.

25. The **DIRECTOR** and **MOVIE** tables have the following column structure:

```
DIRECTOR
DIRECTOR_ID NUMBER PRIMARY KEY
NAME VARCHAR2(64) NOT NULL
MOVIE
MOVIE_ID NUMBER PRIMARY KEY
DIRECTOR_ID NUMBER REFERENCES DIRECTOR
TITLE VARCHAR2(64)
```

Which of the following could utilize a subquery?

- ❑ A. Retrieve all directors sorted by name.
- ❑ B. Retrieve all directors sorted by name who have movies in the **MOVIE** table.
- ❑ C. Retrieve all movie titles.
- ❑ D. Retrieve all movie titles directed by a specified set of directors.
- ❑ E. Retrieve all directors and their respective movie titles.

26. Which of these datatypes are valid?

- ❑ A. **NUMBER(10,2)**
- ❑ B. **NUMBER(4,5)**
- ❑ C. **FLOAT(122,2)**
- ❑ D. **DATE(8)**
- ❑ E. **CHAR(2500)**
- ❑ F. **VARCHAR2**

27. What type of a query is this?

```
SELECT * FROM (SELECT * FROM MOVIE ORDER BY TITLE)
WHERE ROWNUM < 5;
```

- ❑ A. A subquery
- ❑ B. A left outer join
- ❑ C. A right outer join
- ❑ D. A full outer join
- ❑ E. A Top-N query

28. After a user is created, what is the minimum of system privileges required to allow the user to connect to the database? Answer with the name of the privilege, two words only.

29. Which datatype is best used to store very large text objects of well over 4,000 bytes in length?

- ❑ A. **RAW** or **LONG RAW**
- ❑ B. **BLOB**
- ❑ C. **BFILE**

- ❑ D. **CLOB**
- ❑ E. **VARCHAR2(1000000)**

30. This is a table called **MOVIE**:

```
MOVIE_ID        NOT NULL NUMBER PRIMARY KEY
SAGA_ID                  NUMBER Foreign Key
GENRE_ID        NOT NULL NUMBER Foreign Key
RATING_ID       NOT NULL NUMBER Foreign Key
DIRECTOR_ID     NOT NULL NUMBER Foreign Key
STUDIO_ID       NOT NULL NUMBER Foreign Key
TITLE           NOT NULL VARCHAR2(32)
YEAR            NOT NULL NUMBER
RELEASE                  DATE
LIST_PRICE               FLOAT(126)
```

Which of these **CREATE INDEX** and **ALTER INDEX** command sequences will cause errors?

- ❑ A. **CREATE INDEX AK_MOVIE_10 ON MOVIE(GENRE_ID, RATING_ID , DIRECTOR_ID) COMPRESS 4 REVERSE;**
- ❑ B. **CREATE INDEX AK_MOVIE_11 ON MOVIE(GENRE_ID, RATING_ID , DIRECTOR_ID) COMPRESS 2 REVERSE NOSORT;**
- ❑ C. **CREATE INDEX AK_MOVIE_11 ON MOVIE(GENRE_ID, RATING_ID , DIRECTOR_ID) COMPRESS 2 REVERSE;**
  ALTER INDEX AK_MOVIE_11 REBUILD NOSORT;
- ❑ D. **CREATE UNIQUE INDEX AK_MOVIE_12 ON MOVIE(MOVIE_ID);**
- ❑ E. All of the above

31. The **STUDIO** and **MOVIE** tables have the following column structure:

```
STUDIO
STUDIO_ID NUMBER PRIMARY KEY
STUDIO VARCHAR2(64) NOT NULL
MOVIE
MOVIE_ID NUMBER PRIMARY KEY
STUDIO_ID NUMBER REFERENCES STUDIO
TITLE VARCHAR2(64)
```

A report requires a list of studios, listing all movies for each studio, returning the rows in order of studio name, with movies for each studio in descending order of movie title. Also, any studios without movies should not be returned. Which of the following will achieve the required result?

- ❑ A. **SELECT STUDIO, TITLE AS MOVIE FROM STUDIO**
  NATURAL LEFT OUTER JOIN MOVIE
  ORDER BY STUDIO, MOVIE;
- ❑ B. **SELECT STUDIO, TITLE AS MOVIE FROM STUDIO**
  JOIN MOVIE ON(STUDIO_ID)
  ORDER BY STUDIO, MOVIE DESC;
- ❑ C. **SELECT S.STUDIO, M.TITLE AS MOVIE M FROM STUDIO S**
  JOIN MOVIE M USING(M.STUDIO_ID)
  ORDER BY S.STUDIO, M.MOVIE;

- ❑ D. **SELECT STUDIO, TITLE AS MOVIE FROM STUDIO**
  JOIN MOVIE USING(STUDIO_ID)
  ORDER BY STUDIO, MOVIE DESC;
- ❑ E. **SELECT STUDIO, TITLE AS MOVIE FROM STUDIO**
  NATURAL JOIN MOVIE
  ORDER BY STUDIO, MOVIE;

32. Which of the following are valid table object privileges?

- ❑ A. **INSERT**
- ❑ B. **UPDATE**
- ❑ C. **TRUNCATE**
- ❑ D. **READ ONLY**
- ❑ E. **INDEX**

33. How many types of constraints are in this **CREATE TABLE** command?

```
CREATE TABLE PART(
 MOVIE_ID NUMBER NOT NULL
,ACTOR_ID NUMBER NOT NULL
,LEAD_ROLE CHAR(1) DEFAULT 'N' NULL
    CHECK(LEAD_ROLE IN('Y','N'))
,SUPPORTING_ROLE CHAR(1) DEFAULT 'N' NULL
    CHECK(SUPPORTING_ROLE IN('Y','N'))
,CONSTRAINT XPK_PART PRIMARY KEY(MOVIE_ID, ACTOR_ID)
,CONSTRAINT FK_PART_1 FOREIGN KEY(MOVIE_ID)
    REFERENCES MOVIE
,CONSTRAINT FK_PART_2 FOREIGN KEY(ACTOR_ID)
    REFERENCES ACTOR);
```

- ❑ A. 1
- ❑ B. 3
- ❑ C. 4
- ❑ D. None of the above

34. What is the SQL*Plus command allowing output of typed commands and returned results from queries into a file on your computer?

- ❑ A. **PRINT**
- ❑ B. **SET AUTOCOMMIT ON**
- ❑ C. **COLUMN**
- ❑ D. **SPOOL**
- ❑ E. **OUTPUT**

35. What will be the result of this expression?

```
INITCAP(UPPER(LOWER('Hello World')))
```

Type the resulting string as your answer.

36. What will be the value of this sequence after the execution of all these commands, returned by the last line?

```
1.  CREATE SEQUENCE TEST_SEQ START WITH 0 INCREMENT BY -3
        MINVALUE -9 MAXVALUE 10 CYCLE NOCACHE ORDER;
2.  SELECT TEST_SEQ.NEXTVAL FROM DUAL;
3.  SELECT TEST_SEQ.NEXTVAL, TEST_SEQ.NEXTVAL FROM DUAL;
4.  SELECT TEST_SEQ.NEXTVAL FROM DUAL;
5.  SELECT TEST_SEQ.NEXTVAL FROM DUAL;
6.  SELECT TEST_SEQ.NEXTVAL FROM DUAL;
7.  SELECT TEST_SEQ.NEXTVAL FROM DUAL;
8.  SELECT TEST_SEQ.NEXTVAL FROM DUAL;
9.  ALTER SEQUENCE TEST_SEQ INCREMENT BY 5;
10. SELECT TEST_SEQ.NEXTVAL, TEST_SEQ.NEXTVAL FROM DUAL;
11. SELECT TEST_SEQ.NEXTVAL FROM DUAL;
12. SELECT TEST_SEQ.NEXTVAL FROM DUAL;
13. SELECT TEST_SEQ.NEXTVAL FROM DUAL;
```

- ❑ A. **1**
- ❑ B. **-9**
- ❑ C. **0**
- ❑ D. An error will occur

37. This is the **MOVIE** table:

```
MOVIE_ID          NOT NULL NUMBER
TITLE             NOT NULL VARCHAR2(32
YEAR              NOT NULL NUMBER
RELEASE                    DATE
LIST_PRICE                 FLOAT(126)
RANK                       NUMBER
REVIEWS                    NUMBER
REVIEW_RANK                NUMBER(2,1)
```

You want to find all movie titles and years, plus all ranking calculations with a release date between 1998 and 2000, such that the rank divided by the review ranking is greater than 100. Additionally, the sorted order should be in descending order of the ranking calculation expression. Where is this query most likely to go wrong?

```
SELECT TITLE, YEAR, RANK / NVL(REVIEW_RANK, 0) AS RANKPERC
    FROM MOVIE
WHERE TO_NUMBER(TO_CHAR(RELEASE,'YYYY'))
    BETWEEN 1998 AND 2000
AND RANK / NVL(REVIEW_RANK, 1) > 100
ORDER BY RANKPERC;
```

- ❑ A. If the release date is **NULL**, an error could result because NVL is not applied.
- ❑ B. The **TO_NUMBER** conversion function is not required.
- ❑ C. Dividing **RANK** by **REVIEW_RANK** in the **WHERE** clause could cause a division by zero error.
- ❑ D. The **SELECT** list could cause a division by zero error.
- ❑ E. None of the above.

38. How many **NUMBER** datatypes will this table have?

```
CREATE TABLE TEST(A NUMBER, B NUMBER(10,2), C SMALLINT
    , D INTEGER, E FLOAT, F SMALLINT);
```

- ❑ A. 2
- ❑ B. 3
- ❑ C. 4
- ❑ D. 5
- ❑ E. 6

39. Which lines in the following **CREATE TABLE** command produce an error?

```
1. CREATE TABLE RATINGS(
2.      RATING_ID     NUMBER NOT NULL
3.     ,GROUP_ID     NUMBER NULL
4.     ,MPAA         CHAR(5) NULL
5.     ,RATING         VARCHAR2(32) NOT NULL
6.     ,CONSTRAINT     XPK_RATING PRIMARY (RATING_ID)
7.     ,CONSTRAINT     FK_RATING_1 FOREIGN (GROUP_ID) REFERENCES RATING);
```

- ❑ A. 3 and 4
- ❑ B. 2 and 6
- ❑ C. 3 and 7
- ❑ D. 6
- ❑ E. 7
- ❑ F. 6 and 7

40. Is there anything wrong with this query? If so, what?

```
SELECT * FROM(SELECT * FROM SALE)
    WHERE ROWNUM < 5 ORDER BY SALE_PRICE;
```

- ❑ A. There is nothing wrong with this query.
- ❑ B. The subquery will produce an error.
- ❑ C. The Top-N query will be sorted incorrectly.
- ❑ D. The resulting rows will not necessarily be the first five rows.
- ❑ E. Both C and D are true.

41. What are the minimum object privileges required to allow the **NEXTVAL** pseudocolumn to be applied to a sequence?

- ❑ A. **ALTER** and **SELECT**
- ❑ B. **INSERT** and **SELECT**
- ❑ C. **INSERT**
- ❑ D. **ALTER**
- ❑ E. **SELECT**

42. What is the result of this expression?

```
LENGTH(LPAD('This is a string',
    LENGTH(SUBSTR('This is a string', POWER(2, 3)*-1, 4)) * 5
, '*'))
```

- ❑ A. **4**
- ❑ B. **16**
- ❑ C. **20**
- ❑ D. **a string**
- ❑ E. ******This is a string**

43. Which line in this **CREATE VIEW** command will cause an error? Assume that all the underlying table columns exist and are accessible, and that the join is valid.

```
1. CREATE OR REPLACE VIEW myview
2. AS SELECT *
3. FROM MOVIE NATURAL JOIN DIRECTOR
4. WHERE TITLE LIKE '%a%';
```

- ❑ A. 1
- ❑ B. 2
- ❑ C. 3
- ❑ D. 4
- ❑ E. All lines are correct

44. What does this expression produce? Type your answer in as a response.

```
SUBSTR(
    TRANSLATE(
        REPLACE('This is a string', ' ', '')
    , 'ia', 'AI')
, 5, 3)
```

45. What is the result of this expression? Select one answer.

```
TRUNC(ROUND(FLOOR(CEIL(1.2)-.1) + .3445, 3), 2)
```

- ❑ A. **0.34**
- ❑ B. **1.345**
- ❑ C. **1.35**
- ❑ D. **1.3445**
- ❑ E. **1.34**

46. What does this expression evaluate to?

```
SIGN(ABS((MOD(13, 3) * -1)+5))
```

- ❑ A. **-1**
- ❑ B. **0**
- ❑ C. **1**
- ❑ D. **3**
- ❑ E. None of the above

47. What date does this expression return?

```
LAST_DAY(ADD_MONTHS('01-JAN-04',
    MONTHS_BETWEEN('01-JAN-05', '01-JAN-04')))
```

- ❑ A. **01-JAN-04**
- ❑ B. **31-JAN-04**
- ❑ C. **01-JAN-05**
- ❑ D. **31-JAN-05**
- ❑ E. None of the above

48. What is the result returned by the last line in this sequence of commands?

```
1. CREATE SEQUENCE TEST_SEQ START WITH 1 INCREMENT BY 1
       NOMINVALUE MAXVALUE 5 CYCLE NOCACHE ORDER;
2. SELECT TEST_SEQ.NEXTVAL FROM DUAL;
3. SELECT TEST_SEQ.NEXTVAL, TEST_SEQ.NEXTVAL FROM DUAL;
4. SELECT TEST_SEQ.CURRVAL FROM DUAL;
```

- ❑ A. **0**
- ❑ B. **1**
- ❑ C. **2**
- ❑ D. **3**
- ❑ E. None of the above

49. Which of these **CREATE TABLE** statements will create the **MOVIE** table without returning an error? Assume that the **STUDIO** and **DIRECTOR** tables are already properly created with the appropriate matching constraints.

❑ A.
```
CREATE TABLE MOVIE(
 MOVIE_ID NUMBER NOT NULL
,DIRECTOR_ID NUMBER NOT NULL
,STUDIO_ID NUMBER NOT NULL
,TITLE VARCHAR2(32) NOT NULL
,YEAR NUMBER NOT NULL
,CONSTRAINT XPK_MOVIE PRIMARY KEY(MOVIE_ID)
,CONSTRAINT FK_MOVIE_1 FOREIGN KEY(STUDIO_ID)
         REFERENCES STUDIO
,CONSTRAINT FK_MOVIE_2 FOREIGN KEY(DIRECTOR_ID)
         REFERENCES DIRECTOR);
```

❑ B.
```
CREATE TABLE MOVIE(
 MOVIE_ID NUMBER NOT NULL PRIMARY KEY
,DIRECTOR_ID NUMBER NOT NULL
,STUDIO_ID NUMBER NOT NULL
,TITLE VARCHAR2(32) NOT NULL
,YEAR NUMBER NOT NULL
,CONSTRAINT FK_MOVIE_1 FOREIGN KEY(STUDIO_ID)
         REFERENCES STUDIO
,CONSTRAINT FK_MOVIE_2 FOREIGN KEY(DIRECTOR_ID)
         REFERENCES DIRECTOR);
```

❑ C.
```
CREATE TABLE MOVIE(
 MOVIE_ID NUMBER NOT NULL PRIMARY KEY
,DIRECTOR_ID NUMBER NOT NULL REFERENCES DIRECTOR
,STUDIO_ID NUMBER NOT NULL REFERENCES STUDIO
,TITLE VARCHAR2(32) NOT NULL
,YEAR NUMBER NOT NULL);
```

❑ D.
```
CREATE TABLE MOVIE(
 MOVIE_ID NUMBER NOT NULL PRIMARY KEY
,DIRECTOR_ID NUMBER NOT NULL
        REFERENCES DIRECTOR(DIRECTOR_ID)
,STUDIO_ID NUMBER NOT NULL
        REFERENCES STUDIO(STUDIO_ID)
,TITLE VARCHAR2(32) NOT NULL
,YEAR NUMBER NOT NULL);
```

50. A datatype is to be forcibly restricted to contain a number with specific restrictions. The number can be a whole number. The number can also contain three digits to the left of the decimal and two digits to the right of the decimal. What is its correct definition?

❑ A. **NUMBER**

❑ B. **FLOAT**

❑ C. **NUMBER(3,2)**

❑ D. **NUMBER(2,3)**

❑ E. None of the above

51. If you execute these commands, what type of file will be spooled to your hard drive?

```
SPOOL MOVIES.LST;
SET COLSEP ",";
SELECT * FROM MOVIE;
SET COLSEP " ";
SPOOL OFF;
```

❑ A. A text file

❑ B. An output file

❑ C. A comma-separated file with fixed record length

❑ D. A variable-length comma-separated file

❑ E. A and C are correct

52. In the following query which line causes an error?

```
1. SELECT TITLE
2. FROM MOVIE
3. WHERE MOVIE_ID EXISTS
4. (SELECT MOVIE_ID
5. FROM ACTOR);
```

❑ A. 1

❑ B. 2

❑ C. 3

- ❑ D. 4
- ❑ E. 5

53. Which of the following are not restricted to operating on single row subqueries?

- ❑ A. **ANY**
- ❑ B. **SOME**
- ❑ C. **IN**
- ❑ D. **EXISTS**
- ❑ E. **>=**
- ❑ F. **BETWEEN**
- ❑ G. **!=**
- ❑ H. **=**

54. Which of these commands can be used to control DML transactions or transactional behavior?

- ❑ A. **COMMIT**
- ❑ B. **UPDATE**
- ❑ C. **TRUNCATE**
- ❑ D. **INSERT**
- ❑ E. **DELETE**
- ❑ F. **SAVEPOINT**
- ❑ G. **SET TRANSACTION**
- ❑ H. **ROLLBACK**

55. Which of these DML commands can be used to add new rows to a table?

- ❑ A. **INSERT**
- ❑ B. **UPDATE**
- ❑ C. **TRUNCATE**
- ❑ D. **MERGE**
- ❑ E. **COMMIT**

56. Assuming a table is defined by the **CREATE TABLE** statement

```
CREATE TABLE TEST(A NUMBER(8,3));
```

which of these **INSERT** commands will add a row to the table?

- ❑ A. **INSERT INTO TEST VALUES(10000.234);**
- ❑ B. **INSERT INTO TEST VALUES(1000.2345);**
- ❑ C. **INSERT INTO TEST VALUES(10000.2345);**
- ❑ D. **INSERT INTO TEST VALUES(100000.2345);**
- ❑ E. **INSERT INTO TEST VALUES(100000.24);**
- ❑ F. **INSERT INTO TEST VALUES(100000.2);**
- ❑ G. **INSERT INTO TEST VALUES(100000);**

57. This is the **DIRECTOR** table:

```
DIRECTOR_ID        NOT NULL NUMBER PRIMARY KEY
NAME               NOT NULL VARCHAR2(32)
GENDER             NOT NULL CHAR(1) DEFAULT 'M' CHECK
↪(GENDER IN ('M', 'F'))
TALENT                      VARCHAR2(64)
```

Which of these **INSERT** commands will not cause an error when executed? Assume that the sequence exists.

❑ A. `INSERT INTO DIRECTOR(DIRECTOR_ID)`
`VALUES(DIRECTOR_SEQ.NEXTVAL);`

❑ B. `INSERT INTO DIRECTOR(DIRECTOR_ID, NAME)`
`VALUES(DIRECTOR_SEQ.NEXTVAL, 'A new director');`

❑ C. `INSERT INTO DIRECTOR(DIRECTOR_ID, NAME, GENDER, TALENT)`
`VALUES(DIRECTOR_SEQ.NEXTVAL, 'Yet another new director'`
`, NULL, 'Talented');`

❑ D. `INSERT INTO DIRECTOR VALUES(DIRECTOR_SEQ.NEXTVAL`
`, 'And yet another new director', 'M', 'Talented');`

❑ E. `INSERT INTO DIRECTOR VALUES(DIRECTOR_SEQ.NEXTVAL`
`, 'And yet one more new director', 'X', 'Talented');`

❑ F. `INSERT INTO DIRECTOR(DIRECTOR_ID, NAME)`
`VALUES(DIRECTOR_SEQ.NEXTVAL, 'More directors?');`

❑ G. `INSERT INTO DIRECTOR VALUES(DIRECTOR_SEQ.NEXTVAL`
`, 'Even more directors?');`

❑ H. `INSERT INTO DIRECTOR VALUES(DIRECTOR_SEQ.NEXTVAL`
`, 'Even more directors?' , 'M');`

58. Select the queries producing an identical result to that of the query shown, assuming that there is more than one male director:

```
SELECT GENDER, COUNT(GENDER) AS MALES FROM DIRECTOR
WHERE GENDER = 'M' GROUP BY GENDER;
```

❑ A. `SELECT GENDER, COUNT(DISTINCT(GENDER)) AS MALES`
`FROM DIRECTOR WHERE GENDER = 'M' GROUP BY GENDER;`

❑ B. `SELECT DISTINCT GENDER AS MALES FROM DIRECTOR`
`WHERE GENDER = 'M' GROUP BY GENDER;`

❑ C. `SELECT DISTINCT GENDER AS MALES FROM DIRECTOR`
`WHERE GENDER = 'M';`

❑ D. `SELECT GENDER, COUNT(GENDER) AS MALES FROM DIRECTOR`
`GROUP BY GENDER HAVING GENDER = 'M';`

❑ E.
```
SELECT DISTINCT D.GENDER, A.MALES FROM DIRECTOR D
    , (SELECT GENDER, COUNT(GENDER) AS MALES
       FROM DIRECTOR
       GROUP BY GENDER
    ) A
WHERE D.GENDER = A.GENDER;
```

❑ F. None of the above

59. What is the result returned by the last line in this sequence of commands?

```
1. CREATE SEQUENCE TEST_SEQ START WITH 1 INCREMENT BY -1
       MINVALUE -3 MAXVALUE 5 CYCLE NOCACHE ORDER;
2. SELECT TEST_SEQ.NEXTVAL FROM DUAL;
3. SELECT TEST_SEQ.NEXTVAL, TEST_SEQ.NEXTVAL FROM DUAL;
4. SELECT TEST_SEQ.CURRVAL FROM DUAL;
```

- ❑ A. `0`
- ❑ B. `-1`
- ❑ C. `-2`
- ❑ D. `-3`
- ❑ E. None of the above

60. A table contains existing rows. If a constraint is added such that old data is not to be checked and newly inserted rows are to be checked, how should the constraint's state be set?

- ❑ A. **`ENABLE NOVALIDATE`**
- ❑ B. **`ENABLE VALIDATE`**
- ❑ C. **`DISABLE`**
- ❑ D. **`DISABLE NOVALIDATE`**
- ❑ E. None of the above

Answer Key to Practice Test #1

1. B, E
2. E
3. B, C, E
4. A, D
5. A, B, C, D
6. E
7. E
8. A
9. A, B, C, D, E
10. E
11. A
12. D
13. A, C, E
14. D
15. A, B, C, D, E
16. E
17. C, D, E
18. C, D, E
19. D
20. B, E
21. C
22. E
23. C, E
24. C, E
25. B, D, E
26. A, B
27. E
28. `CREATE SESSION`
29. D
30. E
31. D
32. A, B, E
33. C
34. D
35. `Hello World`
36. A
37. D
38. D
39. F
40. E
41. E
42. C
43. E
44. `AsI`
45. E
46. C
47. D
48. C
49. A, B, C, D
50. E
51. E
52. C
53. A, B, C, D
54. A, F, G, H
55. A, D
56. A, B, C
57. B, D, F
58. D, E
59. A
60. A

Question 1

Answers B and E are correct. A is invalid because a date cannot be summed up using SUM. B is correct because a maximum (MAX) value for a group of dates can be found. C is incorrect because aggregation functions cannot be applied in a WHERE clause because it filters rather than groups. D is incorrect because the FROM clause requires a data source, and an aggregation is by no means that. F is incorrect because aggregation functions cannot be nested. There is no such thing as a GROUP BY GROUP BY clause. The initial aggregation would produce a single row, negating the need for aggregation anyway (there would be nothing to aggregate).

Question 2

Answer E is correct. The meaning of the abbreviation DML is Data Manipulation Language.

Question 3

Answers B, C, and E are correct. INSERT and MERGE are DML commands and a ROLLBACK command will undo all changes. CREATE TABLE, CREATE SYNONYM, and TRUNCATE are all DDL commands, forcing a COMMIT to occur automatically. If a ROLLBACK is executed after any of CREATE TABLE, CREATE SYNONYM, or TRUNCATE, no rollback will occur because they have all forced an automatic commit of any changes pending a commit in the current session.

Question 4

Answers A and D are correct. The ORDER BY and DISTINCT clause will sort results. The FROM and OVER clause will not sort results. Because A and D are correct, E is incorrect.

Question 5

Answers A, B, C, and D are correct. None of the queries has a WHERE clause filter. Answer A selects everything based on the asterisk (*), implying all columns. For B the alias makes no difference. For C the schema name makes no difference. D includes all six columns and thus once again there's no difference. E is incorrect because ROWNUM is calculated as the query is being formulated and the ROWNUM tested as being greater than (> 1000000) is nonsensical; thus, no rows are returned.

Question 6

Answer E is correct. Line 1 or line 2 could contain the required comma between the RELEASE and LIST_PRICE columns. However, no syntax error is returned because the LIST_PRICE column will simply be interpreted as a column header name for the RELEASE column. There is nothing wrong with line 3. Line 4 compares a NUMBER field with a string value (WHERE MOVIE_ID > '5'), not a syntax error but bad coding practice. There is nothing wrong with line 5.

Question 7

Answer E is correct. A is incorrect because the user is identified by the operating system and not internally in the Oracle database using the IDENTIFIED BY <password> option. B is functional, but defining the default tablespace as the SYSTEM tablespace can cause contention with metadata. C lacks the CREATE TABLE privilege, prohibiting the user from creating tables. D lacks the CREATE SESSION privilege, preventing the user from connecting to the database altogether.

Question 8

Answer A is correct. The first line contains an undefined alias. Removing the alias and changing the first line from SELECT A.* to SELECT * will remove the syntax error.

Question 9

All answers are correct. All queries simply retrieve various values from the DUAL table. E is simply using various types of subqueries to make multiple retrievals from the DUAL table.

Question 10

Answer E is correct. The NVL function replaces NULL values with zero. Thus, when PRICE is NULL, the expression NVL(price, 0) / NVL(price, 1) will always return zero. Zero multiplied and raised to the power of any number is always 0.

Question 11

Answer A is correct. Line 1 or line 2 should contain the required comma between the RELEASE and LIST_PRICE columns because the LIST_PRICE column is used in the ORDER BY clause. A column contained in the ORDER BY clause is not required to be selected. However, the missing comma effectively renames the RELEASE column as LIST_PRICE. The ORDER BY clause is attempting to divide the RELEASE column, a DATE datatype, by a NUMBER datatype. This causes a datatype error. There is nothing wrong with line 3. Line 4 compares a NUMBER field with a string value (WHERE MOVIE_ID > '5'). This is not a syntax error but it is bad coding practice. There is nothing wrong with line 5.

Question 12

Answer D is correct. By default, NULL values are always sorted last (ORDER BY RELEASE). When using DESC, the sorted order is reversed, returning NULL values first. The NULLS LAST clause overrides all other requirements and returns NULL values at the end. Therefore, last and last is the correct answer.

Question 13

Answers A, C, and E are correct. A is correct because the SUM function is used to aggregate multiple values together as a sum, typically used in tandem with a GROUP BY clause. B is incorrect because ADD_MONTHS is not limited to adding 12 months and can even subtract months from a date. C is correct because LPAD fills a string up to a specified number of characters. D is incorrect because LTRIM removes all occurrences until a set element (characters to be removed) is not found. Thus, LTRIM('iThis is a string','i') returns 'This is a string' and LTRIM('This is a string) returns the string as it is because the first character is *T* and not *i*. E is correct because SIGN(0) = 0 and SIGN(500) = 1; both 0 and 1 are positive numbers.

Question 14

Answer D is correct. The point to this question is knowing the difference between the `CURRVAL` and the `NEXTVAL` pseudocolumns. The first execution of `NEXTVAL` defines a sequence for a session. Executing `CURRVAL` before defining a sequence for a session causes an error. Thus, A and C are incorrect. B is incorrect because `MOVIE_SEQ+1` is syntactically invalid. D is correct because pseudocolumns are accessed in the proper order. E is incorrect because D is correct.

Question 15

All answers are correct. Setting the size of pages to `0` effectively removes page breaks altogether; thus, there are no column headings. Setting headings to `OFF` removes column headings. `PAGES` is simply a shorthand variation of `PAGESIZE`, and the same applies to `HEAD` and `HEA` with respect to `HEADING`.

Question 16

Answer E is correct. E is the correct answer because a `VARCHAR2` variable must have a defined length. Therefore, A is incorrect. C is incorrect because a `CHAR` datatype defaults to a `CHAR(1)` variable. D is incorrect because `FLOAT` defaults to the maximum size of 126 bytes, as does `NUMBER` to 38 bytes.

Question 17

Answers C, D, and E will cause errors. A is correct because it creates Bitmap index on the `GENDER` column, appropriate for a Bitmap index because it contains only two possible values: `M` for Male and `F` for Female. B is correct because Actor names must be unique. C is incorrect because, as can be seen from the data in the question, there are duplicate values for `TYPECAST: Multiple`. D is incorrect because there is no such clause as `OFFLINE`. E is incorrect for the same reason that C is incorrect, even though E is created `ONLINE`.

Question 18

Answers C, D, and E are correct. C is correct because dropping the public synonym is its intent. E is correct because the OR REPLACE and PUBLIC options are used. A and B are incorrect because the OR REPLACE is not used. D is correct but the PUBLIC option is not used. Omitting the PUBLIC option will not cause a syntax error.

Question 19

Answer D is correct. A is incorrect because the PUBLIC synonym requires underlying table access to MOVIES.MOVIE for JOE; JIM already has table access. B is incorrect because it uses a public synonym and access to the underlying table is granted to both users. Both of these facts are inconsistent with tight security requirements. JIM already has access, and thus granting to both users is immaterial, only careless. C is correct but uses a public synonym, not the most secure of available options. D is the best answer because the synonym is most suited to tight security, not being created publicly, and access is granted to JOE only. Because D is correct, E is incorrect.

Question 20

Answers B and E are correct. A is incorrect because FLOAT can be up to 126 bytes. B is correct because DATE datatypes store both date and time. C is incorrect because VARCHAR2 must have a defined size. D is incorrect because CHAR cannot exceed 2000 bytes. E is simply correct.

Question 21

Answer C is correct. Answer A will work because even though the WHERE clause filters out the inserted value, there is no CHECK OPTION validation from the view applied to the INSERT. For B the CHECK OPTION is applied but the STUDIO_ID value inserted is acceptable. For C the CHECK OPTION of < 10 applied to 45 prevents the insertion from occurring. C will cause an error.

Question 22

Answer E is correct. There are no syntax errors. None of answers A, B, C, and D apply. There is something wrong, though. The second index command is attempting to create a second index on the STUDIO_ID column because the primary key has already created an index. The second CREATE INDEX command will therefore produce an error in attempting to create the same index twice. Primary keys create indexes automatically.

Question 23

Answers C and E are correct. Nested tables are dynamic arrays, and VARRAY objects are fixed-length arrays. Thus, A and B are incorrect. A VARRAY object could be used to store large strings, but only as defined by a TYPE structure within each array element of a VARRAY.

Question 24

Answers C and E are correct. The ALTER TABLE command can be used to rename tables, columns, and table constraints. The ALTER VIEW command cannot be used to rename view constraints, or any other constraints. Thus, A and B are true but C is only partly true. D is true because indexes can be renamed using the ALTER INDEX command. E is completely false.

Question 25

Answers B, D, and E are correct. A is incorrect, retrieving only directors and not reading movies at all, thus no subquery:

```
SELECT * FROM DIRECTOR ORDER BY NAME;
```

B is correct because it does not specify to retrieve any movie information, thus a subquery:

```
SELECT * FROM DIRECTOR
   WHERE DIRECTOR_ID IN (SELECT DIRECTOR_ID FROM MOVIE);
```

C is incorrect because only movie information is being retrieved, regardless of directors, thus no subquery:

```
SELECT TITLE FROM MOVIE;
```

D is correct because movies are retrieved based on who directed them:

```
SELECT TITLE FROM MOVIE
    WHERE DIRECTOR_ID IN (1,2,3,4,5);
```

E is correct, even though a join should be used:

```
SELECT * FROM DIRECTOR NATURAL JOIN MOVIE;
```

However, for E an inline view, which is actually a subquery, can also be used such that either of the following queries will suffice:

```
SELECT M.TITLE, D.NAME FROM DIRECTOR D
    , (SELECT * FROM MOVIE) M
WHERE D.DIRECTOR_ID = M.DIRECTOR_ID;

SELECT D.NAME, M.TITLE FROM MOVIE M
    , (SELECT * FROM DIRECTOR) D
 WHERE M.DIRECTOR_ID = D.DIRECTOR_ID;
```

Question 26

Answers A and B are correct. C is incorrect because a FLOAT has only precision and not scale. Scale is used for NUMBER datatypes, implying a fixed number of decimal points. A FLOAT is a floating decimal point number and thus scale is invalid. D is incorrect because a DATE does not require a size. E is incorrect because the maximum size for a CHAR is 2000 bytes. F is incorrect because VARCHAR2 requires length.

Question 27

Answer E is correct. This query is a Top-N query as a whole, containing only a subquery known as an inline view. So A is incorrect. Any form of outer join will include the syntax clause OUTER JOIN or the outer join operator (+) in a WHERE clause. Thus, B, C, and D are all incorrect.

Question 28

The correct answer is the system privilege CREATE SESSION. The CREATE SESSION is the minimum requirement for a new user, allowing that user to connect to the database.

Question 29

Answer D is correct. A CLOB object is used to store very large text strings in binary format. A is incorrect because RAW and LONG RAW datatypes are out of date with the current version of Oracle Database and less manageable than binary large object datatypes such as BLOB datatypes. B is incorrect because BLOB datatypes are generally used to store purely binary data such as multimedia objects. A BFILE datatype is a pointer used to store a reference in a database to an externally stored static multimedia object such as an image. BFILE pointers are the most efficient form of storage for static multimedia objects such as images, which do not change. E is incorrect because the maximum size for a VARCHAR2 datatype is 4,000 bytes.

Question 30

Answer E is correct. All the command sequences will cause errors. Answer A is incorrect because it attempts to compress four columns where there are only three columns; COMPRESS 1 or COMPRESS 2 should be used. B is incorrect because REVERSE and NOSORT options do not apply to the same index. NOSORT assumes rows are already sorted, and REVERSE requires explicit sorting. For C the CREATE INDEX command is valid but the ALTER INDEX command is not, because NOSORT is an invalid option for the ALTER INDEX command. D is incorrect because the MOVIE_ID is shown in the question as the primary key. Oracle Database automatically creates an index for the primary key and does not permit duplicate indexes on the same single or set of columns (ordered the same way).

Question 31

Answer D is correct. A is incorrect because the left outer join returns studios having no movies. B has incorrect syntax because the ON clause requires comparison between two columns, requiring aliases as well. C is incorrectly coded because the USING clause specifies a column list (can be a single column) common to both joined tables, and thus aliases are not allowed. D is correct, returning the intersection, and, unlike B, it joins with the USING clause. E is incorrect because it does not sort the title of the movie in descending order; ascending order is the default.

Question 32

Answers A, B, and E are correct. INSERT allows new row additions, UPDATE allows changes to existing rows, and INDEX allows creation of indexes on a specific table. TRUNCATE is a command in itself and not an object privilege, and READ ONLY is meaningless. Thus, C and D are both invalid answers. The SELECT object privilege allows read access to a table.

Question 33

Answer C is correct. The table contains NOT NULL constraints, primary key constraints, reference constraints (foreign keys), and two check constraints. A, B, and D are thus incorrect.

Question 34

Answer D is correct. When opening an output file, type **SPOOL <filename>**; when closing the file, type **SPOOL OFF**. The output file will be empty until the SPOOL OFF command is executed. A is simply wrong. B is wrong because it turns off automatic COMMIT command execution for all DML activity, this being the recommended setting in a production environment because changes cannot be rolled back. C is wrong because the COLUMN command is used to define headings and format settings for query output columns. E is once again simply wrong because it is non-existent as a command in SQL*Plus.

Question 35

The correct answer is Hello World, in mixed case. LOWER changes all to lowercase. UPPER changes all to uppercase, and INITCAP capitalizes the first letter of each word, returning the original string.

Question 36

Answer A is correct. The sequence of commands is complex, but with a thorough understanding of sequence syntax and the NEXTVAL pseudocolumn, this question is a simple matter of tracing the calculations through the commands.

This question looks complex but it is not—it is merely involved. The sequence starts at 0 counting down in increments of –3, until reaching –9. When –9 is passed, the sequence becomes the MAXVALUE of 10. Line 2 accesses the first sequence value, which is 0. Line 3 increments one and not two increments (NEXTVAL in the same SQL command), setting the sequence to –3. Lines 4 to 8 bump the sequence five times, from –3 to –6, –9, 10 (MAXVALUE), 7, and finally 4. The ALTER SEQUENCE command changes the INCREMENT to 5, resulting in lines 10 to 13 incrementing the sequence four times up to 9, exceeding the MAXVALUE of 10, resulting in two increments from MINVALUE of –9 up to –4 and finally 1. If you do not understand that multiple executions of TEST_SEQ.NEXTVAL in the same SQL command bump the sequence only once, your result is probably answer B (–9). Both answers C and D are incorrect.

Question 37

Answer D is correct. Answer D is the most likely cause of a problem. A will cause a problem because if the release date is NULL, that row will be filtered by the WHERE clause. B is correct but not applicable because removing TO_NUMBER will cause a problem if the BETWEEN expression values are not tested as strings. A problem does not exist for the query as it stands. C is incorrect because the NVL function replaces any zero values with 1. D is correct because NVL replaces NULL values with zero, potentially causing an undefined zero division. Because D is the correct answer, E is incorrect.

Question 38

Answer D is correct. All SMALLINT and INTEGER datatypes are ANSI-compliant standard datatypes and convert to Oracle NUMBER datatypes automatically. Thus, the quantity of NUMBER datatypes is composed of the two NUMBER datatypes, the two SMALLINT datatypes, and the INTEGER datatype.

Question 39

Answer F is correct. Lines 6 and 7 produce errors because the keyword KEY is missing after both keywords PRIMARY and FOREIGN. Thus A, B, C, D and E are all incorrect answers.

Question 40

Answer E is correct. D is correct because the ORDER BY clause should be applied to the subquery. The result of placing the ORDER BY clause after the WHERE clause of the calling query is that the first five rows returned by the unsorted subquery will be returned. If the sorted order is a requirement, the result is spurious and probably useless. A and B are thus incorrect. A more appropriate form of the query would include the required sorted order in the subquery as shown here:

```
SELECT * FROM(SELECT * FROM SALE ORDER BY SALE_PRICE) WHERE ROWNUM < 5;
```

Question 41

Answer E is correct. Granting the SELECT object privilege only on a sequence will allow a different user to access the sequence to obtain either the next value (NEXTVAL) or its current value (CURRVAL).

Question 42

Answer C is correct. When you apply the expression

```
LENGTH(LPAD('This is a string',
    LENGTH(SUBSTR('This is a string', POWER(2, 3)*-1, 4)) * 5
, '*'))
```

the resulting string will be the original string with four * (asterisks) padded to the left side of the string: ****This is a string. The SUBSTR is taken as 2^3, multiplied by –1, searching from the end of the string backward, finding the last eight characters of the string (a string) and selecting the first four of those last eight characters (a st). The resulting four-character string provides the LENGTH function with the value 4, which is then multiplied by 5 to get 20. This string is 16 characters long and thus the LPAD function increases the size of the 16-character string to 20 characters, padding it on the left with * characters: ****This is a string. The final function takes the length of the final string, giving an answer of 20. A is thus completely off and B ignores the LPAD function. D and E both provide different versions of the string at different stages of expression evaluation, but not the final result.

Question 43

Answer E is correct. There is nothing wrong with this CREATE VIEW command.

Question 44

The answer is the string AsI. When you apply the expression

```
SUBSTR(
    TRANSLATE(
        REPLACE('This is a string', ' ', '')
    , 'ia', 'AI')
, 5, 3)
```

the REPLACE function replaces characters with other characters. The REPLACE function in this case changes all space characters to NULL, effectively removing them from the string, leaving the string Thisisastring. The TRANSLATE function does not replace one thing with another but rather translates characters into other characters. In this case the character set ia replaces all occurrences of lowercase *i* and *a* with uppercase *I* and *A*, also switching *I* and *A* around. The string passed to the SUBSTR function is ThAsAsIstrAng. The SUBSTR takes three characters from the fifth position, resulting in a returned value of AsI.

Question 45

Answer E is correct. When you apply the expression

```
TRUNC(ROUND(FLOOR(CEIL(1.2)-.1) + .3445, 3), 2)
```

CEIL rounds up regardless, producing 2. FLOOR rounds down regardless, producing 1 from 2 – .1 (1.9). ROUND will round up 1 + .3445, 1.3445 to three decimal places, producing 1.345. TRUNC will truncate or simply drop characters, with no rounding, from the value 1.345, for two decimal places, leaving the result of 1.34 (no rounding up of 1.345 to 1.35 as for the ROUND function).

Question 46

Answer C is correct. When you apply the expression

```
SIGN(ABS((MOD(13, 3) * -1)+5))
```

MOD is a modulus or remainder function, finding the remainder value of 13 divided by 3: 13 / 3 = 9, remainder 2. Thus MOD(13, 3) = 2. 2 is then multiplied by –1, giving –2, and 5 is added, giving 3. SIGN returns -1 for negative numbers, 0 for 0, and 1 for any positive number other than 0. The result is thus 1.

Question 47

Answer D is correct. When you apply the expression

```
LAST_DAY(ADD_MONTHS('01-JAN-04',
    MONTHS_BETWEEN('01-JAN-05', '01-JAN-04')))
```

the months between the two dates is exactly 12 months. The 12 months are then added to the lower date, yielding the higher date. The last day of the month, or LAST_DAY, returns the last day in January 2005, which is 31-JAN-2005.

Question 48

Answer C is correct. The sequence will start at 1, incrementing by 1, up to a maximum value of 5. If 5 is exceeded, the next value of the sequence goes back to the starting value of 1 (CYCLE). Effectively, there are three sequence increments here and not four. The key to this question is understanding that in line 3, TEST_SEQ.NEXTVAL does not execute twice within the same SQL command. Thus, the answer is 2 (C) and not 3 (D). Options A, B, and E are thus all incorrect.

Question 49

All of answers A, B, C, and D are correct. Each of the four CREATE TABLE commands is a variation on the way of creating the primary and foreign key constraints; all are syntactically valid and all produce the same result.

Question 50

Answer E is correct. None of the definitions apply where the restriction is forcibly applied. The correct definition would be NUMBER(5,2). The two parameters imply precision and scale. Precision dictates the total length of the number (excluding the decimal point); the scale, the number of digits to the right of the decimal point.

Question 51

Answer E is correct. A is correct because you will get a text file, and C is correct because you will get a comma-delimited file (delimiting each column in the MOVIE table); also record lengths will be fixed unless variable-length columns are trimmed of all whitespace and space characters. Thus, D is incorrect. B is a nonsensical answer.

Question 52

Answer C is correct. Line 3 causes an error because EXISTS has only an expression on the right and not two expressions on both the left and right of the EXISTS clause. The IN operator as in *expression* IN (1,2,3,4,5) verifies one expression against another. EXISTS checks for the existence of a result in the subquery, returning a Boolean true or false result.

Question 53

Answers A, B, C, and D are correct. A subquery can return one or more rows, sometimes even no rows. Conditions such as ANY, SOME, ALL, IN, and EXISTS can operate on multiple rows returning subqueries, because they check against multiple values. SOME or ANY implies some or any of a list of elements. IN implies: Is something in a list of elements? EXISTS asks whether something exists within a list of elements, returning a positive or negative answer. Equality, inequality, and range checks (BETWEEN and >=) ask whether an expression matches something. For example, one cannot ask whether something is equal to three different values at the same time. The same applies to inequality and >=. BETWEEN might be a little confusing, but two separate subqueries could be used in the case of BETWEEN. Therefore, answers E, F, G, and H are all incorrect.

Question 54

Answers A, F, G, and H are correct. The COMMIT and ROLLBACK commands both terminate transactions. SAVEPOINT allows rollback to a labeled point within a multiple SQL command transaction. The SET TRANSACTION command is used to control the behavior of specific transactions. UPDATE, INSERT, and DELETE are DML commands forming the steps in a transaction but cannot be used to start, terminate, or manipulate a transaction as a whole. TRUNCATE is a DDL command. Thus B, C, D, and E are all incorrect answers.

Question 55

Answers A and D are correct. The INSERT command is used to add new rows. UPDATE changes existing rows. TRUNCATE destroys rows. MERGE is used to upsert rows where an upsert is an option to add new rows or change existing rows. The COMMIT command permanently saves changes made by other DML commands.

Question 56

Answers A, B, and C are correct. Any number with more than three decimal places will have those decimals rounded to three decimal digits, as in B and C. Answers D, E, F, and G are incorrect because the whole-number portion can be a maximum of five digits. Three decimal places are required, leaving only five digits for the whole-number portion of the number. The resulting inserted values will be 10000.234, 1000.235 (rounded up from 1000.2345), and 10000.235 (also round up), for answers A, B, and C, respectively.

Question 57

Answers B, D, and F are correct. A will not work because the NAME column cannot be NULL. B is fine because the GENDER column has a default setting. C deliberately attempts to set the GENDER column to NULL, violating both NOT NULL and check constraints. D is okay because all NOT NULL constraints are catered for. E attempts to place an X into the GENDER column, violating the check constraint. F is fine, identical to answer B in a syntactical respect. G is erroneous because only two columns are specified, and so is H for the same reason.

Question 58

Answers D and E are correct. The query in the question produces a count of males in the DIRECTOR table. A is incorrect because the DISTINCT clause finds only the first male, and thus one row with one male. Both B and C are incorrect because they find a single row and a single column containing the value M, for male. D finds exactly the same result as the query in question, simply substituting the HAVING clause for the WHERE clause, filtering after all rows are retrieved rather than during the row set construction process. E is also identical but uses a rather convoluted method to find the same result as the query in the question.

Question 59

Answer A is correct. The sequence will start at 1, incrementing by –1, down to a minimum value of –3. If –3 is exceeded, the next value of the sequence goes back to the starting value of 1 (CYCLE). Effectively, there are three sequence increments here and not four. The key to this question is understanding that, in line 3, TEST_SEQ.NEXTVAL does not execute twice within the same SQL command. Thus, the answer is 0 (A) and not -1 (B). Answers C, D, and E are thus all incorrect.

Question 60

Answer A is correct. ENABLE will ensure that the constraint is enabled when new rows are added. NOVALIDATE will ensure that as the constraint is added to the table, existing rows are not validated for the enabling constraint. B thus is incorrect because existing rows would be required to pass the requirements for the constraint being added; otherwise, the constraint creation would fail. DISABLE simply creates a constraint, which exists but does nothing, to existing and new rows. Thus, C is wrong. D is wrong because it instructs Oracle Database to completely ignore the new constraint under all circumstances. E is wrong because A is correct.

Practice Test #2

1. Which of these queries cause errors? Assume that all object names, such as schemas, tables, views, columns, and otherwise, exist in their appropriate places.

   ❑ A. `SELECT * FROM MOVIES.ACTOR;`

   ❑ B. `SELECT MOVIE_ID, TITLE, YEAR FROM MOVIE;`

   ❑ C.
   ```
   SELECT MOVIES.ACTOR.ACTOR_ID, MOVIES.ACTOR.NAME
       FROM MOVIES.ACTOR;
   ```

   ❑ D.
   ```
   SELECT MOVIE_ID, TITLE, YEAR*10
        FROM MOVIES.MOVIE;
   ```

   ❑ E.
   ```
   SELECT TITLE AS MOVIE, NAME AS DIRECTOR
       FROM MOVIE NATURAL JOIN DIRECTOR;
   ```

   ❑ F. None of these queries cause an error.

2. Which two of these queries cause a syntax error?

   ❑ A.
   ```
   SELECT TITLE AS MOVIE, NAME AS DIRECTOR
   FROM MOVIE NATURAL JOIN DIRECTOR
   ORDER BY DIRECTOR, MOVIE;
   ```

   ❑ B.
   ```
   COL MOVIE FORMAT A16
   COL DIRECTOR FORMAT A16
   SELECT TITLE AS MOVIE, NAME AS DIRECTOR
   FROM MOVIE NATURAL JOIN DIRECTOR
   ORDER BY DIRECTOR, MOVIE;
   ```

   ❑ C.
   ```
   SELECT TITLE AS MOVIE, NAME AS DIRECTOR
   FROM MOVIE NATURAL JOIN DIRECTOR
   WHERE DIRECTOR LIKE '%a%'
   ORDER BY DIRECTOR, MOVIE;
   ```

   ❑ D.
   ```
   SELECT TITLE AS MOVIE
   ,RANK+(REVIEWS*REVIEW_RANK) AS RANKING
   , NAME AS DIRECTOR
   FROM MOVIE NATURAL JOIN DIRECTOR
   ORDER BY DIRECTOR, MOVIE, RANKING;
   ```

- ❑ E.
```
SELECT TITLE AS MOVIE,  RANK+(REVIEWS*REVIEW_RANK)
, NAME AS DIRECTOR
FROM MOVIE NATURAL JOIN DIRECTOR
ORDER BY DIRECTOR, MOVIE, RANK+(REVIEWS*REVIEW_RANK);
```
- ❑ F.
```
SELECT TITLE AS MOVIE
, RANK+(REVIEWS*REVIEW_RANK) AS RANKING
, NAME AS DIRECTOR FROM MOVIE NATURAL JOIN DIRECTOR
WHERE RANKING < 100
ORDER BY DIRECTOR, MOVIE, RANKING;
```
- ❑ G.
```
SELECT TITLE AS MOVIE
, RANK+(REVIEWS*REVIEW_RANK)
, NAME AS DIRECTOR
FROM MOVIE NATURAL JOIN DIRECTOR
WHERE RANK+(REVIEWS*REVIEW_RANK) < 100
ORDER BY DIRECTOR, MOVIE, RANK+(REVIEWS*REVIEW_RANK);
```

3. For this query

```
SELECT GENDER, TYPECAST, NAME FROM ACTOR ORDER BY 1, 2, 3;
```

and this data

```
GENDER TYPECAST         NAME
F      Comedian         Teri Garr
F      Multiple         Michelle Pfeiffer
F      Multiple         Sally Field
F      Musical          Irene Cara
F      Science Fiction  Carrie Fisher
F                       Diane Lane
F                       Madelaine Kahn
M      Action Drama     George Clooney
M      Action Drama     Kevin Costner
M      Action Drama     Telly Savalas
M      Action Drama     Tom Hanks
M      Comedian         Carroll O'Connor
M      Comedian         Cloris Leachman
```

which of these queries will retrieve the fewest rows? Select one answer.

- ❑ A. `SELECT DISTINCT GENDER, TYPECAST, NAME FROM ACTOR;`
- ❑ B. `SELECT UNIQUE GENDER, TYPECAST, NAME FROM ACTOR;`
- ❑ C. `SELECT GENDER, TYPECAST, NAME FROM ACTOR;`
- ❑ D. `SELECT DISTINCT(GENDER||TYPECAST||NAME) FROM ACTOR;`
- ❑ E. `SELECT DISTINCT GENDER, TYPECAST FROM ACTOR;`
- ❑ F. `SELECT DISTINCT GENDER FROM ACTOR;`
- ❑ G. `SELECT DISTINCT TYPECAST FROM ACTOR;`

4. Which of these queries will not cause errors? Assume that all schema, table, and column names are valid.

- ❑ A. `SELECT * FROM MOVIE WHERE MOVIES.MOVIE.MOVIE_ID = 1;`
- ❑ B.
```
SELECT * FROM MOVIES.MOVIE
    WHERE MOVIES.MOVIE.MOVIE_ID = 1;
```
- ❑ C.
```
SELECT TITLE FROM MOVIE
    WHERE MOVIES.MOVIE.MOVIE_ID = 1;
```

❑ D. `SELECT MOVIES.MOVIE.TITLE FROM MOVIE`
`WHERE MOVIES.MOVIE.MOVIE_ID = 1;`

❑ E. `SELECT * FROM MOVIE WHERE 1 = MOVIE_ID;`

❑ F. `SELECT * FROM MOVIE M WHERE 1 = MOVIE_ID;`

❑ G. `SELECT * FROM MOVIE WHERE 1 = M.MOVIE_ID;`

❑ H. `SELECT M.TITLE FROM MOVIE M WHERE 1 = M.MOVIE_ID;`

5. Which of these queries will cause a syntax error? Assume that all objects such as tables and columns exist.

❑ A.
```
SELECT * FROM MOVIE
    WHERE MOVIE_ID = 1 AND MOVIE_ID = 2;
```

❑ B.
```
SELECT * FROM MOVIE
    WHERE MOVIE_ID = 1 AND TITLE LIKE '%a%'
    OR YEAR IN(1998, 1999, 2000);
```

❑ C.
```
SELECT * FROM MOVIE
    WHERE MOVIE_ID = 1 OR TITLE LIKE '%a%'
    AND YEAR IN(1998, 1999, 2000);
```

❑ D.
```
SELECT * FROM MOVIE
    WHERE MOVIE_ID = 1 AND TITLE LIKE '%a%'
    AND YEAR IN(1998, 1999, 2000);
```

❑ E.
```
SELECT * FROM MOVIE
    WHERE MOVIE_ID = 1 AND (TITLE LIKE '%a%'
    OR YEAR IN(1998, 1999, 2000));
```

❑ F.
```
SELECT * FROM MOVIE
    WHERE (MOVIE_ID = 1 OR TITLE LIKE '%a%')
    AND YEAR IN(1998, 1999, 2000);
```

❑ G. None of the above

6. Which of the following queries will produce errors? Select one or more. Assume that all objects such as tables and columns exist.

❑ A. `SELECT * FROM MOVIE ORDER BY 1, 2, 3;`

❑ B. `SELECT TITLE FROM MOVIE ORDER BY 2, 1;`

❑ C.
```
SELECT * FROM MOVIE ORDER BY TITLE DESC
    , YEAR ASC, MOVIE_ID NULLS FIRST;
```

❑ D. `SELECT * FROM MOVIE ORDER BY (RANK*REVIEWS)/100;`

❑ E.
```
SELECT TITLE, YEAR, (RANK*REVIEWS)/100 FROM MOVIE
    ORDER BY (RANK*REVIEWS)/100;
```

❑ F.
```
SELECT TITLE AS MOVIE, YEAR, (RANK*REVIEWS)/100
    FROM MOVIE ORDER BY 3, 2, 1;
```

❑ G.
```
SELECT MOVIE_ID, TITLE, YEAR FROM MOVIE
    ORDER BY TITLE DESC, 3 ASC, 1 NULLS FIRST;
```

7. What does the `||` operator do?

❑ A. Adds values together

❑ B. Multiples two numbers

❑ C. Calculates the result of a function

- ❑ D. Concatenates numbers by adding them together mathematically
- ❑ E. None of the above

8. Which of these two queries will retrieve the most and the fewest rows? Select the correct answer.

```
1. SELECT * FROM MOVIE UNION SELECT * FROM MOVIE;
2. SELECT * FROM MOVIE UNION ALL SELECT * FROM MOVIE;
3. SELECT * FROM MOVIE INTERSECT SELECT * FROM MOVIE;
4. SELECT * FROM MOVIE MINUS SELECT * FROM MOVIE;
```

- ❑ A. All queries retrieve the same number of rows.
- ❑ B. All queries retrieve no rows at all.
- ❑ C. Query 2 retrieves the fewest and query 3 the most rows.
- ❑ D. Query 2 retrieves the most and query 3 the fewest rows.
- ❑ E. Query 2 retrieves the most and query 4 the fewest rows.

9. What is the result of this expression?

```
( ( 5 * 3 ) + 12 - ( 6 * ( 2 + 12 ) ) ) / 2 + 4
```

- ❑ A. **0**
- ❑ B. **95**
- ❑ C. **24.5**
- ❑ D. **-24.5**
- ❑ E. None of the above

10. Which movies will this query find?

```
SELECT * FROM MOVIE WHERE TITLE NOT LIKE 'A';
```

- ❑ A. All movies with titles beginning with the letter *A*
- ❑ B. All movies ending with *A*
- ❑ C. Any movie containing an uppercase *A* or lowercase *a*
- ❑ D. All of the above
- ❑ E. None of the above

11. What is a **ROWID** made up of?

- ❑ A. Datafile number relative to tablespace, block number, row number, segment number
- ❑ B. Segment number, datafile number relative to tablespace, block number, row number
- ❑ C. Segment number, datafile number relative to tablespace, row number, block number
- ❑ D. None of the above

12. When first connecting to a session, which commands will cause an error? Assume that the sequence exists and is accessible.

- ❑ A. **SELECT MYSEQ.CURRVAL, MYSEQ.NEXTVAL FROM DUAL;**
- ❑ B. **SELECT MYSEQ.NEXTVAL, MYSEQ.CURRVAL FROM DUAL;**
- ❑ C. **SELECT MYSEQ.CURRVAL, MYSEQ.CURRVAL FROM DUAL;**

❑ D. `SELECT MYSEQ.NEXTVAL, MYSEQ.NEXTVAL , MYSEQ.CURRVAL FROM DUAL;`

❑ E. `SELECT MYSEQ.CURRVAL FROM DUAL;`

13. Which of these `CASE` statement expressions will cause an error?

```
A. SELECT NAME,
    CASE GENDER
        WHEN 'F' THEN 'Female'
        WHEN 'M' THEN 'Male'
        ELSE 'Unknown'
    END
   FROM ACTOR;
```

```
B. SELECT NAME,
    CASE GENDER
        WHEN GENDER = 'F' THEN 'Female'
        WHEN GENDER = 'M' THEN 'Male'
        ELSE 'Unknown'
    END
   FROM ACTOR;
```

```
C. SELECT NAME,
    CASE
        WHEN GENDER = 'F' THEN 'Female'
        WHEN GENDER = 'M' THEN 'Male'
        ELSE 'Unknown'
    END
   FROM ACTOR;
```

❑ A. A

❑ B. B

❑ C. C

❑ D. None of the above

14. Which of these expressions are syntactically valid? Select two answers.

❑ A. `SUBSTRING('This is a string)`

❑ B. `SUBSTR('This is a string')`

❑ C. `SUBSTR("This is a string")`

❑ D. `SUBSTR('This is a string', 5)`

❑ E. `SUBSTR('This is a string', 5, 10)`

15. What string will this expression return?

```
TRIM(BOTH '*' FROM '<comments<')
```

❑ A. `comments`

❑ B. `*comments*`

❑ C. `**comments**`

❑ D. `comments` with three spaces on each side

❑ E. None of the above

16. What is the result of this expression?

```
TRUNC(ROUND(SIGN(FLOOR(CEIL(ABS
    (POWER(2, -3)))/5))+54.355,2),1)
```

- ❑ A. **54.4**
- ❑ B. **54.3**
- ❑ C. **54**
- ❑ D. **55**
- ❑ E. **-1**

17. What is the result of the expression **MOD(LOG(10, 1000), 2)**?

- ❑ A. **2**
- ❑ B. **100**
- ❑ C. **10**
- ❑ D. **1000**
- ❑ E. **1**

18. What value will this query return?

```
SELECT EXTRACT(DAY FROM DATE '2004-06-10')||'/'||
EXTRACT(MONTH FROM DATE '2004-06-10')||'/'||
EXTRACT(YEAR FROM DATE '2004-06-10')
FROM DUAL;
```

- ❑ A. **10th, June 2004**
- ❑ B. **June 10th, 2004**
- ❑ C. **10/6/2004**
- ❑ D. **6/10/2004**
- ❑ E. **10/06/2004**

19. How many tables are being joined in this query?

```
SELECT * FROM DIRECTOR
    NATURAL JOIN MOVIE
        NATURAL JOIN PART
            NATURAL JOIN ACTOR;
```

- ❑ A. 0
- ❑ B. 3
- ❑ C. 5
- ❑ D. 2
- ❑ E. None of the above

20. Which line causes an error and what is the reason?

```
1. SELECT * FROM DIRECTOR
2.     NATURAL JOIN MOVIE
3.         NATURAL JOIN PART USING(MOVIE_ID, ACTOR_ID)
4.             NATURAL JOIN ACTOR;
```

- ❑ A. Line 3 causes an error because the **USING** clause is not required.
- ❑ B. Line 3 causes an error because the **NATURAL** keyword is not required.

- ❑ C. Line 4 causes an error because the **ACTOR** table requires an **ON** clause.
- ❑ D. Line 3 causes an error because the **USING** clause conflicts with all three other **NATURAL** keywords in the query.
- ❑ E. All of the above.

21. Most column names for this join are different except for a **NAME** column on the **ACTOR** and **DIRECTOR** tables. Supposing that you do not want to join using the **NAME** columns, which are the correct versions for the requirements of the join query? Select three answers.

```
1. SELECT * FROM DIRECTOR NATURAL JOIN MOVIE NATURAL JOIN
   PART NATURAL JOIN ACTOR;

2. SELECT * FROM DIRECTOR JOIN MOVIE USING(DIRECTOR_ID)
   JOIN PART USING(MOVIE_ID) JOIN ACTOR USING(ACTOR_ID);

3. SELECT * FROM DIRECTOR D JOIN MOVIE M
   ON(M.DIRECTOR_ID = D.DIRECTOR_ID)
   JOIN PART P ON(P.MOVIE_ID = M.MOVIE_ID)
   JOIN ACTOR A ON(A.ACTOR_ID = P.ACTOR_ID);

4. SELECT * FROM DIRECTOR D, MOVIE M, PART P, ACTOR A
   WHERE M.DIRECTOR_ID = D.DIRECTOR_ID
   AND A.MOVIE_ID = P.MOVIE_ID
   AND P.ACTOR_ID = M.ACTOR_ID;

5. SELECT * FROM DIRECTOR D, MOVIE M, PART P, ACTOR A
   WHERE M.DIRECTOR_ID = D.DIRECTOR_ID
   AND P.MOVIE_ID = M.MOVIE_ID AND A.ACTOR_ID = P.ACTOR_ID;
```

- ❑ A. 1
- ❑ B. 2, 3, and 4
- ❑ C. 1, 3, and 5
- ❑ D. 2, 3, and 5
- ❑ E. None of the above

22. The **ACTOR** table contains 37 actors. Only 3 actors have been given an award and all have the same award. There are 24 types of awards. How many rows will this query produce?

```
SELECT NAME, AWARD FROM ACTOR
    LEFT JOIN RECOGNITION USING(ACTOR_ID)
        FULL JOIN AWARD USING(AWARD_ID);
```

- ❑ A. 37
- ❑ B. 24
- ❑ C. 3
- ❑ D. 1
- ❑ E. 60

23. Which changes could you implement to repair this query, assuming that it is not functioning properly? Also assume that all tables, columns, and relationships between tables exist and are valid using the **NATURAL** keyword. Select more than one answer or select E.

```
SELECT NAME, TITLE, COUNT(SALE_ID)
FROM DIRECTOR NATURAL JOIN MOVIE NATURAL JOIN SALE
WHERE TITLE LIKE '%e%' AND YEAR > 2000 OR YEAR < 2004
GROUP BY TITLE;
```

- ❑ A. **SELECT NAME, TITLE, COUNT(*)**
- ❑ B. **FROM DIRECTOR**
  JOIN MOVIE USING(DIRECTOR_ID)
  JOIN SALE(USING MOVIE_ID)
- ❑ C. **WHERE TITLE LIKE '%e%' AND (YEAR > 2000**
  OR YEAR < 2004)
- ❑ D. **GROUP BY NAME, TITLE;**
- ❑ E. All of the above

24. Which changes should be made to avoid syntax errors in this query? Assume that all tables, columns, and relationships between tables exist and are valid using the **NATURAL** keyword. Select two answers.

```
SELECT NAME, SUBSTR(TITLE, 1, 10) AS AHIT
    , COUNT(TRUNC(SALE_PRICE*1000, -2)) AS SALES
FROM DIRECTOR JOIN MOVIE ON(DIRECTOR_ID)
    JOIN SALE USING(MOVIE_ID)
GROUP BY 1, AHIT
ORDER BY 1, 2;
```

- ❑ A. **SELECT NAME, SUBSTR(TITLE, 1, 10)**
- ❑ B. **JOIN SALE ON(MOVIE_ID)**
- ❑ C. **FROM DIRECTOR JOIN MOVIE USING(DIRECTOR_ID)**
- ❑ D. **GROUP BY 1, SUBSTR(TITLE, 1, 10);**
- ❑ E. **GROUP BY NAME, SUBSTR(TITLE, 1, 10);**

25. For this query

```
SELECT GENDER, TYPECAST, NAME FROM ACTOR ORDER BY 1, 2, 3;
```

and this data

```
G TYPECAST          NAME

F Comedian          Teri Garr
F Multiple          Michelle Pfeiffer
F Multiple          Sally Field
F Musical           Irene Cara
F Science Fiction   Carrie Fisher
F                   Diane Lane
F                   Madelaine Kahn
M Action Drama      George Clooney
M Action Drama      Kevin Costner
M Action Drama      Telly Savalas
M Action Drama      Tom Hanks
M Comedian          Carroll O'Connor
M Comedian          Cloris Leachman
```

which of these queries will retrieve the most rows? Select two or more answers.

- ❑ A. **SELECT DISTINCT GENDER, TYPECAST, NAME FROM ACTOR;**
- ❑ B. **SELECT UNIQUE GENDER, TYPECAST, NAME FROM ACTOR;**
- ❑ C. **SELECT GENDER, TYPECAST, NAME FROM ACTOR;**
- ❑ D. **SELECT DISTINCT(GENDER||TYPECAST||NAME) FROM ACTOR;**
- ❑ E. **SELECT DISTINCT GENDER, TYPECAST FROM ACTOR;**
- ❑ F. **SELECT DISTINCT GENDER FROM ACTOR;**
- ❑ G. **SELECT DISTINCT TYPECAST FROM ACTOR;**

26. Which of these queries will not cause a syntax error but will produce unexpected results? Assume that all objects such as tables and columns exist. Select three answers.

❑ A.
```
SELECT * FROM MOVIE
WHERE MOVIE_ID = 1 AND MOVIE_ID = 2;
```
❑ B.
```
SELECT * FROM MOVIE
WHERE MOVIE_ID = 1 AND TITLE LIKE '%a%'
   OR YEAR IN(1998, 1999, 2000);
```
❑ C.
```
SELECT * FROM MOVIE
WHERE MOVIE_ID = 1 OR TITLE LIKE '%a%'
   AND YEAR IN(1998, 1999, 2000);
```
❑ D.
```
SELECT * FROM MOVIE
WHERE MOVIE_ID = 1 AND TITLE LIKE '%a%'
   AND YEAR IN(1998, 1999, 2000);
```
❑ E.
```
SELECT * FROM MOVIE
WHERE MOVIE_ID = 1 AND (TITLE LIKE '%a%'
   OR YEAR IN(1998, 1999, 2000));
```
❑ F.
```
SELECT * FROM MOVIE
WHERE (MOVIE_ID = 1 OR TITLE LIKE '%a%')
   AND YEAR IN(1998, 1999, 2000);
```

27. This query finds movies spread over 12 different years:

```
SELECT YEAR, COUNT(YEAR) FROM MOVIE GROUP BY YEAR;
```

Using this query, I find that 5 of the 12 years have two movies each:

```
SELECT YEAR, COUNT(YEAR) FROM MOVIE GROUP BY YEAR
   HAVING COUNT(YEAR) > 1;
```

Which of the following queries will return the largest value?

- ❑ A. **SELECT COUNT(DISTINCT(YEAR)) FROM MOVIE;**
- ❑ B. **SELECT COUNT(DISTINCT YEAR) FROM MOVIE;**
- ❑ C. **SELECT COUNT(ALL YEAR) FROM MOVIE;**
- ❑ D. **SELECT COUNT(YEAR) FROM MOVIE;**
- ❑ E. **SELECT COUNT(*) FROM MOVIE;**

28. Which of these are valid Oracle SQL functions?

- ❑ A. **STDEV**
- ❑ B. **STDDEV**
- ❑ C. **VAR**
- ❑ D. **VARIANCE**
- ❑ E. A and C

29. What is wrong with this query?

```
SELECT YEAR, COUNT(YEAR)
FROM MOVIE
WHERE YEAR > 1995
GROUP BY YEAR
HAVING YEAR > 1995;
```

- ❑ A. There is nothing wrong with this query.
- ❑ B. There is a syntax error.
- ❑ C. The **HAVING** clause is superfluous.
- ❑ D. All of the above.
- ❑ E. None of the above.

30. How many of these queries have syntax errors? Assume that all tables, columns, and relationships exist and are correct for the joins in the queries.

```
SELECT REGION, COUNTRY, COUNT(TITLE)
FROM REGION
    JOIN COUNTRY USING (REGION_ID)
        JOIN SALE USING(COUNTRY_ID)
            JOIN MOVIE USING(MOVIE_ID)
GROUP BY ROLLUP(REGION, COUNTRY)
HAVING COUNT(TITLE) > 100
ORDER BY 1, 2;

SELECT REGION, COUNTRY, COUNT(TITLE)
FROM REGION
    JOIN COUNTRY USING (REGION_ID)
        JOIN SALE USING(COUNTRY_ID)
            JOIN MOVIE USING(MOVIE_ID)
GROUP BY CUBE(REGION, COUNTRY)
HAVING REGION LIKE 'S%'
ORDER BY 1, 2;

SELECT REGION, COUNTRY, COUNT(TITLE) AS COUNTER
FROM REGION
    JOIN COUNTRY USING (REGION_ID)
        JOIN SALE USING(COUNTRY_ID)
            JOIN MOVIE USING(MOVIE_ID)
GROUP BY GROUPING SETS((REGION,COUNTRY),(REGION),(COUNTRY))
HAVING REGION LIKE 'S%' AND COUNT(TITLE) > 100
ORDER BY 1, 2;
```

- ❑ A. 1
- ❑ B. 2
- ❑ C. 3

❑ D. None of them

❑ E. There is an improperly coded query but the query will not cause a syntax error.

31. In which of the following clauses can a subquery not be located?

❑ A. **SELECT**

❑ B. **INSERT**

❑ C. **UPDATE**

❑ D. **ORDER BY**

❑ E. **GROUP BY**

❑ F. **CASE**

❑ G. **CREATE TABLE**

32. All subqueries in the following options return more than a single row or more than a single column. Which expression conditions will cause errors? Assume that all tables and columns exist.

❑ A. **WHERE (SELECT * FROM MOVIE) = (SELECT * FROM ACTOR)**

❑ B. **WHERE EXISTS (SELECT MOVIE_ID FROM MOVIE)**

❑ C. **WHERE NOT EXISTS (SELECT MOVIE_ID FROM MOVIE)**

❑ D. **WHERE (SELECT * FROM MOVIE)**
= ALL (SELECT * FROM MOVIE)

❑ E. **WHERE MOVIE_ID = ALL (SELECT * FROM MOVIE)**

❑ F. **WHERE MOVIE_ID = ALL (SELECT MOVIE_ID FROM MOVIE)**

❑ G. None of the above

33. Which line in this query contains an error? Assume that all tables, columns, and relationships between them are valid.

```
1. SELECT *
2. FROM PART
3. WHERE (MOVIE_ID, ACTOR_ID) IN
4. (
5.     SELECT MOVIE_ID, ACTOR_ID
6.     FROM MOVIE NATURAL JOIN PART
7.     NATURAL JOIN ACTOR
8. );
```

❑ A. 3 and 5

❑ B. 6 and 7

❑ C. 8

❑ D. 1 and 3

❑ E. None of the above

34. Which of these queries return errors?

❑ A. **SELECT * FROM MOVIE WHERE EXISTS**
(SELECT RATING_ID FROM RATING);

❑ B. **SELECT * FROM MOVIE M WHERE EXISTS**
(SELECT RATING_ID FROM RATING
WHERE RATING_ID = M.RATING_ID);

- ❑ C. **`SELECT * FROM MOVIE M WHERE RATING_ID IN (SELECT RATING_ID FROM RATING);`**
- ❑ D. **`SELECT * FROM MOVIE M WHERE RATING_ID IN (SELECT RATING_ID FROM RATING WHERE RATING_ID = M.RATING_ID);`**
- ❑ E. None of the above queries returns an error.

35. If the **MOVIE** table contains 17 rows, how many rows will this query return?

```
SELECT MOVIE_ID, TITLE FROM MOVIE
UNION ALL
SELECT MOVIE_ID, TITLE FROM MOVIE
UNION
SELECT MOVIE_ID, TITLE FROM MOVIE
INTERSECT
SELECT MOVIE_ID, TITLE FROM MOVIE
MINUS
SELECT MOVIE_ID, TITLE FROM MOVIE;
```

- ❑ A. 17 rows
- ❑ B. 34 rows
- ❑ C. 0 rows
- ❑ D. 51 rows
- ❑ E. None of the above

36. In the following query the movie genre Non-Action contains seven subsidiary movie genres, but no parent movie genres. How many rows will this query return? The **PARENT_ID** column contains the **GENRE_ID** value for the parent row, of the current **GENRE** table row.

```
SELECT * FROM GENRE
START WITH GENRE = 'Non-Action'
CONNECT BY GENRE_ID = PRIOR PARENT_ID;
```

- ❑ A. 0
- ❑ B. 7
- ❑ C. 49
- ❑ D. All rows in the **GENRE** table
- ❑ E. None of the above

37. Which of these are valid SQL*Plus commands?

- ❑ A. **SHOW ALL**
- ❑ B. **SHOW L**
- ❑ C. **SHOW LINESIZE**
- ❑ D. **SHOW PAGESIZE LINESIZE**
- ❑ E. **SHOW**

38. Which of these are valid SQL*Plus commands?

❑ A. **SET LINESIZE=132**

❑ B. **SET LINESIZE = 132**

❑ C. **SET LINES 132**

❑ D. **SET LINESIZE 132**

❑ E. All of the above

39. Which of these commands will execute a SQL*Plus script?

❑ A. **RUN**

❑ B. **STARTUP**

❑ C. **@@**

❑ D. **!!**

❑ E. **EXEC**

40. Which of these SQL*Plus commands are not available in iSQL*Plus?

❑ A. **SET LINESIZE 132**

❑ B. **PASSWORD**

❑ C. **SET SQLPROMPT '>>'**

❑ D. **SET SPOOL ON**

❑ E. **SET SPOOL OFF**

41. Assume that all database objects exist and are accessible. This is the **ACTOR** table:

```
ACTOR_ID NOT NULL NUMBER Primary Key
NAME NOT NULL VARCHAR2(32)
GENDER NOT NULL CHAR(1) DEFAULT 'M'
TYPECAST VARCHAR2(64)
```

Which of these commands contain errors?

❑ A.
```
INSERT INTO ACTOR
    VALUES(ACTOR_SEQ.NEXTVAL, 'Actor name');
```

❑ B.
```
INSERT INTO ACTOR
    VALUES(ACTOR_SEQ.NEXTVAL, 'Actor name', 'F');
```

❑ C.
```
INSERT INTO ACTOR(ACTOR_ID, NAME)
    VALUES(ACTOR_SEQ.NEXTVAL, 'Actor name');
```

❑ D.
```
INSERT INTO ACTOR(ACTOR_ID, NAME, TYPECAST)
    VALUES(ACTOR_SEQ.NEXTVAL, 'Actor name'
    , 'Multi talented');
```

❑ E.
```
INSERT INTO ACTOR
    VALUES(ACTOR_SEQ.NEXTVAL, 'Actor name', 'F'
    , 'Multiple');
```

42. All rows in the **MOVIE** table have **SALE_DATE** dates in the years 2003, 2004, and 2005. Examine this SQL command:

```
INSERT
 WHEN TO_CHAR(SALE_DATE, 'YYYY') = '2003' THEN INTO SALE2003
 WHEN TO_CHAR(SALE_DATE, 'YYYY') = '2004' THEN INTO SALE2004
 WHEN TO_CHAR(SALE_DATE, 'YYYY') = '2005' THEN INTO SALE2005
SELECT * FROM SALE;
```

If there are 1000 rows in the **SALE** table, what will be the result of this query?

```
SELECT TO_CHAR(SALE_DATE, 'YYYY') FROM SALE2003
INTERSECT
SELECT TO_CHAR(SALE_DATE, 'YYYY') FROM SALE2004
INTERSECT
SELECT TO_CHAR(SALE_DATE, 'YYYY') FROM SALE2005;
```

- ❑ A. 1000 rows
- ❑ B. The sum of all rows in all three tables **SALE2003**, **SALE2004**, and **SALE2005**
- ❑ C. 0 rows
- ❑ D. The count of rows in the **SALE2003** table
- ❑ E. None of the above

43. Which of these SQL commands will cause an error? Select all that apply. Assume that all tables and columns are valid.

- ❑ A. **UPDATE STUDIO SET STUDIO = UPPER(STUDIO);**
- ❑ B. **UPDATE STUDIO A SET A.STUDIO = (SELECT UPPER(STUDIO) FROM STUDIO WHERE STUDIO_ID = A.STUDIO_ID);**
- ❑ C.
```
UPDATE SALE A SET (A.SALE_PRICE, A.SALE_DATE) =
    (SELECT NVL(LIST_PRICE, 0), NVL(RELEASE, SYSDATE)
       FROM MOVIE WHERE MOVIE_ID = A.MOVIE_ID);
```
- ❑ D.
```
UPDATE SALE A SET (A.SALE_PRICE, A.SALE_DATE) =
    (SELECT NVL(LIST_PRICE, 0), NVL(RELEASE, SYSDATE)
       FROM MOVIE WHERE MOVIE_ID = A.MOVIE_ID
          AND TO_CHAR(SALE_DATE,'YYYY')='2003')
    , (A.SALE_PRICE, A.SALE_DATE) =
      (SELECT NVL(LIST_PRICE, 0), NVL(RELEASE, SYSDATE)
       FROM MOVIE WHERE MOVIE_ID = A.MOVIE_ID
          AND TO_CHAR(SALE_DATE,'YYYY')='2004');
```
- ❑ E. None of the above

44. Which of these commands removes the largest number of rows from the table? Assume that the table and all columns exist and that there are no constraint issues involved.

- ❑ A. **DELETE FROM MOVIE;**
- ❑ B. ***DELETE ALL FROM MOVIE;**
- ❑ C. **TRUNCATE MOVIE;**
- ❑ D. **TRUNCATE TABLE MOVIE;**
- ❑ E. All of the above remove the same number of rows.

45. How many rows will be added to the **STUDIO** table by these commands? Assume that the rows to be added do not yet exist and that all table and column names are valid.

```
INSERT INTO STUDIO VALUES(500, 'Studio 500');
INSERT INTO STUDIO VALUES(501, 'Studio 501');
SAVEPOINT INSERTDONE;
INSERT INTO STUDIO VALUES(502, 'Studio 502');
INSERT INTO STUDIO VALUES(503, 'Studio 503');
INSERT INTO STUDIO VALUES(504, 'Studio 504');
DELETE FROM STUDIO WHERE STUDIO_ID BETWEEN 502 AND 503;
ROLLBACK TO SAVEPOINT INSERTDONE;
```

❑ A. 2 rows

❑ B. 5 rows

❑ C. 3 rows

❑ D. 0 rows

❑ E. None of the above

46. User A does this in his session:

```
LOCK TABLE SALE EXCLUSIVE NOWAIT;
DELETE FROM SALE;
ROLLBACK;
```

Immediately after the first user executes the preceding commands, a second user, User B, executes these commands in a different session:

```
DELETE FROM SALE;
ROLLBACK;
```

Which user's commands will complete first? Answer by entering A or B.

47. Which lines are incorrect for this command?

```
1. CREATE TABLE ACTORS(
2.     ACTOR_ID      NUMBER NOT NULL
3.     NAME          VARCHAR2(32) NOT NULL
4.    ,GENDER        CHAR(1) DEFAULT 'M' NOT NULL
5.    ,TYPECAST      VARCHAR2(64) NULL);
```

❑ A. 1 or 2

❑ B. 2 and 3

❑ C. 2 or 3

❑ D. 4 and 1

❑ E. 3

48. Examine the following sequence of commands. There are 17 rows in the **DIRECTOR** table, all of which contain the value **M** in the **GENDER** column. Which two of these commands will cause errors?

```
1. CREATE TABLE PERSON(
      PERSON_ID NUMBER NOT NULL PRIMARY KEY
    , NAME VARCHAR2(32) NOT NULL
    , GENDER CHAR(1) DEFAULT 'U' NOT NULL);

2. INSERT INTO PERSON
      SELECT DIRECTOR_ID, NAME, 'U' FROM DIRECTOR;
```

```
3. ALTER TABLE PERSON MODIFY(GENDER DEFAULT 'M');

4. INSERT INTO PERSON VALUES(501, 'A Person', 'G');
5. COMMIT;

6. ALTER TABLE PERSON ADD CONSTRAINT GENDERCHECK
       CHECK(GENDER IN('M', 'F')) ENABLE VALIDATE;

7. INSERT INTO PERSON VALUES(502, 'A Person', 'G');
8. COMMIT;

9. ALTER TABLE PERSON ADD CONSTRAINT GENDERCHECK
       CHECK(GENDER IN('M', 'F')) ENABLE NOVALIDATE;

10. INSERT INTO PERSON VALUES(502, 'A Person', 'G');
    COMMIT;
```

- ❑ A. 1 and 2
- ❑ B. 2 and 4
- ❑ C. 6 and 10
- ❑ D. 9 and 10
- ❑ E. None of the above

49. Which of these are not constraint states?

- ❑ A. **DEFERRABLE**
- ❑ B. **INITITALLY IMMEDIATE**
- ❑ C. **NOCOMMIT**
- ❑ D. **ENABLE**
- ❑ E. **DISABLE**
- ❑ F. **NOVALIDATE**
- ❑ G. **NOLOGGING**

50. Which of these commands are valid?

- ❑ A. **ALTER TABLE STUDIO RENAME COLUMN STUDIO TO STUDIO_NAME;**
- ❑ B. **ALTER TABLE STUDIO RENAME TO STUDIOS;**
- ❑ C. **ALTER TABLE MOVIES RENAME CONSTRAINT UK_MOVIES TO PK_MOVIES;**
- ❑ D. All of the above

51. Which of these **CREATE INDEX** commands will cause an error?

- ❑ A. **CREATE INDEX AK_MOVIE ON MOVIE(RANK) ONLINE;**
- ❑ B. **CREATE INDEX AK_MOVIE ON MOVIE (TITLE, YEAR, RANK) COMPRESS 1;**
- ❑ C. **CREATE INDEX AK_MOVIE ON MOVIE (TITLE, YEAR, RANK) COMPRESS 3;**
- ❑ D. **CREATE INDEX AK_MOVIE ON MOVIE (TITLE, YEAR, RANK) COMPRESS 4;**
- ❑ E. **CREATE INDEX AK_MOVIE ON MOVIE(RANK) OFFLINE;**

52. Which of these **CREATE INDEX** commands will cause errors? Assume that the index **AK_MOVIE** exists and that it contains three columns.

- ❑ A. **ALTER INDEX AK_MOVIE RENAME INDEX TO AK_MOVIE_1;**
- ❑ B. **ALTER INDEX REBUILD ONLINE REVERSE;**
- ❑ C. **ALTER INDEX AK_MOVIE NOCOMPRESS NOPARALLEL;**
- ❑ D. **ALTER INDEX AK_MOVIE COMPRESS 2;**
- ❑ E. All of the above

53. What will be the final value of the sequence from all the commands listed here?

```
CREATE SEQUENCE NEW_SEQ START WITH 1
    INCREMENT BY 1 NOMAXVALUE NOCYCLE;
SELECT NEW_SEQ.NEXTVAL, NEW_SEQ.NEXTVAL FROM DUAL;
SELECT NEW_SEQ.CURRVAL FROM DUAL;
```

- ❑ A. **0**
- ❑ B. **1**
- ❑ C. **2**
- ❑ D. **3**
- ❑ E. None of the above

54. Under what circumstance could this **CREATE VIEW** fail to create the view **MYMOVIES**?

```
CREATE FORCE VIEW MYMOVIES AS SELECT * FROM MOVIES;
```

- ❑ A. If the **MOVIES** table does not exist
- ❑ B. If the **MOVIES** table exists
- ❑ C. If the **MYMOVIES** view does not exist
- ❑ D. If the **MYMOVIES** view exists
- ❑ E. None of the above

55. Which of these SQL*Plus commands is invalid? Assume that all user passwords are **password** unless otherwise specified and that the TNS name for the database is **TEST**. Assume that user **SYSTEM** is granted the same privileges as the **SYS** user.

- ❑ A. **CONNECT SYS/password@TEST AS SYSDBA**
- ❑ B. **CONNECT SYS/password@TEST AS SYSOPER**
- ❑ C. **CONNECT SYSTEM/password@TEST**
- ❑ D. **CONNECT SYSTEM/password@TEST AS SYSDBA**
- ❑ E. **CONNECT SYS/password@TEST**

56. Assume that all user passwords are **password** unless otherwise specified and that the TNS name for the database is **TEST**. Also assume that the

MOVIES schema **MOVIE** table (**MOVIES.MOVIE**) exists. And assume that the users **ANNE** and **ANGELA** do not exist. These commands are executed:

```
CONNECT SYS/password@TEST AS SYSDBA
CREATE USER ANNE IDENTIFIED BY ANNE;
CREATE USER ANGELA IDENTIFIED BY ANGELA;
GRANT CREATE SESSION TO ANNE, ANGELA;
GRANT SELECT ON MOVIES.MOVIE TO ANNE;
CONNECT ANNE/ANNE@TEST
GRANT SELECT ON MOVIES.MOVIE TO ANGELA;
CONNECT ANGELA/ANGELA@TEST
SELECT * FROM MOVIES.MOVIE;
```

Which users will have access to the **MOVIES** schema **MOVIE** table (**MOVIES.MOVIE**)?

- ❑ A. **SYS**
- ❑ B. **ANNE**
- ❑ C. **ANGELA**
- ❑ D. All of the above

57. Assume that all user passwords are **password** unless otherwise specified and that the TNS name for the database is **TEST**. And assume that the users **ANNE** and **ANGELA** do not exist. These commands are executed:

```
1. CONNECT SYS/password@TEST AS SYSDBA
2. CREATE USER ANNE IDENTIFIED BY ANNE;
3. CREATE USER ANGELA IDENTIFIED BY ANGELA;
4. GRANT CREATE SESSION, UNLIMITED TABLESPACE
       TO ANNE, ANGELA;
5. GRANT CREATE TABLE TO ANNE WITH ADMIN OPTION;
6. CONNECT ANNE/ANNE@TEST
7. CREATE TABLE TABLE1(COL1 NUMBER, COL2 CHAR(5));
8. GRANT CREATE TABLE TO ANGELA;
9. CONNECT SYS/password@TEST AS SYSDBA
10. REVOKE CREATE TABLE FROM ANNE;
11. CONNECT ANGELA/ANGELA@TEST
12. CREATE TABLE TABLE2(COL1 NUMBER, COL2 CHAR(5));
```

Which line will cause an error?

- ❑ A. 4
- ❑ B. 5
- ❑ C. 7
- ❑ D. 8
- ❑ E. 12
- ❑ F. None of the above

58. What will this query return? Type your answer.

```
SELECT DECODE(DUMMY, 'X', 'DUMMY', 'UNKNOWN') FROM DUAL;
```

59. Which lines cause errors?

```
1. CREATE TABLE TEST(
2.       ID NUMBER
3.     , TEXT1 VARCHAR2(5000)
4.     , TEXT2 CHAR(4000)
5.     , AMOUNT FLOAT);
```

- ❑ A. 1
- ❑ B. 2
- ❑ C. 3
- ❑ D. 4
- ❑ E. 5

60. What is another but syntactically invalid term used to describe the **MERGE** command? Type your answer.

Answer Key to Practice Test #2

1. F
2. C, F
3. F
4. B, E, F, H
5. G
6. B
7. E
8. E
9. D
10. E
11. B
12. C, E
13. B
14. D, E
15. A
16. B
17. E
18. C
19. E
20. D
21. D
22. E
23. C, D
24. C, E
25. A, B, C, D
26. A, B, C
27. C, D, E
28. B, D
29. C
30. E
31. E
32. A, D, E
33. E
34. E
35. C
36. E
37. A, C, D
38. C, D
39. A, C
40. B, C, D, E
41. A, B
42. C
43. D
44. A, D
45. A
46. A
47. C
48. C
49. C, G
50. D
51. D, E
52. E
53. B
54. D
55. E
56. A, B
57. F
58. DUMMY
59. C, D
60. Upsert

Question 1

Answer F is correct. All queries are valid and none causes an error. Query A is a simple "get all columns from a table" query. B is similar except that it retrieves three specific columns. C references all columns by tables and schemas and a table's by schemas, not causing an issue. D contains a schema name referencing the table, which incidentally does not have to be used by selected columns. D also contains a simple expression on the `YEAR` column. E renames columns retrieved using the `AS` clause.

Question 2

Answers C and F are correct. Query A is sorting by the renamed columns. B is assigning specific formatting to renamed columns and sorting by those renamed columns. C causes an error because a column rename using the `AS` clause cannot be used in the `WHERE` clause. D uses the column rename from the `AS` clause as a reference to the `SELECT` list expression. E includes the same expression in both the `SELECT` list and the `ORDER BY` clause. F causes an error for the same reason that C does. G shows that a `SELECT` list expression can be included as the expression in the `WHERE` clause.

Question 3

Answer F is correct. F and G both execute `DISTINCT` on a single column and thus are most likely to find the fewest number of rows. Looking at the data, you should see that there are two values for `GENDER`, `M` and `F`; and that there are six values for `TYPECAST`, `Comedian`, `Multiple`, `Action Drama`, `Musical`, `Science Fiction`, and `NULL`. F will therefore find two unique values and G will find five unique values. F will retrieve the fewest rows.

Question 4

Answers B, E, F, and H are correct. A, C, D, and G will all cause an error for the same reason: mixing up aliases and schema names. A, C, and D attempt to access the `MOVIES` schema, in the `WHERE` clause, without specifying the `MOVIES` schema in the `FROM` clause. G uses an alias in the `WHERE` clause without declaring the alias in the `FROM` clause. B and H are correct because aliases are used as specified in the FROM clause. E uses no aliases. F declares an alias but the query does not absolutely require its use.

Question 5

Answer G is correct. None of these queries will cause a syntax error. However, A attempts to find two different rows at once and will find no rows. B and C include AND and OR logical operators in the WHERE clause with no parentheses to determine precedence and will thus produce spurious results.

Question 6

Answer B is correct. B produces an error because it attempts to sort two columns by position (ORDER BY 2, 1) where only a single column is retrieved, the TITLE column. Query A is fine because all columns are retrieved. Of course, if the MOVIE table had only two columns, A would have the same error as B. C sorts by multiple columns and adjusts various aspects of sorted order. D sorts by an expression not in the SELECT list where E also retrieves that same expression. F uses positional parameters for columns, renamed columns, and expressions. G retrieves specific columns and changes sort order specifics similar to C.

Question 7

Answer E is correct. The || operator is called the concatenation operator and is used to concatenate strings together. String concatenation is a process of adding the contents of one string onto the end of another, with no interference between the two strings in the concatenated result. Thus, 'This is a '||'string' will return the string This is a string. A, B, C, and D all imply simple arithmetic, which has absolutely nothing to do with the concatenation of strings.

Question 8

Answer E is correct. Note that all queries are using a different set operator to merge rows from the same table, the MOVIE table. Therefore, INTERSECTION will always be the number of rows in the table because rows selected on either side of the intersection are identical, and thus intersecting rows will result in exactly half the number of rows from both tables merged together. Therefore, `UNION` finds the same as the intersection because `UNION` finds all distinct rows from the two merged queries. `UNION ALL` finds all duplicate values, thus all rows in both queries or the rows in the table multiplied by 2. Thus, query 2 will find the most rows. The `MINUS` operator attempts to return rows in one query not in the other. Because rows are from the same table, `MINUS` will not return any rows. Therefore, query 4 returns the fewest rows. The result is that query 2 returns the most rows and query 4 returns the fewest rows.

Question 9

Answer D is correct. This question is about precedence. Evaluate all expressions, starting with the most deeply embedded and working your way outward. Remember that `*` and `/` have higher precedence than `+` and `-`.

Question 10

Answer E is correct. None of the solutions presented are correct. This query will find all movies not titled *A*. Because there are unlikely to be any movies called *A*, it is likely that all movies will be found. None of the given answers in A, B, or C suffices, and thus none of the answers is correct. D assumes that all of A, B, and C are correct and thus D is incorrect as well. Generally, the `LIKE` operator is used with pattern matching characters `%` and `_`. Rather than using `NOT LIKE 'A'` it is better to use `= 'A'`.

Question 11

Answer B is correct. A `ROWID` pointer value consists of four values: segment number (indicates a table or another database object), datafile number relative to a tablespace, a block number, and a row number.

Question 12

Answers C and E are correct. As a general rule, a sequence must be defined for a newly connected session using the `NEXTVAL` pseudocolumn. The first access to a sequence using the `CURRVAL` pseudocolumn, without having first accessed the sequence using the `NEXTVAL` pseudocolumn, returns a `sequence not` yet defined for this session error. Also note that any NEXTVAL access to the same sequence within a single SELECT command will increment the sequence only once. It follows, therefore, that including both NEXTVAL and CURRVAL pseudocolumns in the same SELECT command, in any order, will execute NEXTVAL and thus not produce an error, even if CURRVAL is executed before NEXTVAL. So for A, B, and D the execution of CURRVAL does not cause an error because NEXTVAL is executed. However, C and E execute CURRVAL only and thus both cause an error.

Question 13

Answer B is correct. A is a simple CASE statement expression that simply checks a single expression against a number of other expressions. C is a searched CASE statement expression, verifying multiple conditions. A condition consists of a comparison between two expressions. B is attempting to do both a simple and a searched CASE statement expression at the same time and is thus syntactically invalid. This makes D an incorrect answer as well.

Question 14

Answers D and E are correct. A is incorrect because the SUBSTRING function does not exist and should be typed as SUBSTR. Also, the string is not terminated with a closing single quote ('), and there are not enough parameters for the SUBSTR function. B is incorrect because there are not enough parameters. C is incorrect because strings are delimited not using double quotes (") in Oracle Database, but using single quotes ('). D selects a substring from the fifth character position, returning " is a string". E selects a substring from the fifth position for 10 characters, returning "is a stri".

Question 15

Answer A is correct. The string comments will be returned. The TRIM function can trim leading, trailing, or both from a string. If all options are omitted, such as in TRIM('   a test   '), then the TRIM function removes all spaces at the start and end of the string, leaving spaces within the string. B and C leave some of the asterisks (*) behind and are thus incorrect. D is incorrect because the TRIM function removes characters, not replaces characters. E is incorrect because A is correct.

Question 16

Answer B is correct. The result is obtained by evaluating all functions and arithmetic within the expression. Remember precedence rules in that `*` and `/` have higher precedence than `+` and `-`, plus functions have highest precedence in this expression unless overridden by a parenthesized sub-expression. This question simply tests your knowledge of what the different functions do. `POWER` raises to a power. `ABS` finds the absolute value. `FLOOR` rounds down to the nearest integer regardless of the value of the rounded decimal. `CEIL` does the opposite of `FLOOR` by rounding up. `SIGN` finds `-1` for negative and `0` or `1` for positive numbers. `ROUND` performs mathematical rounding. `TRUNC` chops off decimals with no rounding.

Question 17

Answer E is correct. `LOG(10, 1000)` finds a logarithm which returns `3` because $10^3 = 1000$, or `POWER(10, 3)` = 1000. The `MOD` function is a modulus or remainder function, finding the remainder as the result of a division. Thus, `MOD(3, 2)` = 3/2 with 1 left over, leaving the result of `1`.

Question 18

Answer C is correct. The `EXTRACT` function can be used to return parts of dates. The expression returns numerical values, with padding or trimming, in the order of day, month, and year, separating each with a `/` character.

Question 19

Answer E is correct. Four tables are being joined: `DIRECTOR`, `MOVIE`, `PART`, and `ACTOR`.

Question 20

Answer D is correct. Line 3 contains both the `NATURAL` keyword and the `USING` clause. Using the `NATURAL` keyword excludes use of the `USING` or `ON` clauses. If the `NATURAL` keyword is used in a query, all joins must be joined using the

NATURAL keyword; no use of the USING clause or the ON clause will be allowed. All other answers, A, B, C, and D, are incorrect because D is the correct answer.

Question 21

Answer D is correct. Queries 2, 3, and 5 meet requirements. Query 1 does not meet requirements because use of the NATURAL keyword will join the DIRECTOR and ACTOR tables using the NAME column in both tables. There is no sense in joining actors and directors based on their names because the two tables do not necessarily contain the same people. Some actors become directors, but it is a rarity only for the most successful. Query 4 is incorrect because it has a mix-up with table aliases in the last two lines of its WHERE clause. Query 2 will cause a syntax error.

Question 22

Answer E is correct. Thirty-seven actors are left outer joined to the RECOGNITION table where three actors are recognized. This left outer join simply finds all actors or 37 rows. The full outer join merges rows from the AWARD table and the result of the left outer join. Because there are 24 awards, and 1 award is already allocated to three actors, the full outer join adds awards not yet retrieved by the left outer join, 23 rows. The resulting row count is 37 + 23 = 60 rows.

Question 23

Answers C and D are correct. C will not cause a syntax error but the parentheses are required around either the AND conjunction expressions or the OR conjunction expressions. The WHERE clause as it stands is likely to produce a meaningless result. The GROUP BY clause will cause a syntax error because two columns are not aggregated in the SELECT column list and both must be grouped on. Answer A will not make any difference because the correct GROUP BY clause in D finds the correct groupings to apply the COUNT function to. E is incorrect because only C and D are correct.

Question 24

Answers C and E are correct. C is correct because in the query the ON clause should specify as <expression> <condition> <expression>, as in MOVIE.DIRECTOR_ID = DIRECTOR.DIRECTOR_ID. Changing ON to USING executes the join based on the DIRECTOR_ID column in both tables. D is partially correct, replacing the AHIT column name, but it includes the column position of 1 for the NAME column, allowed only in the ORDER BY clause. Answer A will make no difference. B will cause another error (see the explanation for C).

Question 25

Answers A, B, C, and D are correct. Answer A retrieves unique values for all three columns. B does exactly the same thing except using the UNIQUE version of the DISTINCT clause. For both A and B no uniqueness or distinction is applied because, according to the data, there is none. In other words, A and B retrieve all rows because the names of actors are all unique values. C simply retrieves all rows, the same answer as A and B. D wraps the entire column set into a single string, applying the DISTINCT clause, producing the same result as A, B, and C, all rows. E, F, and G remove values because they reduce the number of columns, retaining one or more columns containing duplicate values. Because A, B, C, and D are the same, and greater than E, F, and G, then it follows that A, B, C, and D produce the most rows.

Question 26

Answers A, B, and C are correct. Answer A is completely pointless because it attempts to find two different rows at the same time, resulting in no rows. B and C include both AND and OR logical operators in the WHERE clause, but no parentheses to determine precedence, thus producing spurious results.

Question 27

Answers C, D, and E are correct. A and B find unique values using DISTINCT, and thus all movies occurring twice are counted as one. Thus, A and B will return a count of 12. C, D, and E, on the other hand, find all movies, regardless of duplication, all retrieving a count of 17.

Question 28

Answers B and D are correct. The functions STDDEV and VARIANCE exist. STDEV and VAR do not exist and therefore A, C, and E are all incorrect.

Question 29

Answer C is correct. The WHERE clause and the HAVING clause are filtering exactly the same rows. The only difference is that the WHERE clause is filtering rows selected by the query, and the HAVING clause is filtering aggregated groups produced by the GROUP BY clause. The query will not produce an error but it is doing extra work. Additionally, it is more efficient and better SQL coding practice to filter with the WHERE clause rather than the HAVING where possible and appropriate.

Question 30

Answer E is correct. D is correct but parts of the HAVING clause excluding group functions (REGION LIKE 'S%') would be more efficiently served in the WHERE clause, as shown in the following alteration of the third query:

```
SELECT REGION, COUNTRY, COUNT(TITLE) AS COUNTER
FROM REGION
    JOIN COUNTRY USING (REGION_ID)
        JOIN SALE USING(COUNTRY_ID)
            JOIN MOVIE USING(MOVIE_ID)
WHERE REGION LIKE 'S%'
GROUP BY GROUPING SETS((REGION, COUNTRY), (REGION), (COUNTRY))
HAVING COUNT(TITLE) > 100
ORDER BY 1, 2;
```

Question 31

Answer E is correct. The following clauses can contain subqueries: the SELECT clause list, the INSERT VALUES clause, the UPDATE SET clause, an ORDER BY clause, a CASE expression, and the CREATE TABLE command.

Question 32

Answers A, D, and E are correct. Answer A is correct because it is invalid syntax, containing multiple-row, multiple-column subqueries on both sides of the condition, an equals sign, which expects a scalar value on both sides of the comparison. B is valid syntax because it checks for existence within a set of values. C is valid syntax, being a logical opposite of B. D is invalid syntax and thus a correct answer, because a scalar value expression is required on the left and a single column (can have multiple rows) is required on the right. E is invalid syntax and thus a correct answer, because a single column (can have multiple rows) is required on the right. F is valid syntax because syntax errors in D and E are corrected. G is not a correct answer because A, D, and E are correct.

Question 33

Answer E is correct. There is nothing wrong with this query. Syntactically, the query is correct. The calling query WHERE clause is validating the combination of two columns against a multiple-column, multiple-row join subquery.

Question 34

Answer E is correct. None of these queries returns an error. Answers A and C contain regular subqueries, and B and D contain correlated subqueries. Both IN and EXISTS can compare against correlated subqueries or regular subqueries.

Question 35

Answer C is correct. Note that all four queries access the same two columns from the same table. The UNION ALL operator will return all 34 rows from both queries. UNION removes all duplicates from the 34 rows and the new query, resulting in the unique 17 rows from all 51 rows read. INTERSECT finds rows common to both, effectively the same query, once again returning all 17 rows. MINUS removes rows from the previous result, using the last query, all 17 rows. Thus, the result is 0 rows returned.

Question 36

Answer E is correct. The PRIOR operator should be applied to the parent row, not the child row as in this case. Thus,

```
CONNECT BY GENRE_ID = PRIOR PARENT_ID
```

should be replaced with

```
CONNECT BY PRIOR GENRE_ID = PARENT_ID
```

indicating that the GENRE_ID column in the parent row is the parent of the PARENT_ID column value for the current row. One row will be returned indicated by the START WITH clause, the row containing the movie genre Non-Action.

Question 37

Answers A, C, and D are correct. B will produce an error and E will do nothing at all. SHOW ALL shows all SQL*Plus environment settings. SHOW LINESIZE displays the current LINESIZE setting. SHOW PAGESIZE LINESIZE displays the value of both the LINESIZE and PAGESIZE parameters.

Question 38

Answers C and D are correct. The equals sign is not required for the SQL*Plus SET command. Obviously, E is incorrect because A and B are incorrect.

Question 39

Answers A and C are correct. Scripts can be executed in SQL*Plus using the RUN, START, @, or @@ commands. For B the STARTUP command is used to start up a database. D is a nonsensical answer because it does not exist as a SQL*Plus command. The EXEC command is used to execute PL/SQL procedures.

Question 40

Answers B, C, D, and E are correct. Answer A contains the only option among these that is allowed in iSQL*Plus. PASSWORD is not allowed because a special screen is used in iSQL*Plus. The SQLPROMPT command is pointless because iSQL*Plus does not contain a prompt. The SPOOL command is not permitted in iSQL*Plus for security reasons. iSQL*Plus is a browser tool directly accessing a database. Allowing unknown browser users to use the SPOOL command would give access to the database server operating system and I/O subsystem. This would be a serious security issue.

Question 41

Answers A and B are correct. Answer A contains no column list specification and therefore must contain all the columns in the table; it does not. B is invalid syntax for the same reason that A is. C, D, and E are all valid INSERT commands.

Question 42

Answer C is correct. Rows are split based on the year in the SALE_DATE column, into three separate tables, by the multiple table INSERT command. The result is that all rows in each of the three separate tables have dates with different years. The second query attempts to find rows in the three tables intersecting based on the year in each date. Because there are no intersecting years across the three tables, the result of the query must be 0 rows.

Question 43

Answer D is correct. A updates a single column. B updates a single column with a subquery. C updates two columns with a multiple column subquery. D is invalid syntax and thus the correct answer, because the same two column sets are updated twice in the single UPDATE command: SET (A.SALE_PRICE, A.SALE_DATE).

Question 44

Answers A and D are correct. Thus E is incorrect. B contains incorrect syntax and should be the same as A without the incorrectly included ALL clause (non-existent for the DELETE command). The TRUNCATE command in C should be written as that in D, including the keyword TABLE.

Question 45

Answer A is correct. The first set of two INSERT commands adds two rows. The second set of three INSERT commands adds three rows. The DELETE command removes two rows. The ROLLBACK TO SAVEPOINT command undoes the three INSERT commands and the single DELETE command executed after the SAVEPOINT command. The result is the first two rows created by the first two INSERT commands.

Question 46

The Answer is A. User A ensures that his command will complete first by locking the table in exclusive mode (allowing read access only to the table for other users). After User A's ROLLBACK command is completed, User B's session will emerge from wait mode and execute User B's sequence of commands.

Question 47

Answer C is correct. Line 3 is missing a comma. Thus, E could be correct but the comma could be placed at the end of line 1 or the start of line 2, splitting the definitions of the ACTOR_ID and NAME columns appropriately.

Question 48

Answer C is correct. Line 6 will cause an error because it attempts to create a validated constraint on existing rows (ENABLE VALIDATE) where those rows contain GENDER column values of U and G, not in the CHECK constraint set of M and F. Line 10 causes a similar problem in that it attempts to add a row with GENDER value G where only M and F are allowed.

Question 49

Answers C and G are correct. NOCOMMIT and NOLOGGING are not available as constraint states.

Question 50

Answer D is correct. All of A, B, and C are correct. Tables, columns, and constraints can be renamed.

Question 51

Answers D and E are correct. A and B will not cause an error. For A an index can be built with the `ONLINE` option, preventing interference with DML activity during the build of the index. For B `COMPRESS 1` compresses the first indexed column. For C, even though there are only three columns in the index, `COMPRESS 3` will not cause an error. For D only three columns are indexed, and thus `COMPRESS 4` is invalid. For E, there is no such option as `OFFLINE`.

Question 52

Answer E is correct. All four of the `CREATE INDEX` commands in A, B, C, and D will cause a syntax error. Answer A attempts to rename an index with incorrect syntax. The command should be this:

```
ALTER INDEX AK_MOVIE RENAME TO AK_MOVIE_1;
```

B is incorrect because no index is named. C is incorrect because it is missing the `REBUILD` option and should be written this way:

```
ALTER INDEX AK_MOVIE REBUILD NOCOMPRESS NOPARALLEL;
```

The `REBUILD` option is also missing in D and should be written like this:

```
ALTER INDEX AK_MOVIE REBUILD COMPRESS 2;
```

Question 53

Answer B is correct. The sequence is created with a starting value of `1`. The first increment will not change the sequence because its starting value will be its first value, namely `1`, set by `START WITH 1`. The two `NEXTVAL` pseudocolumn executions for the first query increment the sequence only once because both `NEXTVAL` executions are in the same query. The `CURRVAL` pseudocolumn merely displays the current value of the sequence without incrementing it.

Question 54

Answer D is correct. If the MYMOVIES view exists, then the view could use the OR REPLACE optional keywords to overwrite the existing view as shown here:

```
CREATE OR REPLACE FORCE VIEW MYMOVIES AS SELECT * FROM MOVIES;
```

The FORCE option will create the view even if the underlying MOVIES table does not exist but will return a view created with complication errors message.

Question 55

Answer E is correct. The SYS user must be connected as SYSDBA or SYSOPER. The SYSTEM user can be connected only as SYSDBA, or SYSOPER is granted the SYSDBA and SYSOPER privileges, the same privileges as the SYS user.

Question 56

Answers A and B are correct. ANGELA will not have access to the MOVIES.MOVIE table because ANNE is not allowed to grant access for that table to ANGELA. ANNE would be allowed to grant access to ANGELA if she was granted the privilege herself with the WITH GRANT OPTION like this:

```
GRANT SELECT ON MOVIES.MOVIE TO ANNE WITH GRANT OPTION;
```

Question 57

Answer F is correct. ANNE is granted the CREATE TABLE privilege including the WITH ADMIN OPTION, allowing her to grant the CREATE TABLE privilege to ANGELA. The CREATE TABLE privilege is then revoked from ANNE. However, a REVOKE command does not cascade through users granted system privileges by ANNE, and thus ANGELA retains the CREATE TABLE PRIVILEGE and can still create tables even though ANNE no longer can. Note that when revoked, system privileges are not cascaded, whereas revoked object privileges are cascaded.

Question 58

The answer is DUMMY. The DUAL table contains a single row and a single column called DUMMY, with the value X in the DUMMY column. The DECODE function returns the string DUMMY if the value X is found and the string UNKNOWN if otherwise.

Question 59

Answers C and D are correct. The maximum length for a VARCHAR2 datatype is 4000 characters, and the maximum length for a CHAR datatype is 2000 characters.

Question 60

The answer is Upsert. *Upsert* is a term sometimes used to describe the combination of an INSERT and an UPDATE command. When rows are found in the target table, they are updated. When rows are not found in the target table, they are added.

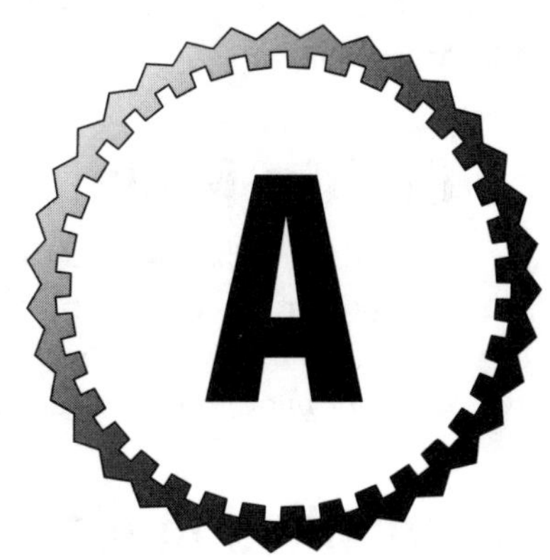

CD Contents and Installation Instructions

The CD features an innovative practice test engine powered by MeasureUp, giving you yet another effective tool to assess your readiness for the exam. The CD also includes a helpful "Need to Know More?" appendix that will break down by chapter extra resources you can visit if some of the topics in this book are still unclear to you.

Multiple Test Modes

MeasureUp practice tests are available in Study, Certification, Custom, Adaptive, Missed Question, and Non-Duplicate question modes.

Study Mode

Tests administered in Study Mode allow you to request the correct answer(s) and explanation for each question during the test. These tests are not timed. You can modify the testing environment *during* the test by clicking the Options button.

Certification Mode

Tests administered in Certification Mode closely simulate the actual testing environment you will encounter when taking a certification exam. These tests do not allow you to request the answer(s) or explanation for each question until after the exam.

Custom Mode

Custom Mode allows you to specify your preferred testing environment. Use this mode to specify the objectives you want to include in your test, the timer length, and other test properties. You can also modify the testing environment *during* the test by clicking the Options button.

Adaptive Mode

Tests administered in Adaptive Mode closely simulate the actual testing environment you will encounter when taking an adaptive exam. After answering a question, you are not allowed to go back; you are only allowed to move forward during the exam.

Missed Question Mode

Missed Question Mode allows you to take a test containing only the questions you missed previously.

Non-Duplicate Mode

Non-Duplicate Mode allows you to take a test containing only questions not displayed previously.

Question Types

The practice question types simulate the real exam experience.

Random Questions and Order of Answers

This feature helps you learn the material without memorizing questions and answers. Each time you take a practice test, the questions and answers appear in a different randomized order.

Detailed Explanations of Correct and Incorrect Answers

You'll receive automatic feedback on all correct and incorrect answers. The detailed answer explanations are a superb learning tool in their own right.

Attention to Exam Objectives

MeasureUp practice tests are designed to appropriately balance the questions over each technical area covered by a specific exam.

Installing the CD

The minimum system requirements for the CD-ROM are as listed here:

- Windows 95, 98, ME, NT4, 2000, or XP
- 7MB disk space for testing engine
- An average of 1MB disk space for each test

If you need technical support, please contact MeasureUp at 678-356-5050 or email support@measureup.com. Additionally, you'll find Frequently Asked Questions (FAQs) at www.measureup.com.

To install the CD-ROM, follow these instructions:

1. Close all applications before beginning this installation.
2. Insert the CD into your CD-ROM drive. If the setup starts automatically, go to step 6. If the setup does not start automatically, continue with step 3.
3. From the Start menu, select Run.
4. Click Browse to locate the MeasureUp CD. In the Browse dialog box, from the Look In drop-down list, select the CD-ROM drive.
5. In the Browse dialog box, double-click on `Setup.exe`. In the Run dialog box, click OK to begin the installation.
6. On the Welcome Screen, click Next.

7. To agree to the Software License Agreement, click Yes.
8. On the Choose Destination Location screen, click Next to install the software to `C:\Program Files\MeasureUp Practice Tests\Launch`.

If you cannot locate MeasureUp Practice Tests through the Start menu, see the section later in this Appendix titled "Creating a Shortcut to the MeasureUp Practice Tests."

9. On the Setup Type screen, select Individual Typical Setup. Click Next to continue.
10. On the Select Features screen, click the check box next to the test(s) you purchased. After you have checked your test(s), click Next.
11. On the Enter Text screen, type the password provided in this receipt, and click Next. Follow this step for any additional tests.
12. On the Select Program Folder screen, verify that the Program Folder is set to MeasureUp Practice Tests, and click Next.
13. After the installation is complete, verify that Yes, I Want to Restart My Computer Now is selected. If you select No, I Will Restart My Computer Later, you will not be able to use the program until you restart your computer.
14. Click Finish.
15. After restarting your computer, choose Start, Programs, MeasureUp Practice Tests, Launch.
16. On the MeasureUp welcome screen, click Create User Profile.
17. In the User Profile dialog box, complete the mandatory fields and click Create Profile.
18. Select the practice test you want to access, and click Start Test.

Creating a Shortcut to the MeasureUp Practice Tests

To create a shortcut to the MeasureUp Practice Tests, follow these steps:

1. Right-click on your desktop.
2. From the shortcut menu select New, Shortcut.

3. Browse to `C:\Program Files\MeasureUp Practice Tests` and select the `MeasureUpCertification.exe` or `Localware.exe` file.
4. Click OK.
5. Click Next.
6. Rename the shortcut MeasureUp.
7. Click Finish.

After you have completed step 7, use the MeasureUp shortcut on your Desktop to access the MeasureUp products you ordered.

Technical Support

If you encounter problems with the MeasureUp test engine on the CD-ROM, you can contact MeasureUp at 678-356-5050 or email support@measureup.com. Technical support hours are from 8 a.m. to 5 p.m. EST Monday through Friday. Additionally, you'll find Frequently Asked Questions (FAQs) at www.measureup.com.

If you'd like to purchase additional MeasureUp products, telephone 678-356-5050 or 800-649-1MUP (1687), or visit www.measureup.com.

Need to Know More?

Chapter 1

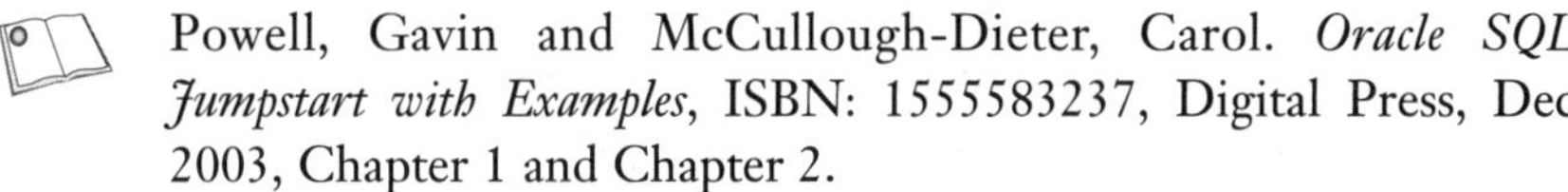

Powell, Gavin and McCullough-Dieter, Carol. *Oracle SQL Jumpstart with Examples*, ISBN: 1555583237, Digital Press, Dec 2003, Chapter 1 and Chapter 2.

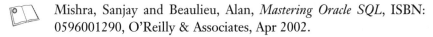

Mishra, Sanjay and Beaulieu, Alan, *Mastering Oracle SQL*, ISBN: 0596001290, O'Reilly & Associates, Apr 2002.

Kyte, Thomas, *Expert One on One Oracle*, ASIN: 1861004826, APress, Jun 2001. This book gives general Oracle Database details.

Powell, Gavin, *Introduction to Oracle 9i: SQL Tutorials VTC Training CD*, ISBN: 1932072241, VTC, Mar 2003.

Oracle documentation is bundled with the software or available online:

http://otn.oracle.com

Oracle documentation has a link called List of Books. Specific manuals within List of Books are *Concepts*, *SQL*Plus Quick Reference*, *SQL*Plus User's Guide and Reference*, for new features, *What's New in SQL Reference* inside the *SQL Reference* manual, *Oracle Enterprise Manager Concepts Guide*, and *Net Services Administrator's Guide*. The Oracle Enterprise Manager help files bundled with Oracle software are a good self-training resource.

Search the Web using specific terms:

http://www.yahoo.com

http://www.google.com

Chapter 2

Powell, Gavin and McCullough-Dieter, Carol. *Oracle SQL Jumpstart with Examples*, ISBN: 1555583237, Digital Press, Dec 2003, Chapter 4.

Mishra, Sanjay and Beaulieu, Alan, *Mastering Oracle SQL*, ISBN: 0596001290, O'Reilly & Associates, Apr 2002.

Kyte, Thomas, *Expert One on One Oracle*, ASIN: 1861004826, APress, Jun 2001. This book gives general Oracle Database details.

Powell, Gavin, *Introduction to Oracle 9i: SQL Tutorials VTC Training CD*, ISBN: 1932072241, VTC, Mar 2003.

SELECT Statements:

http://www.oracledbaexpert.com/oracle/ocp/TheSELECTStatement.html

Oracle documentation is bundled with the software or available online:

http://otn.oracle.com

Oracle documentation has a link called List of Books. Specific manuals within List of Books are *SQL Reference* and *Reference*. Search the *SQL Reference* manual for the keyword SELECT.

Search the Web using specific terms:

http://www.yahoo.com

http://www.google.com

Chapter 3

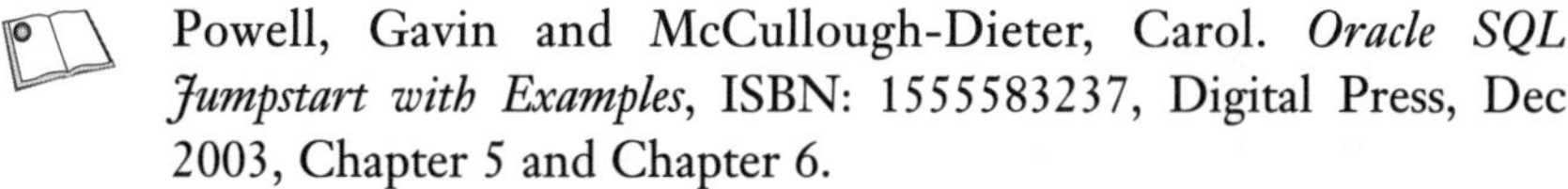

Powell, Gavin and McCullough-Dieter, Carol. *Oracle SQL Jumpstart with Examples*, ISBN: 1555583237, Digital Press, Dec 2003, Chapter 5 and Chapter 6.

Mishra, Sanjay and Beaulieu, Alan, *Mastering Oracle SQL*, ISBN: 0596001290, O'Reilly & Associates, Apr 2002.

Kyte, Thomas, *Expert One on One Oracle*, ASIN: 1861004826, APress, Jun 2001. This book gives general Oracle Database details.

Powell, Gavin, *Introduction to Oracle 9i: SQL Tutorials VTC Training CD*, ISBN: 1932072241, VTC, Mar 2003.

Filtering and Sorting:

http://www.oracledbaexpert.com/oracle/ocp/FilteringAndSorting.html

Oracle documentation is bundled with the software or available online:

http://otn.oracle.com

Oracle documentation has a link called List of Books. Specific manuals within List of Books are *SQL Reference* and *Reference*. Search the *SQL Reference* manual for the keyword SELECT.

Search the Web using specific terms:

http://www.yahoo.com

http://www.google.com

Chapter 4

Powell, Gavin and McCullough-Dieter, Carol. *Oracle SQL Jumpstart with Examples*, ISBN: 1555583237, Digital Press, Dec 2003, Chapter 7 and Chapter 14.

Mishra, Sanjay and Beaulieu, Alan, *Mastering Oracle SQL*, ISBN: 0596001290, O'Reilly & Associates, Apr 2002.

Kyte, Thomas, *Expert One on One Oracle*, ASIN: 1861004826, APress, Jun 2001. This book gives general Oracle Database details.

Powell, Gavin, *Introduction to Oracle 9i: SQL Tutorials VTC Training CD*, ISBN: 1932072241, VTC, Mar 2003.

SELECT Statements:

http://www.oracledbaexpert.com/oracle/ocp/TheSELECTStatement.html

Oracle documentation is bundled with the software or available online:

http://otn.oracle.com

Oracle documentation has a link called List of Books. Specific manuals within List of Books are *SQL Reference* and *Reference*. Search the *SQL Reference* manual for the keyword SELECT.

Search the Web using specific terms:

http://www.yahoo.com

http://www.google.com

Chapter 5

Powell, Gavin and McCullough-Dieter, Carol. *Oracle SQL Jumpstart with Examples*, ISBN: 1555583237, Digital Press, Dec 2003, Chapter 9.

Mishra, Sanjay and Beaulieu, Alan, *Mastering Oracle SQL*, ISBN: 0596001290, O'Reilly & Associates, Apr 2002.

Kyte, Thomas, *Expert One on One Oracle*, ASIN: 1861004826, APress, Jun 2001. This book gives general Oracle Database details.

Powell, Gavin, *Introduction to Oracle 9i: SQL Tutorials VTC Training CD*, ISBN: 1932072241, VTC, Mar 2003.

SELECT Statements:

http://www.oracledbaexpert.com/oracle/ocp/Functions.html

Oracle documentation is bundled with the software or available online:

http://otn.oracle.com

Oracle documentation has a link called List of Books. A specific manual within List of Books is *SQL Reference*. Search the *SQL*

Reference manual for the name of any functions, or check in Chapter 6 of the manual.

Search the Web using specific terms:

http://www.yahoo.com

http://www.google.com

Chapter 6

Powell, Gavin and McCullough-Dieter, Carol. *Oracle SQL Jumpstart with Examples*, ISBN: 1555583237, Digital Press, Dec 2003, Chapter 10.

Mishra, Sanjay and Beaulieu, Alan, *Mastering Oracle SQL*, ISBN: 0596001290, O'Reilly & Associates, Apr 2002.

Kyte, Thomas, *Expert One on One Oracle*, ASIN: 1861004826, APress, Jun 2001. This book gives general Oracle Database details.

Powell, Gavin, *Introduction to Oracle 9i: SQL Tutorials VTC Training CD*, ISBN: 1932072241, VTC, Mar 2003.

SELECT Statements:

http://www.oracledbaexpert.com/oracle/ocp/Joins.html

Oracle documentation is bundled with the software or available online:

http://otn.oracle.com

Oracle documentation has a link called List of Books. A specific manual within List of Books is *SQL Reference*. Search the *SQL Reference* manual for the keyword SELECT.

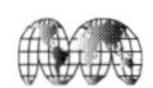

Search the Web using specific terms:

http://www.yahoo.com

http://www.google.com

The American National Standards Institute (ANSI) website is http://www.ansi.org.

Chapter 7

Powell, Gavin and McCullough-Dieter, Carol. *Oracle SQL Jumpstart with Examples*, ISBN: 1555583237, Digital Press, Dec 2003, Chapter 11.

Mishra, Sanjay and Beaulieu, Alan, *Mastering Oracle SQL*, ISBN: 0596001290, O'Reilly & Associates, Apr 2002.

Kyte, Thomas, *Expert One on One Oracle*, ASIN: 1861004826, APress, Jun 2001. This book gives general Oracle Database details.

Powell, Gavin, *Introduction to Oracle 9i: SQL Tutorials VTC Training CD*, ISBN: 1932072241, VTC, Mar 2003.

SELECT Statements:

http://www.oracledbaexpert.com/oracle/ocp/Aggregation.html

Oracle documentation is bundled with the software or available online:

http://otn.oracle.com

Oracle documentation has a link called List of Books. A specific manual within List of Books is *SQL Reference*. Search the *SQL Reference* manual for the keyword SELECT. Also see the "Operators" section in the *SQL Reference* manual under the section title "Set Operators."

Search the Web using specific terms:

http://www.yahoo.com

http://www.google.com

Chapter 8

Powell, Gavin and McCullough-Dieter, Carol. *Oracle SQL Jumpstart with Examples*, ISBN: 1555583237, Digital Press, Dec 2003, Chapter 12 and Chapter 13.

Powell, Gavin. *Oracle High Performance Tuning for 9i and 10g*, ISBN: 1555583059, Digital Press, Jun 2004, Part II.

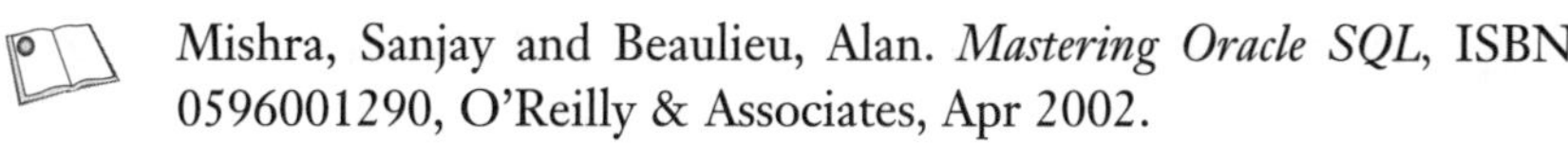

Mishra, Sanjay and Beaulieu, Alan. *Mastering Oracle SQL*, ISBN: 0596001290, O'Reilly & Associates, Apr 2002.

Kyte, Thomas. *Expert One on One Oracle*, ASIN: 1861004826, APress, Jun 2001. This book gives general Oracle Database details.

Powell, Gavin. *Introduction to Oracle 9i: SQL Tutorials VTC Training CD*, ISBN: 1932072241, VTC, Mar 2003.

Subqueries:

http://www.oracledbaexpert.com/oracle/ocp/Subqueries.html

Oracle documentation is bundled with the software or available online:

http://otn.oracle.com

Oracle documentation has a link called List of Books. A specific manual within List of Books is *SQL Reference*. Search the *SQL Reference* manual for the keyword SELECT. Also see the "SQL Functions" section in the *SQL Reference* manual under the section titles "Aggregate Functions" and "Analytic Functions."

Search the Web using specific terms:

http://www.yahoo.com

http://www.google.com

Chapter 9

Powell, Gavin and McCullough-Dieter, Carol. *Oracle SQL Jumpstart with Examples*, ISBN: 1555583237, Digital Press, Dec 2003, Chapter 1 and Chapter 8.

Mishra, Sanjay and Beaulieu, Alan. *Mastering Oracle SQL*, ISBN: 0596001290, O'Reilly & Associates, Apr 2002.

Kyte, Thomas. *Expert One on One Oracle*, ASIN: 1861004826, APress, Jun 2001. This book gives general Oracle Database details.

Powell, Gavin. *Introduction to Oracle 9i: SQL Tutorials VTC Training CD*, ISBN: 1932072241, VTC, Mar 2003.

SQL*Plus Formatting:

http://www.oracledbaexpert.com/oracle/ocp/SQLPlusFormatting.html

Oracle documentation is bundled with the software or available online:

http://otn.oracle.com

Oracle documentation has a link called List of Books. Specific manuals within List of Books are *SQL*Plus Quick Reference* and *SQL*Plus User's Guide and Reference*.

Search the Web using specific terms:

http://www.yahoo.com

http://www.google.com

Chapter 10

Powell, Gavin and McCullough-Dieter, Carol. *Oracle SQL Jumpstart with Examples*, ISBN: 1555583237, Digital Press, Dec 2003, Chapter 15.

Mishra, Sanjay and Beaulieu, Alan. *Mastering Oracle SQL*, ISBN: 0596001290, O'Reilly & Associates, Apr 2002.

Kyte, Thomas. *Expert One on One Oracle*, ASIN: 1861004826, APress, Jun 2001. This book gives general Oracle Database details.

Powell, Gavin. *Introduction to Oracle 9i: SQL Tutorials VTC Training CD*, ISBN: 1932072241, VTC, Mar 2003.

DML:

http://www.oracledbaexpert.com/oracle/ocp/DML.html

Oracle documentation is bundled with the software or available online:

http://otn.oracle.com

Oracle documentation has a link called List of Books. Search within *SQL Reference* for commands such as `INSERT`, `UPDATE`, `DELETE`, `MERGE`, `TRUNCATE`, `COMMIT`, `ROLLBACK`, and `SET TRANSACTION`.

Search the Web using specific terms:

http://www.yahoo.com

http://www.google.com

Chapter 11

Powell, Gavin and McCullough-Dieter, Carol. *Oracle SQL Jumpstart with Examples*, ISBN: 1555583237, Digital Press, Dec 2003, Chapter 16, Chapter 18, and Chapter 20.

Mishra, Sanjay and Beaulieu, Alan. *Mastering Oracle SQL*, ISBN: 0596001290, O'Reilly & Associates, Apr 2002.

Kyte, Thomas. *Expert One on One Oracle*, ASIN: 1861004826, APress, Jun 2001. This book gives general Oracle Database details.

Powell, Gavin. *Introduction to Oracle 9i: SQL Tutorials VTC Training CD*, ISBN: 1932072241, VTC, Mar 2003.

DML:

http://www.oracledbaexpert.com/oracle/ocp/Tables.html

and

http://www.oracledbaexpert.com/oracle/ocp/Constraints.html

Oracle documentation is bundled with the software or available online:

http://otn.oracle.com

Oracle documentation has a link called List of Books. Search within *SQL Reference* for commands such as CREATE TABLE, ALTER TABLE, DROP TABLE, and TRUNCATE TABLE. There is also a section called "Datatypes."

Search the Web using specific terms:

http://www.yahoo.com

http://www.google.com

Chapter 12

Powell, Gavin and McCullough-Dieter, Carol. *Oracle SQL Jumpstart with Examples*, ISBN: 1555583237, Digital Press, Dec 2003, Chapter 19, Chapter 21, and Chapter 22.

Mishra, Sanjay and Beaulieu, Alan. *Mastering Oracle SQL*, ISBN: 0596001290, O'Reilly & Associates, Apr 2002.

Kyte, Thomas. *Expert One on One Oracle*, ASIN: 1861004826, APress, Jun 2001. This book gives general Oracle Database details.

Powell, Gavin. *Introduction to Oracle 9i: SQL Tutorials VTC Training CD*, ISBN: 1932072241, VTC, Mar 2003.

DML:

http://www.oracledbaexpert.com/oracle/ocp/Indexes.html

and

http://www.oracledbaexpert.com/oracle/ocp/SequencesSynonymsAndViews.html

Oracle documentation is bundled with the software or available online:

http://otn.oracle.com

Oracle documentation has a link called List of Books. Search within *SQL Reference* for the commands `CREATE VIEW`, `ALTER VIEW`, `DROP VIEW`, `CREATE INDEX`, `ALTER INDEX`, `DROP INDEX`, `CREATE SEQUENCE`, `ALTER SEQUENCE`, `DROP SEQUENCE`, `CREATE SYNONYM`, and `DROP SYNONYM`.

Search the Web using specific terms:

http://www.yahoo.com

http://www.google.com

Chapter 13

Powell, Gavin and McCullough-Dieter, Carol. *Oracle SQL Jumpstart with Examples*, ISBN: 1555583237, Digital Press, Dec 2003, Chapter 23.

Mishra, Sanjay and Beaulieu, Alan. *Mastering Oracle SQL*, ISBN: 0596001290, O'Reilly & Associates, Apr 2002.

Kyte, Thomas. *Expert One on One Oracle*, ASIN: 1861004826, APress, Jun 2001. This book gives general Oracle Database details.

Powell, Gavin. *Introduction to Oracle 9i: SQL Tutorials VTC Training CD*, ISBN: 1932072241, VTC, Mar 2003.

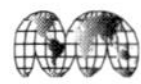

DML:

http://www.oracledbaexpert.com/oracle/ocp/UsersAndSecurity.html

Oracle documentation is bundled with the software or available online:

http://otn.oracle.com

Oracle documentation has a link called List of Books. Search within *SQL Reference* for commands such as CREATE USER, CREATE ROLE, GRANT, and REVOKE.

Search the Web using specific terms:

http://www.yahoo.com

http://www.google.com

Chapters 14–17

These are your practice exam chapters.

Glossary

' (single quote)

The single quote character is used extensively in Oracle SQL syntax to delimit strings.

" (double quote)

Double quotes are occasionally used in SQL*Plus. They are necessary in column names and headers that contain spaces. For example, the only way to name a column in a `CREATE TABLE` command as `"My Column"` is by enclosing it in double quotes.

!=

Anti equivalence or inequality implies two expressions being compared for inequality or not being equal to each other (`!=`, `<>`, or `^=`).

=

Equality (`=`) is when two expressions are compared for being equal to each other.

&, &&, DEFINE, and UNDEFINE

`DEFINE` and `UNDEFINE` are used to define (create) and undefine (remove) script variables, respectively. `&` and `&&` ampersand characters are used to refer to variable names in scripts.

*

The asterisk or `*` character is used in Oracle SQL syntax in two places: (1) the select list of a `SELECT` statement when all columns are to be retrieved, (2) as a multiplication operator in arithmetic expressions.

@, @@, RUN, and START

These commands are all used to execute scripts from SQL*Plus.

^=

Anti equivalence or inequality implies two expressions being compared for inequality or not being equal to each other (`!=`, `<>`, or `^=`).

<

Range implies that one expression is greater than (>), less than (<), less than or equal to (=>), or greater than or equal to (>=).

<=

Range implies that one expression is greater than (>), less than (<), less than or equal to (=>), or greater than or equal to (>=).

<>

Anti equivalence or inequality implies two expressions being compared for inequality or not being equal to each other (!=, <>, or ^=).

>

Range implies that one expression is greater than (>), less than (<), less than or equal to (=>), or greater than or equal to (>=).

>=

Range implies that one expression is greater than (>), less than (<), less than or equal to (=>), or greater than or equal to (>=).

1st Normal Form

1st Normal Form, also known as First Normal Form, eliminates repeating groups by dividing a single entity into two separate entities, usually connecting the two new entities with a one-to-many relationship. Both entities get primary keys. The entity on the many side of the relationship has a foreign key. The foreign key column contains copies of primary key values of the entity on the one side of the relationship.

2nd Normal Form

2nd Normal Form, also known as Second Normal Form, eliminates redundant data by separating an entity into two entities in which the 1st Normal Form entity contains columns not dependent on the primary key, or only a part of a composite primary key. Unlike 1st Normal Form, in which repetitive rows are spread to a new entity, for 2nd Normal Form repeated rows are consolidated to a new entity. In simpler terms, 2nd Normal Form usually creates many-to-one relationships between dynamic and static data, separating static data into the new entity.

3rd Normal Form

3rd Normal Form, also known as Third Normal Form, expects all non-key fields to be dependent on the primary key with no transitive dependencies. A transitive dependency determines that when a given column X depends on the key and column Y depends on column X, then column Y depends on the key through column X. Column Y is transitively dependent on the key.

4th Normal Form

4th Normal Form, also known as Fourth Normal Form, disperses multivalued facts in a single entity into separate entities.

5th Normal Form

5th Normal Form, also known as Fifth Normal Form, covers anything already missed by 1st, 2nd, 3rd, and 4th Normal Forms.

aggregate function

These functions summarize repeating groups in a row set into distinct groups, aggregating repetitive values into items such as sums or averages. Aggregation is another term used to describe grouping or aggregate functions. An aggregation is a process of grouping rows from their individual rows into fewer groups. Aggregation functions fall into several categories: simple summaries, simple statistics, statistical distributions, and rankings.

alias

An alias is a shorthand or secondary name, which can be applied to the columns in a query table if defined in the `FROM` clause. An alias can be used to access columns retrieved in the query. An alias can be defined for a table or an object in the `FROM` clause. Columns can be accessed within the `SELECT` list, `ORDER BY` clause, `WHERE` clause, and other clauses using columns prefixed by an alias, in the form `<alias>.<column>`. Depending on the contents of the query, aliases declared for tables do not always have to prefix a column. If multiple tables are retrieved from, multiple aliases can be used. Only columns can be aliased because they refer to an aliased table. Expressions containing multiple columns cannot be aliased as a whole, but only the columns within those expressions. So the expression `(<column1> * <column2>)`, `<alias>.(<column1> * <column2>)` is syntactically invalid, whereas `(<alias>.<column1> * <alias>.<column2>)` is valid.

ALL

The `ALL` keyword is the default for numerous options and functions, including the `COUNT` function. The expression `COUNT(ALL <expression>)` retrieves a count of all rows including all repetitions. On the contrary, `COUNT(DISTINCT <expression>)` counts only unique expressions.

ALL comparison

The `ANY`, `SOME`, and `ALL` comparisons all check an expression for membership in a set or list of elements. `ANY` and `SOME` are the same and allow a response when any element in the set matches. `ALL` produces a response only when all elements in a set match an expression.

analytical function

Unlike aggregates, which summarize repetitions into unique items, analytics create subset summaries within aggregates. Analytical functions can utilize most aggregation functions applying an `OVER` clause. Analysis allows more extensive examination of groups and subgroups within groups. Analytical aggregations can be cumulative, centered, moving, or summary in nature. This type of SQL functionality is OLAP in nature. Analytical functions can be used to create a window over ranges of rows. The window can be moved, varied in size, or determined by a measure such as time.

AND logical condition

AND is applied as <expression> AND <expression>, implying that both expressions must yield a true result for <expression> AND <expression> to yield a true result. Of the three logical conditions—NOT, AND, and OR—NOT has highest precedence (is processed first), followed by AND and then OR.

ANSI join format

9i ANSI join syntax joins tables in the FROM clause of a query. ANSI join syntax can perform full outer joins.

Anti join

Anti joins combine rows using inequality (!=, <>, or NOT).

ANY comparison

The ANY, SOME, and ALL comparisons all check an expression for membership in a set or list of elements. ANY and SOME are the same and allow a response when any element in the set matches. ALL produces a response only when all elements in a set match an expression.

arithmetic operator

The arithmetic operators *, /, +, and - are used to perform simple arithmetic calculations on numeric values. The * and / operators have equal precedence, as do + and -. The * and / operators have higher precedence than + and -.

ASC

An ascending sort can be set within an ORDER BY clause by assigning the ASC modifier to each column in the ORDER BY clause expressions list. ASC is the default and is thus not required to be specified, unless perhaps reading directly from an index that is created as sorted in descending order.

ascending sort

An ascending sort can be set within an ORDER BY clause by assigning the ASC modifier to each column in the ORDER BY clause expressions list. ASC is the default and is thus not required to be specified, unless perhaps directly reading from an index that is sorted in descending order.

asterisk (*)

The asterisk or * character is used in Oracle SQL syntax in two places: (1) the select list of a SELECT statement when all columns are to be retrieved, (2) as a multiplication operator in arithmetic expressions.

Backus-Naur Form

See the section in Chapter 1 called “Syntax Conventions Used in This Book” for details on the Backus-Naur Form syntax notation convention.

BETWEEN

[NOT] BETWEEN verifies expressions between a range of two values.

build and document phase

The building and documentation phase is the third step in the system development cycle. The building and documentation phase converts the technical design document into executable software code and data structures. Thus, the building process is the construction of Oracle databases and software applications.

Cartesian Product

A Cartesian Product is the mathematical term for a cross join. A cross join joins all rows in one table to all rows in another table, having the effect of creating a product or multiplication of the number of rows in both tables. Thus, a Cartesian Product of two tables, each containing 10 rows, results in a join containing 100 rows.

CASE expression

A CASE statement can be embedded in a SQL statement and is thus an inline CASE statement expression. A CASE statement is a similar programming construct to that of an IF-THEN-ELSE statement.

check constraint

A check constraint validates a value setting for a column such that the column value in every row must conform to the specified condition.

cluster

A cluster is used to create groupings of frequently accessed columns, both indexed and non-indexed columns, from one or more tables. A cluster is a form of a pre-constructed data set. Clusters are often used to pre-create or pre-execute joins, allowing for faster read access to join results because the join does not have to be re-executed; the cluster is read. The resulting effect is that when the cluster is being read, the processing time required to create the join is avoided. Clusters are often used to increase performance in data warehouses where large amounts of data are read at once.

column (in a table or view)

Tables are divided into columns and rows. Columns impose structure and datatype specifics onto each of the column values in a row. Columns are also known as fields or attributes.

COLUMN

The COLUMN command allows alteration of the output format for columns returned by a query.

Column list

This is the part of a SELECT command listing column to be retrieved by a query. When more than one column is retrieved, the columns become a list of columns or a Column list.

COMMIT

This command permanently stores changes to the database.

comparison condition

Comparison conditions allow two expressions to be compared with each other in various ways. These different methods of comparison depend on the comparison condition used, such as =, <>, LIKE, and EXISTS.

composite query

A composite query concatenates the rows from two queries in which column numbers retrieved (SELECT list elements) and datatypes match. Set operators UNION, UNION ALL, INTERSECT, and MINUS are used to create concatenations between two queries.

compound expression

A compound expression is a combination or concatenation of multiple simple expressions.

concatenation operator

Oracle SQL has a special string concatenation operator denoted by two pipe characters, ||. String concatenation is the process of adding two strings together.

condition

A condition is used to test the existence of a condition, between two expressions. Conditions can be divided up into comparison conditions, logical conditions, XML conditions, and object collection conditions.

CONNECT

The CONNECT command is used to connect a user or schema to a database of the following form: CONNECT <user>/<password>[@TNS] [AS { SYSDBA | SYSOPER }]. The DISCONNECT command is used to disconnect a session from a database.

CONNECT BY

The CONNECT BY clause is used in hierarchical queries defining columns to link parent and child rows together.

CONNECT role

The CONNECT role contains minimum system privileges applicable to power end users.

constraint

Constraints constrain, restrict, or apply rules both within and between tables.

conversion function

These functions convert between different datatypes. Datatype conversion functions are used to change values from one datatype to another. For example, TO_CHAR(SYSDATE) will convert a date datatype value into a string containing a date. Datatype conversion functions can be divided into string conversions, number conversions, datetime conversions, functions concerned with ROWIDS or hexadecimals, character set conversions, and finally there are also some obscure datatype conversion functions.

correlated subquery

A correlated subquery simply allows the passing of a referential value to a subquery such that the subquery can reference each row of the calling query.

CREATE ROLE

The CREATE ROLE command is used to create roles. Roles are used for convenience, grouping privileges together.

CREATE TABLE

A table can be created using the CREATE TABLE command.

CREATE USER

The CREATE USER command is used to create database users.

CREATE VIEW

A view can be created using the CREATE VIEW command.

cross join

A cross join joins all rows in one table to all rows in another table. For example, when joining two tables as a cross join, each containing 10 rows, the cross join will contain 100 rows. A cross join has no join specification other than both table names, simply combining all rows from both tables by returning every row in one table joined with every row in the other table.

CUBE clause

9i The GROUP BY clause can be extended with OLAP functionality using the ROLLUP and CUBE clauses. The results of ROLLUP and CUBE clauses can be filtered with the GROUPING SETS clause. In their most simplistic forms, the ROLLUP and CUBE clauses can be used to produce super-aggregates. A super-aggregate is an aggregate of an aggregate, allowing creation of groups within groups. The CUBE clause goes a little further and deeper than the ROLLUP clause by allowing production of cross-tabulation reports, generating combinations of all possible values. A cross-tabulation report is a multiple-dimensional report. In lay terms, the CUBE clause allows subtotals for groups within a set of groups, plus subtotals between different groups, followed by grand totals.

CURRVAL

<sequence>.CURRVAL finds the current value for a sequence.

CURSOR expression

A cursor can be nested inside a calling SQL statement and can be passed to a function as a REF CURSOR.

Data Definition Language

DDL (Data Definition Language) commands are used to create or change metadata objects. DDL commands commit all pending changes to the database automatically and cannot be rolled back.

Data Manipulation Language

DML (Data Manipulation Language) commands change data in the database. These commands are INSERT, UPDATE, DELETE, and MERGE. DML commands can be committed permanently using the COMMIT command and undone using the ROLLBACK command. Unlike DDL commands, DML commands do not commit automatically for all pending changes. The SELECT command is neither a DML nor a DDL command because it only retrieves data from a database.

database consistency

Multiple users accessing the same data need to be able to see the state of the database at a specific point in time. If one user makes changes without committing those changes, another user will see the data as it was before the changes were made, until the first user stores those changes.

datatype

Special datatypes can be created using the CREATE TYPE command, allowing construction of user-defined types and structures. Also, binary objects such as BLOB binary objects can be used to store binary data such as multimedia.

datetime expression

A datetime expression places a date into varying datetime datatypes, such as LOCAL, DBTIMEZONE, or SESSIONTIMEZONE.

datetime function

These functions accept date value parameters. Datetime conversion functions convert datatypes between dates, strings, and some unusual interval datetime representation. For example, TO_CHAR(SYSDATE, 'J') will return the Julian number representation of the date value retrieved by the SYSDATE function.

DDL

DDL (Data Definition Language) commands are used to create or change metadata objects. DDL commands commit all pending changes to the database automatically and cannot be rolled back.

DEFAULT

In Oracle9i default values can now be set explicitly using INSERT and UPDATE commands, utilizing DEFAULT settings made by the CREATE TABLE and ALTER TABLE DDL commands.

default tablespaces

Default tablespaces can be set when creating a user with the CREATE USER command. If default tablespaces are not set, the SYSTEM tablespace is used, causing possible conflict between user data and database metadata.

deficient in information

This term applies to outer joins using the Oracle syntax and not ANSI join syntax. The side of a join deficient in information acquires the outer join operator or (+) in the WHERE clause because it has missing rows.

DELETE

The DELETE command can be used to remove one, some, or all rows from a table.

Denormalization

Denormalization is most often the opposite of Normalization and is more commonly used in data warehouse or reporting environments. Denormalization decreases granularity. Granularity is the scope of a definition for any particular thing. The more granular a data model is the easier it becomes to manage, up to a point. Over granular structures tend to create complexity and hurt performance. Denormalization is often used when the rules of Normalization have been over-zealously applied. Other Denormalizing and granularity reduction techniques involve making copies or summaries of parts of tables in other tables, among other options, plus various specialized Oracle Database objects such as clusters, IOTs, and materialized views.

DESC

A descending sort can be set within an ORDER BY clause by assigning the DESC modifier to each column in the ORDER BY clause expressions list.

descending sort

A descending sort can be set within an ORDER BY clause by assigning the DESC modifier to each column in the ORDER BY clause expressions list.

design phase

The design phase is the second step in the system development cycle. The design phase covers technical design documentation. Technical design documentation is a direct successor to and is produced from the user requirements and system specifications.

DISABLE

DISABLE is a constraint state that switches a constraint off or disables a trigger. Thus, a constraint will not be applied and a trigger will not be fired.

DISCONNECT

Whereas the CONNECT command connects a user to a database, the DISCONNECT command is used to terminate a session. CONNECT connects a user to a database.

DISTINCT

The DISTINCT clause functions by returning the first element of each repeating group from multiple repeating groups.

DISTINCT

The DISTINCT and UNIQUE clauses are synonymous; they perform exactly the same function, finding unique values only.

DML

DML (Data Manipulation Language) commands change data in the database. These commands are INSERT, UPDATE, DELETE, and MERGE. DML commands can be committed permanently using the COMMIT command and undone using the ROLLBACK command. Unlike DDL commands, DML commands do not commit automatically for all pending changes. The SELECT command is neither a DML nor a DDL command because it only retrieves data from a database.

double quote (")

Double quotes are occasionally used in SQL*Plus. They are necessary in column names and headers that contain spaces. For example, the only way to name a column in a CREATE table command as "My Column" is by enclosing it in double quotes.

DUAL table

The DUAL table is a dummy table used for executing any SQL command not requiring a database object such as a table or a view as a row source.

ENABLE

ENABLE is a constraint state that switches a constraint on or enables a trigger.

enforcing Referential Integrity

Referential Integrity is enforced in one of three ways. It can be implemented in a database using constraints or triggers, or even outside the database in application coding. The most effective method for implementing Referential Integrity in an Oracle database is by using constraints (see Chapter 11, "Tables, Datatypes, and Constraints [DDL]"). Constraints are centralized, standardized, the best option for performance, and easy to change.

entity

An entity is synonymous with a table. In general, an entity refers to a data model and a table refers to a metadata object.

Entity Relationship Diagram

An Entity Relationship Diagram (ERD) represents the structural contents (columns) in tables for an entire schema, in a database. Additionally, the ERD includes schematic representations of relationships between entities, represented by various types of relationships, plus primary and foreign keys.

environmental settings

An environmental setting allows a connected SQL*Plus instance to be formatted in a specific manner. SQL*Plus environmental settings are set for each instantiation of a SQL*Plus execution and not the duration of a session, unless otherwise altered within that session.

equi join

Equi joins combine rows using equality (=).

ERD

An Entity Relationship Diagram (ERD) represents the structural contents (columns) in tables for an entire schema, in a database. Additionally, the ERD includes schematic representations of relationships between entities, represented by various types of relationships, plus primary and foreign keys.

EXISTS

The [NOT] EXISTS comparison condition is used to test for membership of an expression within a set or list of expressions.

EXIT

The EXIT command is used to exit and shut down a SQL*Plus instance. When SQL*Plus shuts down, an implicit COMMIT and automatic DISCONNECT are executed.

expression

An expression is a combination of other expressions or values, evaluating to a single value. Expressions can be categorized into simple expressions, compound expressions, expression lists, CURSOR expressions, and CASE expressions.

expressions list

An expression list is a list of comma-delimited expressions, those expressions being any other expression type.

filtered query (filtering)

Filtering implies selecting a subset of rows or removing a subset of rows from the source. Filtering is done in Oracle using the WHERE clause for basic query rows retrieved, and using the HAVING clause to remove groups from an aggregated query.

Flashback query

9i Flashback queries allow querying of data in a database at a specified point in time or at a specific data change point in the past, a consistent data snapshot.

foreign key

Foreign key columns contain copies of primary key values, uniquely identified in parent entities, representing the child or sibling side of what is most commonly a one-to-many relationship.

foreign key constraint

A foreign key is a type of constraint in which foreign key columns contain copies of primary key values, uniquely identified in parent entities, representing the child or sibling side of what is most commonly a one-to-many relationship.

FROM clause

The FROM clause is the section of a query primarily used to declare which tables to select data from. For the ANSI standard join syntax, the FROM clause includes table join specifications.

full outer join

A full outer join includes the intersection from two tables plus rows missing on both the left and the right of the join. Thus, a full outer join is the combination of the intersection, the left and right outer joins.

function

A function is a programming unit returning a single value, allowing values to be passed in as parameters. The parameters can change the outcome or return result of a function. The beauty of a function is that it is self-contained and can thus be embedded in an expression. By definition, in Oracle SQL an expression is a SQL code command or even another function. For Oracle SQL, functions can be divided into single row, aggregate, analytical, and object reference functions.

grant privilege

Granting privileges to a user involves giving a user more powerful access to database objects. The `GRANT` command is used to assign privileges to users.

GROUP BY clause

The `GROUP BY` clause is used to aggregate or group together. `GROUP BY` is a `SELECT` statement extension clause allowing grouping and aggregating of repetitions into summary values. The `GROUP BY` clause can be used in conjunction with a multitude of Oracle built-in functions, and even user-defined functionality written in PL/SQL. The `GROUP BY` clause itself can also be extended with filtering using the `HAVING` clause and various OLAP type modifications using the `ROLLUP`, `CUBE`, and `GROUPING SETS` clauses. In addition, the `OVER` clause can be applied, transforming aggregate functions into analytical functions.

grouping functions

Grouping functions apply aggregation and analysis and thus produce groupings of rows, resulting in fewer rows returned by a query.

grouping query

A grouping query groups or aggregates from a larger number of rows into a smaller number of summarized rows. Grouping queries are executed using the `GROUP BY` clause in tandem with specialized aggregation functions and various `GROUP BY` clause extensions such as `ROLLUP`, `CUBE`, and the `SPREADSHEET (MODEL)` clause.

GROUPING SETS clauses
The GROUPING SETS clause can be used to filter out the results of ROLLUP and CUBE clauses.

HAVING clause
The HAVING clause is used to filter out unwanted groups and is thus applied to groups returned by the GROUP BY clause.

hierarchical query
Hierarchical queries can be used to retrieve data from hierarchical row sets and organize results into hierarchical output. What is a hierarchy? A hierarchy is like an inverted tree with branches containing finer detail as you progress farther toward the leaves of the tree.

hierarchical query operators
The hierarchical query operator PRIOR works in tandem with the CONNECT BY clause, causing a column in a currently processed row to be connected with a row in a column from a parent row.

IN
[NOT] IN is used to test for membership of an expression within a set or list of expressions.

index
Indexes are shortened and better-organized partial copies of tables, used for fast access to table data.

Index Organized Table (IOT)
An IOT contains all table rows and columns but is sorted and organized in the manner of an index. An IOT can be very efficient if the IOT is accessed in the sorted order.

inline constraint
An inline constraint is created when a column is created and applies to a single column.

inline view
An inline view is a subquery nested in the FROM clause of a calling query. Values are retrieved from the subquery by assigning an alias to the subquery as a whole.

inner join
An inner join is an intersection, combining only matching rows from two tables based on column values to form an intersection between the two tables.

INSERT
The INSERT command allows addition of new rows to one or many tables at once.

intersection
Intersection is a term from mathematical set theory referring to items common to two sets (existing in both sets).

interval expression
These expressions can be used to express intervals between dates.

IS NULL

NULL values are tested for using the IS NULL comparison. When testing for NULL, IS NULL implies equal to NULL and IS NOT NULL implies not equal to NULL. In other words, = NULL and != NULL are both syntactically invalid and will cause errors. The correct syntax is IS [NOT] NULL, where [NOT] is optional.

iSQL*Plus

iSQL*Plus means "Internet SQL*Plus" and is a browser-enabled form of SQL*Plus. iSQL*Plus can be used just like SQL*Plus, running SQL commands and generating reporting in HTML format.

iterative

Iterative means that a process can be repeated over and over again.

join

The term *join* is applied to a query, which joins one or more tables in a single query. A joined query retrieves rows from more than a single row source (table), merging results together. Joins can be built in various ways, including set intersections and three types of outer joins.

join query

A joined query implies that the rows from more than a single row source (table) are merged together. Joins can be built in various ways, including set intersections and three types of outer joins.

left outer join

A left outer join is the intersection between two tables plus all rows from the left-side table but not in the right-side table.

LEVEL

The LEVEL pseudocolumn returns the level of a row in a hierarchical query in tandem with the CONNECT BY clause and other hierarchical query clauses and operators.

LIKE

[NOT] LIKE uses special wild characters performing pattern matching between expressions. The % (percentage) character attempts to match zero or more characters in a string, and the _ (underscore) character matches exactly one character in a string.

listener process

On the database server side there is a listener process that listens for incoming connection requests from client machines. The configuration file for the listener resides on the server as $ORACLE_HOME/network/admin/listener.ora.

logical condition

Logical conditions allow conjunctions between two expression comparisons in the form of AND and OR. The NOT condition by itself can check for falsity of a Boolean expression. NOT has highest precedence (is processed first), followed by AND and then OR. NOT is applied as <expression> NOT <expression> or AND NOT <expression comparison> or OR NOT <expression comparison>.

materialized view

A materialized view is a physically preconstructed view of data containing data copied into the materialized view. Materialized views can be highly efficient in read-only environments and are often used for replication, for distribution, and in data warehouses.

MERGE

The MERGE command performs what is called an upsert between a source and a target table. In an upsert, existing rows are updated and new rows are added.

metadata

Metadata is the data about the data. Where users change data in tables, the metadata is the structure for the tables. Tables are the containers for user data. Metadata includes the definitional structures for all database objects such as indexes, views, and synonyms.

multiple column subquery

A multiple column subquery returns more than a single value, in one or more rows.

multiple row subquery

A multiple row subquery simply returns more than one row, containing one or more columns.

multiple table INSERT

Multiple table INSERT commands allow insertions into more than one table using the same INSERT command. Multiple table INSERT commands can be either conditional (determining which table is added to for a particular row) or non-conditional (adding each row to all tables at once). A conditional multiple table INSERT command can be used to spread rows from one table into many. A non-conditional multiple table INSERT command can be used to add rows from multiple tables into a single table.

NATURAL keyword

A join is created "naturally" using the ANSI join syntax NATURAL keyword, matching same column names between two joined tables. A join using the NATURAL keyword can be either an inner join or an outer join.

nested subquery

A nested subquery is a subquery nested down to multiple levels. In effect, a nested query can contain multiples of other types of subqueries in multiple nested layers of subqueries.

nested table

A nested table is a dynamic array. A dynamic array is an array with an undetermined and flexible number of elements.

NEXTVAL

<sequence>.NEXTVAL finds the next sequential value for a sequence.

Normal Forms

Normal Forms are the steps contained within the process of Normalization. Normal Forms are cumulative such that a data model in 3rd Normal Form is in both 2nd and 1st Normal Forms, but not 4th or 5th Normal Form.

normalization

Normalization is the process of simplifying the structure of data. Denormalization is the opposite of Normalization. Normalization increases granularity and Denormalization decreases granularity. Granularity is the scope of a definition for any particular thing. The more granular a data model is the easier it becomes to manage, up to a point.

NOT logical condition

NOT is applied as <expression> NOT <expression>, or AND NOT <expression>, or OR NOT <expression>. NOT simply implies that the expression must yield a false result to produce a true result. Of the three logical conditions—NOT, AND, and OR—NOT has highest precedence (is processed first), followed by AND and then OR.

NOT NULL constraint

A NOT NULL constraint implies that a column must have a value placed into it; otherwise an error will be returned.

NOVALIDATE

NOVALIDATE is a constraint state that does not require existing rows to comply with an enabled constraint, only new rows.

NULL

NULL is both a value and a PL/SQL command. NULL is nothing and does nothing. NULL is not the same as a space character or a zero value. A NULL valued column is a column that has never been initialized with any value. The NVL and NVL2 functions are often used to control query results when NULL values are encountered. Similarly, SET NULL can be used to achieve the same effect in SQL*Plus.

NULLS FIRST

By default, NULL values are sorted with the ORDER BY clause to appear last because they cannot be sorted. In the case of an ascending index, NULL values will appear last. The NULLS FIRST option is best used to return sorted values first for an ascending sort.

NULLS LAST

By default, NULL values are sorted with the ORDER BY clause to appear last because they cannot be sorted. In the case of a descending index, NULL values will appear first. The NULLS LAST option can be used to return sorted values last for a descending sort.

object expression

Object expressions include various object methodology expressions such as type constructors, variables, and object access expressions.

object privilege

Object privileges provide DML capable access to user objects such as read and write access to tables using the SELECT, INSERT, UPDATE, and DELETE privileges.

object reference function

These functions use pointers to reference values. Commonly, object reference functions either reference objects or dereference values from objects.

object-relational data model

The object-relational data model is the combination of relational and object data models, two completely contradictory methodologies. The object-relational data model includes the capability to store large binary objects in or as pointed to from inside a database. Additionally, Oracle Database does allow type definitions, collection management, and extensive object-like coding in PL/SQL. However, object-like capabilities in Oracle Database fall far short of the capabilities of Java or an object database.

OLAP

OLAP (Online Analytical Processing) functionality provides rapid interactive analysis of data into multiple dimensions, usually involving extremely large databases. The objective of analysis is to highlight trends, patterns, and exceptions.

ON clause

The ON clause is ANSI standard join format and allows exact column join specification when you want to include one or more columns in a join that have different names in different tables.

operator

Operators are used to perform operations on arguments passed to them. Operators can be divided up into arithmetic operators, the concatenation operator, set operators, and hierarchical query operators.

OR logical condition

OR is applied as `<expression> OR <expression>`, implying that either expression must yield a true result for `<expression> OR <expression>` to yield a true result. Of the three logical conditions—NOT, AND, and OR—NOT has highest precedence (is processed first), followed by AND and then OR.

Oracle Enterprise Manager

Oracle Enterprise Manager provides a complete suite of tools and programs for accessing, maintaining, tuning, and administering an Oracle database.

Oracle Enterprise Manager Console

The Oracle Enterprise Manager Console allows access to all the multifarious array of applications available from within Oracle Enterprise Manager. Oracle Enterprise Manager truly is an enterprise-wide Oracle software management tool, as its name describes. Oracle Enterprise Manager capabilities include navigation across all applications and databases within an enterprise, job scheduling, automated event management and detection, instance management, schema management, security management, storage management, distribution management, data warehouse management, workspaces management, and XML management. Additionally, there are various add-on options, such as change management, automated tuning, and problem detection.

Oracle join format

Oracle join syntax joins tables using both the `FROM` clause and the `WHERE` clause of a query. Oracle join syntax uses the `(+)` operator, sometimes called the outer join operator. The outer join operator is placed on either side of a comparison of two expressions in the `WHERE` clause of a query, never on both sides. As a result, a full outer join is not possible using the Oracle join syntax. The join operator is placed on the side of the join deficient in information. The side deficient in information is the side of the join containing rows outside the intersection, which are to be included in a left or right outer join.

Oracle SQL

Oracle SQL is an Oracle Database–specific flavor of SQL.

ORDER BY clause

Rows in a query are sorted according to the sequence of elements listed in the `ORDER BY` clause, from left to right. Therefore, the leftmost `ORDER BY` clause element is the most significant sort parameter, and the rightmost element is the least important sort parameter. Remember the sequence for `WHERE`, `GROUP BY`, and `ORDER BY` clauses. The `WHERE` clause is always first and the `ORDER BY` clause is always last.

out-of-line constraint

An out-of-line constraint is created a little like a table column is created, after all columns are created, on one or more of the columns within the `CREATE TABLE` command.

outer join

An outer join is an intersection plus rows outside the intersection.

OVER clause

The `OVER` clause allows a function to execute on the results of a query, allowing a moving window with the windowing clause. The windowing clause applies to a starting row or a range between two rows, within a row set returned by a query. The window can effectively slide through the range of rows or a partition among a group of partitions. Window start and end points can be specified as unbounded (start or finish), the current row, or with an expression.

parallel query

A parallel query is a query that can be executed on more than one CPU at the same time. Parallel queries are most effective when used on multiple CPU platforms, including Oracle Partitioning.

partition

A partition, or Oracle Partitioning, is a method by which datafiles can be physically broken up into more manageable parts, or partitions. Both tables and indexes can be created as partitioned objects. Oracle Partitioning allows division of objects into separate physical files and layers. The separate layers can be executed on as individual partitions or simultaneously in parallel.

precedence

Precedence implies that one expression has priority over another, and that expression is executed first.

primary key

A primary key uniquely identifies each row in a table. The entity on the many side of the relationship has a foreign key. The foreign key column contains primary key values of the entity on the one side of the relationship.

primary key constraint

A primary key is a type of constraint in which the primary key uniquely identifies each row in a table. The entity on the many side of the relationship has a foreign key. The foreign key column contains primary key values of the entity on the one side of the relationship.

PRIOR

The `PRIOR` operator is used in conjunction with the `CONNECT BY` clause in hierarchical queries. The `PRIOR` operator always refers to a parent row of the curent row.

private synonym

A synonym is created as private by default and is accessible only to the user creating the synonym or any user receiving privileges on the synonym. A private synonym can link to an object in a different schema, assuming that appropriate privileges are available. Both private and public synonyms, whomever granted to, still require granting of access privileges to underlying objects.

production phase

The production phase is the fifth and final step in the system development cycle. The production phase is when applications come into use in the real world. Application support is passed over to production support, and applications are released to the general user population.

pseudocolumn

A pseudocolumn is not a real column in a table, thus the term *pseudo*: false or counterfeit. A pseudocolumn is retrieved in a tool such as SQL*Plus much like a column in a table, generated by Oracle Database during the processing of a query. A pseudocolumn is selected from using a SELECT command, much like a table is accessed using a standard syntax SELECT statement, typically selected from the DUAL table or embedded within a query or DML statement.

public synonym

A public synonym is available to all users and is created using the PUBLIC keyword. Both private and public synonyms, whomever granted to, still require granting of access privileges to underlying objects.

query

A query is a statement interrogating the database and returning information. Most often, tables are interrogated and rows from those tables are returned. Queries can be both simple and complex.

range join

Range joins combine rows using a range of values (<, >, <=, >=, or BETWEEN).

ranking functions

A ranking function is used to assess the ranking or the importance of a value within a set of values.

RDBMS

RDBMS is an abbreviation for relational database management system. A relational database contains tables with data. The management system part is the part allowing you access to that database and the power to manipulate both the database and the data contained within it. A relational database is called a relational database due to setlike relationships established between tables. These relationships are based on the rules of Normalization.

REF constraint

A REF constraint or REF column is defined in Oracle documentation as a type of integrity constraint. In reality, a REF column is an object pointer to rows in another table. For more details and examples using REF constraints, see my book *Oracle SQL Jumpstart with Examples*, ISBN: 1555583237, by Gavin Powell and Carol McCullough-Dieter. Look specifically in Chapter 16, "Datatypes and Collections," under the section "Using the REF Datatype."

Referential Integrity

Referential Integrity usually validates one-to-many relationships. This validation is a process of making sure that related primary and foreign key column values actually exist. For instance, a foreign key value cannot be added to a table unless the related primary key value exists in the parent table. Similarly, deleting a primary key value necessitates removing all rows in subsidiary tables containing that primary key value in foreign key columns. Additionally, it follows that preventing the deletion of a primary key row is not allowed if a foreign key value exists elsewhere.

regular subquery

A regular query is the opposite of a correlated query in that values are not passed between calling query and subquery, and thus there is not correlation.

relational data model

The relational data model allows the creation of entities related through primary and foreign keys, validated using Referential Integrity.

relational database management system

A relational database contains tables with data. The management system part is the part allowing you access to that database and the power to manipulate both the database and the data contained within it. A relational database is called a relational database due to setlike relationships established between tables. These relationships are based on the rules of Normalization.

repeating groups

A repeating group is a row that is duplicated. A duplicated row is a row with the same values, repeating for each row, or a subset of columns within each row.

RESOURCE role

The RESOURCE role contains system privileges applicable to developers, such as CREATE TABLE, CREATE SEQUENCE, and CREATE CLUSTER.

revoke privilege

Revoking a privilege removes a previously granted privilege from a user. The REVOKE command is used to remove privileges, the opposite of the GRANT command. The GRANT command increases access permissions for a user and the REVOKE command decreases access permissions for a user.

right outer joins

A right outer join is the intersection plus all rows in the right-side table but not in the left-side table.

role

Both system and object privileges can be grouped together into what is called a role. A role applies a set of privileges to a user or group of users performing a specific function.

ROLLBACK

This command undoes any database changes not yet committed to the database using the COMMIT command, or an inadvertent implicit commit caused by a DDL command, or disconnection from a session.

ROLLUP clause

9i The GROUP BY clause can be extended with OLAP functionality using the ROLLUP and CUBE clauses. The results of ROLLUP and CUBE clauses can be filtered with the GROUPING SETS clause. In their most simplistic forms, the ROLLUP and CUBE clauses can be used to produce super-aggregates. A super-aggregate is an aggregate of an aggregate, allowing creation of groups within groups. In lay terms, the ROLLUP clause can be used to produce subtotals and grand totals for groups within a query.

row

Tables are divided into columns and rows. Columns impose structure and datatype specifics onto each of the column values in a row. Rows are also known as tuples (database design) and records (a programming naming convention).

ROWID

A ROWID is a datatype containing a relative row pointer most commonly used by Oracle Database internally. For instance, indexes contain values of indexed columns plus a ROWID pointer value back to the row in the table indexed.

ROWNUM

A ROWNUM is a pseudocolumn returning a sequence number for rows returned by a query, as the rows are returned.

SAVEPOINT

This command allows for partial rollback within a transaction back to a defined label.

scalar subquery

A scalar subquery simply returns a single value, a scalar value, or even a Boolean TRUE or FALSE. In SQL statements in which only a single value is required, an error will be returned when more than one item is returned to a calling query from a subquery.

scalar subquery expression

A scalar subquery is an expression, returning a single column value from one row where no rows returned results in a NULL value.

schema

In terms of Oracle metadata, a schema is the same object as a user. A schema contains tables and the relationships between those tables. The meaning of the word *schema* is model, diagram, or diagrammatic representation.

scripting

Scripts can be output from SQL*Plus using the SPOOL command. The EDIT command can be used to edit scripts from within SQL*Plus.

SELECT

The SELECT statement is the core of what makes up a query. A SELECT statement is made up of columns retrieved, a FROM clause (where columns are retrieved from), and various optional additions and modifiers, such as a WHERE clause, an ORDER BY clause, and a GROUP BY clause. The SELECT list is the list of items retrieved. The SELECT list can consist of an asterisk (*) and one or more columns or expressions. An asterisk is used as a substitution character representing all available columns in the object or objects retrieved from. Because a SELECT statement does not change data, only reading a database, it is neither a DML nor a DDL command. This is the basic syntax: `SELECT columns ... FROM tables ... [WHERE ...] [GROUP BY ...] [ORDER BY ...]`.

self join

A self join joins rows in a table to other rows in the same table.

semi join

Set membership or semi joins combine rows based on subset membership. They are called semi joins because they join only for the purposes of validation and do not return a joined set of column values.

sequence

A sequence is an internal counter often used to populate primary and foreign surrogate key columns for Referential Integrity.

session

A session is created when a user connects to a database.

set operators

Set operators merge multiple compatible queries into a single resulting row set. Oracle set operators are UNION, UNION ALL, INTERSECT, and MINUS.

simple expression

A simple expression contains a single value such as a number, a string, or a pseudocolumn.

simple query

This is a query simply retrieving one or more columns and/or expressions from a single table or other selectable database object.

single quote (')

The single quote character is used extensively in Oracle SQL syntax to delimit strings.

simple statistical functions

Simple statistical functions perform basic tasks such as calculations of standard deviations and variances.

simple summary functions

Simple summary functions perform basic tasks such as counting, averaging, or summing up.

single row function
Single row functions can be used to execute an operation on each row of a query. In other words, a single row function can be used to execute the same operation for every row a query retrieves. Single row functions can be divided into categories of string functions, number functions, datetime functions, datatype conversions, and miscellaneous functions. Single row functions operate within or as expressions on each row of a SQL statement. By definition, a function is a piece of compiled or interpreted code used to do some processing and return a value. Because a function returns a value, it can be embedded into an expression.

single row subquery
A single row subquery returns an entire row or a single iteration of a set of columns to a calling query.

single table INSERT
A single table `INSERT` command allows adding of rows to one table at a time.

SOME comparison
The `ANY`, `SOME`, and `ALL` comparisons all check an expression for membership in a set or list of elements. `ANY` and `SOME` are the same and allow a response when any element in the set matches. `ALL` produces a response only when all elements in a set match an expression.

sorted query
Sorting a query involves reordering the sequence in which rows are returned using the `ORDER BY` clause.

sorting
Rows in a query are sorted according to the sequence of elements listed in the `ORDER BY` clause, from left to right. Therefore, the leftmost `ORDER BY` clause element is the most significant sort parameter, and the rightmost element is the least important sort parameter. Automatic sorting can be performed without the use of the `ORDER BY` clause when sorting is inherent to indexes, `WHERE` clause filters, the `GROUP BY` clause, and `DISTINCT`, among others. However, note that relying on indirect sorting methods is risky, especially for cases of sorting performed on more than a single column at the same time.

SQL
SQL is an abbreviation for Structured Query Language, the language used to access data in a relational database. SQL is pronounced “ess-queue-ell” or “sequel”.

SQL*Plus
SQL*Plus can be executed either from a shell using `SQLPLUS.EXE` or in a window using `SQLPLUSW.EXE`.

SQL*Plus Worksheet
SQL*Plus Worksheet comes packaged with Oracle Enterprise Manager and provides a much more user-friendly form of SQL*Plus.

star (*)

The asterisk or * character is used in Oracle SQL syntax in two places: (1) the select list of a SELECT statement when all columns are to be retrieved, (2) as a multiplication operator in arithmetic expressions.

statistical distributions

Statistical distribution functions help to assess where values are within a distribution of a set of values.

strategy and analysis phase

The strategy and analysis phase is the first step in the system development cycle. This step analyzes user requirements and produces a system specification.

string function

A string function takes a string as a parameter and returns either a number or a string result.

Structured Query Language

SQL is an abbreviation for Structured Query Language, the language used to access data in a relational database.

subquery

A subquery is a query contained within another query, a calling query. Subqueries can be built in numerous shapes and forms. A subquery is, as the term implies, one query called from another. Subqueries can retrieve a single value, multiple columns, or multiple rows, and can even be used to create tables. Subqueries can also be embedded in most parts of DML and SELECT statement syntax elements, plus subqueries can have values passed into them from calling queries.

synonym

A synonym provides object transparency, being a substitute or an easier-to-use name for an object within any accessible schema.

SYS user

This user is the most powerful user in an Oracle Database and is a database administration super user. The SYS user is generally used to perform the most high-level administration tasks, such as shutting down and starting up a database.

system development cycle

Oracle Corp. classifies the system development cycle as consisting of five distinct steps. The term *iterative* is used to imply that the distinct steps can be revisited more than once, either in part or as a whole, and not necessarily in any particular sequence. The steps in the system development cycle are strategy and analysis, design, build and document, transition, and production.

system privilege

System privileges allow access to change metadata such as creating tables and indexes. When privileges are allocated to developers, system privileges such as `CREATE ANY TABLE`, `CREATE ANY INDEX`, `EXECUTE ANY PROCEDURE`, `CREATE ROLE`, and `CREATE SEQUENCE` could be granted.

SYSTEM user

The `SYSTEM` user is intended as a less powerful version of the `SYS` user. The `SYSTEM` user is used to perform less drastic tasks than those of the `SYS` user, such as creation of new users.

table

Tables are divided into columns and rows. Columns impose structure and datatype specifics onto each of the column values in a row.

TNS

The simplest network naming method is something Oracle calls the Transparent Network Substrate (TNS), or just “local naming method.” TNS is defined by a configuration file on a client machine called `$ORACLE_HOME/network/admin/tnsnames.ora`.

Top-N query

A Top-N query retrieves the top-n rows from a query. It uses what is called an inline view to retrieve rows initially. An inline view is a subquery embedded in the `FROM` clause of a calling query. The calling query has a `ROWNUM` restriction applied to it as in the following example: `SELECT * FROM (SELECT * FROM MOVIE ORDER BY TITLE) WHERE ROWNUM < 10`. Notice how the `WHERE` clause is contained outside the inline view, maintaining the proper sort order.

transaction

A transaction in Oracle SQL is a sequence of one or more commands in which changes are not as yet committed permanently to thc database. A transaction is completed when changes are committed or undone (rolled back).

transaction control

A transaction is composed of one or more DML commands that make database changes. A transaction is completed on the execution of a COMMIT or ROLLBACK command, manually or automatically. The concept of transactional control is that SQL allows sets of commands to be permanently stored all at once, or undone all at once.

transition phase

The transition phase is the fourth step in the system development cycle. The transition phase involves user acceptance testing and any final modifications as a result of discrepancies (bugs) found during testing.

Transparent Network Substrate

The simplest network naming method is something Oracle calls the Transparent Network Substrate (TNS). TNS is defined by a configuration file on a client machine called $ORACLE_HOME/network/admin/tnsnames.ora.

TRUNCATE

TRUNCATE deletes *all* the rows in a table without the option to undo the TRUNCATE command and retrieve the rows again. The TRUNCATE command has syntax equally simplistic as that of the DELETE command with respect to simple removal of rows from a table. TRUNCATE is a faster option for clearing out a table than the DELETE command. However, TRUNCATE is a DDL command and cannot be rolled back. DELETE is a DML command and can be rolled back.

tuple

A tuple is another name for a row in a table. A tuple is essentially an iteration of a column structure in a table, namely a row.

UPDATE

The UPDATE command is used to change existing row values in tables. The UPDATE command can be used to change a single row, multiple rows, or even all the rows in a table with a single command.

user

A schema is a logical structure for the data contained in a database. That schema can contain many types of objects. When users connect to an Oracle Database, the users connect to their schema (synonymous with a user). That schema may or may not contain a set of objects such as tables. It is possible to create a user that does not contain any schema elements (not tables).

USING clause

The USING clause is ANSI standard join format and allows forcing of one or more columns to be joined on, avoiding same-named columns containing different data to be excluded from a join.

VALIDATE

VALIDATE is a constraint state that requires that all rows comply with a constraint. If a constraint is enabled on a table with existing data, VALIDATE will cause all existing rows to be validated against the constraint, as the constraint is created. If any rows fail to comply, the constraint creation will fail as well.

variable substitution

Variable substitution allows for named variables to be placeholders for values in scripts.

VARRAY

A VARRAY is a fixed-length array. A fixed-length array has a predetermined, fixed number of elements.

view

A view is a logical overlay containing a query, executed whenever the view is accessed. Repeated query execution can make views very inefficient in busy environments.

virtual column

Virtual columns are created by assigning aliases to columns.

WHERE clause

The WHERE clause is an optional part of SELECT statements, UPDATE commands, and DELETE commands. The WHERE clause allows inclusion of wanted rows and filtering out of unwanted rows. Basic syntax for the WHERE clause includes a single expression-to-expression comparison of the following form: WHERE <expression> <comparison> <expression>. Multiple comparisons can be made using logical condition conjunctions in the form of AND [NOT] or OR [NOT]: WHERE <expression> <comparison> <expression> AND ....

WITH clause

9i The WITH clause allows for the creation of named subqueries. The results of named queries can be accessed by subsequent queries with the same query, using the named query columns retrieved by the WITH clause queries.

XMLDATA

XMLDATA is an XMLType datatype attribute allowing access to the underlying storage structure of binary stored XML documents.

Index

SYMBOLS

A

B - C

D

E

F

G

N

O

Q

R

S

T

U

V

W - X - Y - Z